Angel Cup

3

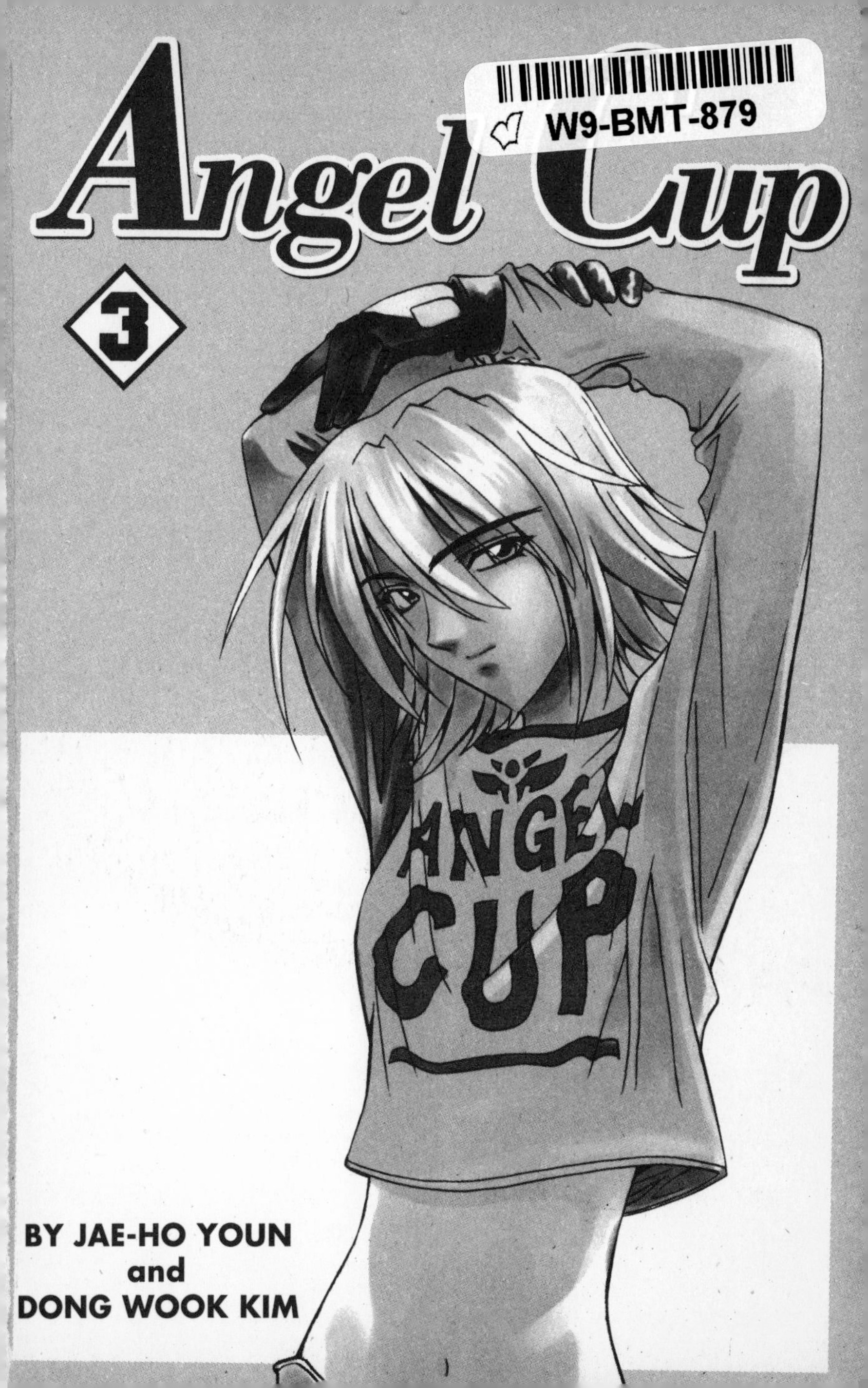
ANGEL
CUP

BY JAE-HO YOUN
and
DONG WOOK KIM

Angel Cup Volume 3
Created By Jae-ho Youn

Translation - Jumi V. Yang
English Adaptation - Hope Donovan
Retouch and Lettering - Star Print Brokers
Production Artist - Courtney Geter
Graphic Designer - Fawn Lau

Editor - Katherine Schilling
Digital Imaging Manager - Chris Buford
Pre-Production Supervisor - Erika Terriquez
Art Director - Anne Marie Horne
Production Manager - Elisabeth Brizzi
Managing Editor - Vy Nguyen
VP of Production - Ron Klamert
Editor-in-Chief - Rob Tokar
Publisher - Mike Kiley
President and C.O.O. - John Parker
C.E.O. and Chief Creative Officer - Stuart Levy

A **TOKYOPOP** Manga

TOKYOPOP and are trademarks or registered trademarks of TOKYOPOP Inc.

TOKYOPOP Inc.
5900 Wilshire Blvd. Suite 2000
Los Angeles, CA 90036

E-mail: info@TOKYOPOP.com
Come visit us online at www.TOKYOPOP.com

ISBN: 978-1-59532-305-7

First TOKYOPOP printing: February 2007
10 9 8 7 6 5 4 3 2 1
Printed in the USA

Volume 3

written by Dong Wook Kim
illustrated by Jae-Ho Youn

HAMBURG // LONDON // LOS ANGELES // TOKYO

ANGEL CUP STORY SO FAR...

⚽ So-jin's boyfriend thinks he's got the perfect girl – funny, energetic, and cute! Little does he know that this girl's got burning passion for soccer that puts the World Cup players to shame! And though the school she's just transferred to didn't have its own girls' soccer team, she made sure that all changed...

So-jin, and her quickly assembled teammates challenged the cocky boys' team to a game of futsal. The bet? If the girls win, they get their team. If they lose...let's just say So-jin gets a lesson in proper housecleaning.

After an epic game of head-butting and bruised pride, the girls lose by two points. But the journey's far from over. It's still safe to say that So-jin's got herself a dedicated team, and the boys definitely got a lesson in respect. Now that So-jin's said so long to her boyfriend, and Shin-bee collapsed from a mysterious heart-condition while Akira watches on...

THE GIRLS

So-jin

An energetic and tough girl who's determined to start an official girls' soccer team at her new high school. She considered Shin-bee her chief rival before she quit the sport after junior high.

Shin-bee

A quiet and passive girl who was known as the MVP during her soccer career in junior high. Though she swore off the game forever, she managed to step onto the field again to lead the girls' team to a near victory. An unexplained heart condition has left her unconscious after the game...

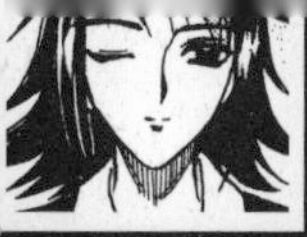

Cool and calm on the outside, but raging and tough on the inside, Yee-ju has a natural gift as goalie for the team with her experience in the sport of handball.

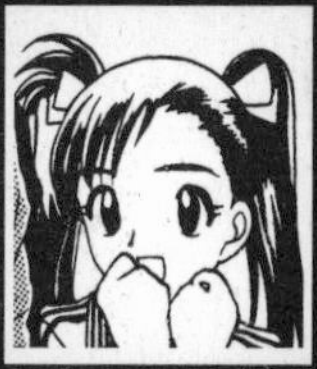

Soo-hee

Soft-spoken and faithful lapdog to Yee-ju, Soo-hee is desperate to prove herself to her teammates, even if it means taking a nasty hit to the face during the game.

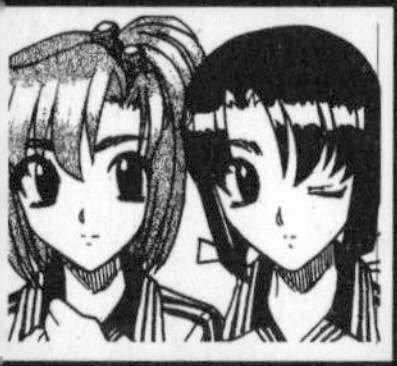

Mi-ae & Mi-rae

One's a bubble-brained ditz who makes up for brains with a bouncing rack, while the other's a no-nonsense strategist. But together, these two twins can take the field with their killer combos.

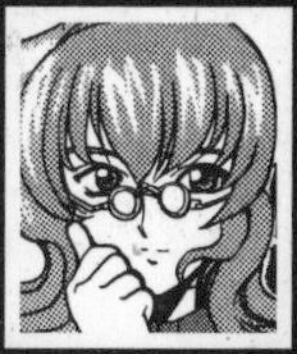

Chae-young

The kindhearted but klutzy granddaughter of the rich Yoon Kang-ui, and coach for the girls' team. She watches eagerly from the sidelines as the game reveals her future team's true potential.

VS. THE BOYS...

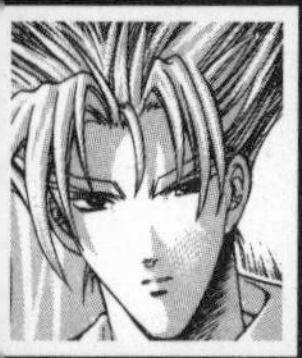

Joon-suh

Popular boy-hottie of the school and captain of the boys' soccer team. He's a fierce player, but has an honorable attitude for the sport.

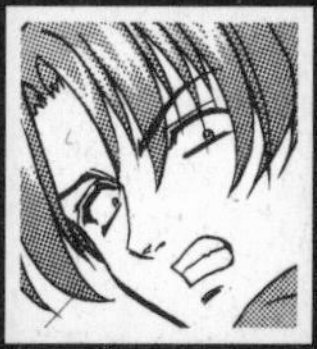

In-hyuk

Joon-suh's lackey, and meanest player on the team. His unbeatable hate for women keeps him from ever taking a girls' soccer team seriously. Keep your guard up when he's on the field, because he'll be the first to throw fouls.

Chairman Yoon Kang-ui

The dying chairman of the powerful Dae Han group who donated a hefty portion of his money to forming a girls' soccer league. His reasons may go

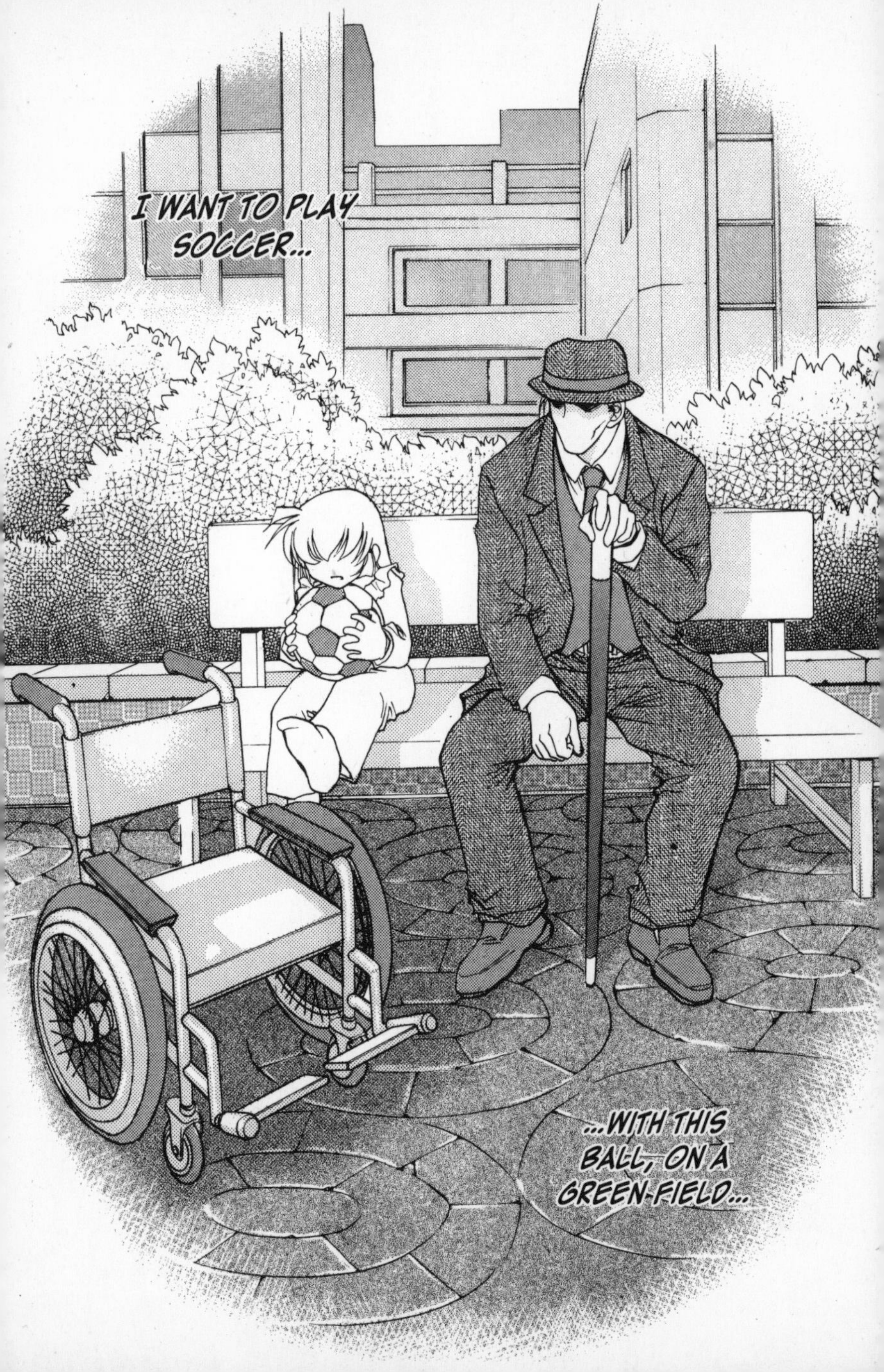
I WANT TO PLAY SOCCER...
...WITH THIS BALL, ON A GREEN FIELD...

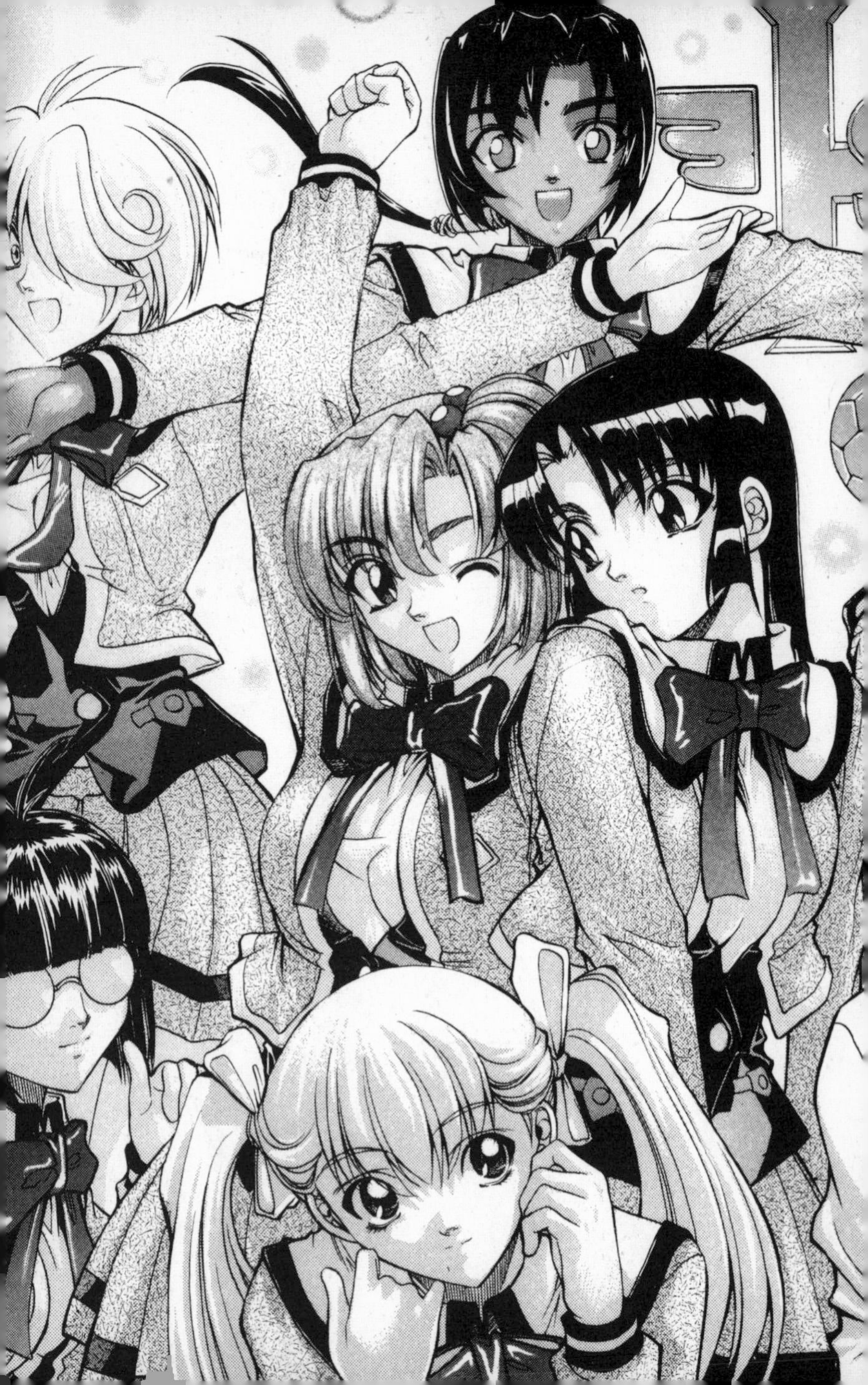

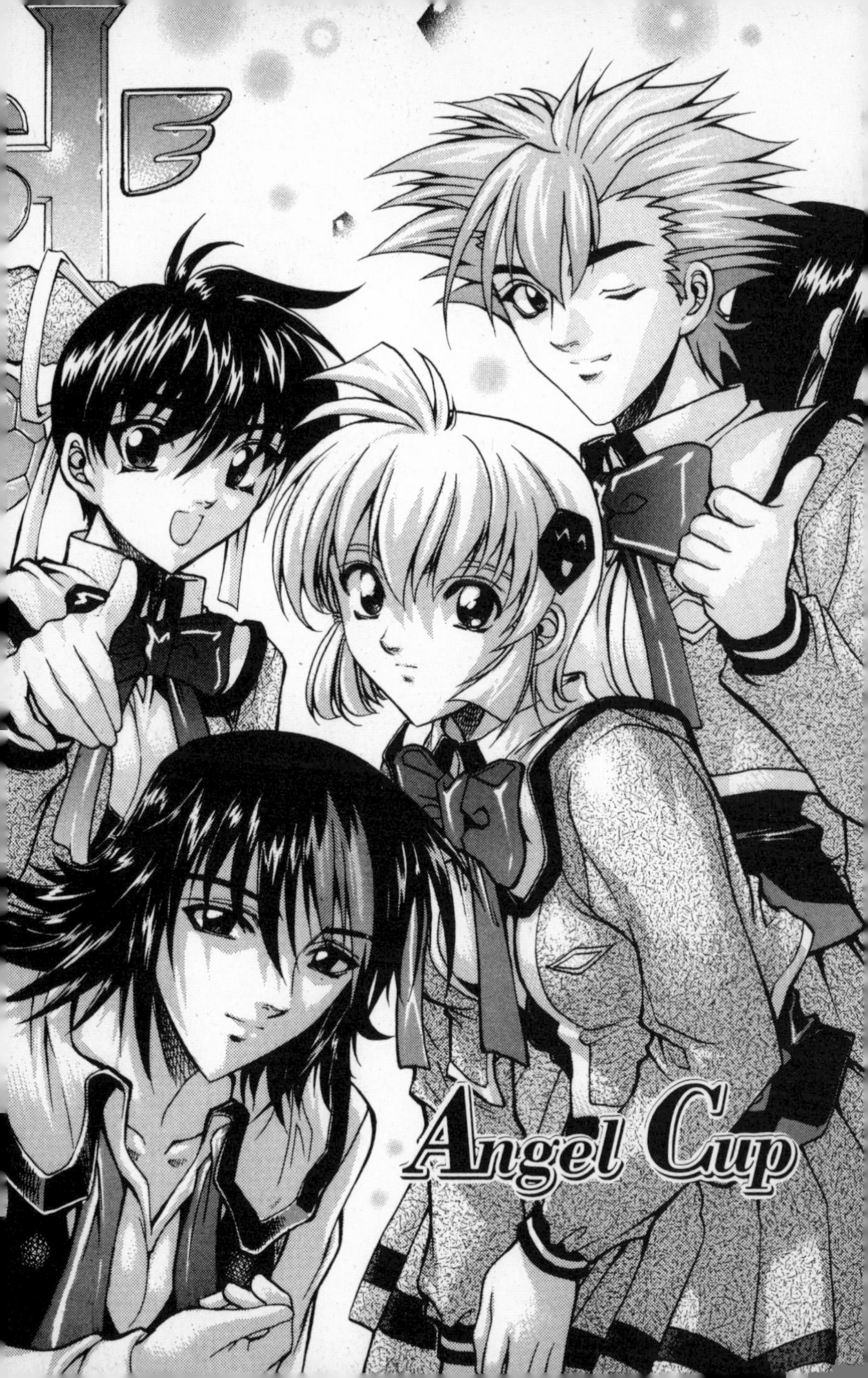
Angel Cup

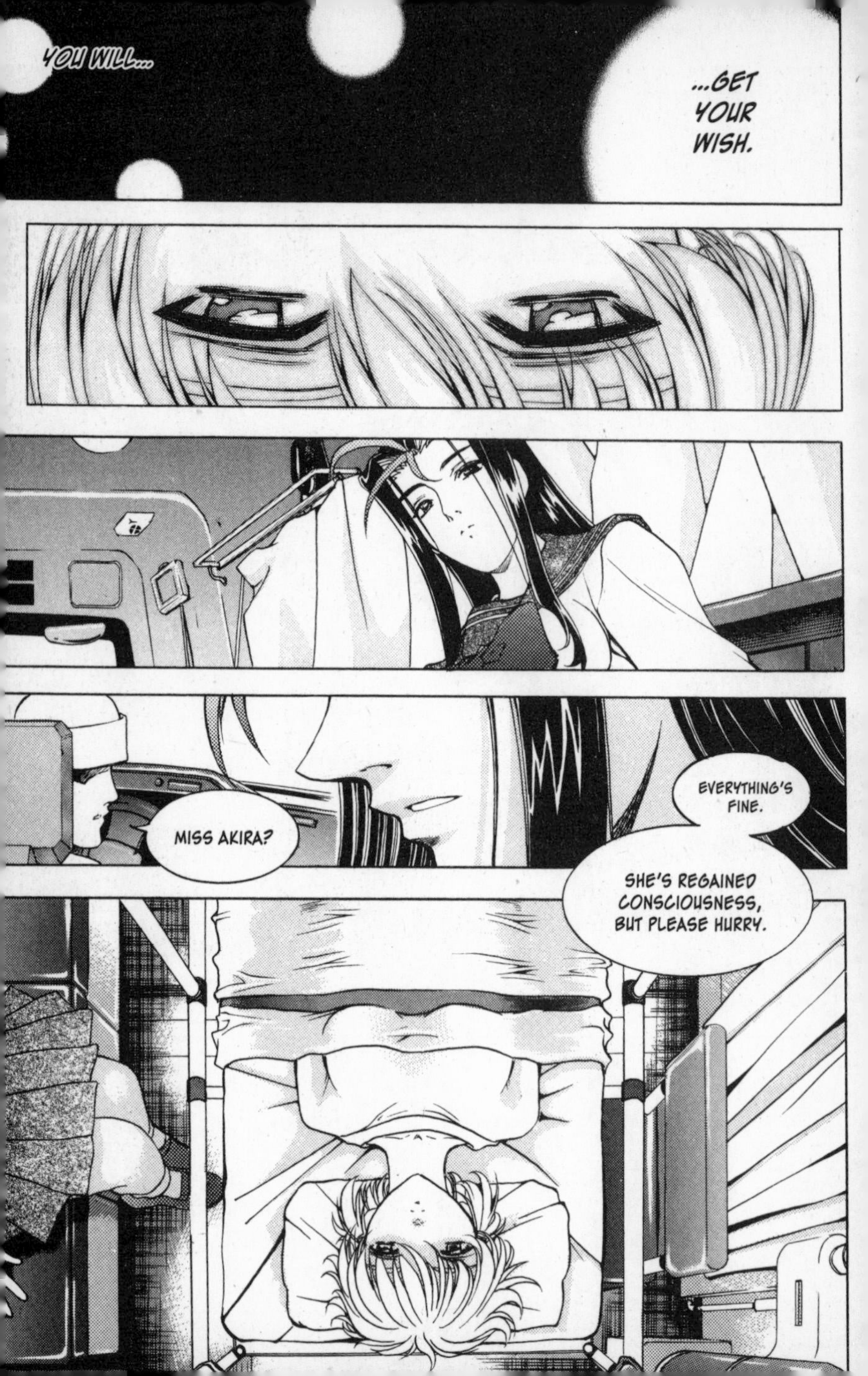
YOU WILL...
...GET YOUR WISH.
MISS AKIRA?
EVERYTHING'S FINE.
SHE'S REGAINED CONSCIOUSNESS, BUT PLEASE HURRY.

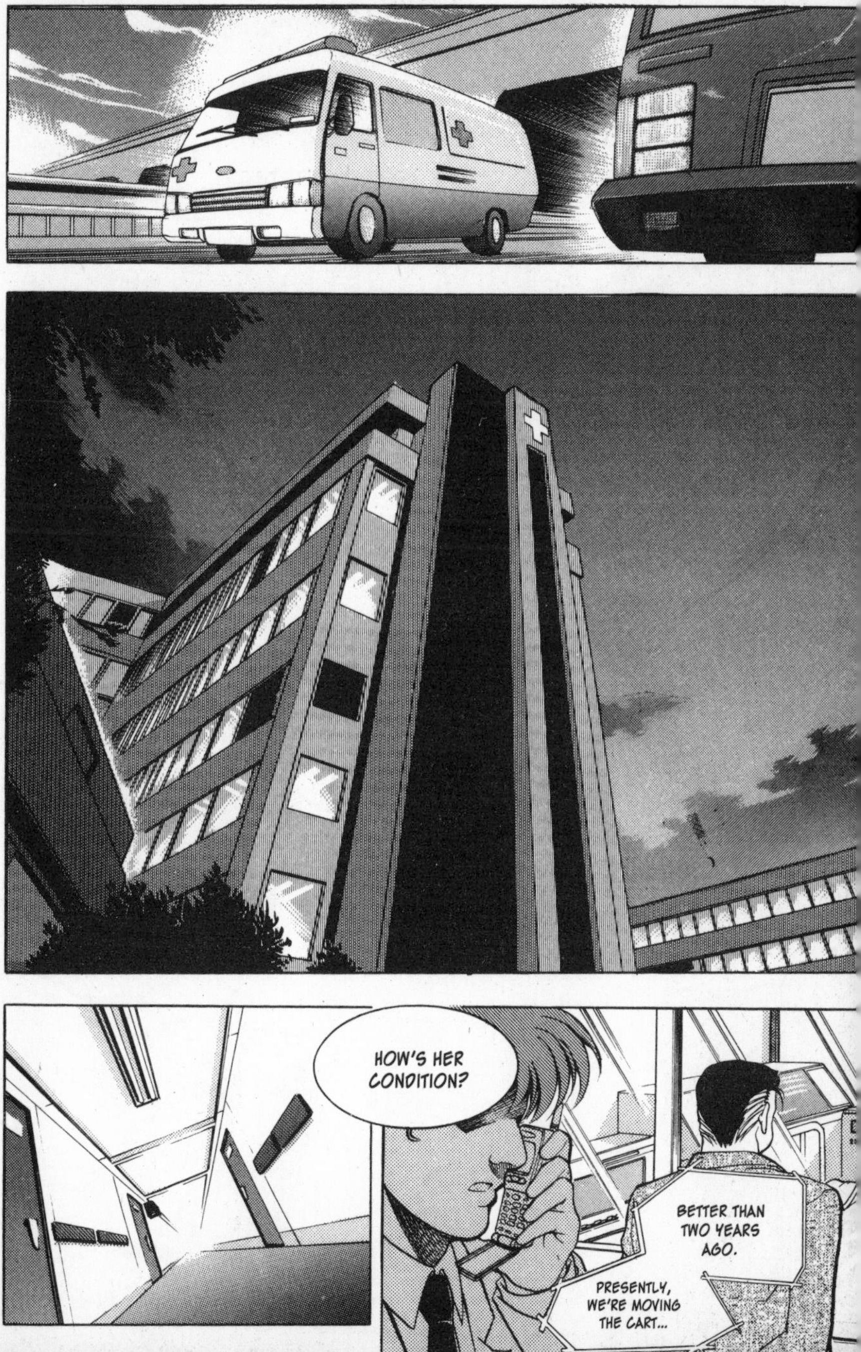
HOW'S HER CONDITION?
BETTER THAN TWO YEARS AGO.
PRESENTLY, WE'RE MOVING THE CART...

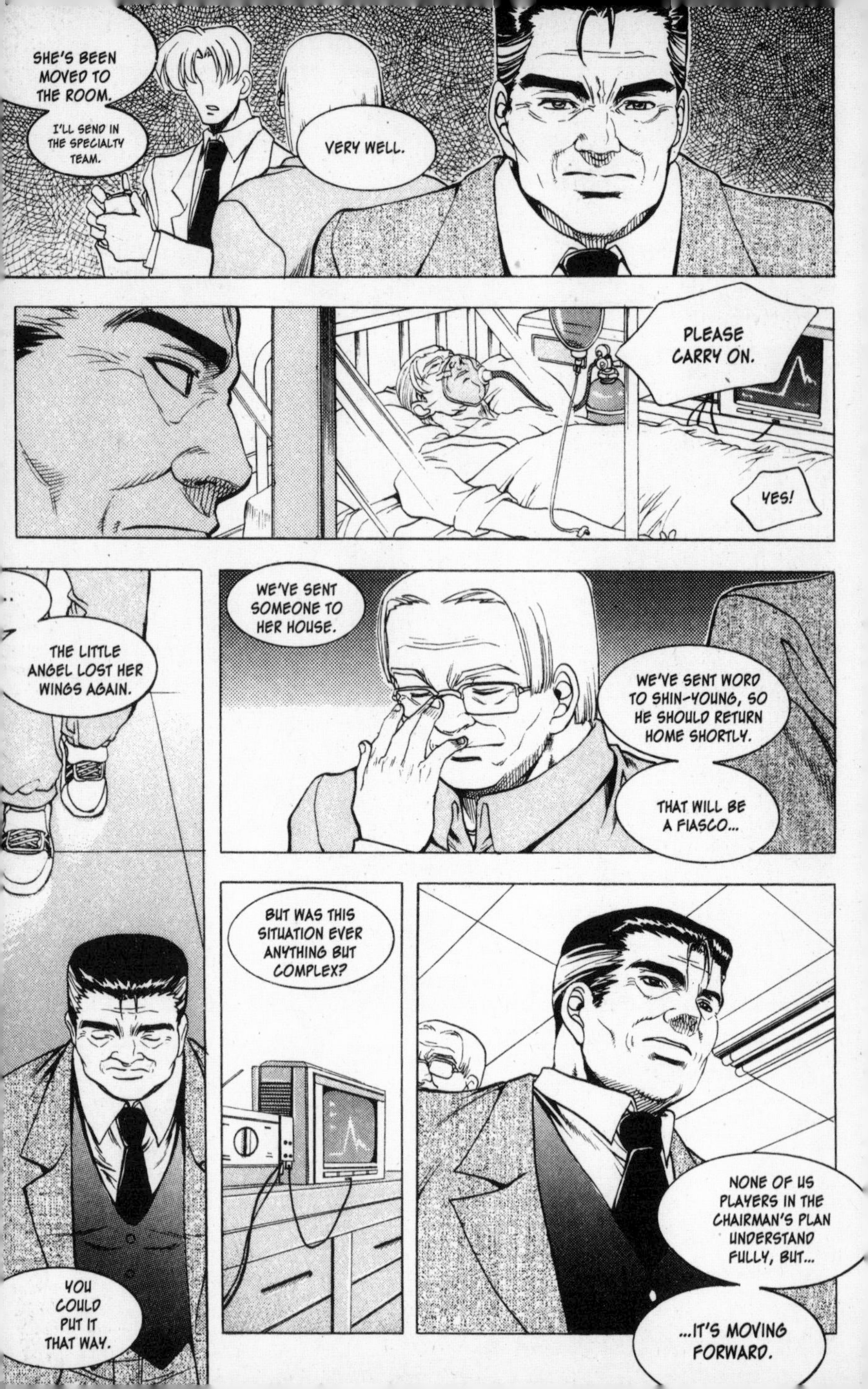
SHE'S BEEN MOVED TO THE ROOM.
I'LL SEND IN THE SPECIALTY TEAM.
VERY WELL.
PLEASE CARRY ON.
YES!
...
THE LITTLE ANGEL LOST HER WINGS AGAIN.
WE'VE SENT SOMEONE TO HER HOUSE.
WE'VE SENT WORD TO SHIN-YOUNG, SO HE SHOULD RETURN HOME SHORTLY.
THAT WILL BE A FIASCO...
YOU COULD PUT IT THAT WAY.
BUT WAS THIS SITUATION EVER ANYTHING BUT COMPLEX?
NONE OF US PLAYERS IN THE CHAIRMAN'S PLAN UNDERSTAND FULLY, BUT...
...IT'S MOVING FORWARD.

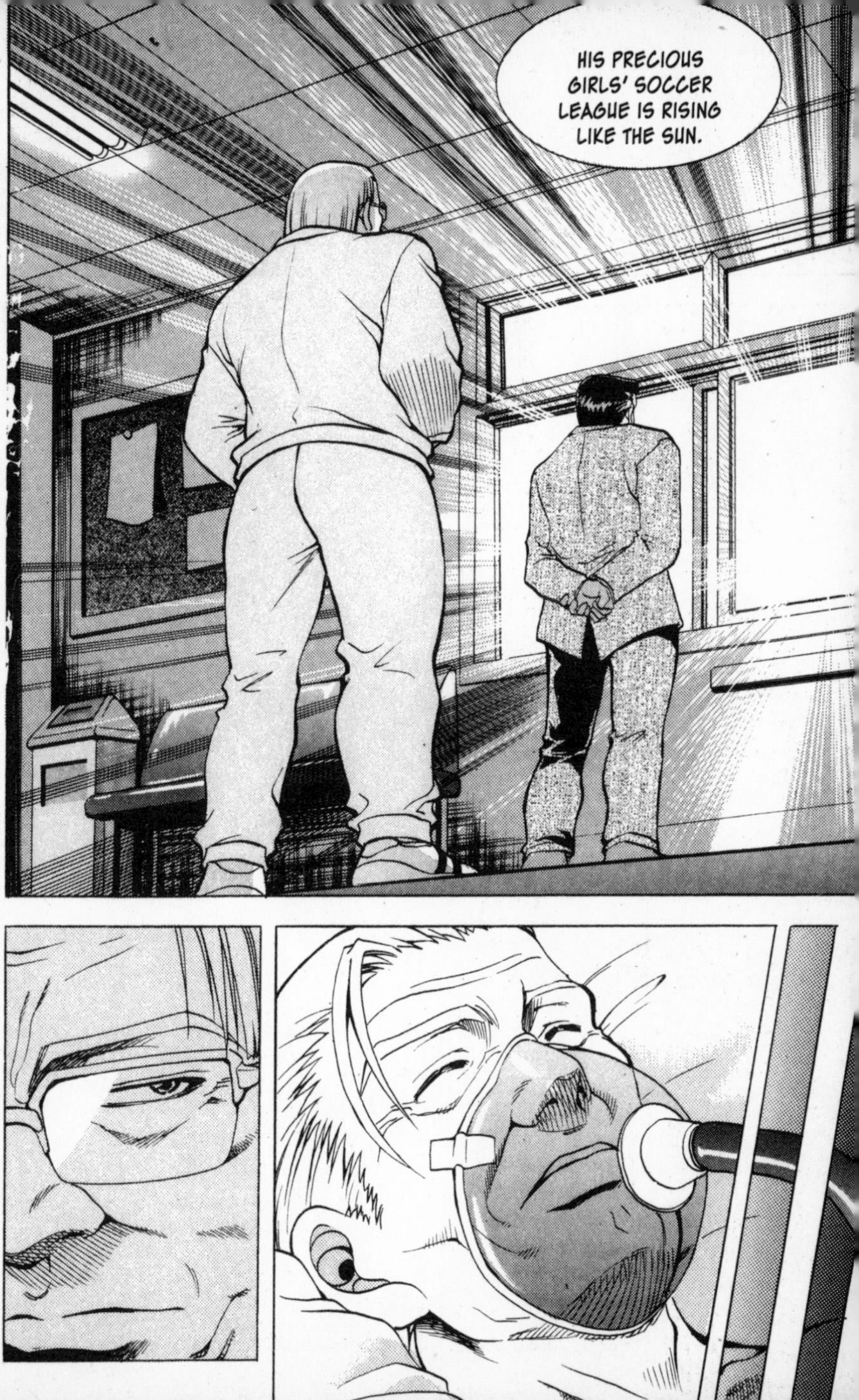
HIS PRECIOUS GIRLS' SOCCER LEAGUE IS RISING LIKE THE SUN.

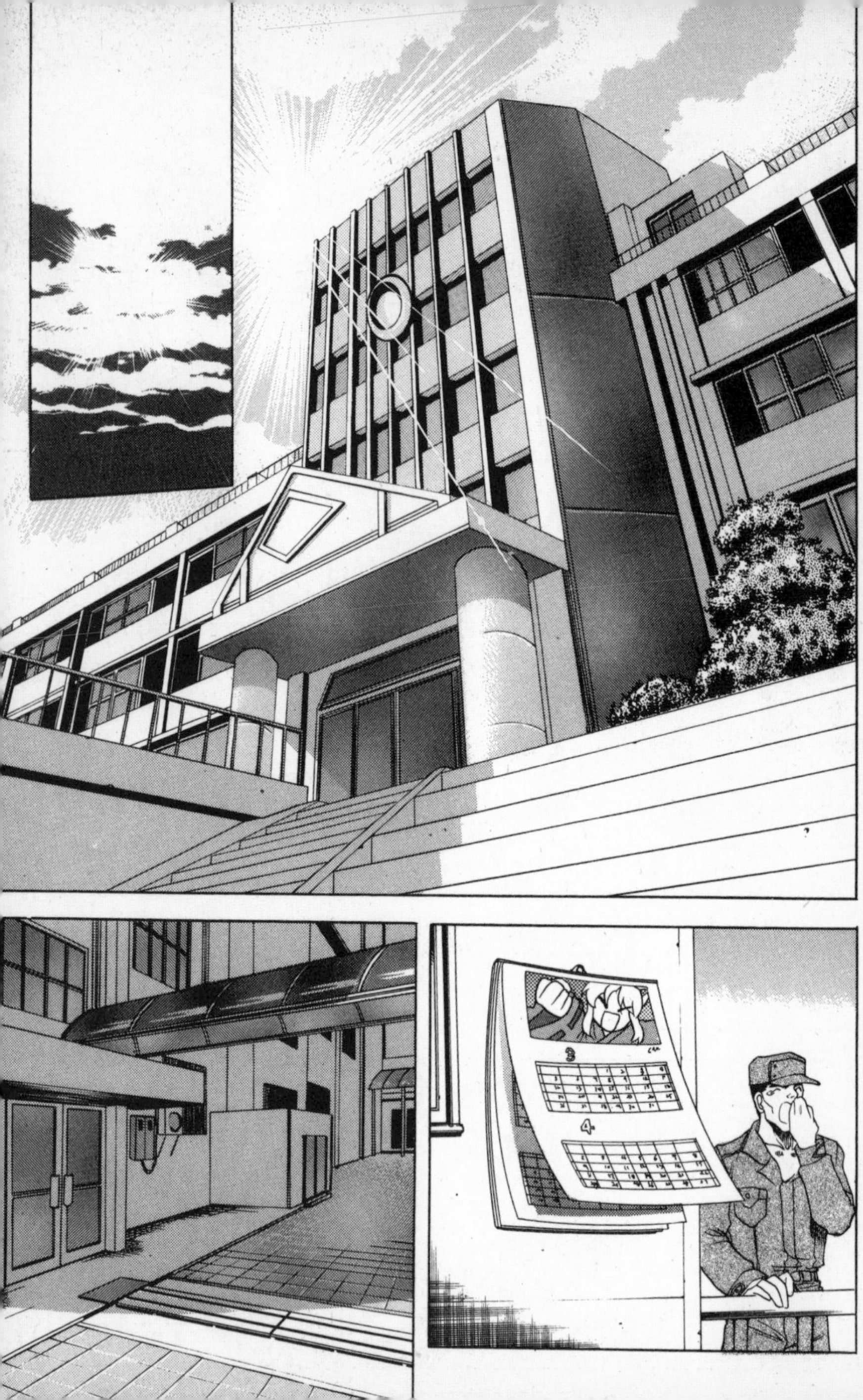

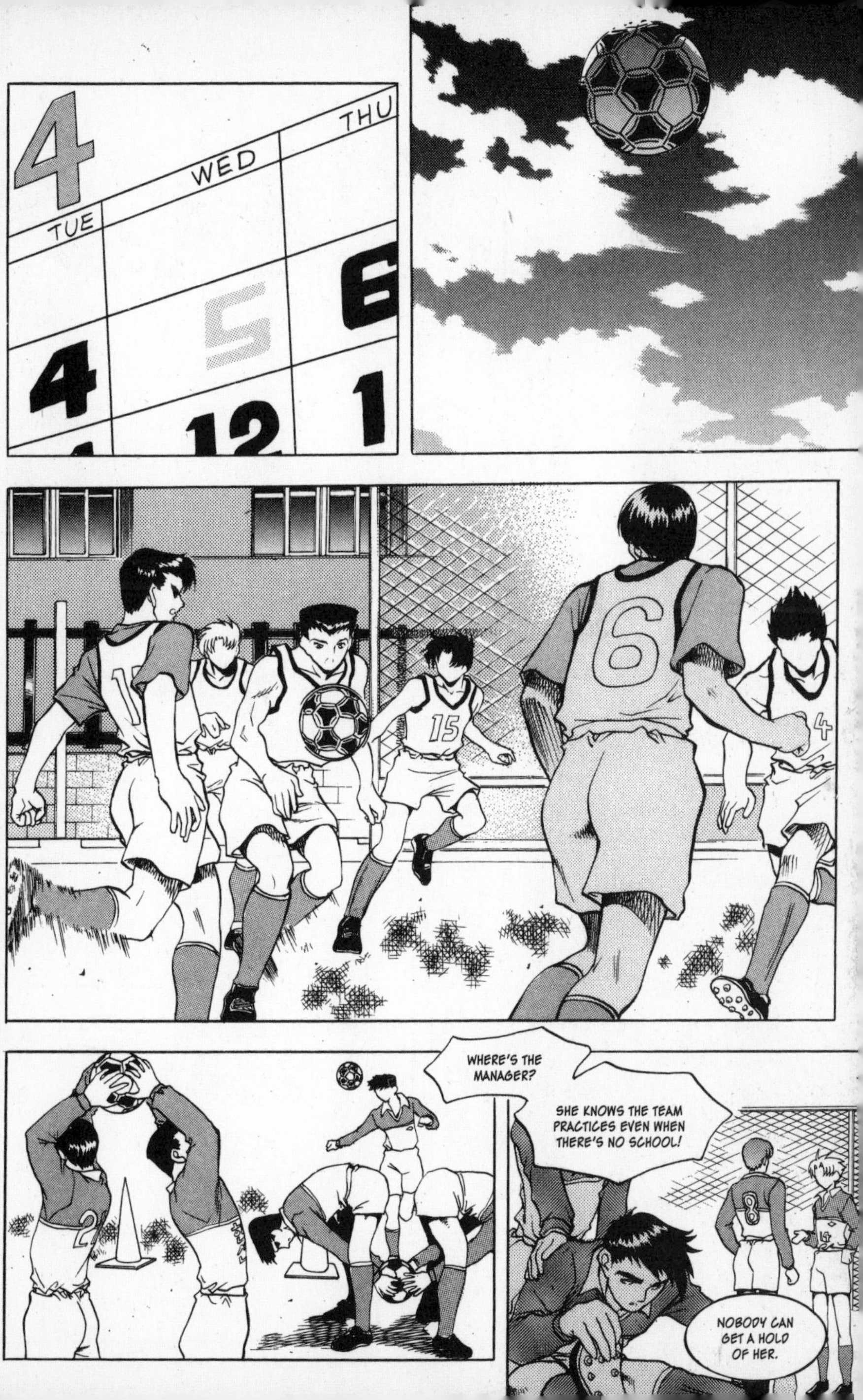
4
TUE
WED
THU
6
5
4
12
1
WHERE'S THE MANAGER?
SHE KNOWS THE TEAM PRACTICES EVEN WHEN THERE'S NO SCHOOL!
NOBODY CAN GET A HOLD OF HER.

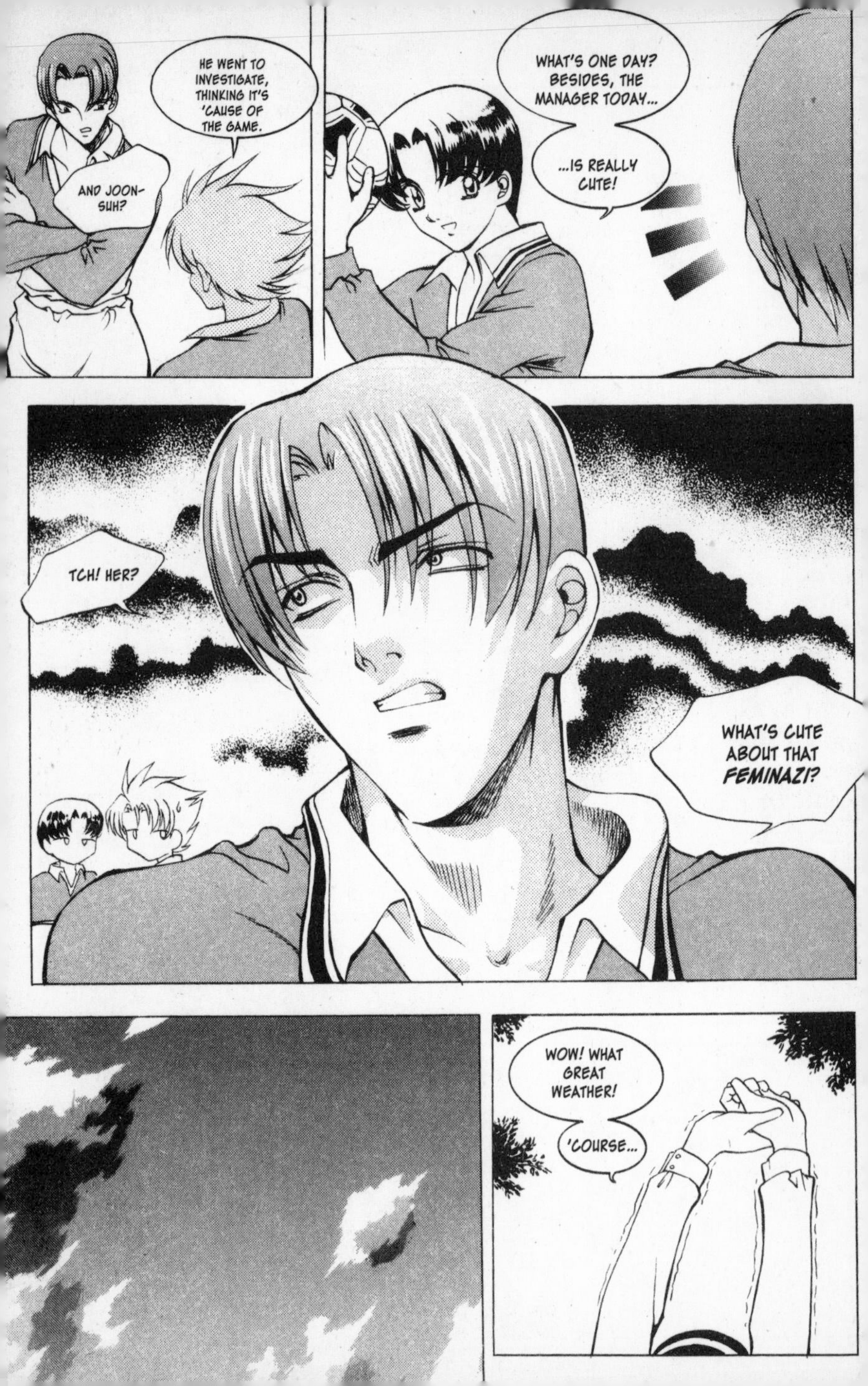
HE WENT TO INVESTIGATE, THINKING IT'S 'CAUSE OF THE GAME.
AND JOON-SUH?
WHAT'S ONE DAY? BESIDES, THE MANAGER TODAY...
...IS REALLY CUTE!
TCH! HER?
WHAT'S CUTE ABOUT THAT FEMINAZI?
WOW! WHAT GREAT WEATHER!
'COURSE...

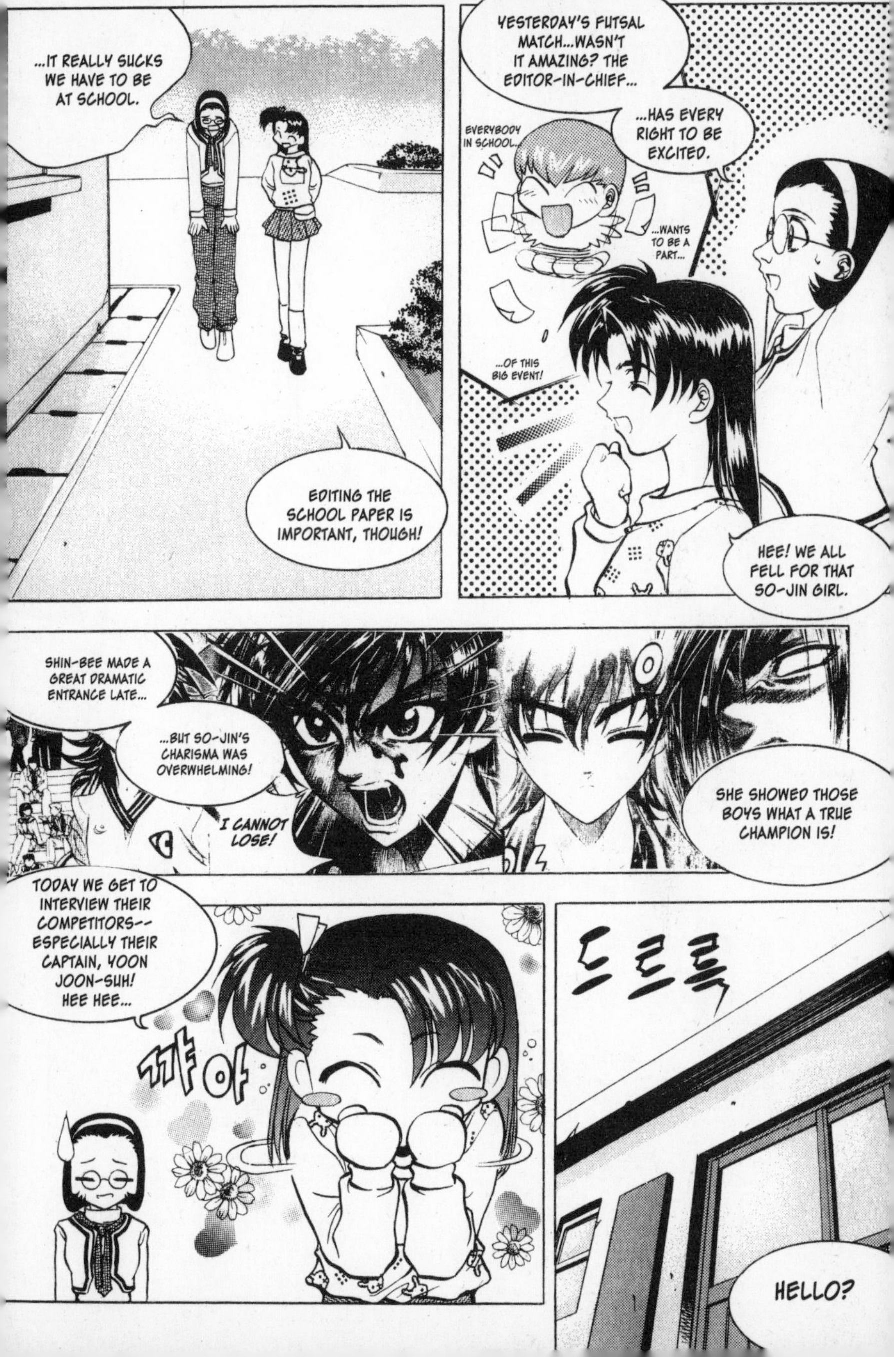
...IT REALLY SUCKS WE HAVE TO BE AT SCHOOL.
EDITING THE SCHOOL PAPER IS IMPORTANT, THOUGH!
YESTERDAY'S FUTSAL MATCH...WASN'T IT AMAZING? THE EDITOR-IN-CHIEF...
...HAS EVERY RIGHT TO BE EXCITED.
EVERYBODY IN SCHOOL...
...WANTS TO BE A PART...
...OF THIS BIG EVENT!
HEE! WE ALL FELL FOR THAT SO-JIN GIRL.
SHIN-BEE MADE A GREAT DRAMATIC ENTRANCE LATE...
...BUT SO-JIN'S CHARISMA WAS OVERWHELMING!
I CANNOT LOSE!
SHE SHOWED THOSE BOYS WHAT A TRUE CHAMPION IS!
TODAY WE GET TO INTERVIEW THEIR COMPETITORS--ESPECIALLY THEIR CAPTAIN, YOON JOON-SUH! HEE HEE...
꺄 아
드르륵
HELLO?

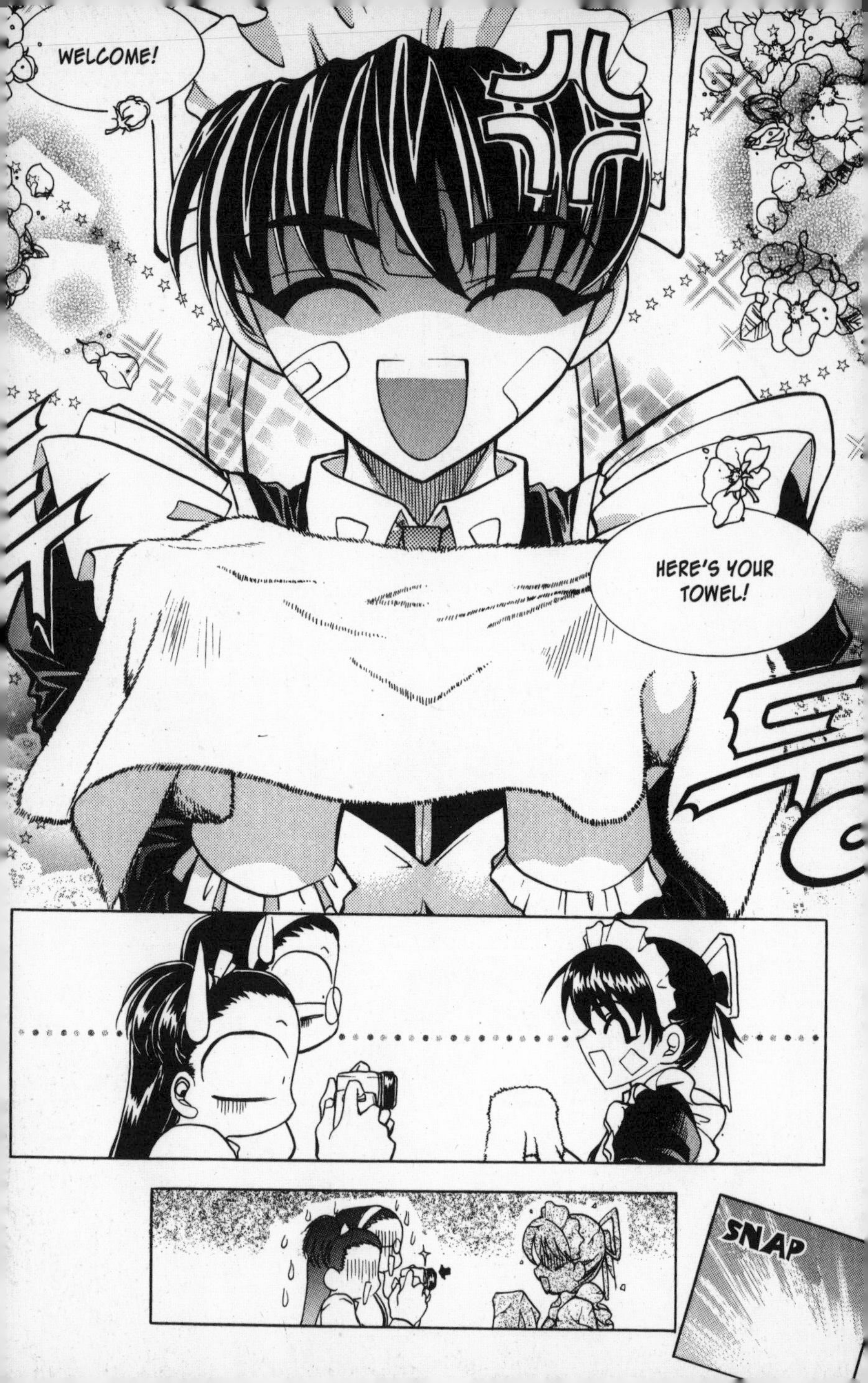
WELCOME!
HERE'S YOUR TOWEL!
SNAP

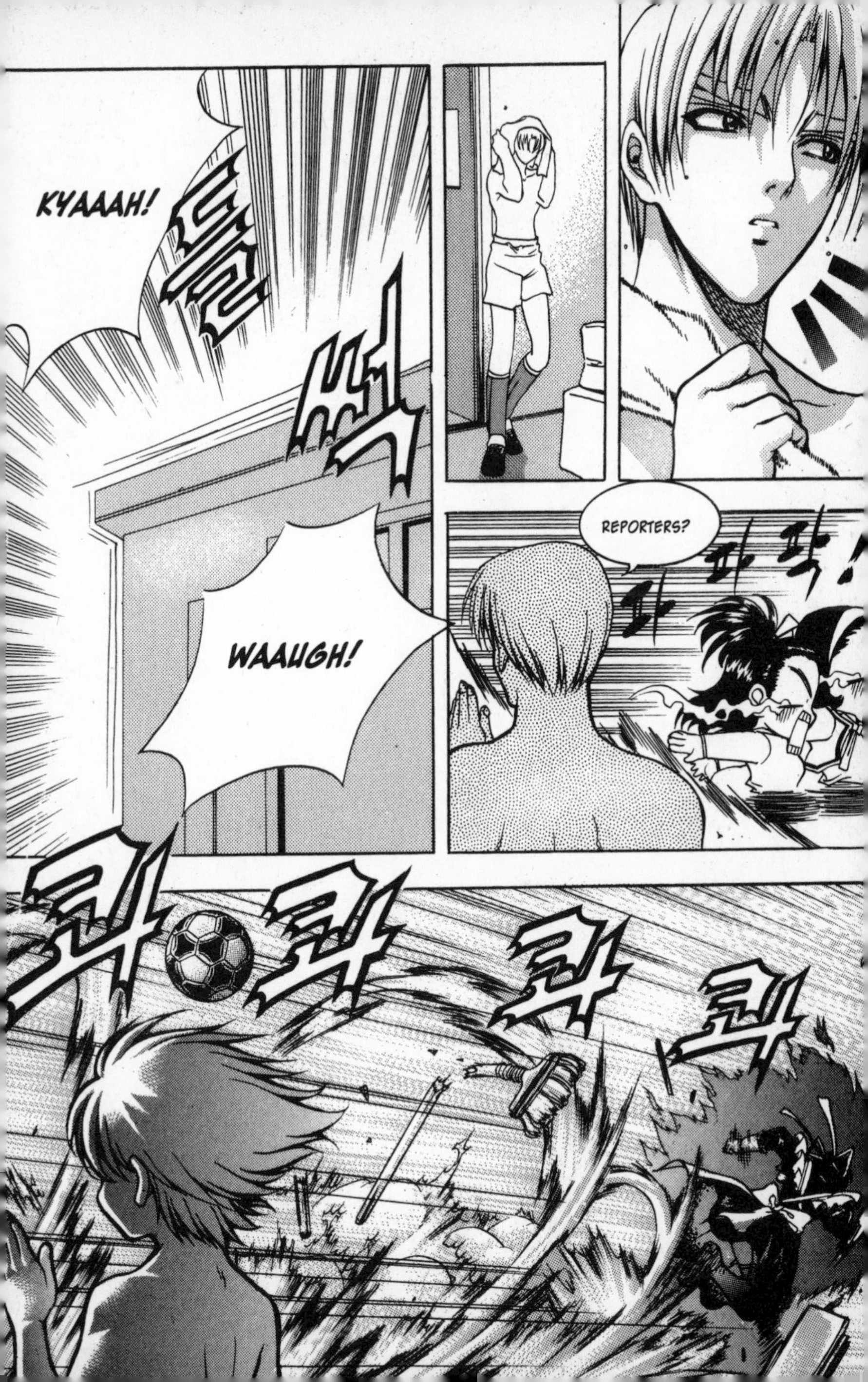
KYAAAH!
WAAUGH!
REPORTERS?
파파팍!
콰콰콰콰

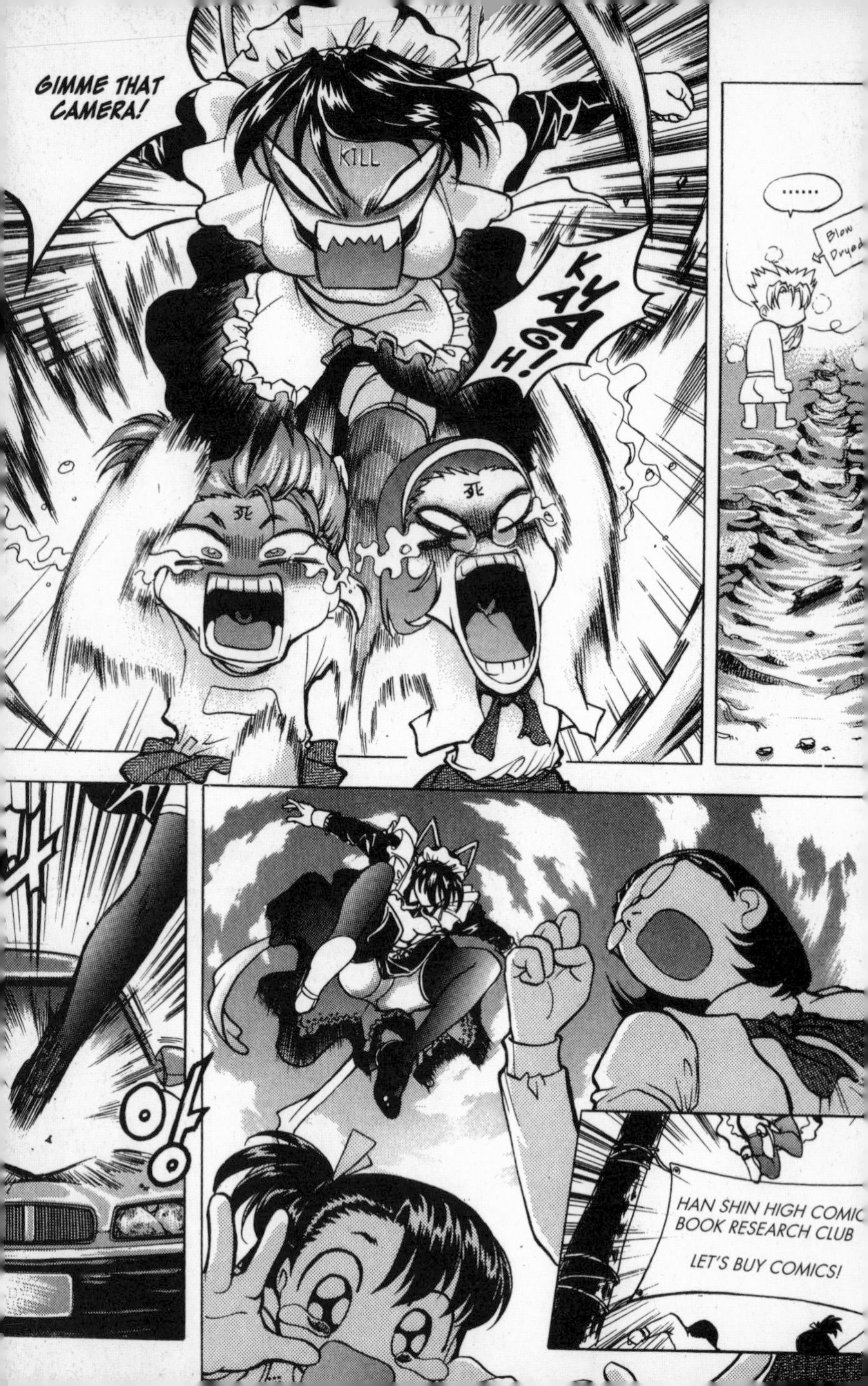
GIMME THAT CAMERA!
KILL
KYAAAGH!
......
Blow Dryed
HAN SHIN HIGH COMIC BOOK RESEARCH CLUB
LET'S BUY COMICS!

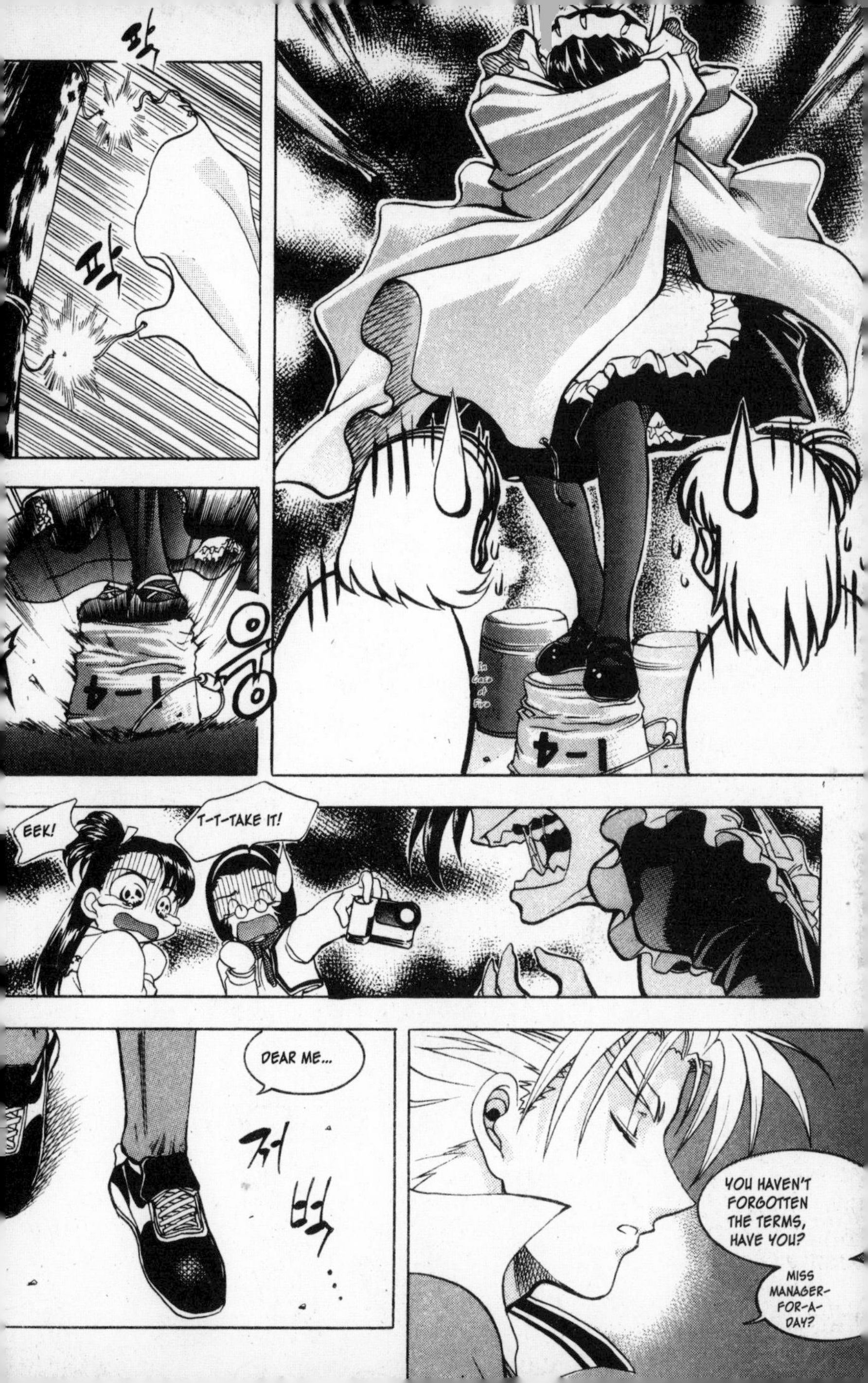
팍
팍
In Case of Fire
EEK!
T-T-TAKE IT!
DEAR ME...
저벅
YOU HAVEN'T FORGOTTEN THE TERMS, HAVE YOU?
MISS MANAGER-FOR-A-DAY?

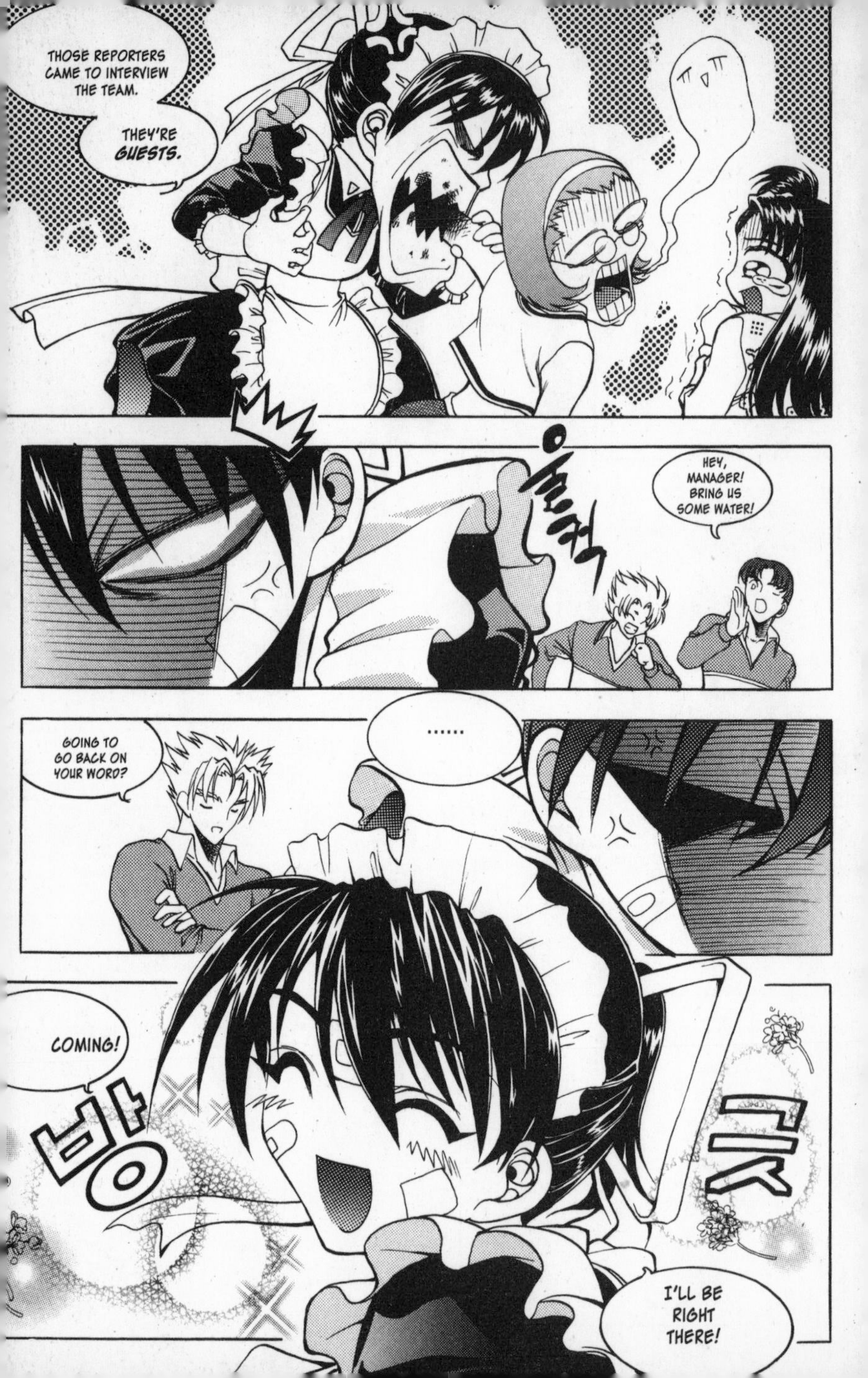
THOSE REPORTERS CAME TO INTERVIEW THE TEAM.
THEY'RE *GUESTS.*
HEY, MANAGER! BRING US SOME WATER!
GOING TO GO BACK ON YOUR WORD?
......
COMING!
방
긋
I'LL BE RIGHT THERE!

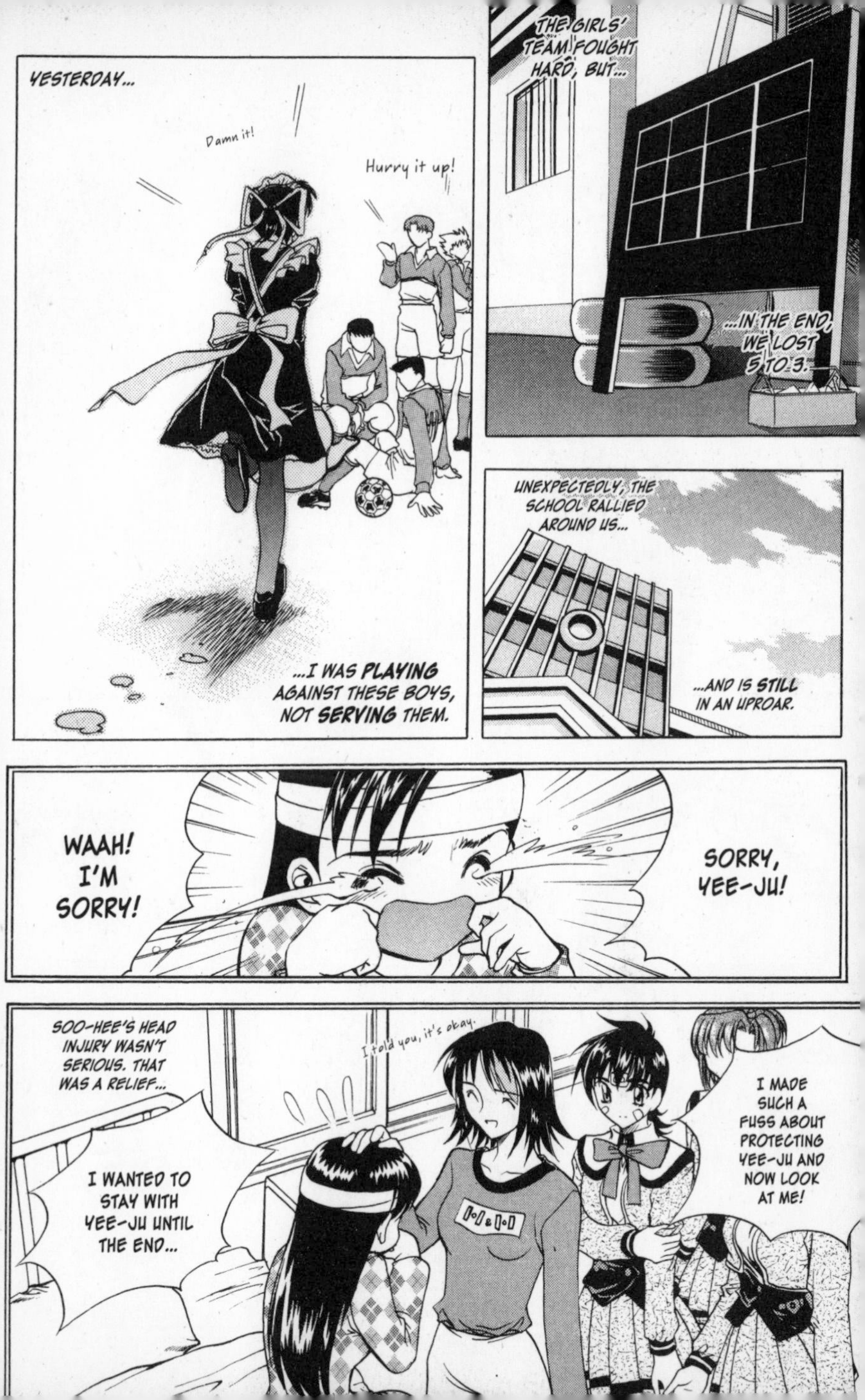

YESTERDAY...
Damn it!
Hurry it up!
...I WAS PLAYING AGAINST THESE BOYS, NOT SERVING THEM.
THE GIRLS' TEAM FOUGHT HARD, BUT...
...IN THE END, WE LOST 5 TO 3.
UNEXPECTEDLY, THE SCHOOL RALLIED AROUND US...
...AND IS STILL IN AN UPROAR.
WAAH! I'M SORRY!
SORRY, YEE-JU!
SOO-HEE'S HEAD INJURY WASN'T SERIOUS. THAT WAS A RELIEF...
I WANTED TO STAY WITH YEE-JU UNTIL THE END...
I told you, it's okay.
I MADE SUCH A FUSS ABOUT PROTECTING YEE-JU AND NOW LOOK AT ME!

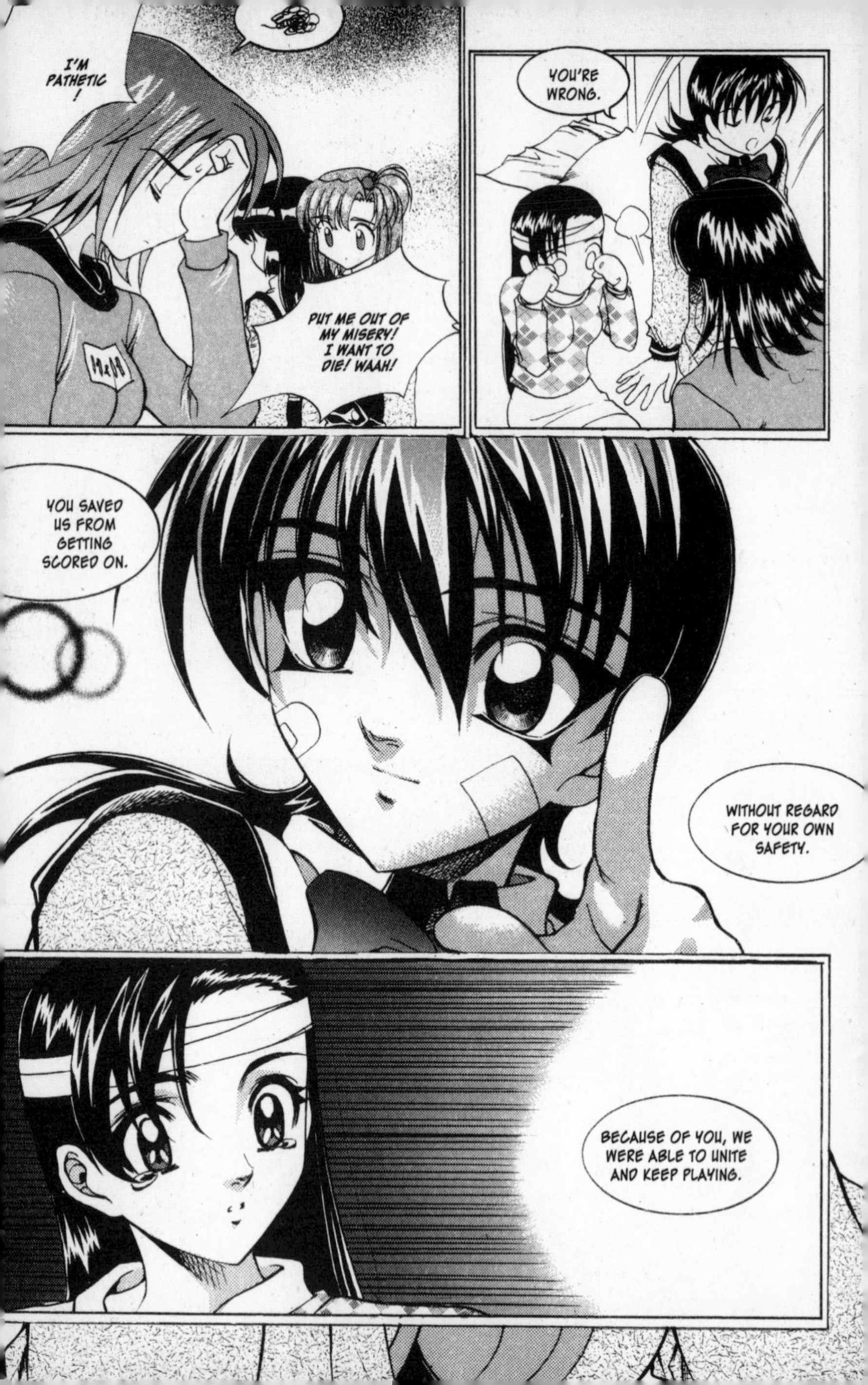
I'M PATHETIC!
PUT ME OUT OF MY MISERY! I WANT TO DIE! WAAH!
YOU'RE WRONG.
YOU SAVED US FROM GETTING SCORED ON.
WITHOUT REGARD FOR YOUR OWN SAFETY.
BECAUSE OF YOU, WE WERE ABLE TO UNITE AND KEEP PLAYING.

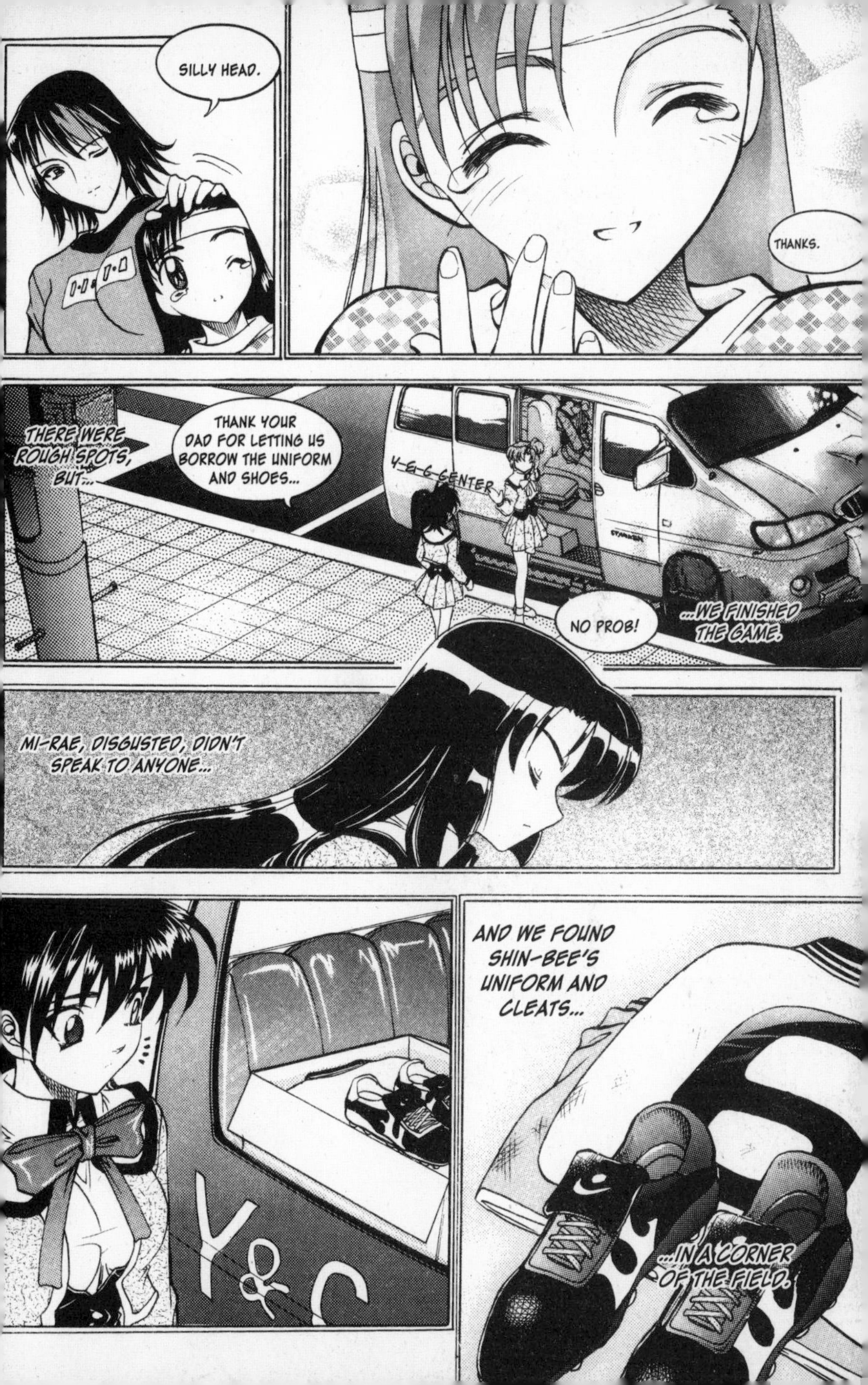
SILLY HEAD.
THANKS.
THERE WERE ROUGH SPOTS, BUT...
THANK YOUR DAD FOR LETTING US BORROW THE UNIFORM AND SHOES...
NO PROB!
...WE FINISHED THE GAME.
MI-RAE, DISGUSTED, DIDN'T SPEAK TO ANYONE...
Y&C
AND WE FOUND SHIN-BEE'S UNIFORM AND CLEATS...
...IN A CORNER OF THE FIELD.

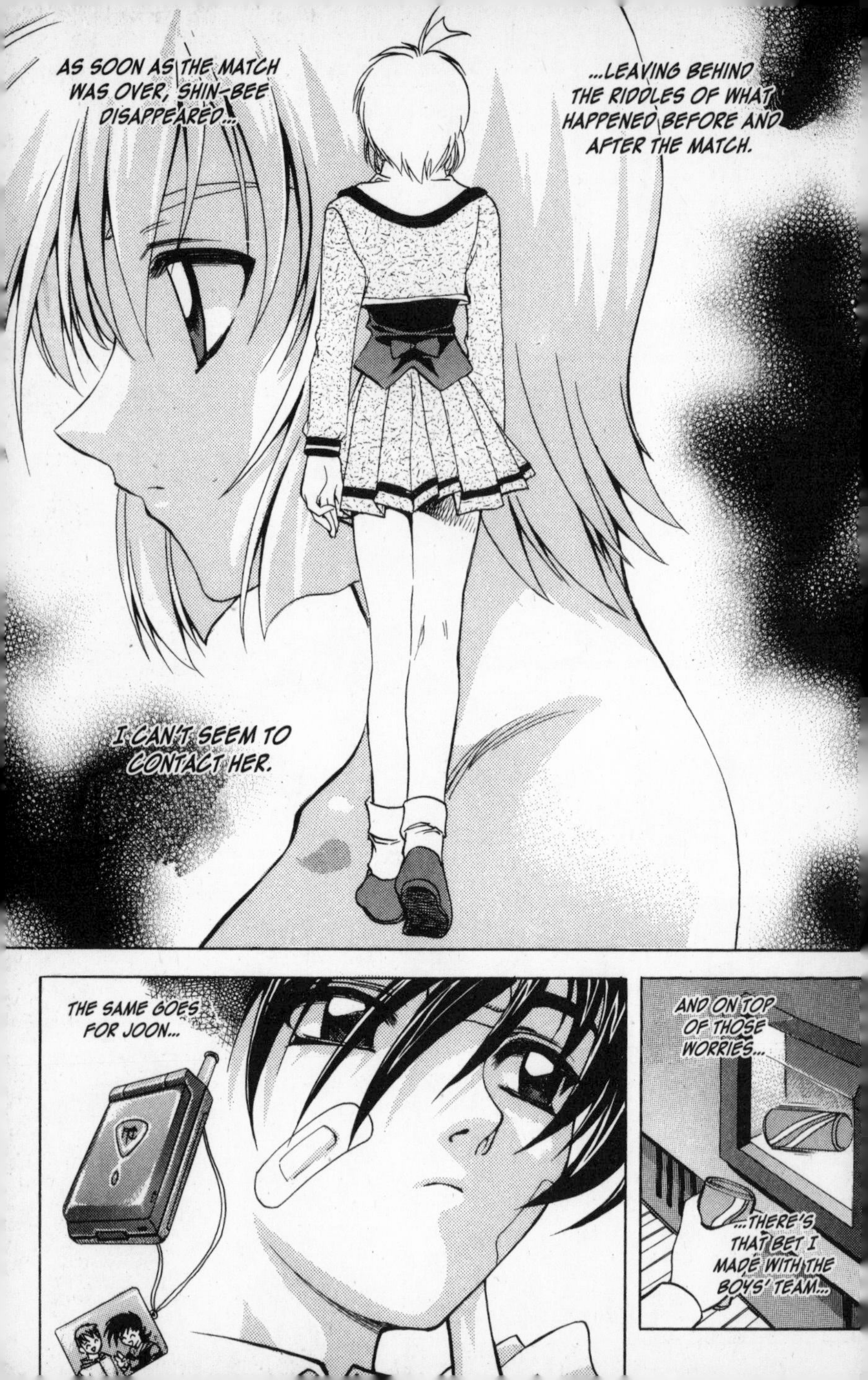
AS SOON AS THE MATCH WAS OVER, SHIN-BEE DISAPPEARED...
...LEAVING BEHIND THE RIDDLES OF WHAT HAPPENED BEFORE AND AFTER THE MATCH.
I CAN'T SEEM TO CONTACT HER.
THE SAME GOES FOR JOON...
AND ON TOP OF THOSE WORRIES...
...THERE'S THAT BET I MADE WITH THE BOYS' TEAM...

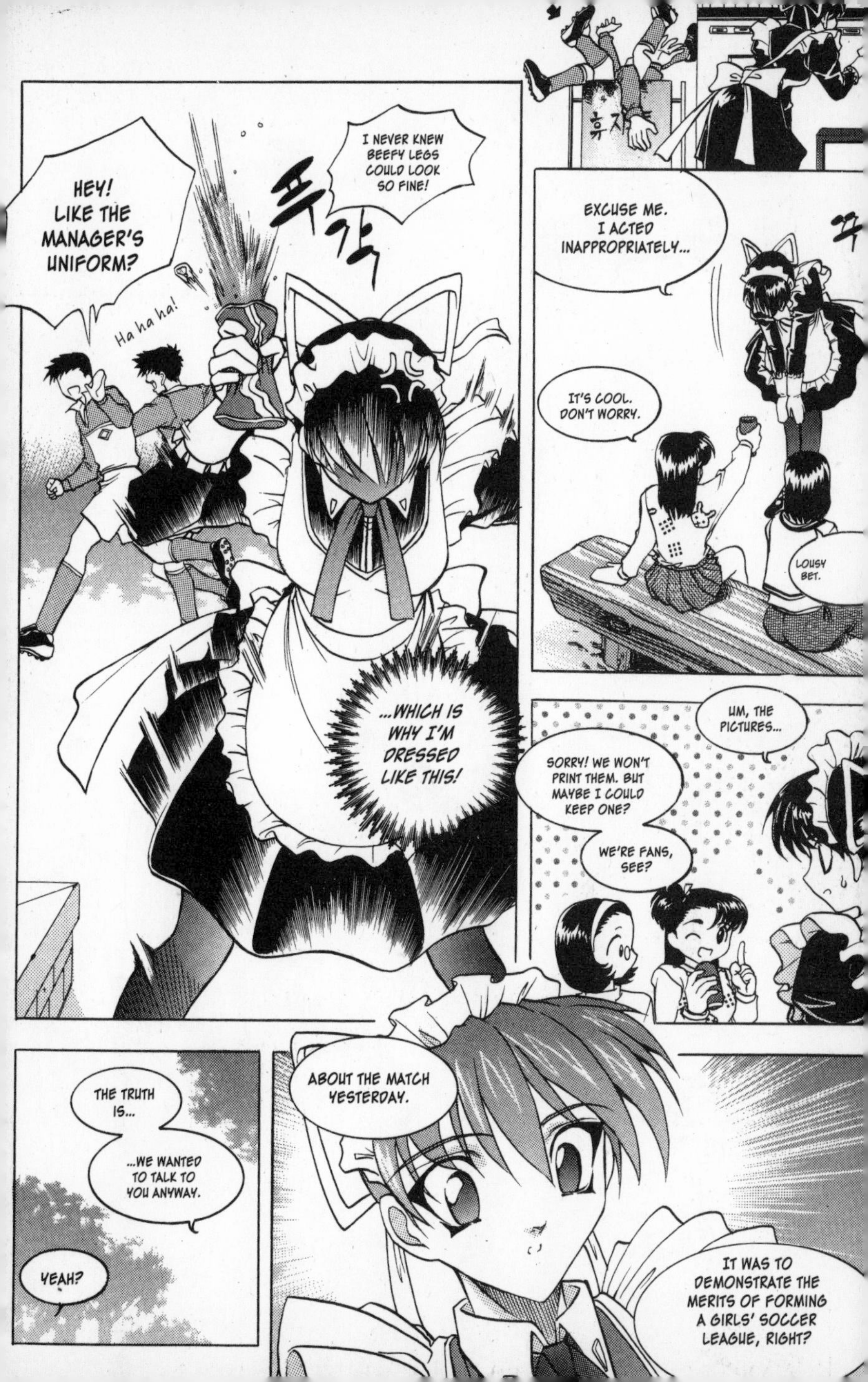
HEY! LIKE THE MANAGER'S UNIFORM?
Ha ha ha!
I NEVER KNEW BEEFY LEGS COULD LOOK SO FINE!
...WHICH IS WHY I'M DRESSED LIKE THIS!
EXCUSE ME. I ACTED INAPPROPRIATELY...
IT'S COOL. DON'T WORRY.
LOUSY BET.
UM, THE PICTURES...
SORRY! WE WON'T PRINT THEM. BUT MAYBE I COULD KEEP ONE?
WE'RE FANS, SEE?
THE TRUTH IS...
...WE WANTED TO TALK TO YOU ANYWAY.
YEAH?
ABOUT THE MATCH YESTERDAY.
IT WAS TO DEMONSTRATE THE MERITS OF FORMING A GIRLS' SOCCER LEAGUE, RIGHT?

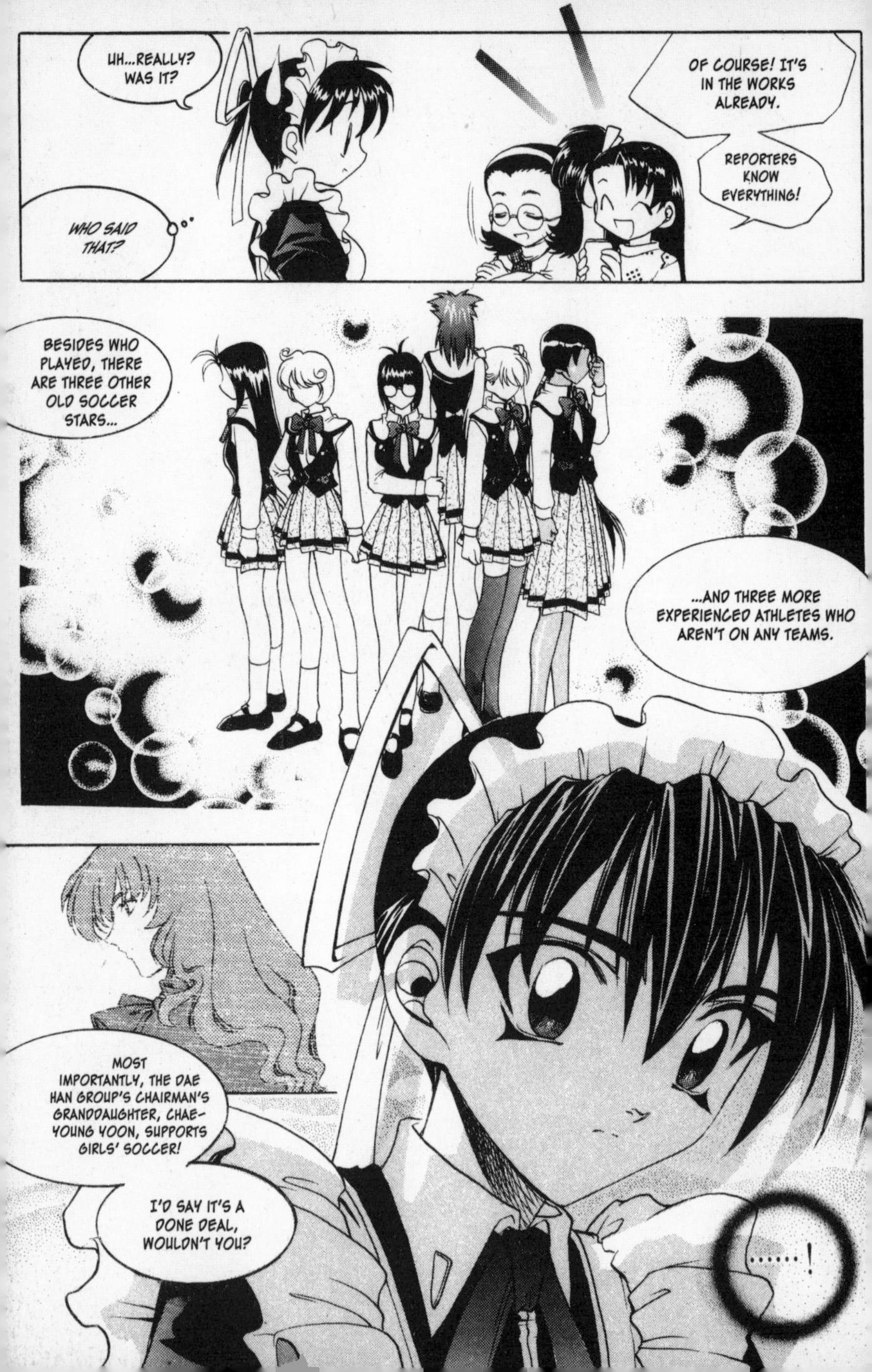
UH...REALLY? WAS IT?
WHO SAID THAT?
OF COURSE! IT'S IN THE WORKS ALREADY.
REPORTERS KNOW EVERYTHING!
BESIDES WHO PLAYED, THERE ARE THREE OTHER OLD SOCCER STARS...
...AND THREE MORE EXPERIENCED ATHLETES WHO AREN'T ON ANY TEAMS.
MOST IMPORTANTLY, THE DAE HAN GROUP'S CHAIRMAN'S GRANDDAUGHTER, CHAE-YOUNG YOON, SUPPORTS GIRLS' SOCCER!
I'D SAY IT'S A DONE DEAL, WOULDN'T YOU?
......!

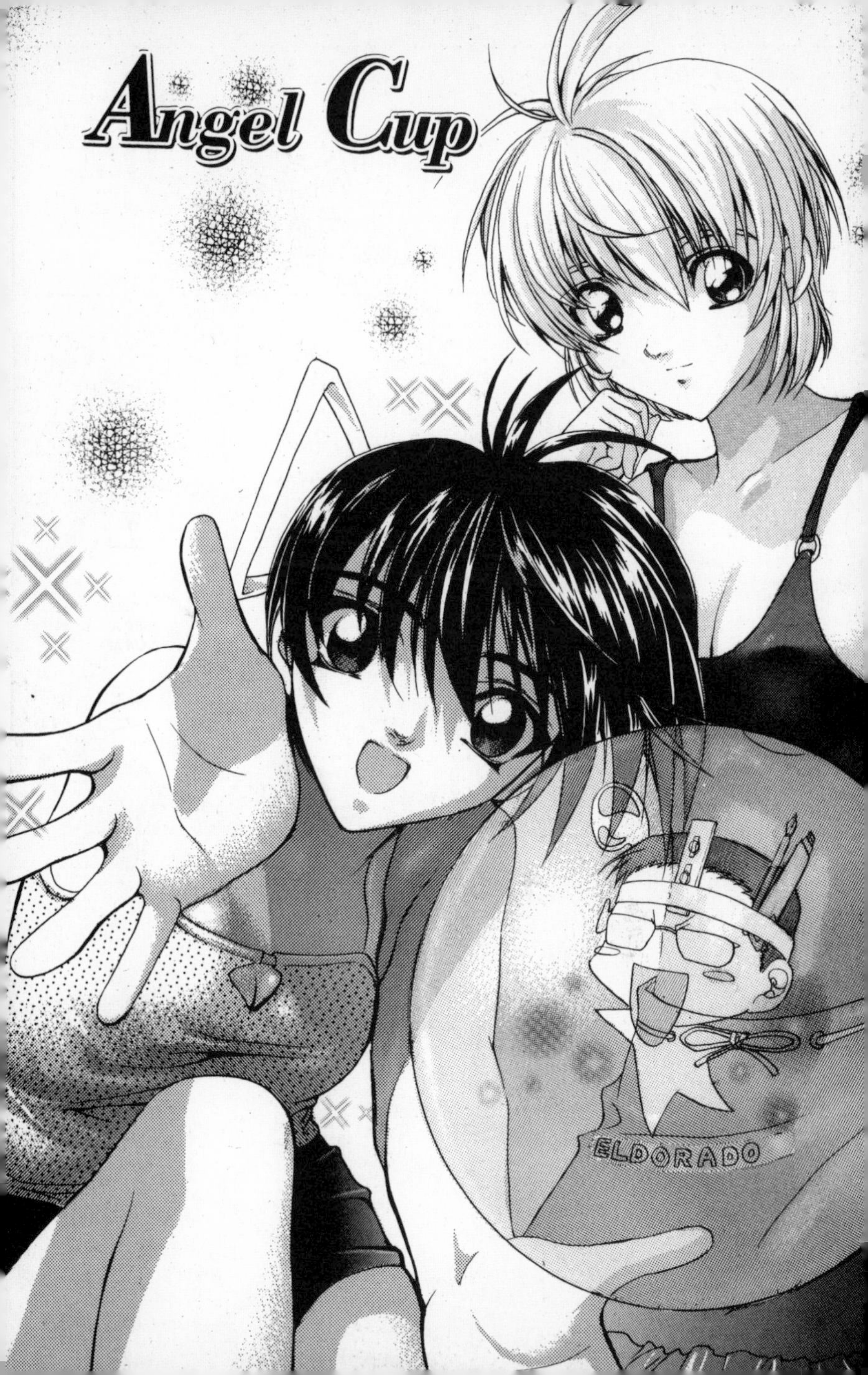
Angel Cup
ELDORADO

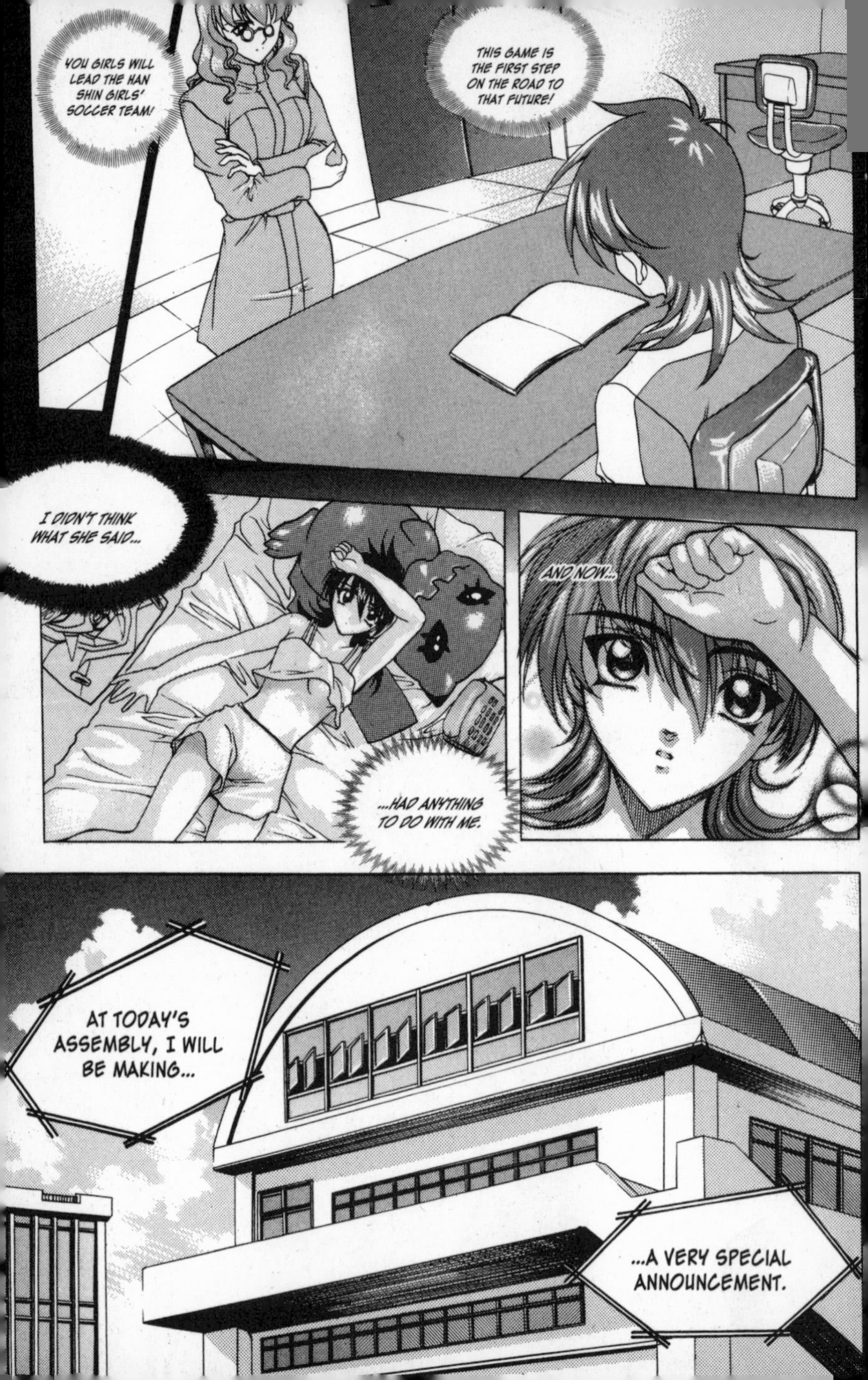
YOU GIRLS WILL LEAD THE HAN SHIN GIRLS' SOCCER TEAM!
THIS GAME IS THE FIRST STEP ON THE ROAD TO THAT FUTURE!
I DIDN'T THINK WHAT SHE SAID...
...HAD ANYTHING TO DO WITH ME.
AND NOW...
AT TODAY'S ASSEMBLY, I WILL BE MAKING...
...A VERY SPECIAL ANNOUNCEMENT.

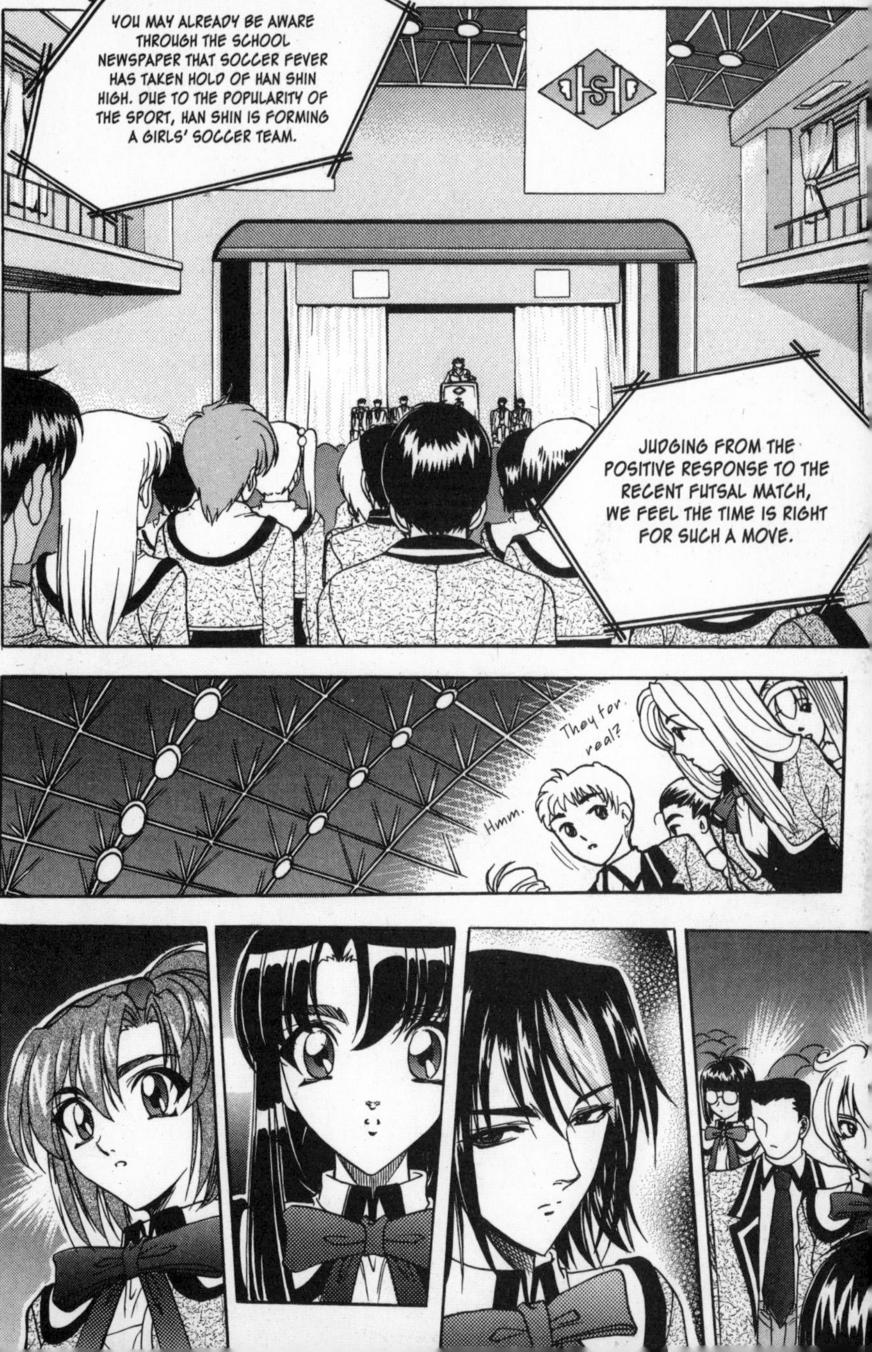
YOU MAY ALREADY BE AWARE THROUGH THE SCHOOL NEWSPAPER THAT SOCCER FEVER HAS TAKEN HOLD OF HAN SHIN HIGH. DUE TO THE POPULARITY OF THE SPORT, HAN SHIN IS FORMING A GIRLS' SOCCER TEAM.
JUDGING FROM THE POSITIVE RESPONSE TO THE RECENT FUTSAL MATCH, WE FEEL THE TIME IS RIGHT FOR SUCH A MOVE.
They for real?
Hmm.

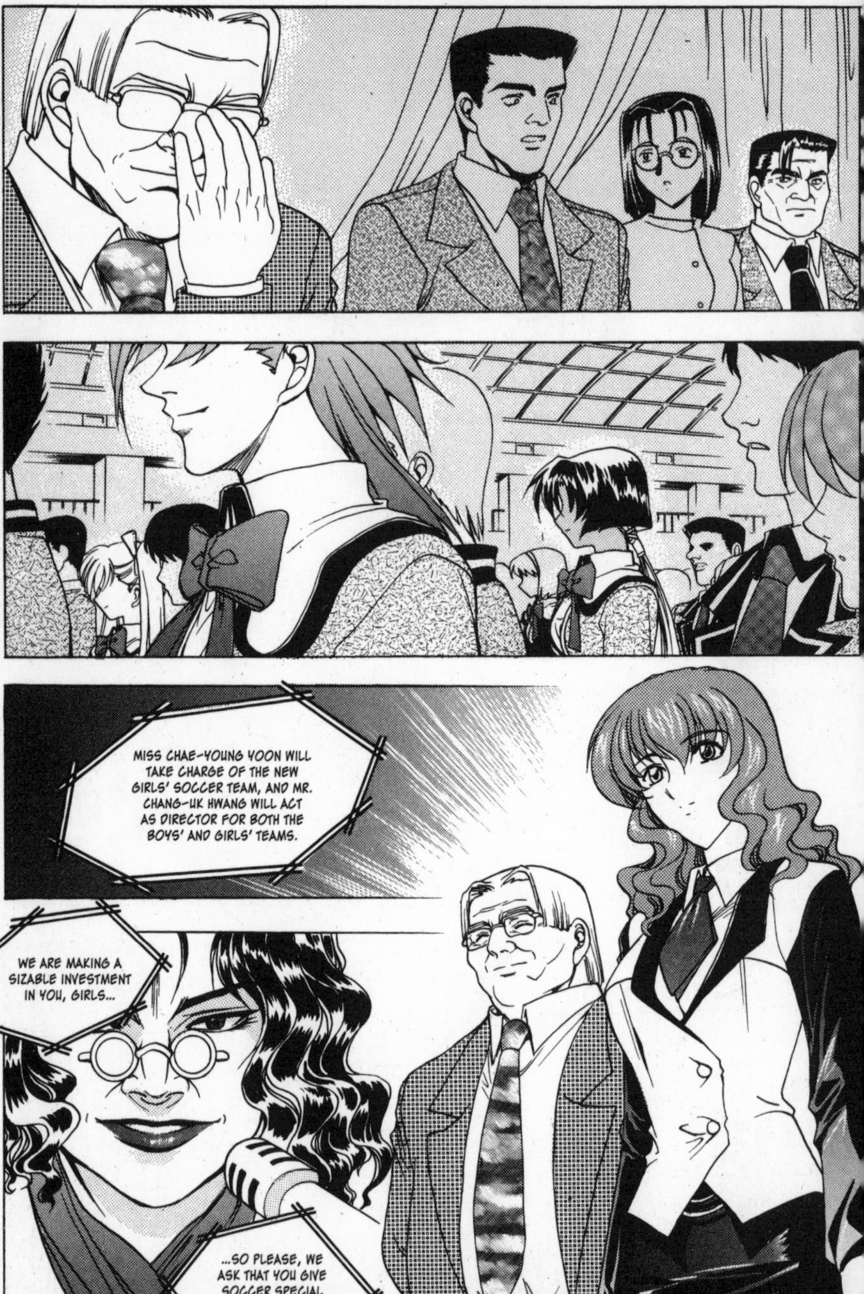
MISS CHAE-YOUNG YOON WILL TAKE CHARGE OF THE NEW GIRLS' SOCCER TEAM, AND MR. CHANG-UK HWANG WILL ACT AS DIRECTOR FOR BOTH THE BOYS' AND GIRLS' TEAMS.
WE ARE MAKING A SIZABLE INVESTMENT IN YOU, GIRLS...
...SO PLEASE, WE ASK THAT YOU GIVE SOCCER SPECIAL CONSIDERATION.

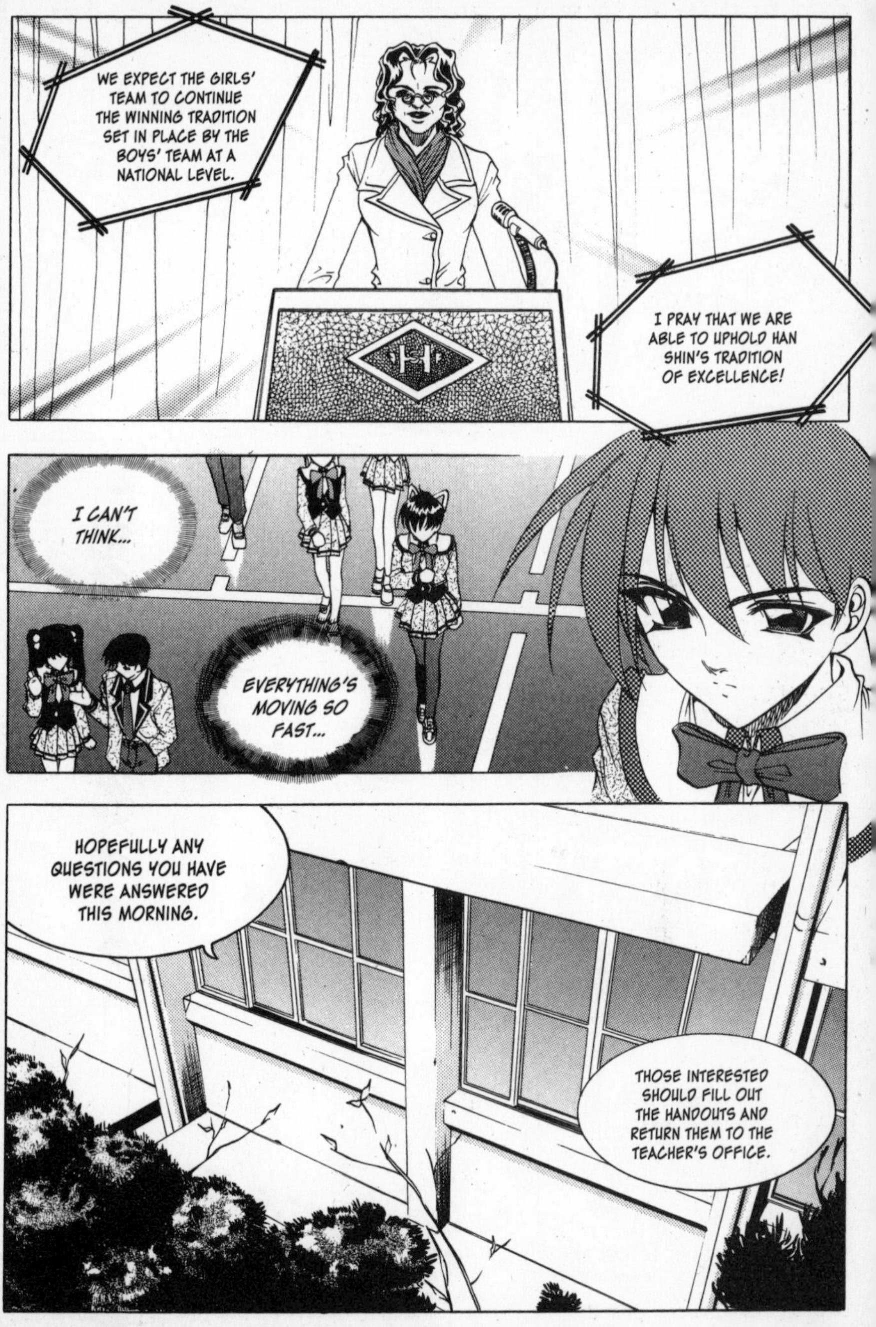
WE EXPECT THE GIRLS' TEAM TO CONTINUE THE WINNING TRADITION SET IN PLACE BY THE BOYS' TEAM AT A NATIONAL LEVEL.
I PRAY THAT WE ARE ABLE TO UPHOLD HAN SHIN'S TRADITION OF EXCELLENCE!
I CAN'T THINK...
EVERYTHING'S MOVING SO FAST...
HOPEFULLY ANY QUESTIONS YOU HAVE WERE ANSWERED THIS MORNING.
THOSE INTERESTED SHOULD FILL OUT THE HANDOUTS AND RETURN THEM TO THE TEACHER'S OFFICE.

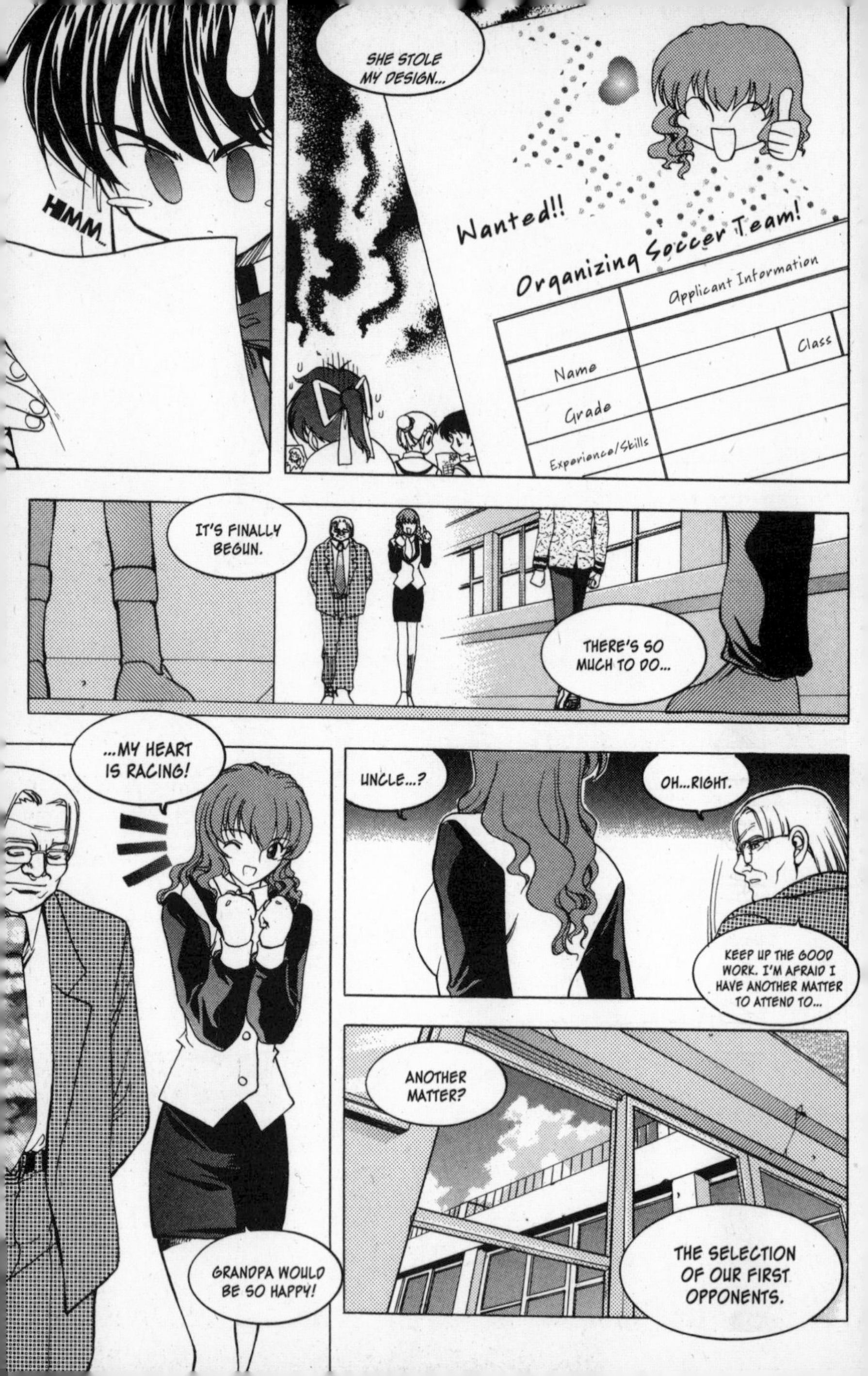
HMM...
SHE STOLE MY DESIGN...
Wanted!!
Organizing Soccer Team!
Applicant Information
Name
Class
Grade
Experience/Skills
IT'S FINALLY BEGUN.
THERE'S SO MUCH TO DO...
...MY HEART IS RACING!
GRANDPA WOULD BE SO HAPPY!
UNCLE...?
OH...RIGHT.
KEEP UP THE GOOD WORK. I'M AFRAID I HAVE ANOTHER MATTER TO ATTEND TO...
ANOTHER MATTER?
THE SELECTION OF OUR FIRST OPPONENTS.

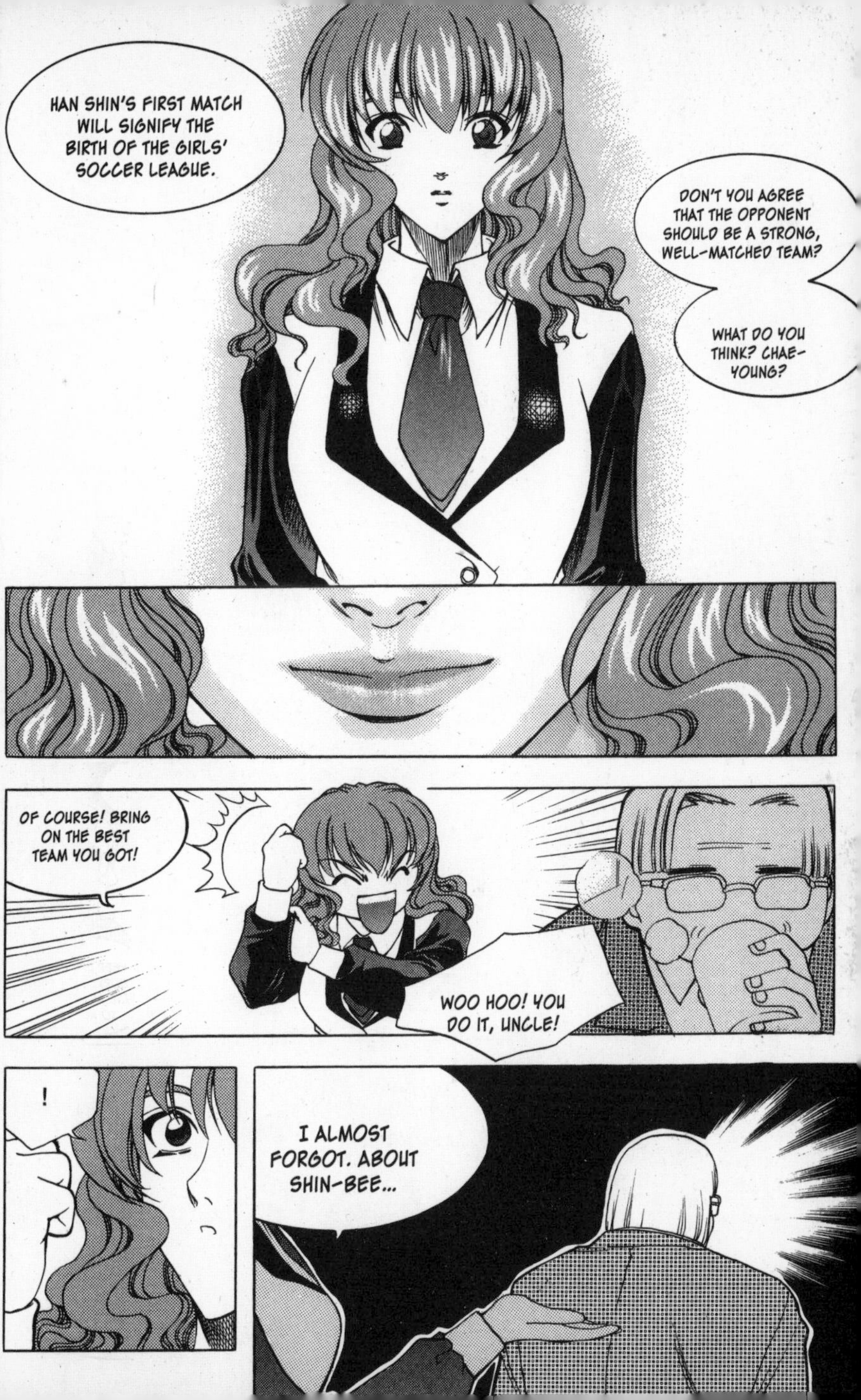
HAN SHIN'S FIRST MATCH WILL SIGNIFY THE BIRTH OF THE GIRLS' SOCCER LEAGUE.
DON'T YOU AGREE THAT THE OPPONENT SHOULD BE A STRONG, WELL-MATCHED TEAM?
WHAT DO YOU THINK? CHAE-YOUNG?
OF COURSE! BRING ON THE BEST TEAM YOU GOT!
WOO HOO! YOU DO IT, UNCLE!
!
I ALMOST FORGOT. ABOUT SHIN-BEE...

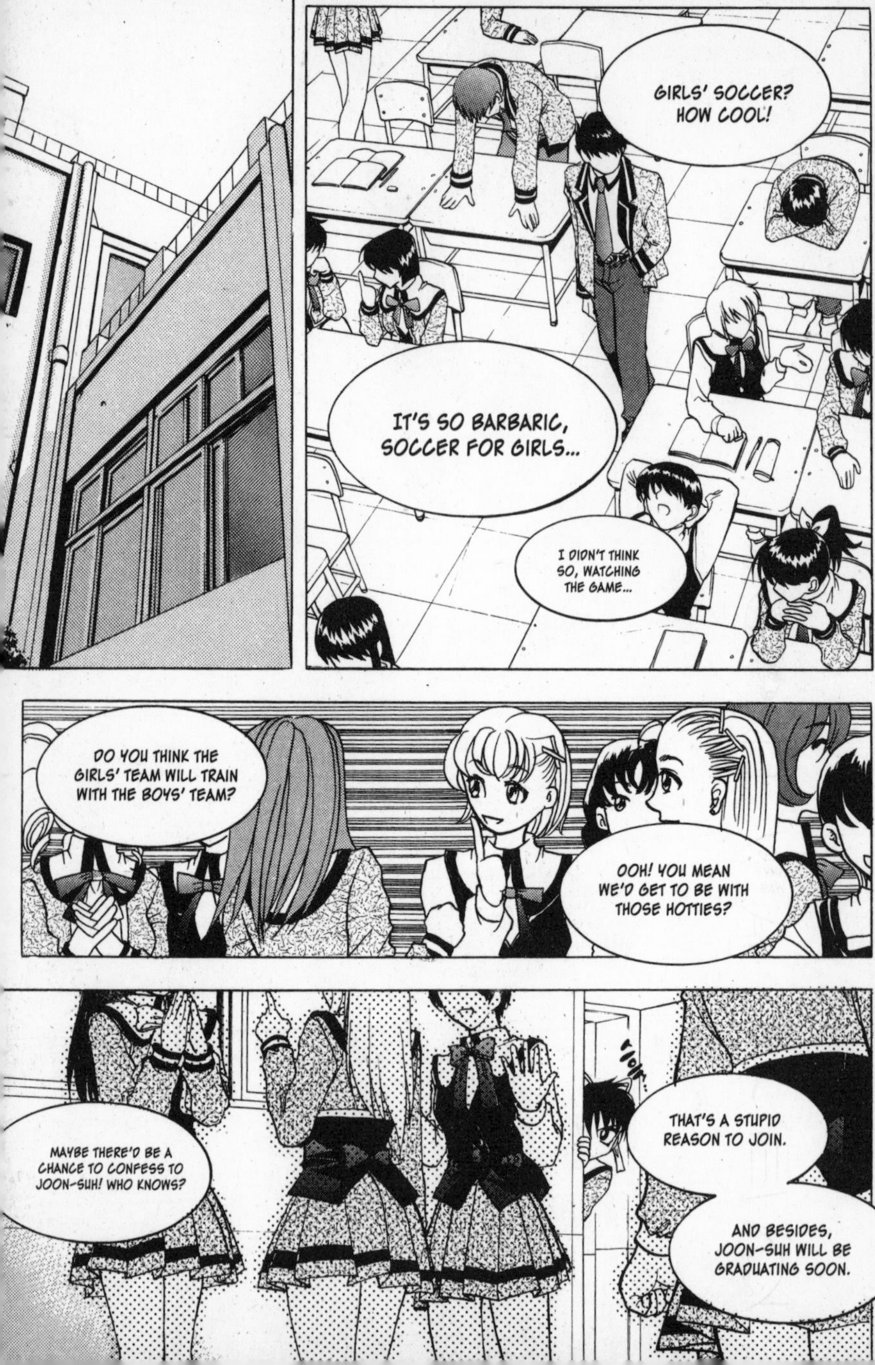
GIRLS' SOCCER? HOW COOL!
IT'S SO BARBARIC, SOCCER FOR GIRLS...
I DIDN'T THINK SO, WATCHING THE GAME...
DO YOU THINK THE GIRLS' TEAM WILL TRAIN WITH THE BOYS' TEAM?
OOH! YOU MEAN WE'D GET TO BE WITH THOSE HOTTIES?
MAYBE THERE'D BE A CHANCE TO CONFESS TO JOON-SUH! WHO KNOWS?
THAT'S A STUPID REASON TO JOIN.
AND BESIDES, JOON-SUH WILL BE GRADUATING SOON.

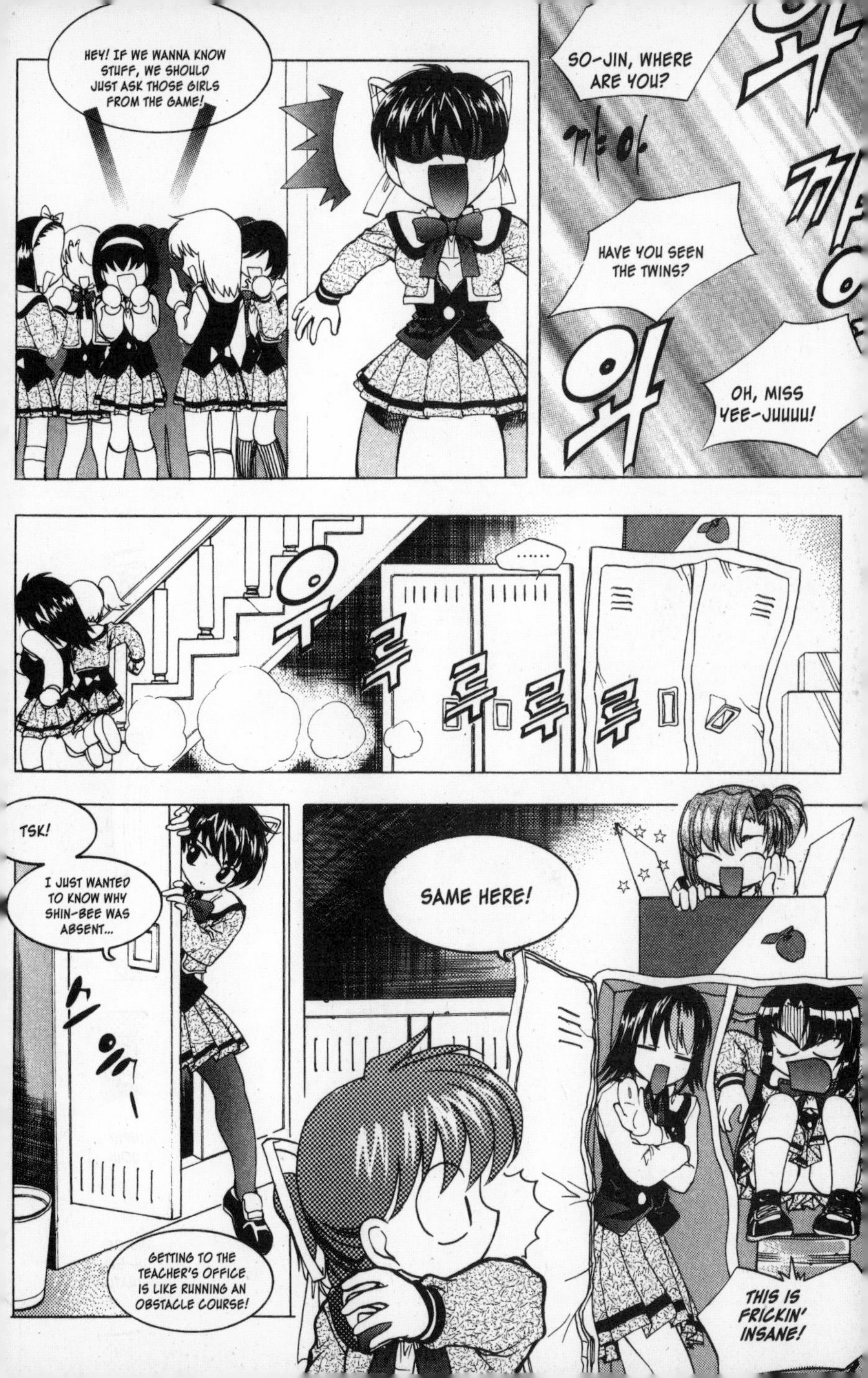
HEY! IF WE WANNA KNOW STUFF, WE SHOULD JUST ASK THOSE GIRLS FROM THE GAME!
SO-JIN, WHERE ARE YOU?
HAVE YOU SEEN THE TWINS?
OH, MISS YEE-JUUUU!
......
TSK!
I JUST WANTED TO KNOW WHY SHIN-BEE WAS ABSENT...
GETTING TO THE TEACHER'S OFFICE IS LIKE RUNNING AN OBSTACLE COURSE!
SAME HERE!
THIS IS FRICKIN' INSANE!

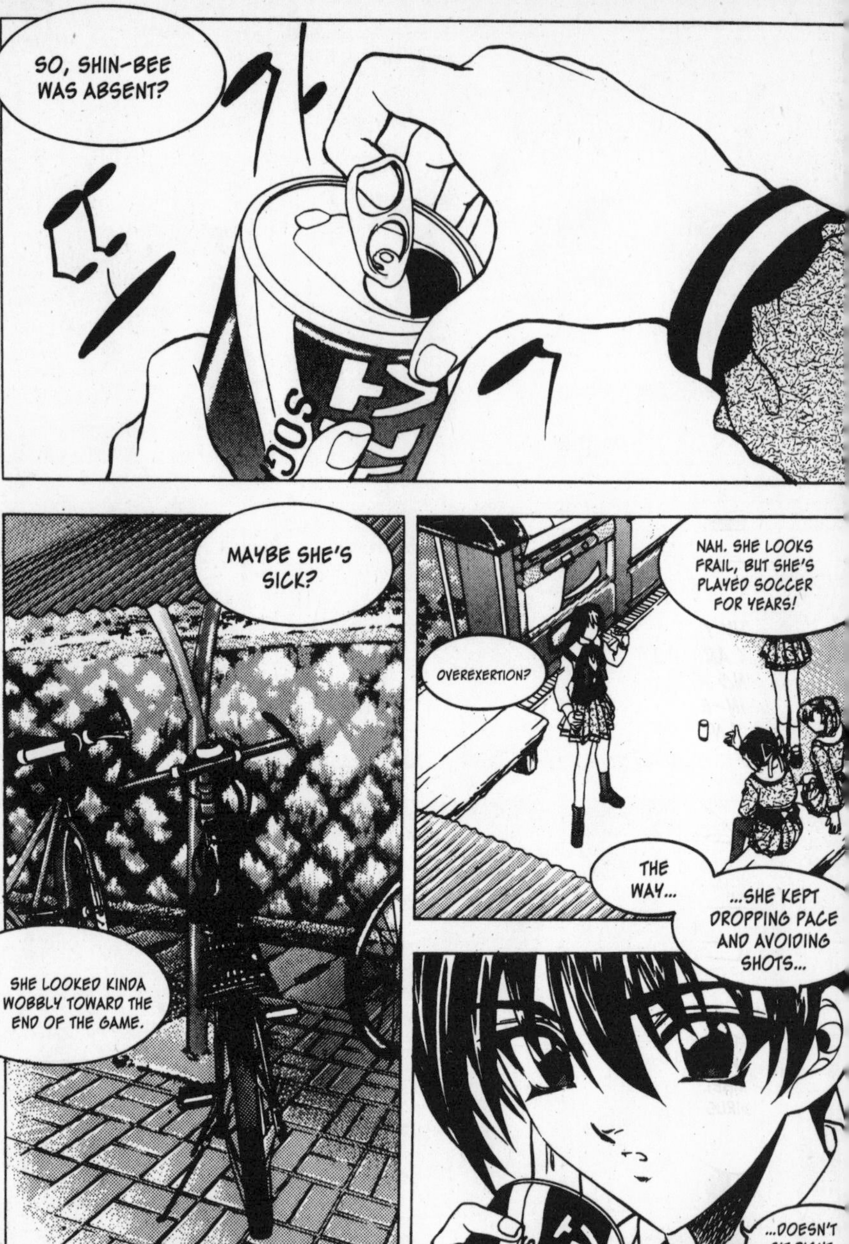
SO, SHIN-BEE WAS ABSENT?
MAYBE SHE'S SICK?
SHE LOOKED KINDA WOBBLY TOWARD THE END OF THE GAME.
NAH. SHE LOOKS FRAIL, BUT SHE'S PLAYED SOCCER FOR YEARS!
OVEREXERTION?
THE WAY...
...SHE KEPT DROPPING PACE AND AVOIDING SHOTS...
...DOESN'T SIT RIGHT WITH ME.

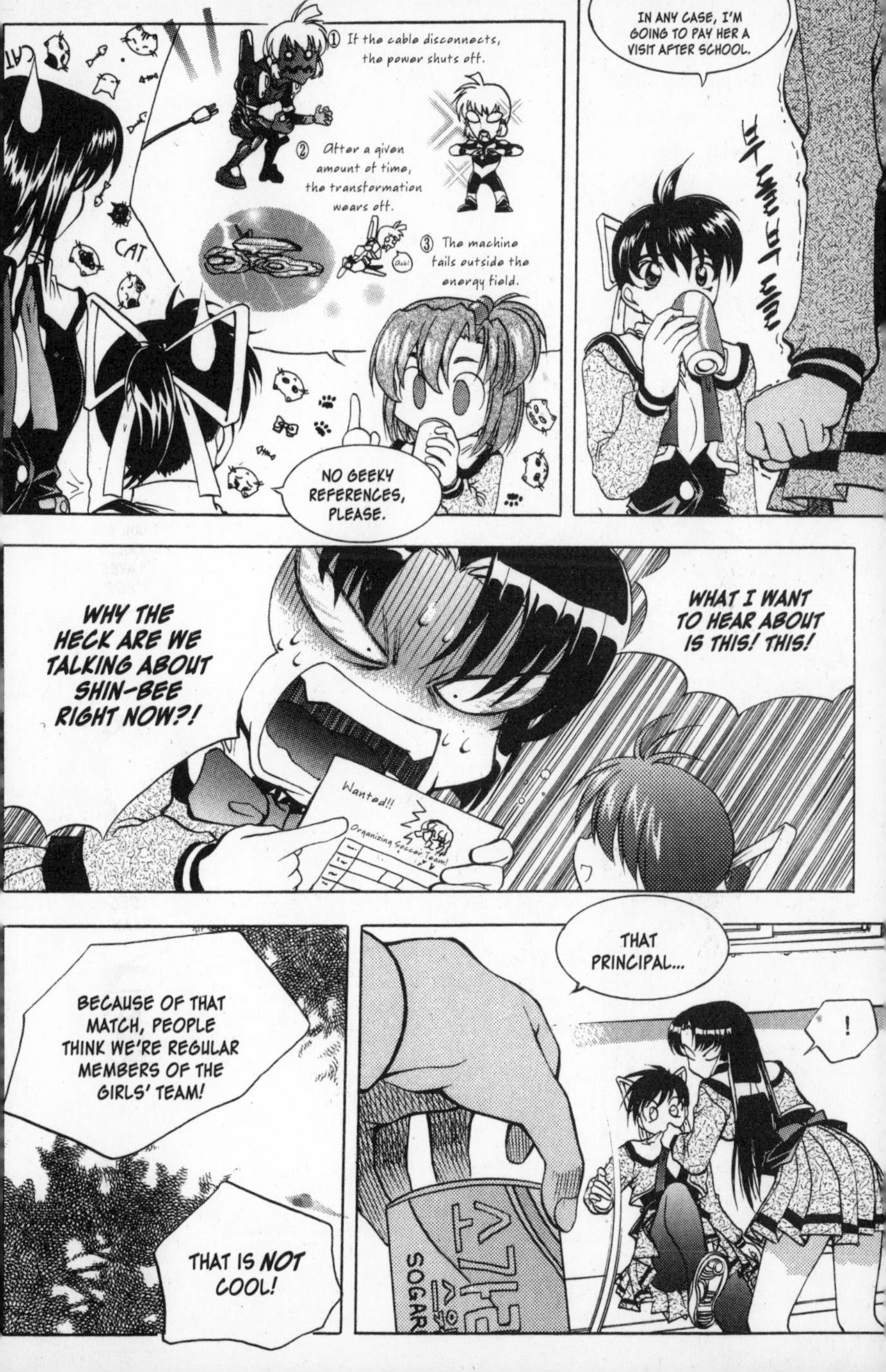
CAT
CAT
① If the cable disconnects, the power shuts off.
② After a given amount of time, the transformation wears off.
③ The machine fails outside the energy field.
NO GEEKY REFERENCES, PLEASE.
IN ANY CASE, I'M GOING TO PAY HER A VISIT AFTER SCHOOL.
WHY THE HECK ARE WE TALKING ABOUT SHIN-BEE RIGHT NOW?!
WHAT I WANT TO HEAR ABOUT IS THIS! THIS!
Wanted!!
Organizing Soccer Team!
BECAUSE OF THAT MATCH, PEOPLE THINK WE'RE REGULAR MEMBERS OF THE GIRLS' TEAM!
THAT IS *NOT* COOL!
THAT PRINCIPAL...
!
SOGAR

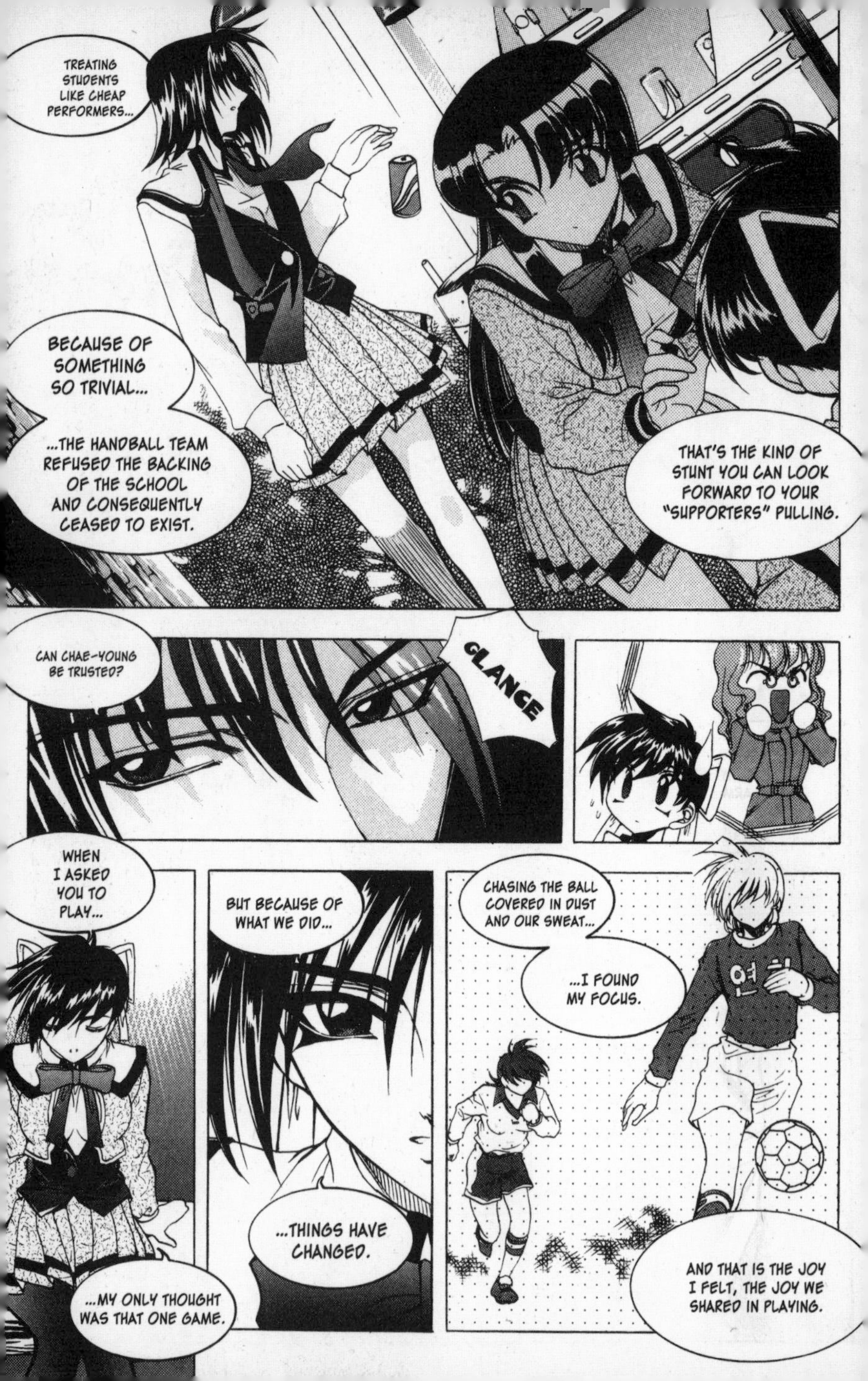
TREATING STUDENTS LIKE CHEAP PERFORMERS...
BECAUSE OF SOMETHING SO TRIVIAL...
...THE HANDBALL TEAM REFUSED THE BACKING OF THE SCHOOL AND CONSEQUENTLY CEASED TO EXIST.
THAT'S THE KIND OF STUNT YOU CAN LOOK FORWARD TO YOUR "SUPPORTERS" PULLING.
CAN CHAE-YOUNG BE TRUSTED?
GLANCE
WHEN I ASKED YOU TO PLAY...
...MY ONLY THOUGHT WAS THAT ONE GAME.
BUT BECAUSE OF WHAT WE DID...
...THINGS HAVE CHANGED.
CHASING THE BALL COVERED IN DUST AND OUR SWEAT...
...I FOUND MY FOCUS.
AND THAT IS THE JOY I FELT, THE JOY WE SHARED IN PLAYING.

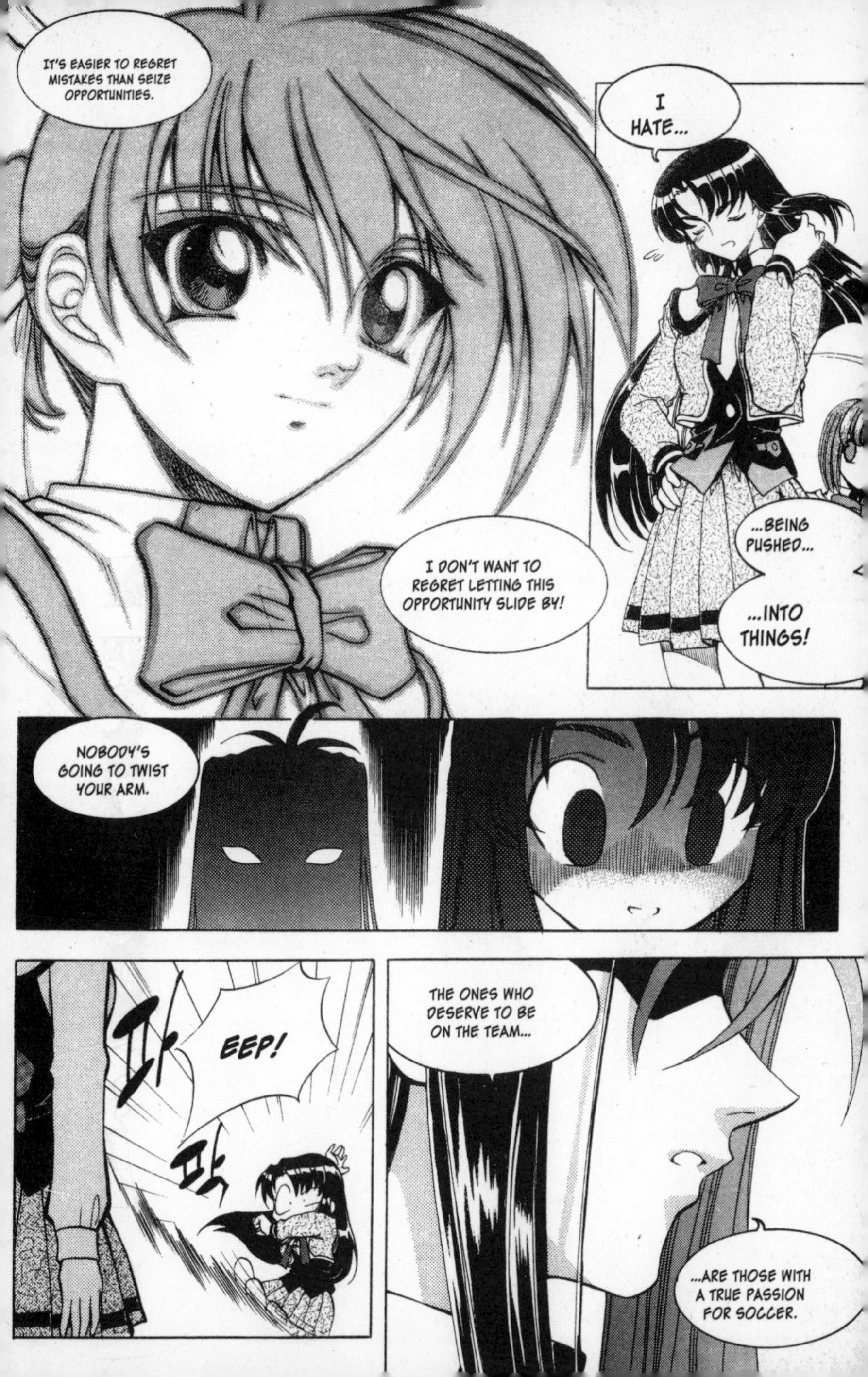
IT'S EASIER TO REGRET MISTAKES THAN SEIZE OPPORTUNITIES.
I DON'T WANT TO REGRET LETTING THIS OPPORTUNITY SLIDE BY!
I HATE...
...BEING PUSHED...
...INTO THINGS!
NOBODY'S GOING TO TWIST YOUR ARM.
EEP!
THE ONES WHO DESERVE TO BE ON THE TEAM...
...ARE THOSE WITH A TRUE PASSION FOR SOCCER.

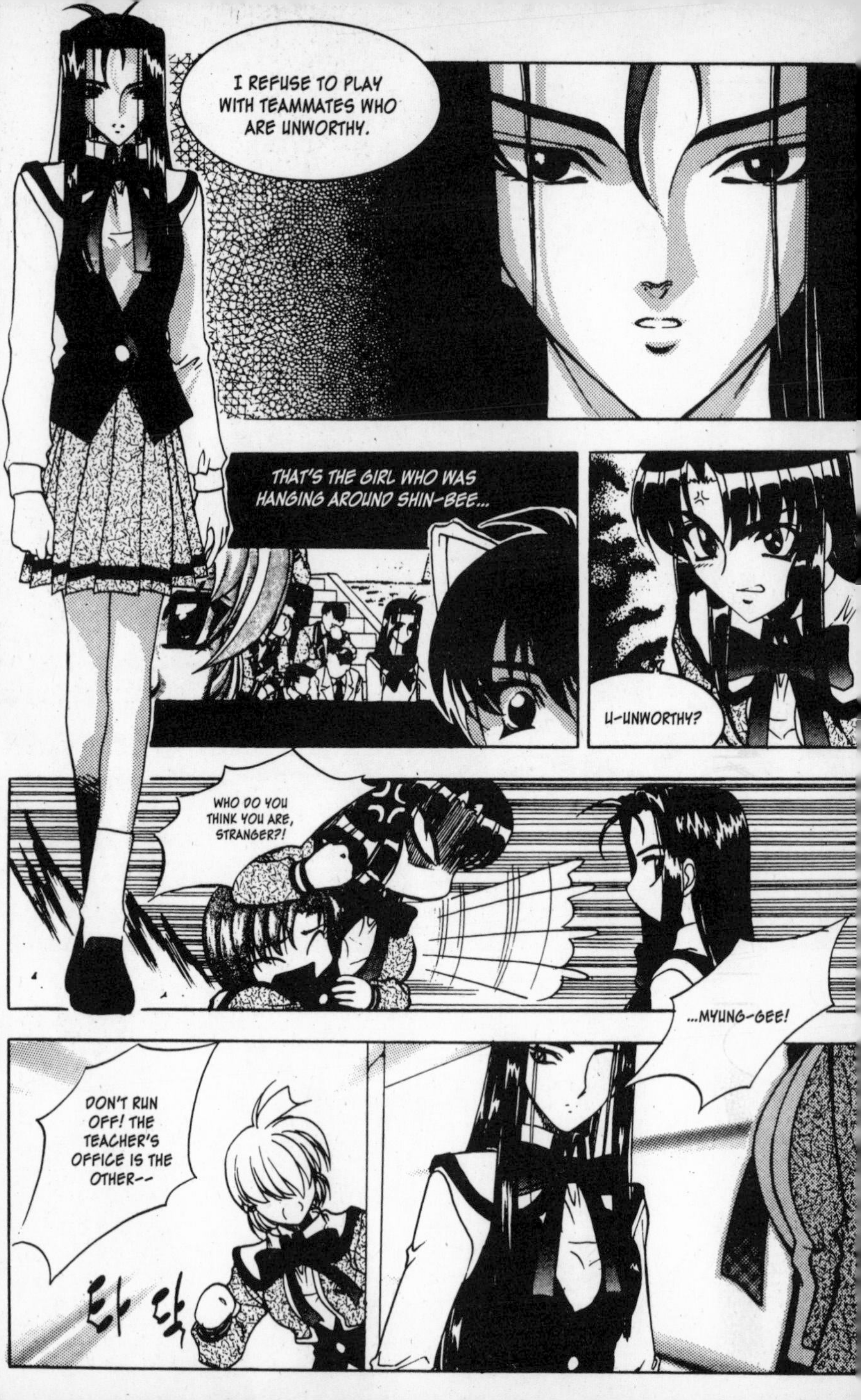
I REFUSE TO PLAY WITH TEAMMATES WHO ARE UNWORTHY.
THAT'S THE GIRL WHO WAS HANGING AROUND SHIN-BEE...
U-UNWORTHY?
WHO DO YOU THINK YOU ARE, STRANGER?!
...MYUNG-GEE!
DON'T RUN OFF! THE TEACHER'S OFFICE IS THE OTHER--
타 닥

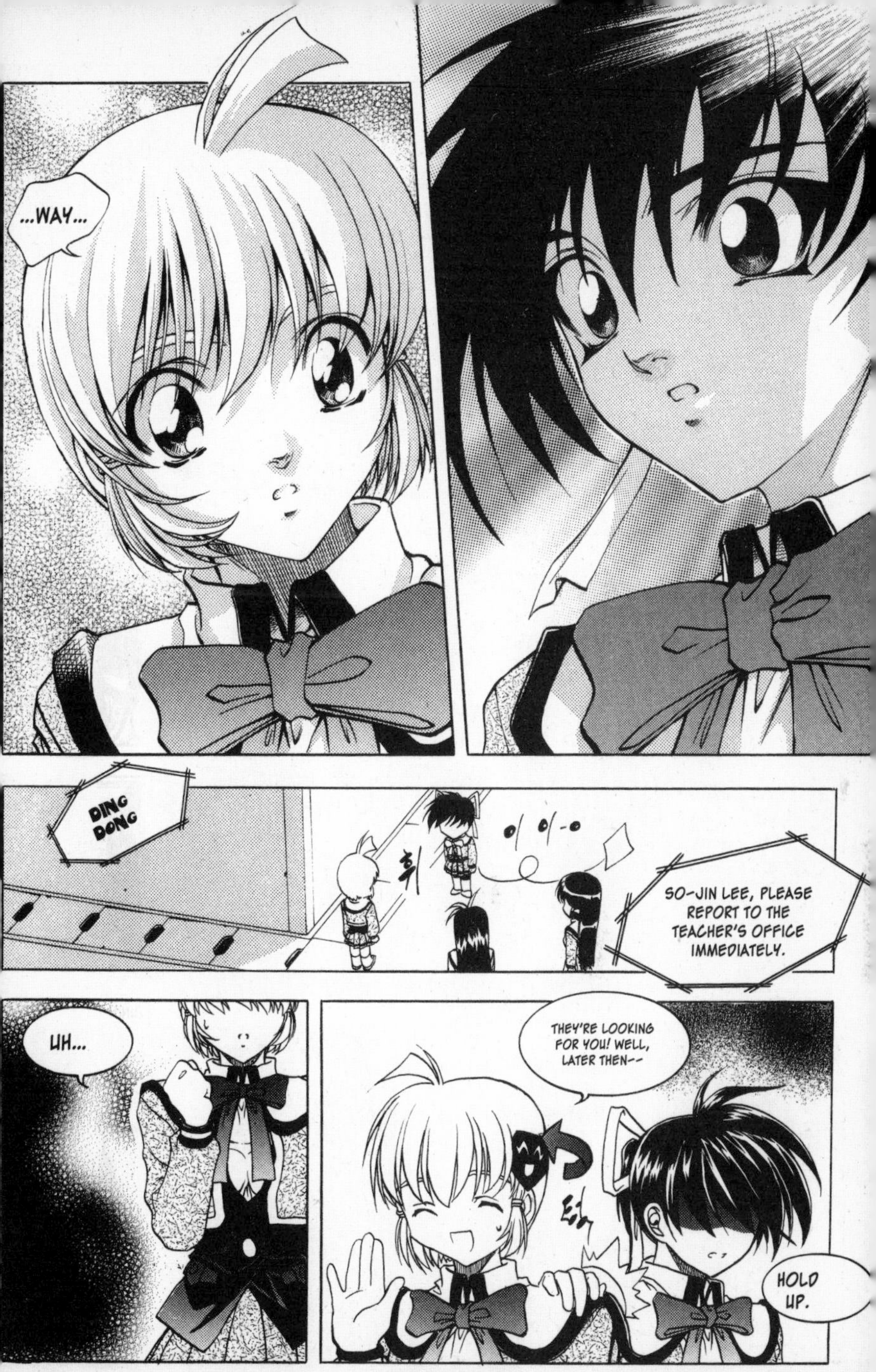
...WAY...
DING DONG
SO-JIN LEE, PLEASE REPORT TO THE TEACHER'S OFFICE IMMEDIATELY.
UH...
THEY'RE LOOKING FOR YOU! WELL, LATER THEN--
HOLD UP.

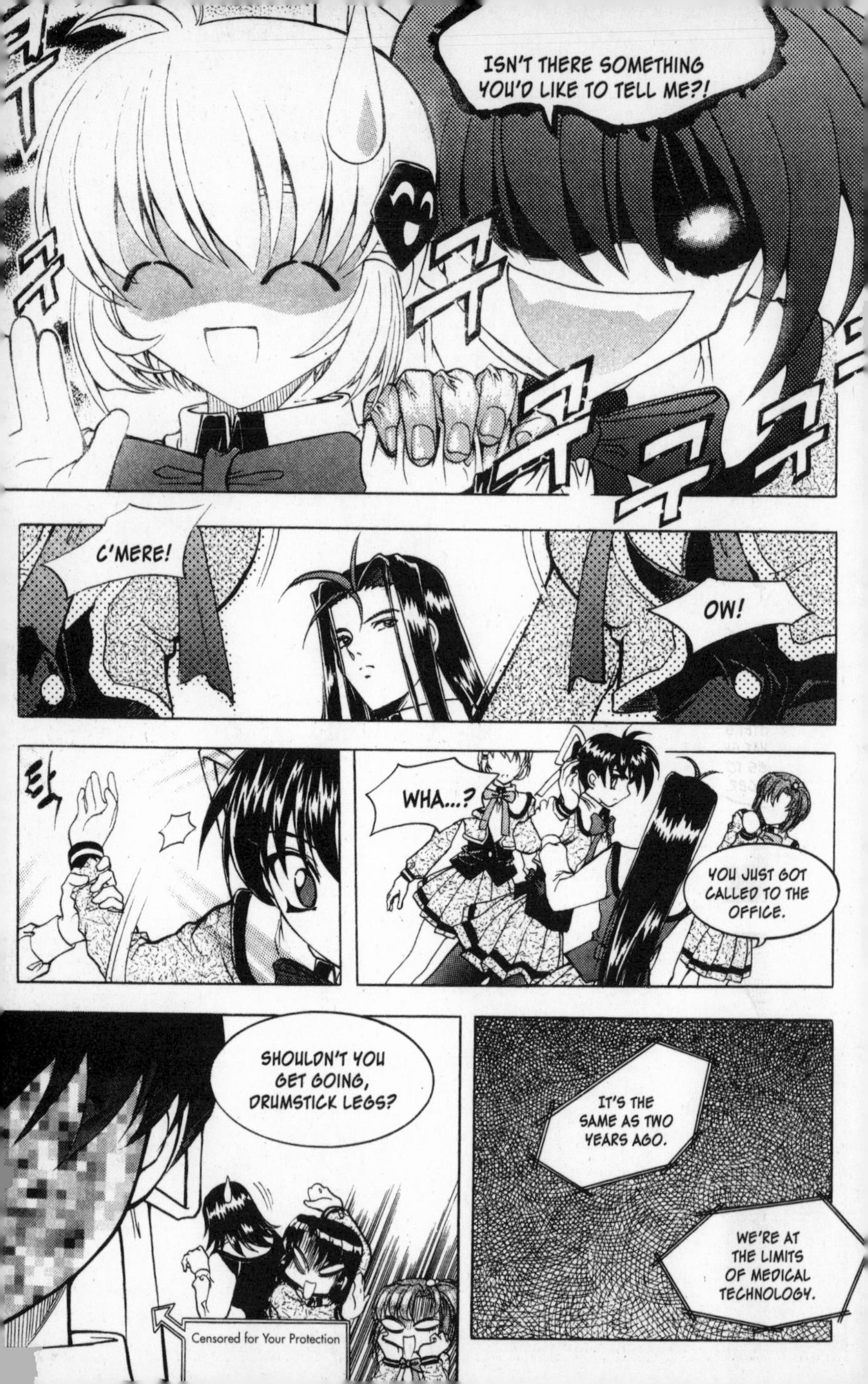
ISN'T THERE SOMETHING YOU'D LIKE TO TELL ME?!
C'MERE!
OW!
탁
WHA...?
YOU JUST GOT CALLED TO THE OFFICE.
SHOULDN'T YOU GET GOING, DRUMSTICK LEGS?
Censored for Your Protection
IT'S THE SAME AS TWO YEARS AGO.
WE'RE AT THE LIMITS OF MEDICAL TECHNOLOGY.

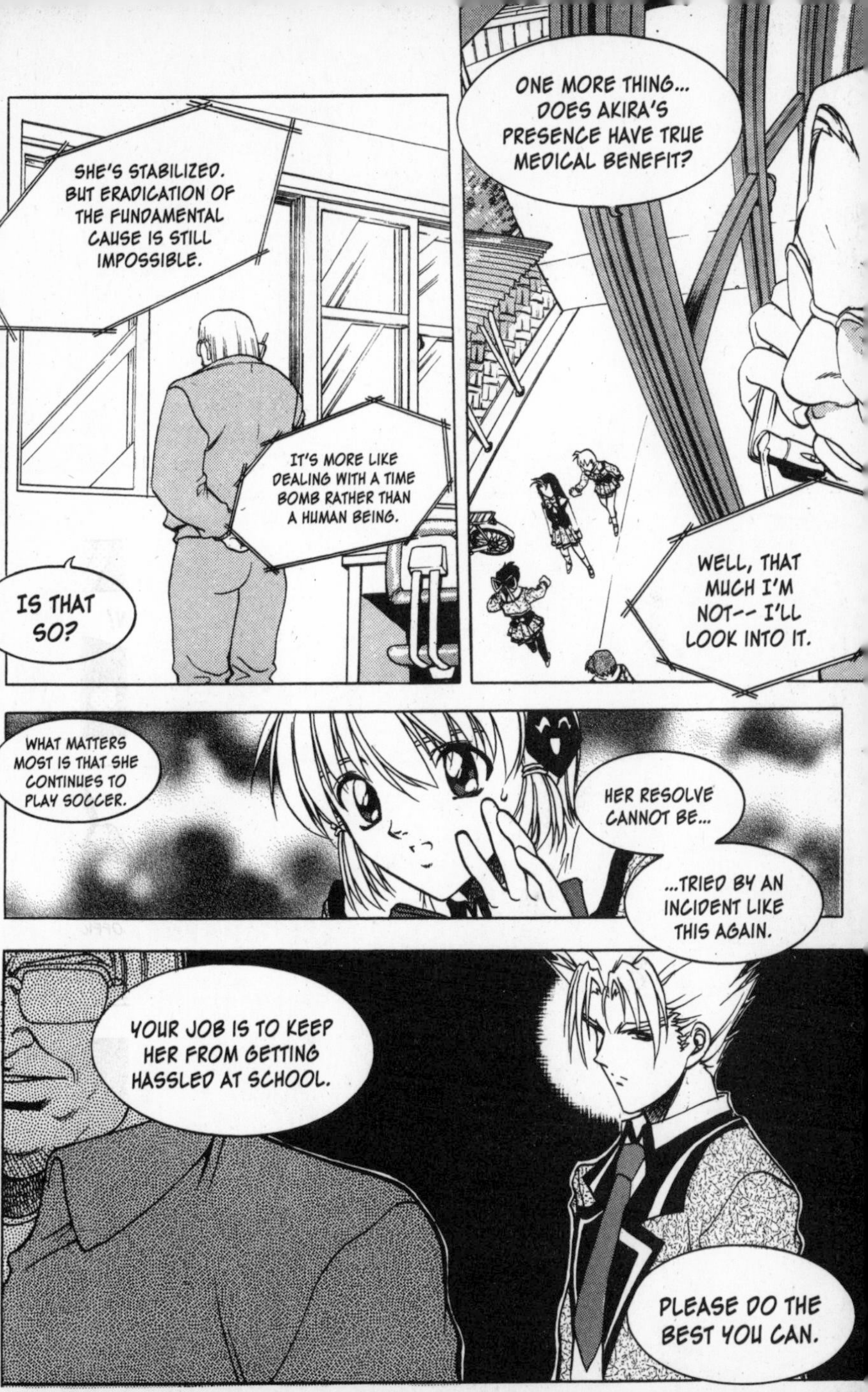
SHE'S STABILIZED. BUT ERADICATION OF THE FUNDAMENTAL CAUSE IS STILL IMPOSSIBLE.
IT'S MORE LIKE DEALING WITH A TIME BOMB RATHER THAN A HUMAN BEING.
IS THAT SO?
ONE MORE THING... DOES AKIRA'S PRESENCE HAVE TRUE MEDICAL BENEFIT?
WELL, THAT MUCH I'M NOT-- I'LL LOOK INTO IT.
WHAT MATTERS MOST IS THAT SHE CONTINUES TO PLAY SOCCER.
HER RESOLVE CANNOT BE...
...TRIED BY AN INCIDENT LIKE THIS AGAIN.
YOUR JOB IS TO KEEP HER FROM GETTING HASSLED AT SCHOOL.
PLEASE DO THE BEST YOU CAN.

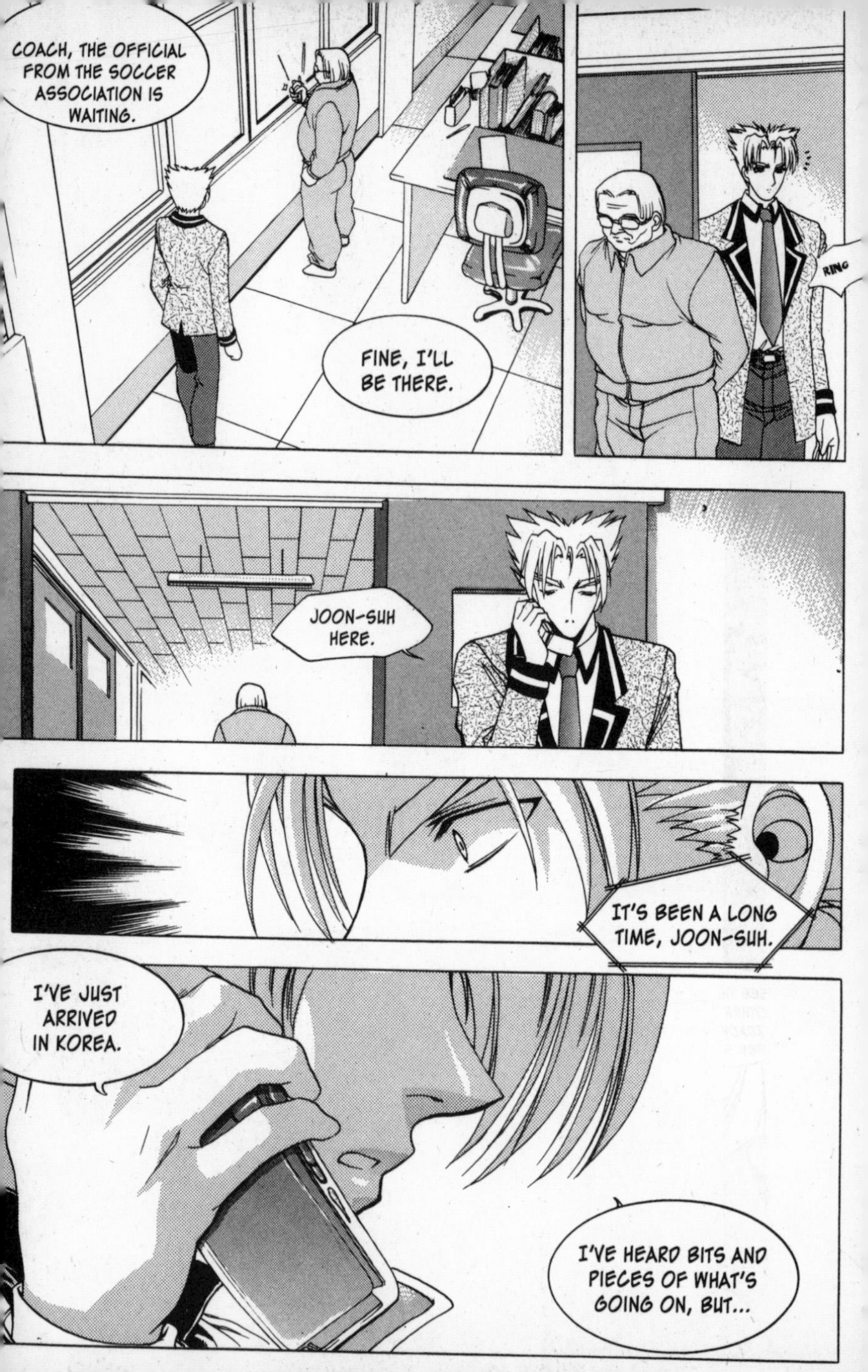
COACH, THE OFFICIAL FROM THE SOCCER ASSOCIATION IS WAITING.
FINE, I'LL BE THERE.
RING
JOON-SUH HERE.
IT'S BEEN A LONG TIME, JOON-SUH.
I'VE JUST ARRIVED IN KOREA.
I'VE HEARD BITS AND PIECES OF WHAT'S GOING ON, BUT...

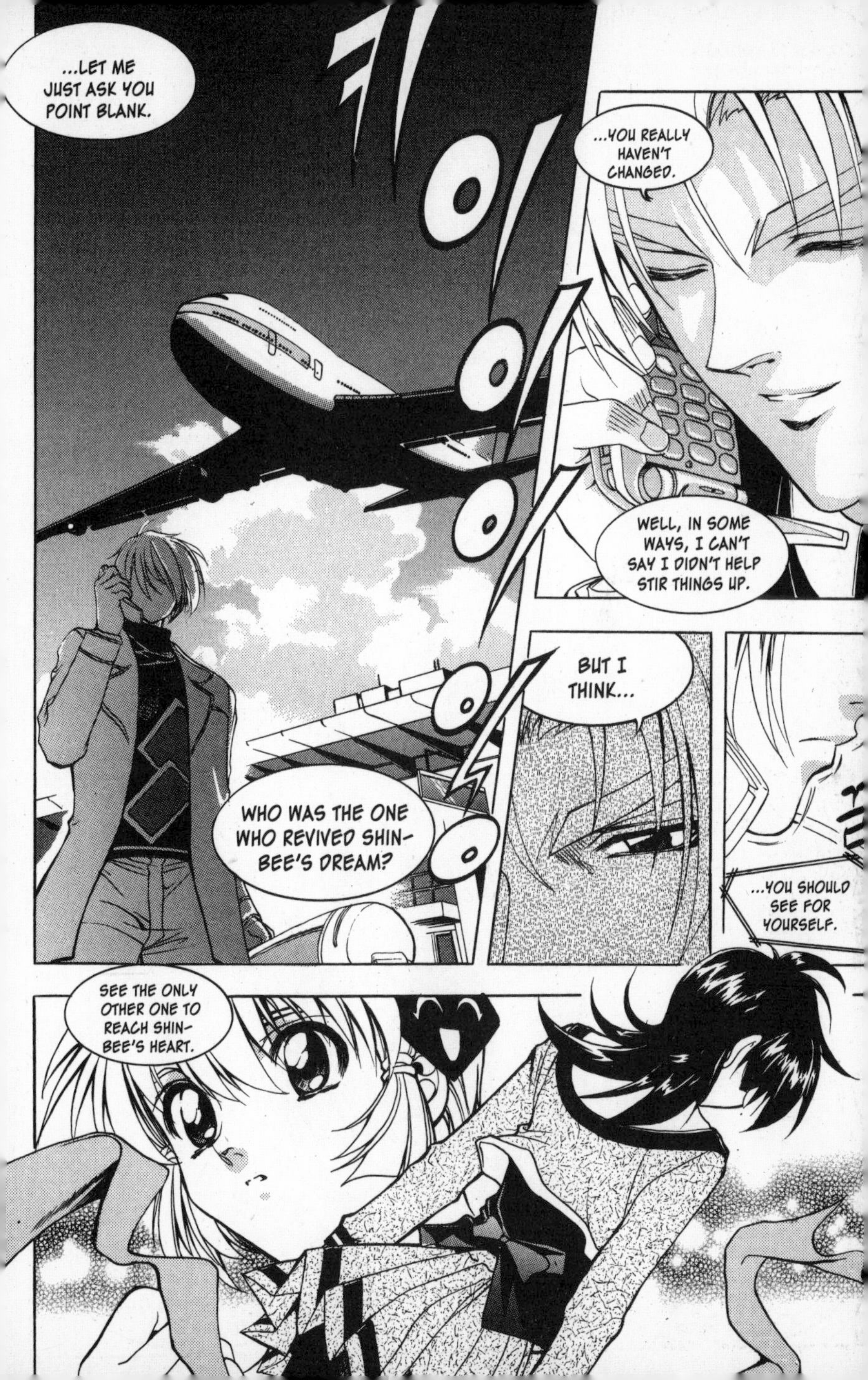
...LET ME JUST ASK YOU POINT BLANK.
WHO WAS THE ONE WHO REVIVED SHIN-BEE'S DREAM?
...YOU REALLY HAVEN'T CHANGED.
WELL, IN SOME WAYS, I CAN'T SAY I DIDN'T HELP STIR THINGS UP.
BUT I THINK...
...YOU SHOULD SEE FOR YOURSELF.
SEE THE ONLY OTHER ONE TO REACH SHIN-BEE'S HEART.

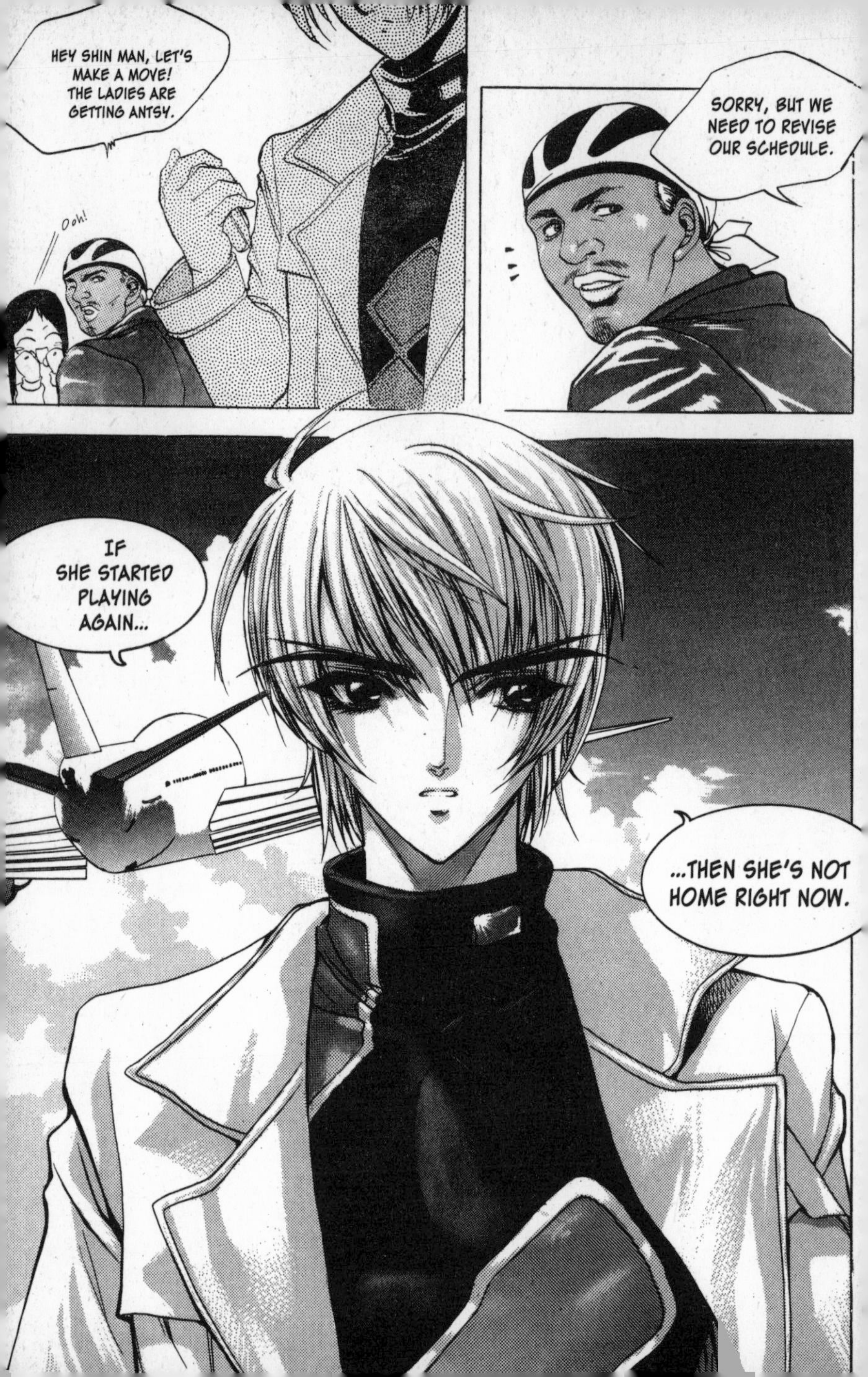
HEY SHIN MAN, LET'S MAKE A MOVE! THE LADIES ARE GETTING ANTSY.
Ooh!
SORRY, BUT WE NEED TO REVISE OUR SCHEDULE.
IF SHE STARTED PLAYING AGAIN...
...THEN SHE'S NOT HOME RIGHT NOW.

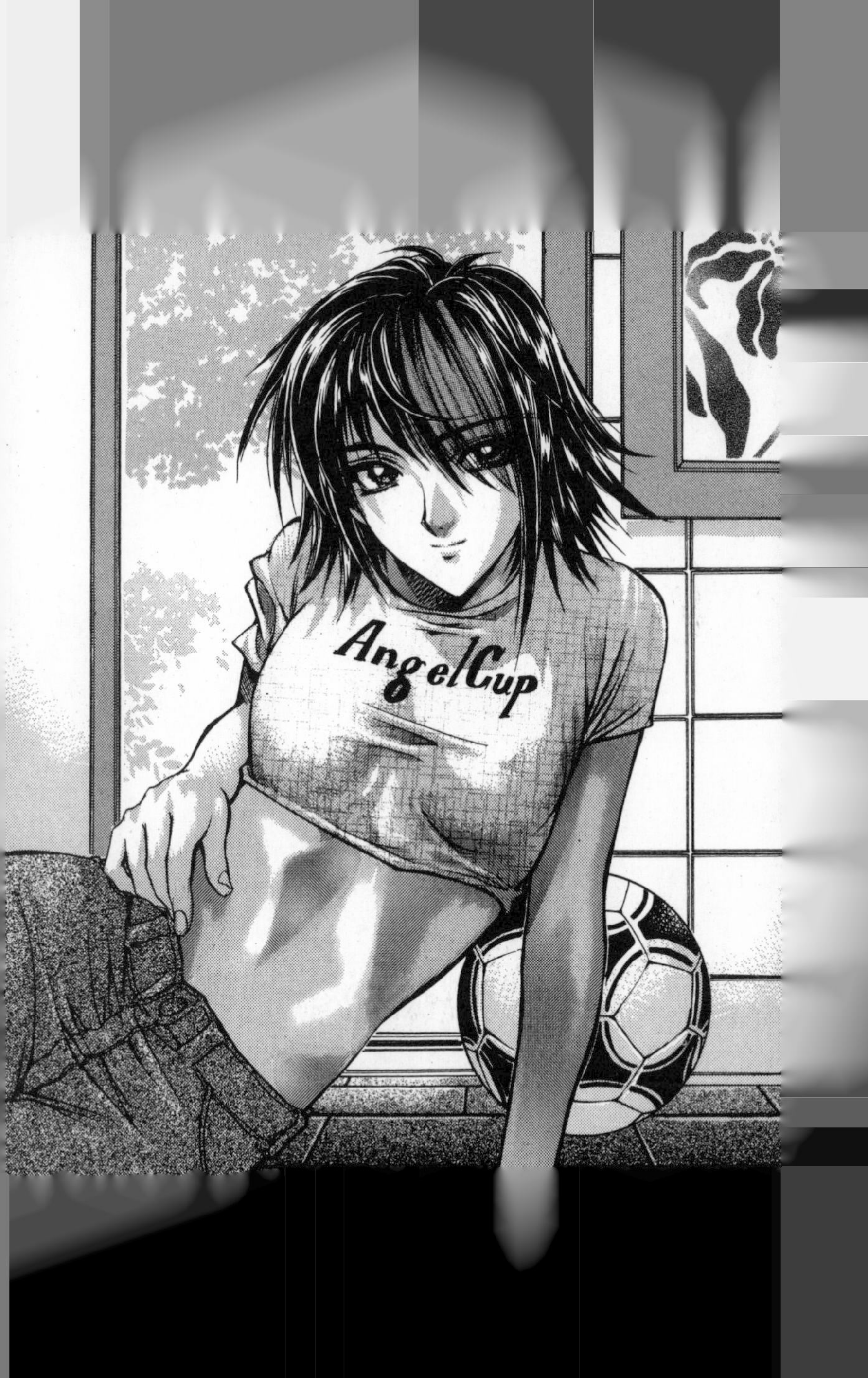
AngelCup

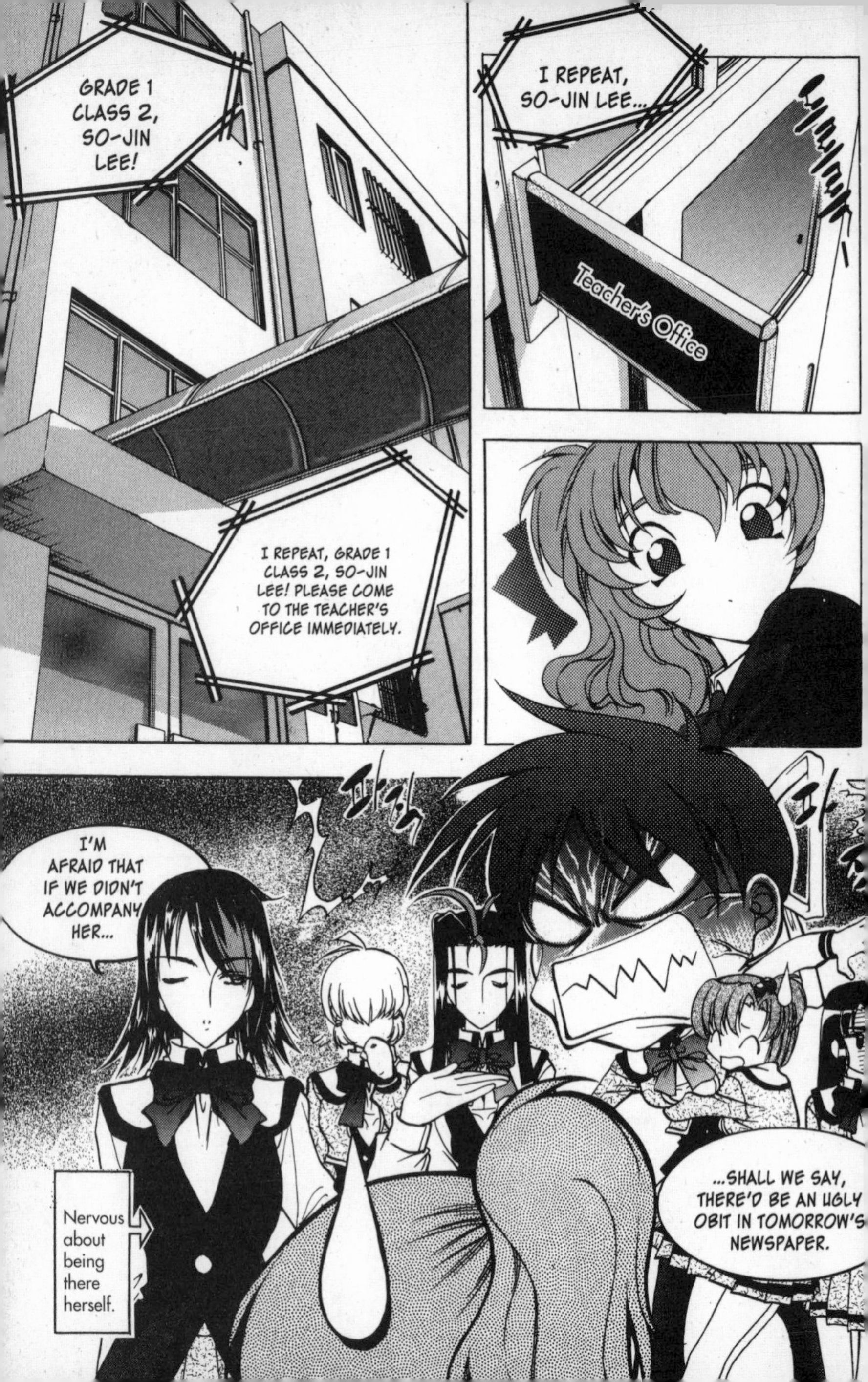
GRADE 1 CLASS 2, SO-JIN LEE!
I REPEAT, GRADE 1 CLASS 2, SO-JIN LEE! PLEASE COME TO THE TEACHER'S OFFICE IMMEDIATELY.
I REPEAT, SO-JIN LEE...
Teacher's Office
I'M AFRAID THAT IF WE DIDN'T ACCOMPANY HER...
Nervous about being there herself.
...SHALL WE SAY, THERE'D BE AN UGLY OBIT IN TOMORROW'S NEWSPAPER.

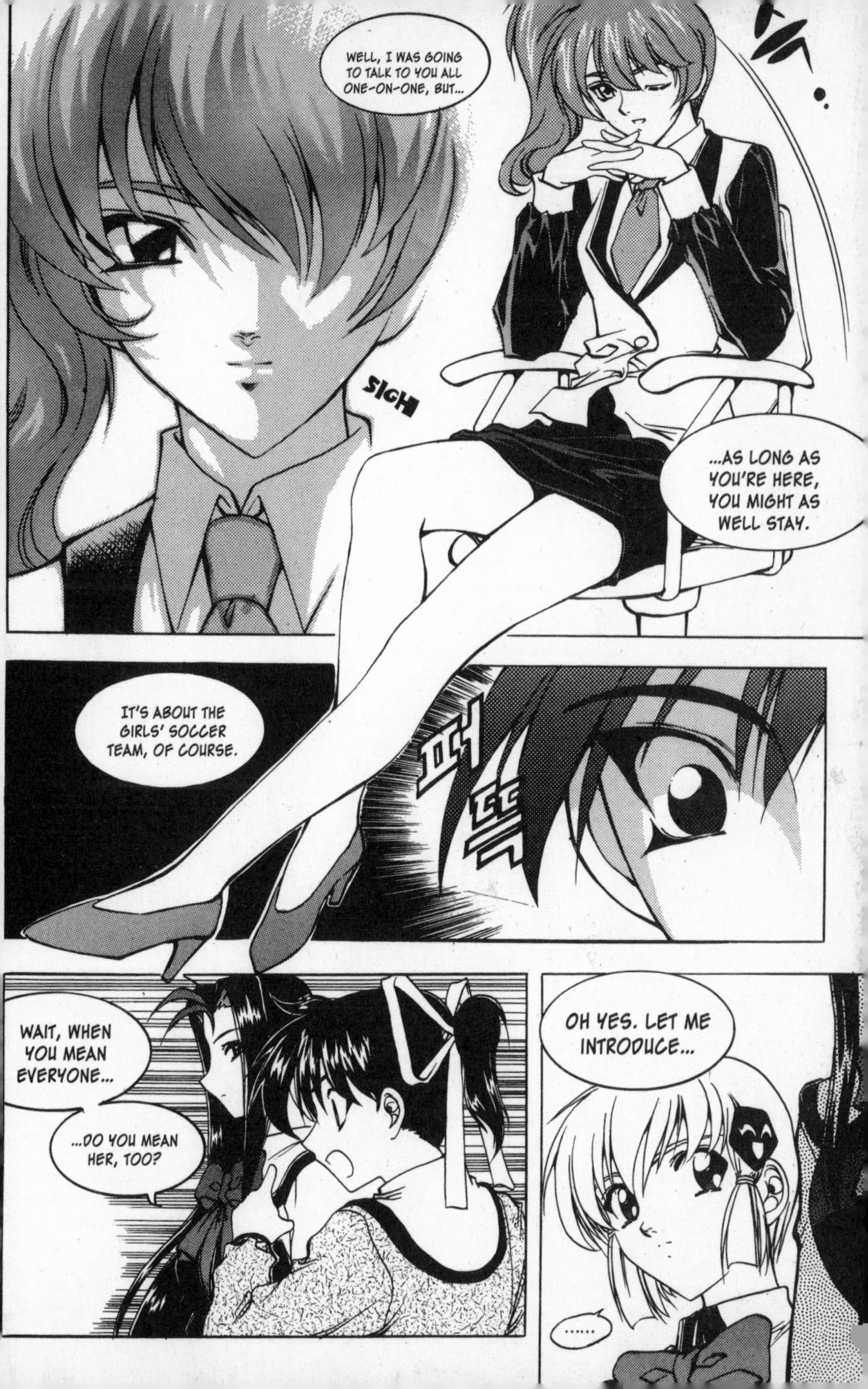
WELL, I WAS GOING TO TALK TO YOU ALL ONE-ON-ONE, BUT...
SIGH
...AS LONG AS YOU'RE HERE, YOU MIGHT AS WELL STAY.
IT'S ABOUT THE GIRLS' SOCCER TEAM, OF COURSE.
WAIT, WHEN YOU MEAN EVERYONE...
...DO YOU MEAN HER, TOO?
OH YES. LET ME INTRODUCE...
......

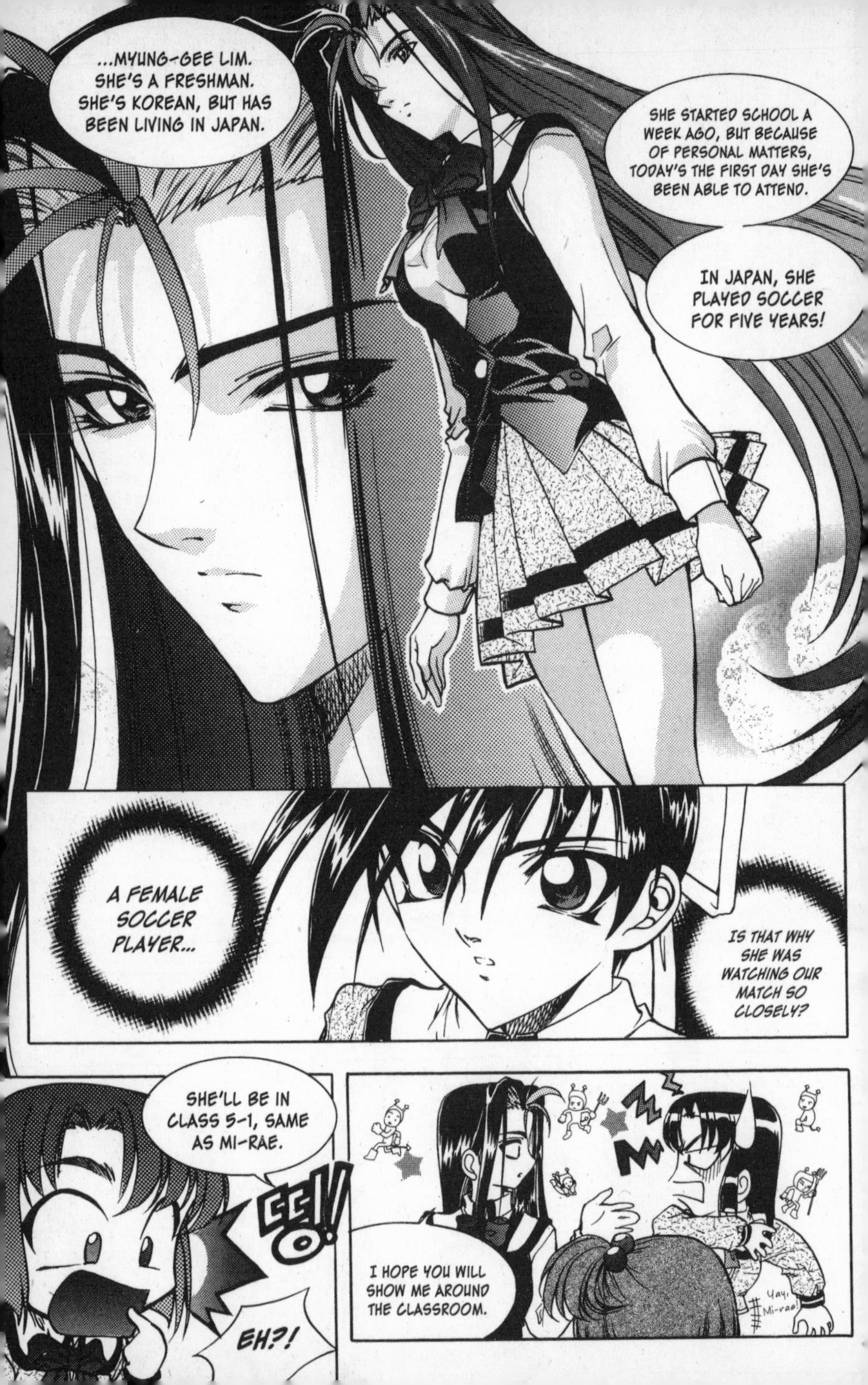
...MYUNG-GEE LIM. SHE'S A FRESHMAN. SHE'S KOREAN, BUT HAS BEEN LIVING IN JAPAN.
SHE STARTED SCHOOL A WEEK AGO, BUT BECAUSE OF PERSONAL MATTERS, TODAY'S THE FIRST DAY SHE'S BEEN ABLE TO ATTEND.
IN JAPAN, SHE PLAYED SOCCER FOR FIVE YEARS!
A FEMALE SOCCER PLAYER...
IS THAT WHY SHE WAS WATCHING OUR MATCH SO CLOSELY?
SHE'LL BE IN CLASS 5-1, SAME AS MI-RAE.
뜽!!
EH?!
I HOPE YOU WILL SHOW ME AROUND THE CLASSROOM.
Yay, Mi-rae!

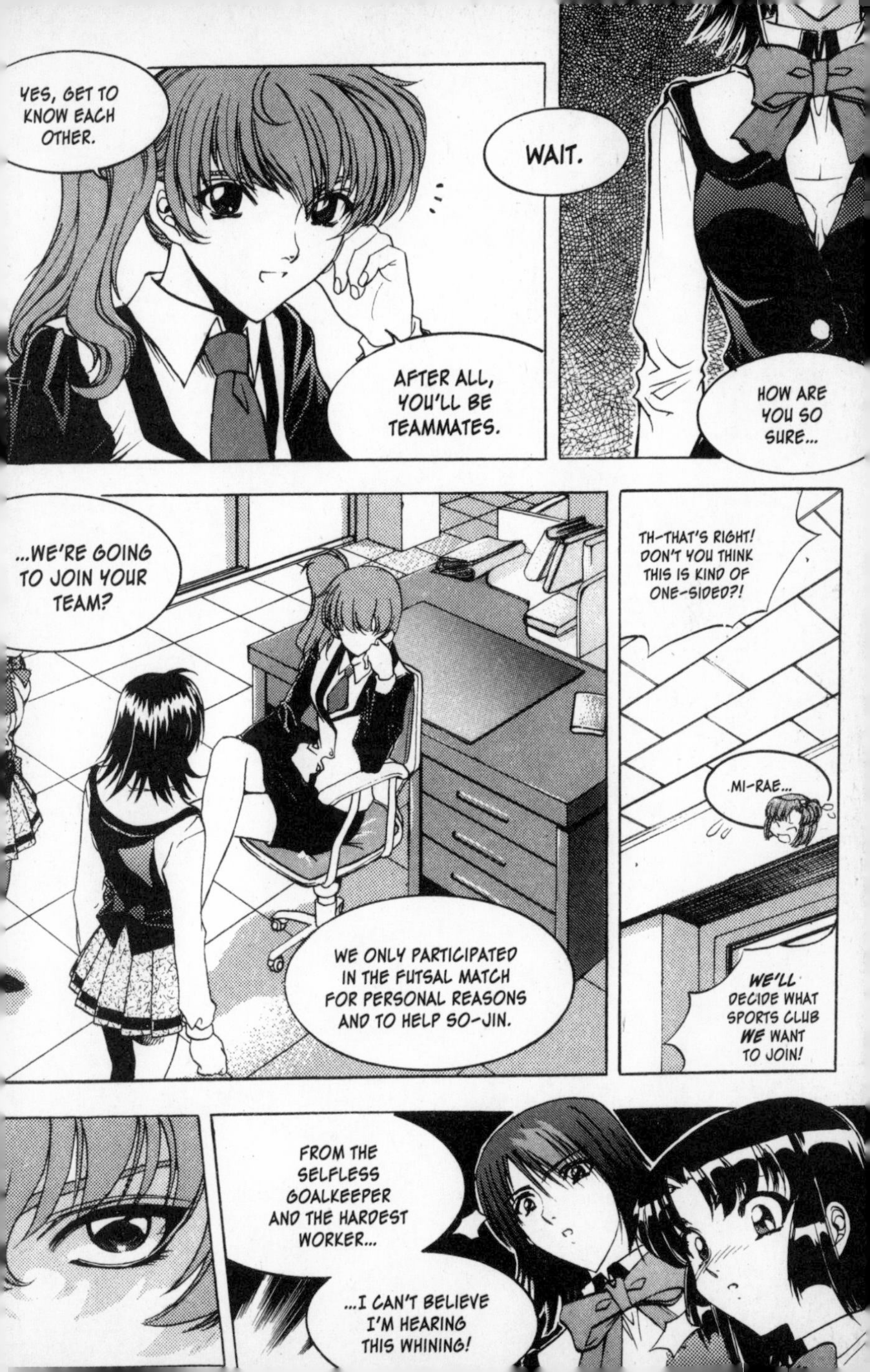
YES, GET TO KNOW EACH OTHER.
AFTER ALL, YOU'LL BE TEAMMATES.
WAIT.
HOW ARE YOU SO SURE...
...WE'RE GOING TO JOIN YOUR TEAM?
WE ONLY PARTICIPATED IN THE FUTSAL MATCH FOR PERSONAL REASONS AND TO HELP SO-JIN.
TH-THAT'S RIGHT! DON'T YOU THINK THIS IS KIND OF ONE-SIDED?!
MI-RAE...
WE'LL DECIDE WHAT SPORTS CLUB *WE* WANT TO JOIN!
FROM THE SELFLESS GOALKEEPER AND THE HARDEST WORKER...
...I CAN'T BELIEVE I'M HEARING THIS WHINING!

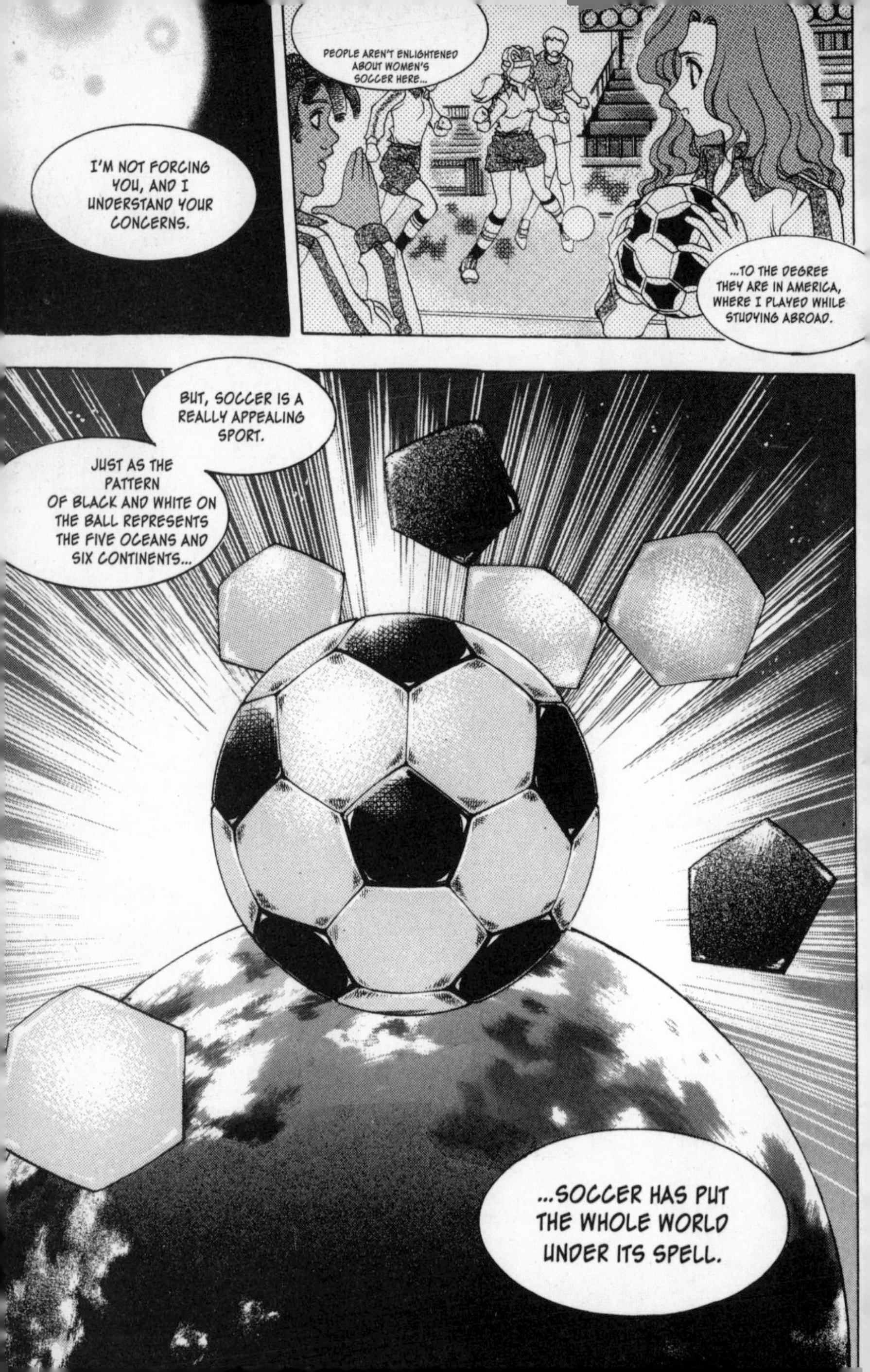
I'M NOT FORCING YOU, AND I UNDERSTAND YOUR CONCERNS.
PEOPLE AREN'T ENLIGHTENED ABOUT WOMEN'S SOCCER HERE...
...TO THE DEGREE THEY ARE IN AMERICA, WHERE I PLAYED WHILE STUDYING ABROAD.
BUT, SOCCER IS A REALLY APPEALING SPORT.
JUST AS THE PATTERN OF BLACK AND WHITE ON THE BALL REPRESENTS THE FIVE OCEANS AND SIX CONTINENTS...
...SOCCER HAS PUT THE WHOLE WORLD UNDER ITS SPELL.

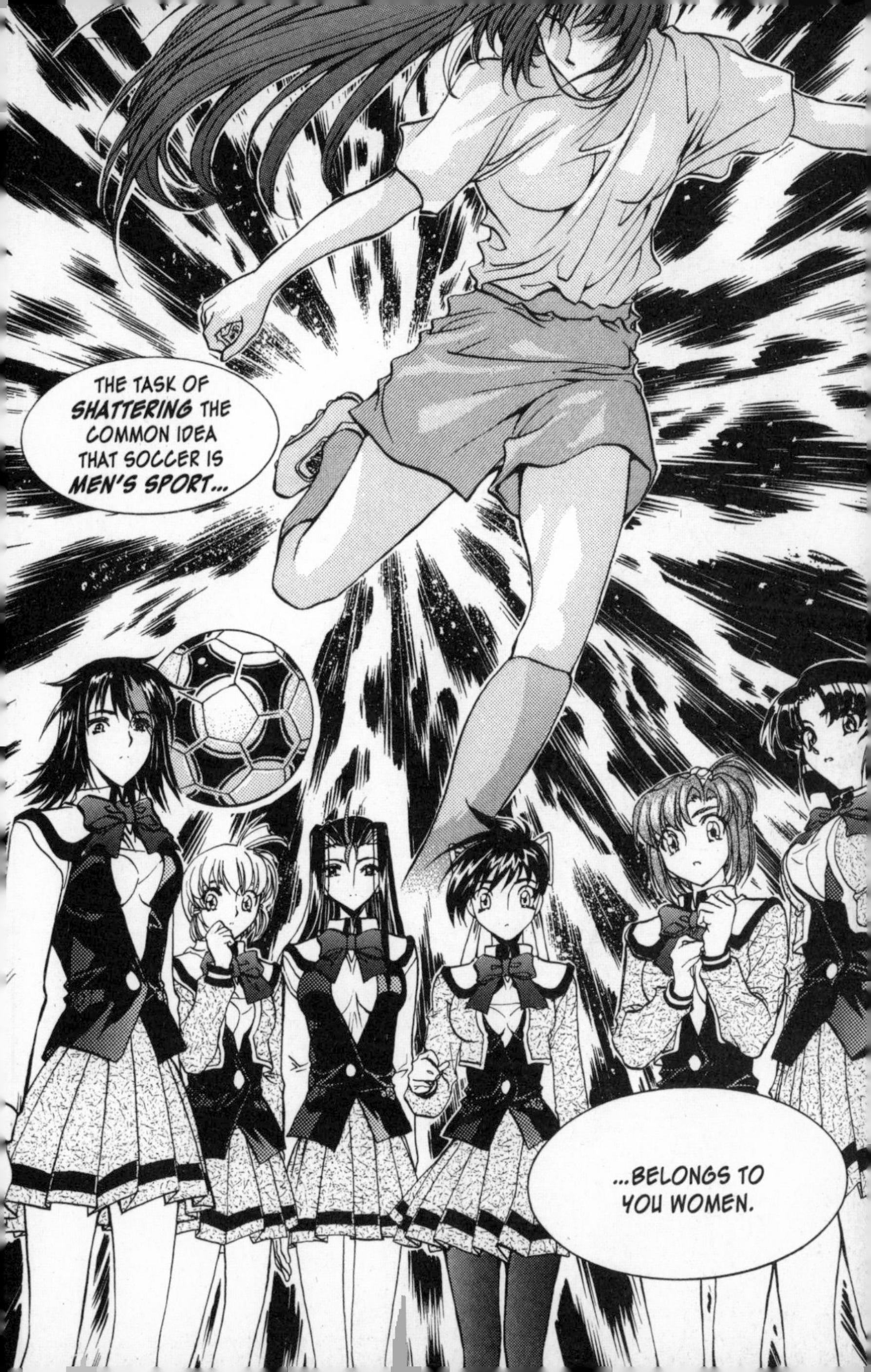
THE TASK OF SHATTERING THE COMMON IDEA THAT SOCCER IS MEN'S SPORT...
...BELONGS TO YOU WOMEN.

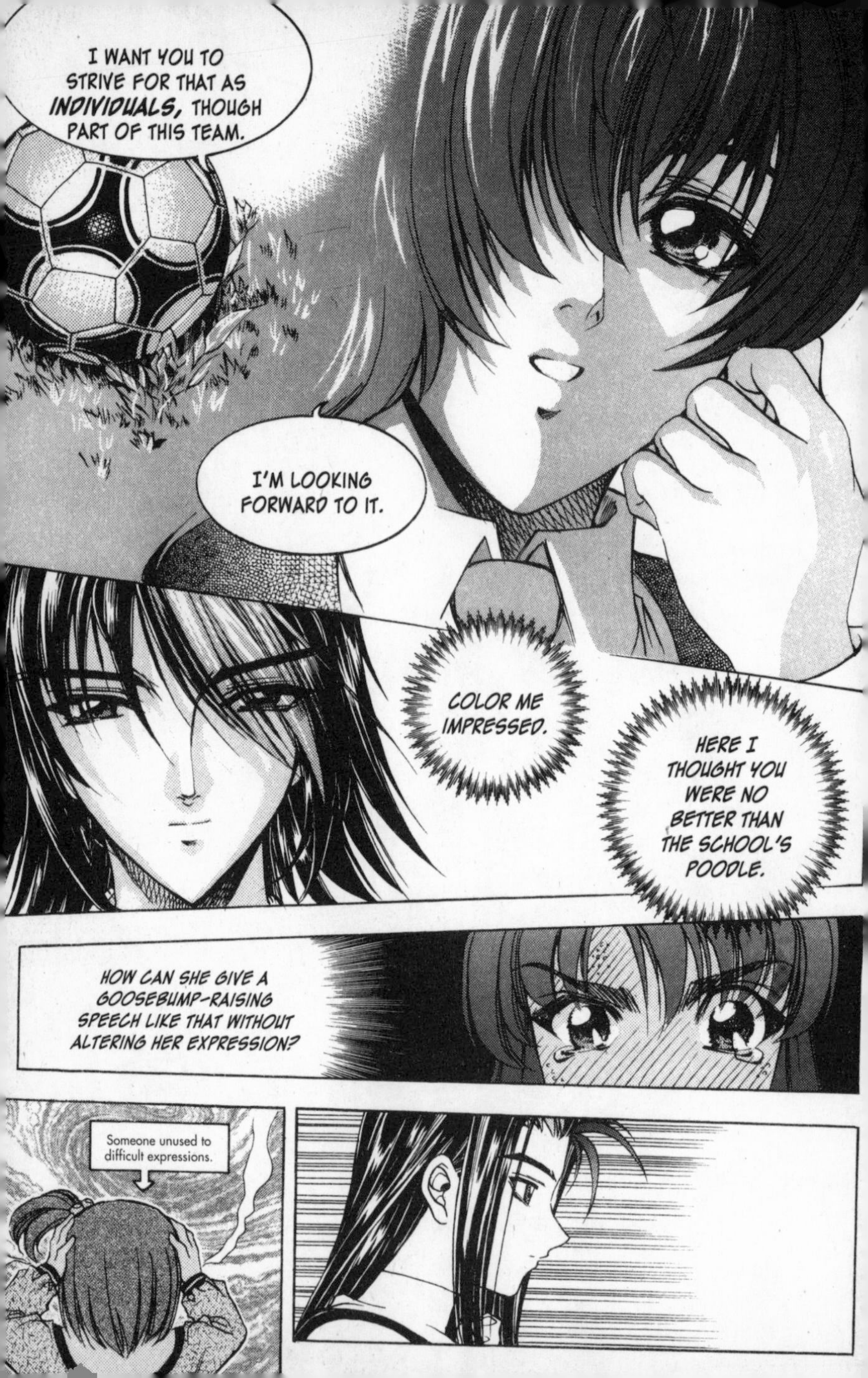
I WANT YOU TO STRIVE FOR THAT AS *INDIVIDUALS,* THOUGH PART OF THIS TEAM.
I'M LOOKING FORWARD TO IT.
COLOR ME IMPRESSED.
HERE I THOUGHT YOU WERE NO BETTER THAN THE SCHOOL'S POODLE.
HOW CAN SHE GIVE A GOOSEBUMP-RAISING SPEECH LIKE THAT WITHOUT ALTERING HER EXPRESSION?
Someone unused to difficult expressions.

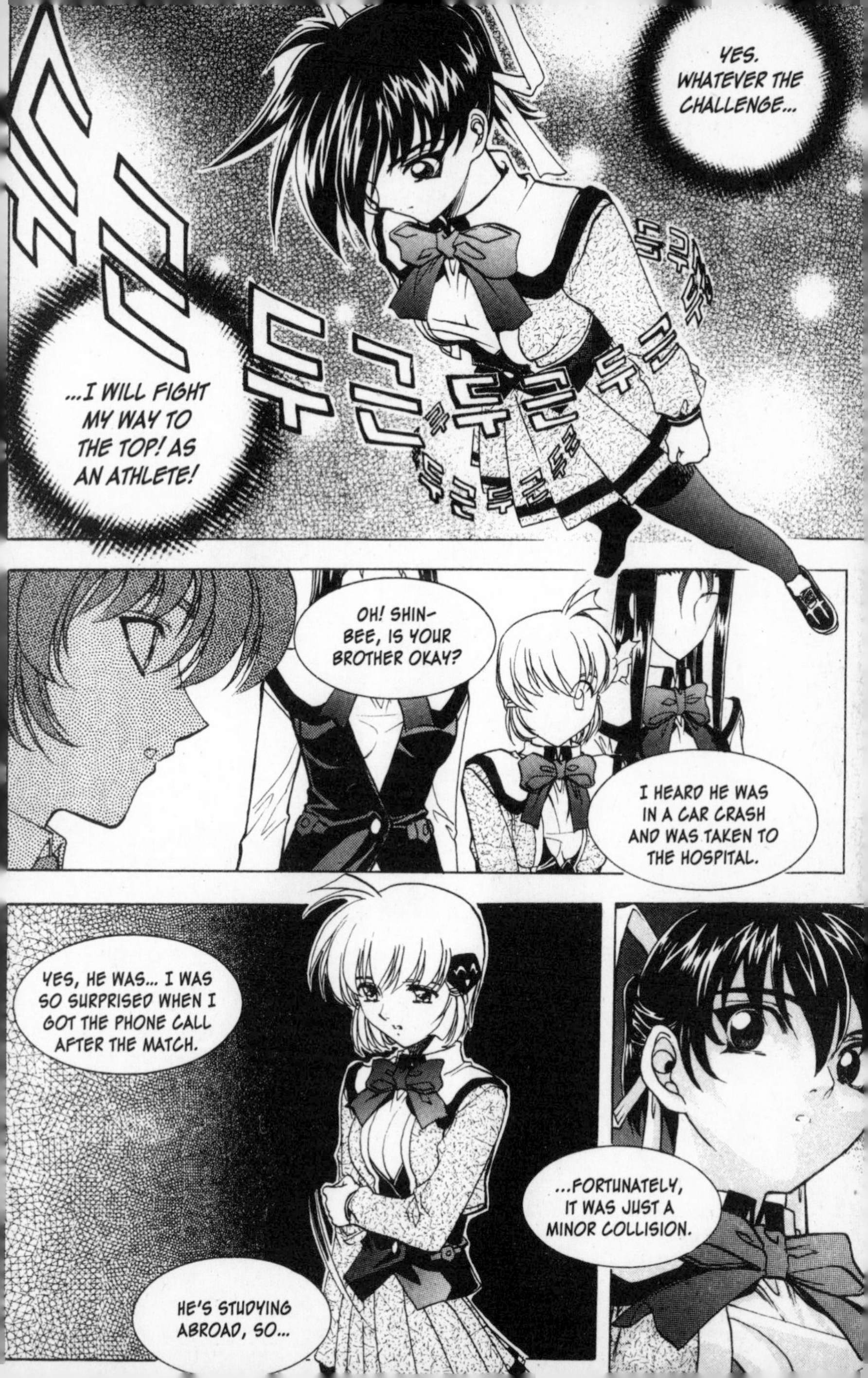
YES. WHATEVER THE CHALLENGE...
...I WILL FIGHT MY WAY TO THE TOP! AS AN ATHLETE!
OH! SHIN-BEE, IS YOUR BROTHER OKAY?
I HEARD HE WAS IN A CAR CRASH AND WAS TAKEN TO THE HOSPITAL.
YES, HE WAS... I WAS SO SURPRISED WHEN I GOT THE PHONE CALL AFTER THE MATCH.
HE'S STUDYING ABROAD, SO...
...FORTUNATELY, IT WAS JUST A MINOR COLLISION.

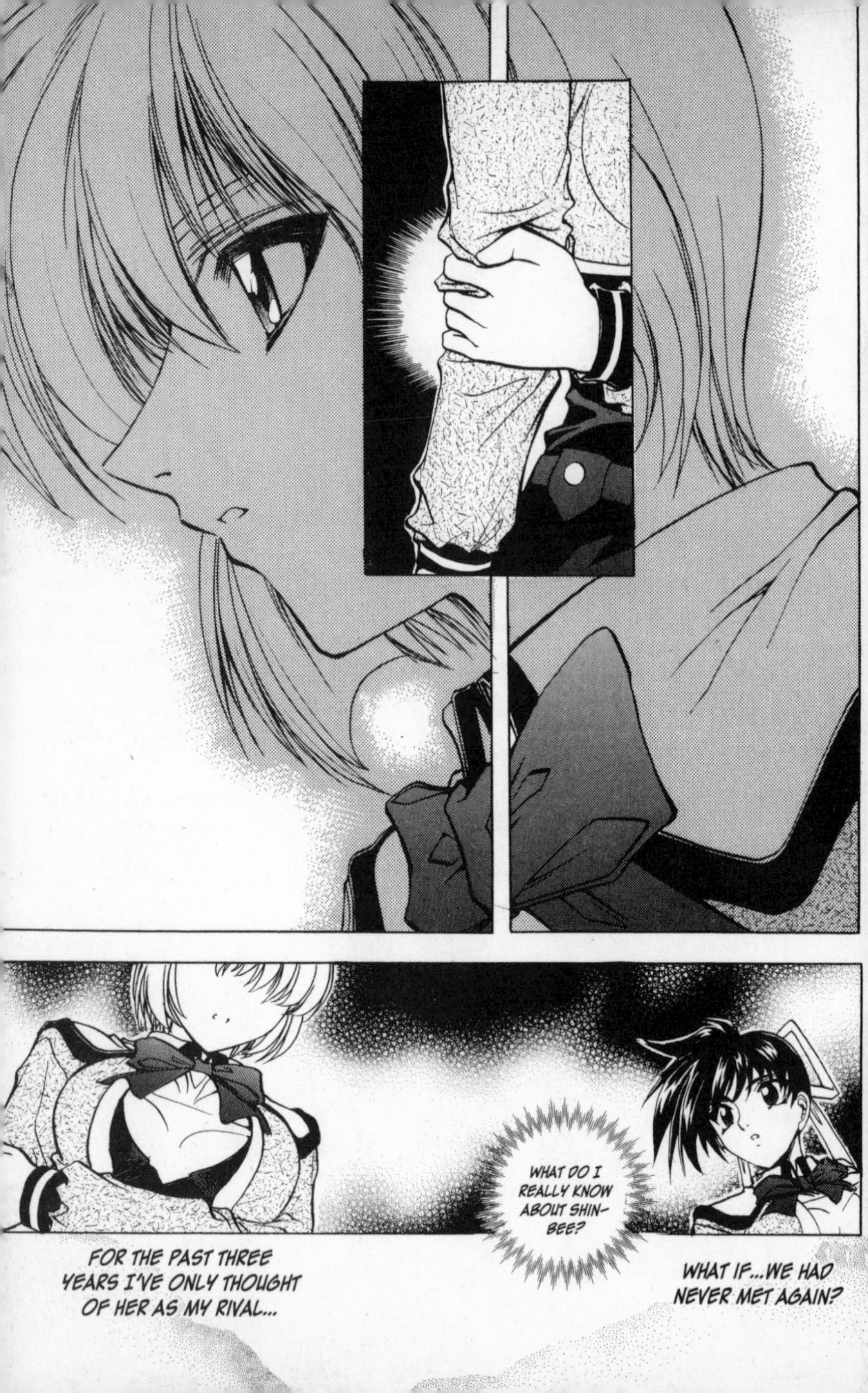
FOR THE PAST THREE YEARS I'VE ONLY THOUGHT OF HER AS MY RIVAL...
WHAT DO I REALLY KNOW ABOUT SHIN-BEE?
WHAT IF...WE HAD NEVER MET AGAIN?

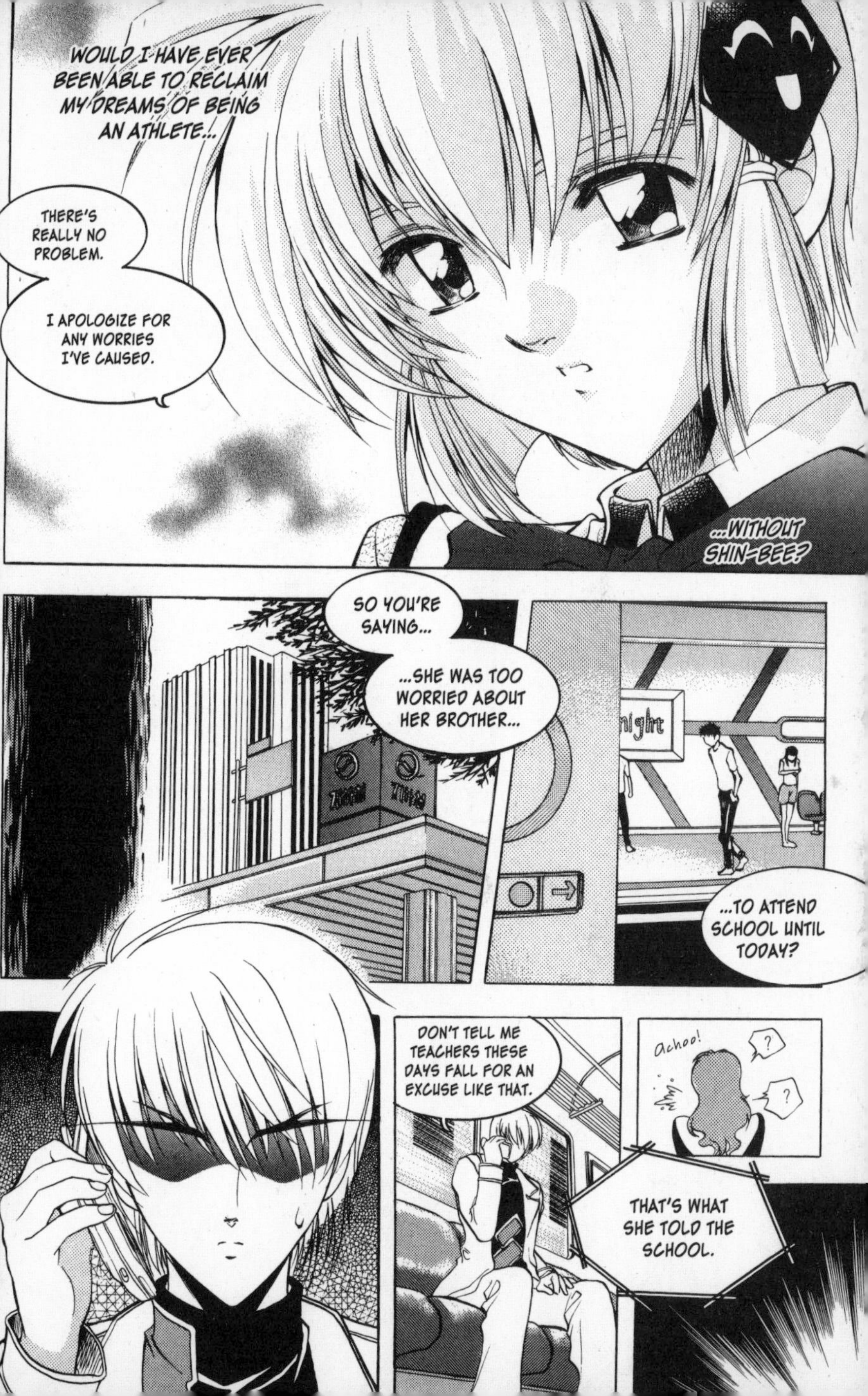
WOULD I HAVE EVER BEEN ABLE TO RECLAIM MY DREAMS OF BEING AN ATHLETE...
THERE'S REALLY NO PROBLEM.
I APOLOGIZE FOR ANY WORRIES I'VE CAUSED.
...WITHOUT SHIN-BEE?
SO YOU'RE SAYING...
...SHE WAS TOO WORRIED ABOUT HER BROTHER...
night
...TO ATTEND SCHOOL UNTIL TODAY?
DON'T TELL ME TEACHERS THESE DAYS FALL FOR AN EXCUSE LIKE THAT.
achoo!
?
?
THAT'S WHAT SHE TOLD THE SCHOOL.

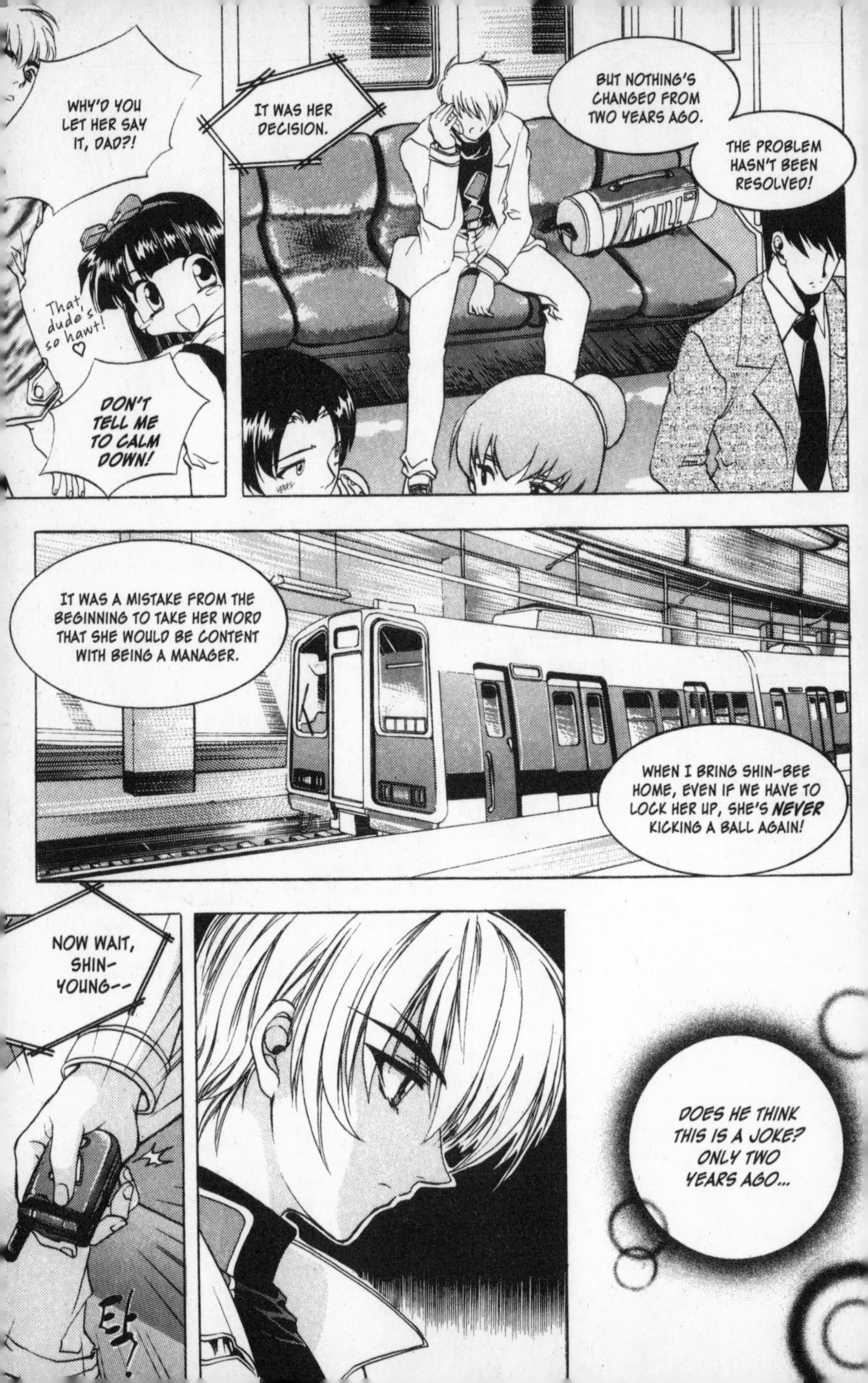
WHY'D YOU LET HER SAY IT, DAD?!
That dude's so hawt! ♡
DON'T TELL ME TO CALM DOWN!
IT WAS HER DECISION.
BUT NOTHING'S CHANGED FROM TWO YEARS AGO.
THE PROBLEM HASN'T BEEN RESOLVED!
IT WAS A MISTAKE FROM THE BEGINNING TO TAKE HER WORD THAT SHE WOULD BE CONTENT WITH BEING A MANAGER.
WHEN I BRING SHIN-BEE HOME, EVEN IF WE HAVE TO LOCK HER UP, SHE'S NEVER KICKING A BALL AGAIN!
NOW WAIT, SHIN-YOUNG--
DOES HE THINK THIS IS A JOKE? ONLY TWO YEARS AGO...

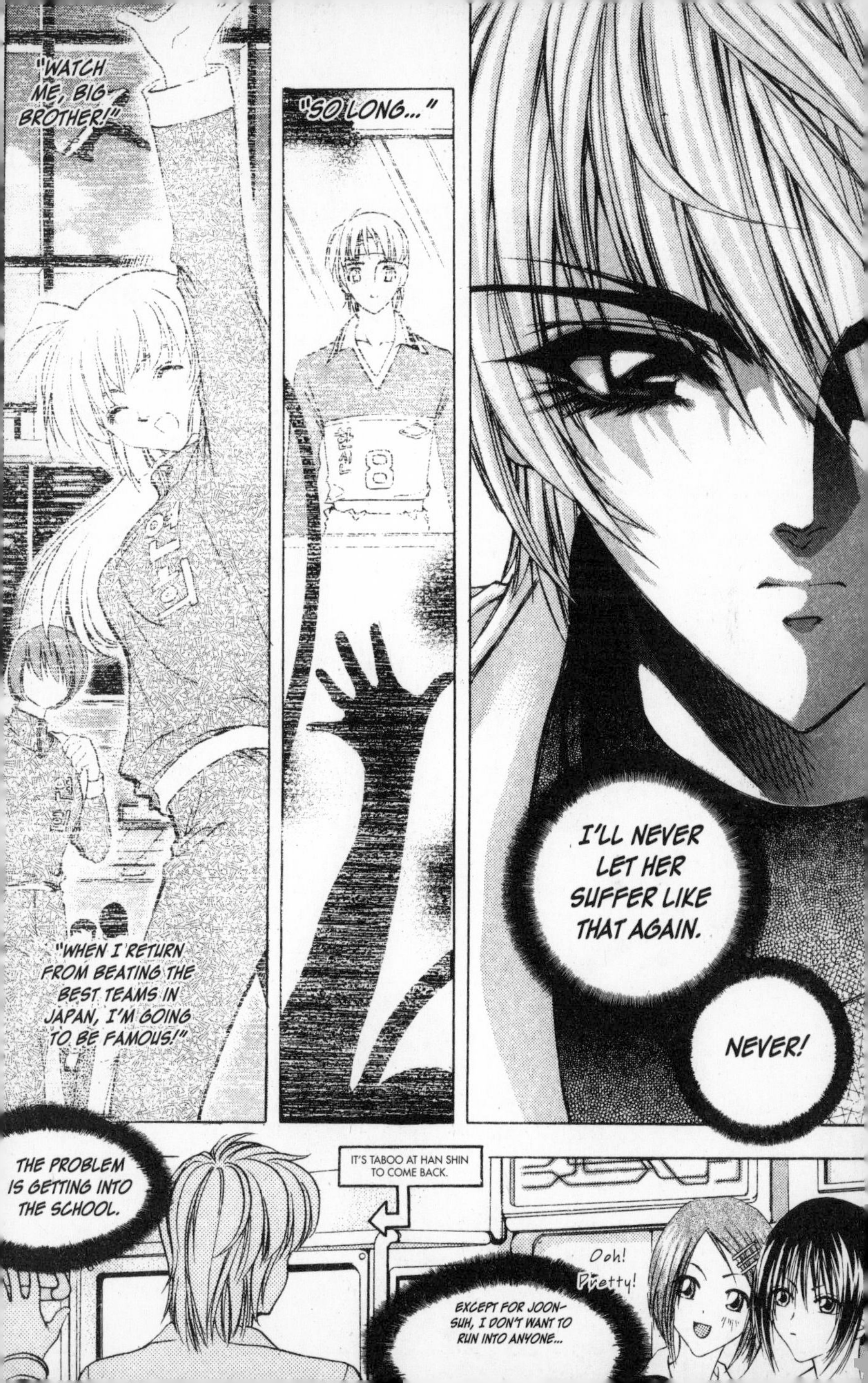
"WATCH ME, BIG-BROTHER!"
"WHEN I RETURN FROM BEATING THE BEST TEAMS IN JAPAN, I'M GOING TO BE FAMOUS!"
"SO LONG..."
I'LL NEVER LET HER SUFFER LIKE THAT AGAIN.
NEVER!
THE PROBLEM IS GETTING INTO THE SCHOOL.
IT'S TABOO AT HAN SHIN TO COME BACK.
EXCEPT FOR JOON-SUH, I DON'T WANT TO RUN INTO ANYONE...
Ooh!
Pretty!

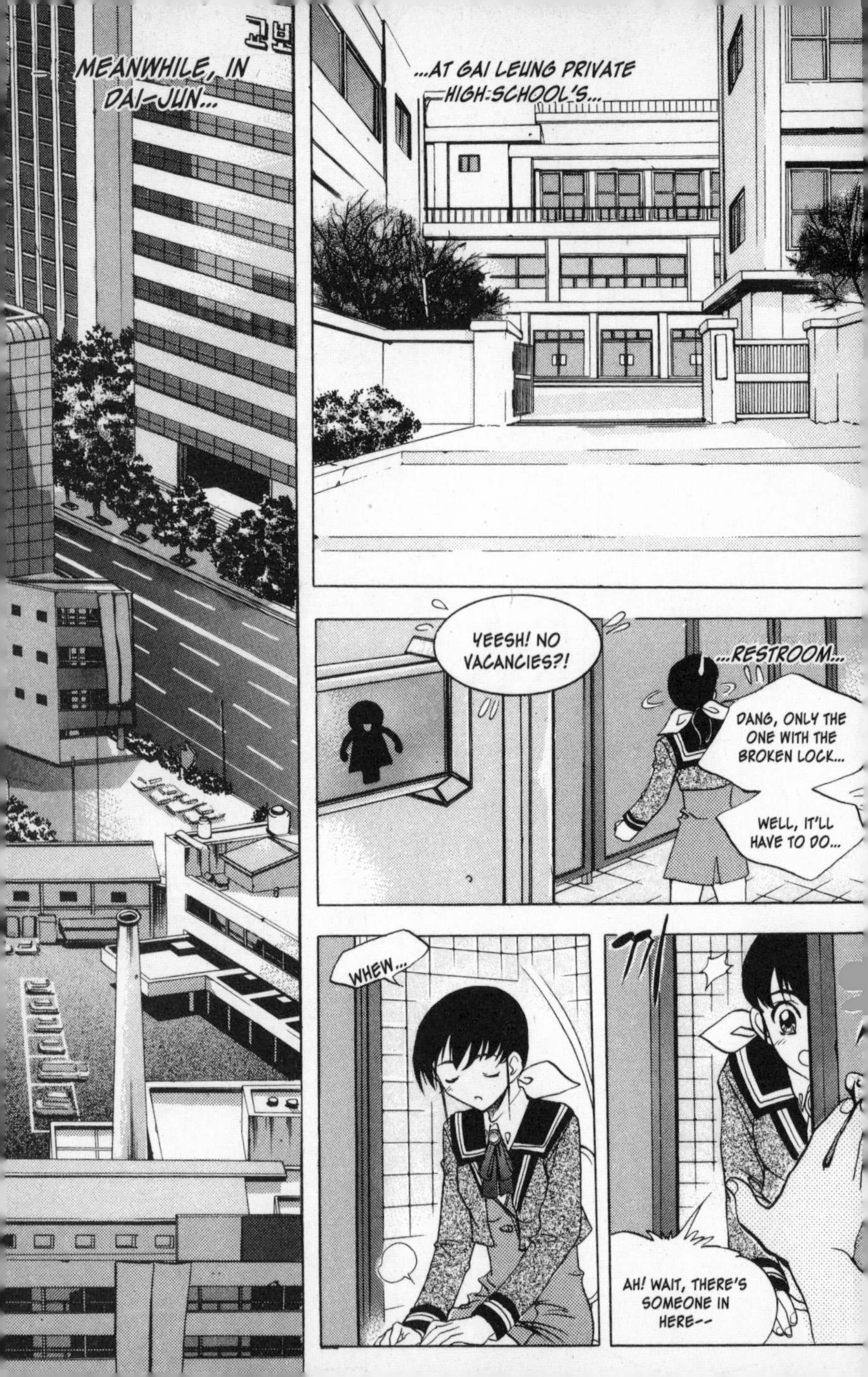
MEANWHILE, IN DAI-JUN...
...AT GAI LEUNG PRIVATE HIGH-SCHOOL'S...
...RESTROOM...
YEESH! NO VACANCIES?!
DANG, ONLY THE ONE WITH THE BROKEN LOCK...
WELL, IT'LL HAVE TO DO...
WHEW...
AH! WAIT, THERE'S SOMEONE IN HERE--

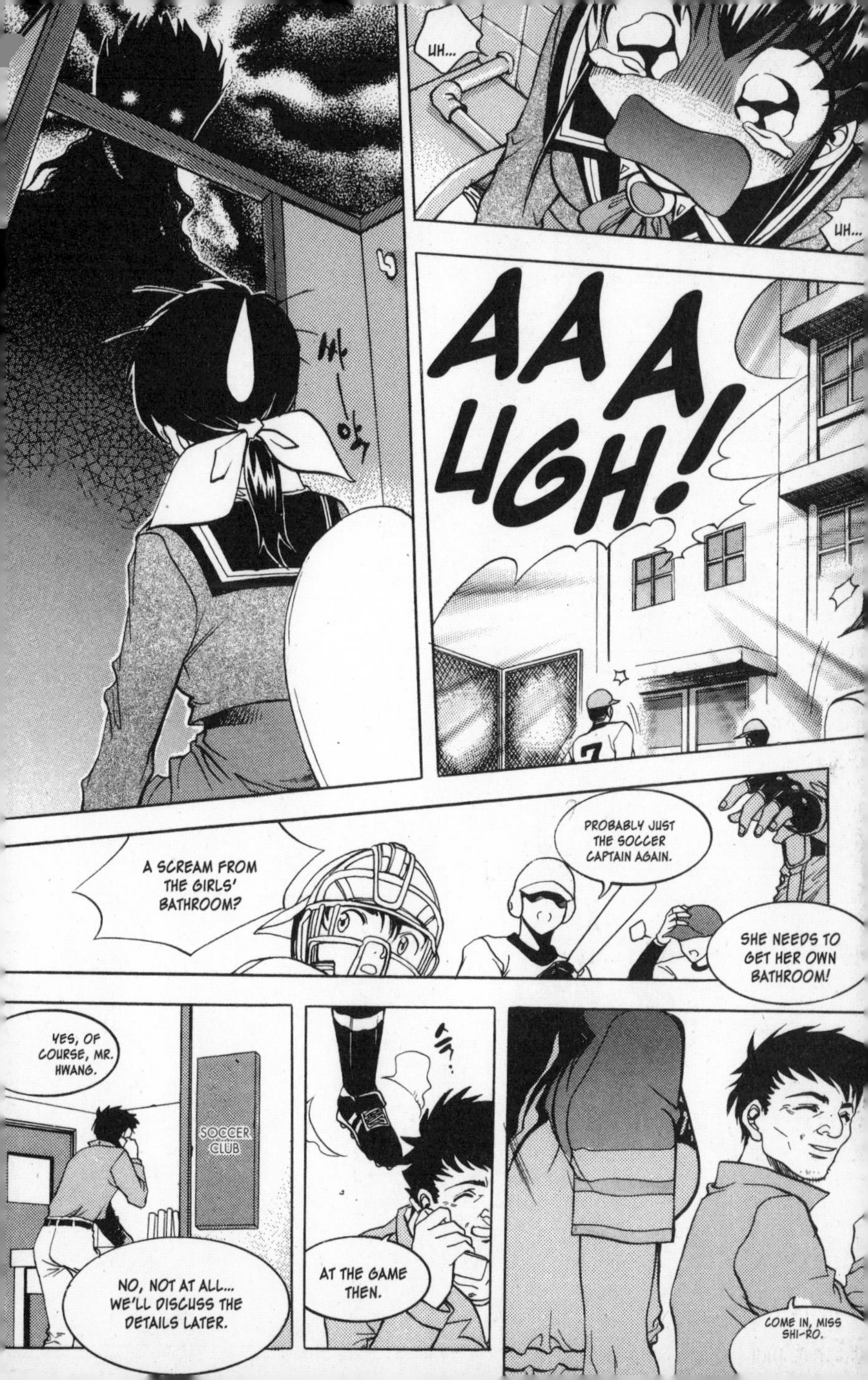
UH...
UH...
AAAUGH!
A SCREAM FROM THE GIRLS' BATHROOM?
PROBABLY JUST THE SOCCER CAPTAIN AGAIN.
SHE NEEDS TO GET HER OWN BATHROOM!
YES, OF COURSE, MR. HWANG.
SOCCER CLUB
NO, NOT AT ALL... WE'LL DISCUSS THE DETAILS LATER.
AT THE GAME THEN.
COME IN, MISS SHI-RO.

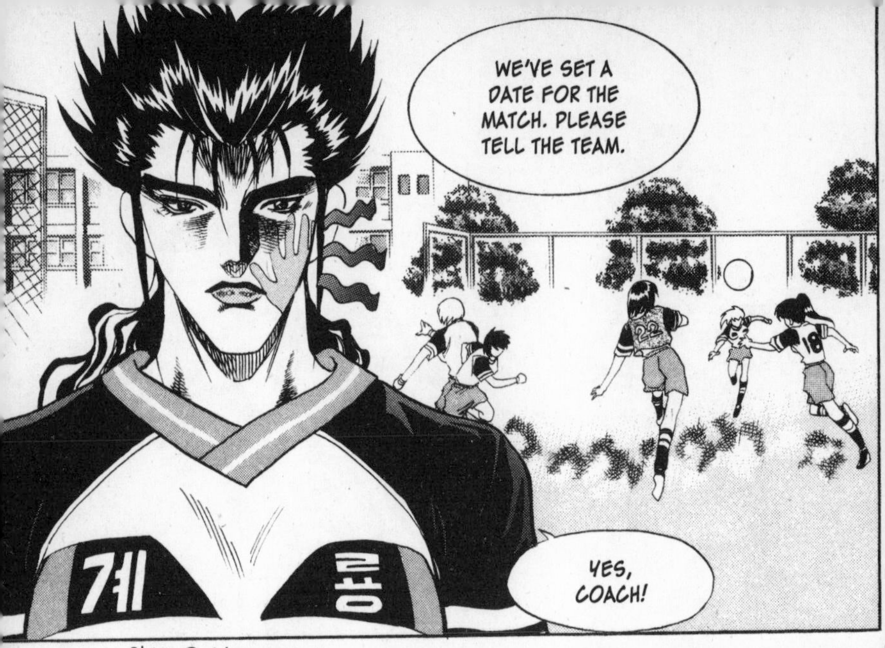
WE'VE SET A DATE FOR THE MATCH. PLEASE TELL THE TEAM.
YES, COACH!

Shirt: Gai Leung

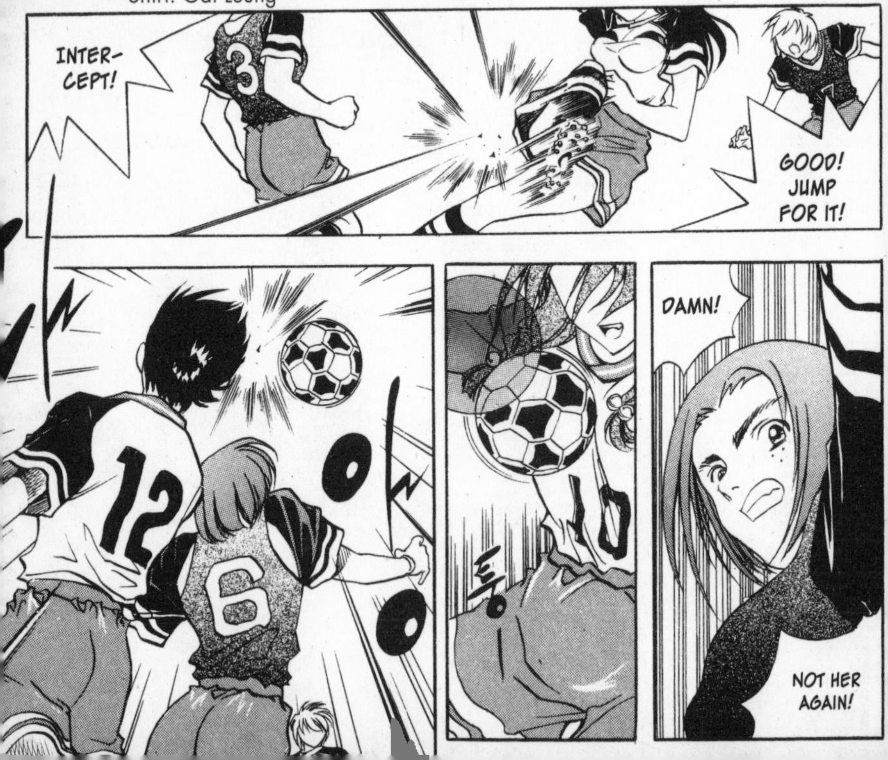
INTER-CEPT!
GOOD! JUMP FOR IT!
DAMN!
NOT HER AGAIN!

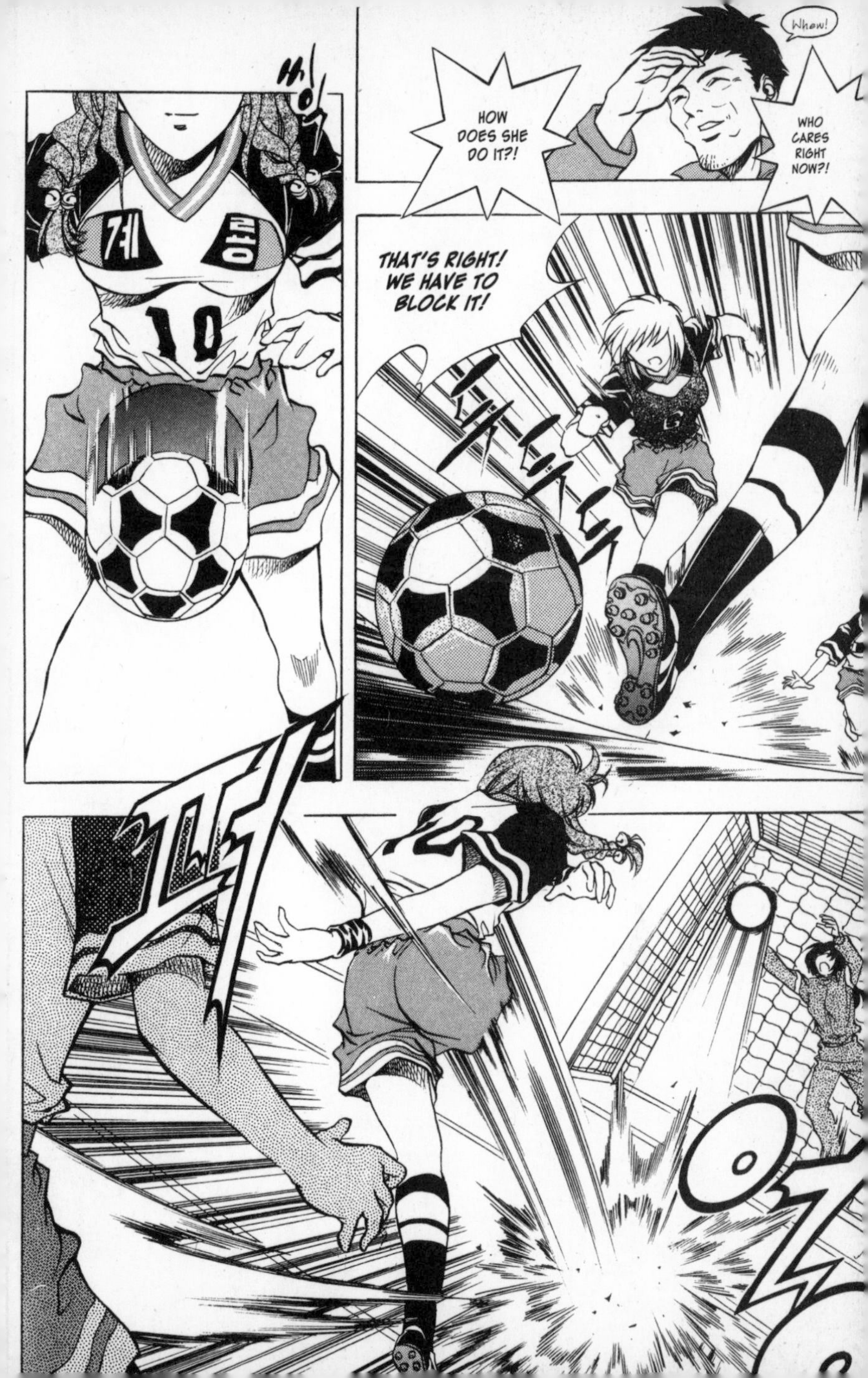
HOW DOES SHE DO IT?!
Whew!
WHO CARES RIGHT NOW?!
THAT'S RIGHT! WE HAVE TO BLOCK IT!

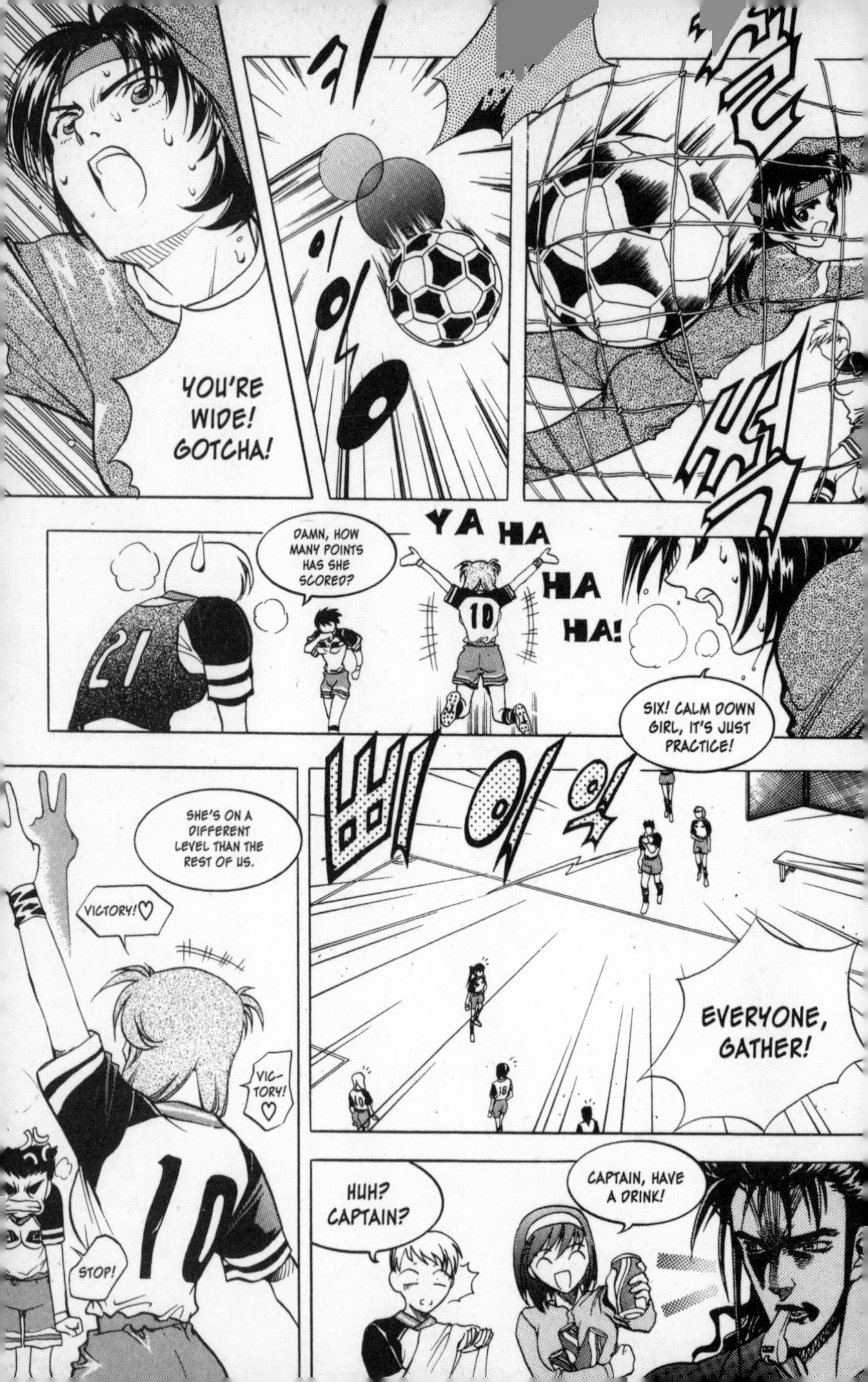
YOU'RE WIDE! GOTCHA!
DAMN, HOW MANY POINTS HAS SHE SCORED?
YA HA HA HA HA!
SIX! CALM DOWN GIRL, IT'S JUST PRACTICE!
SHE'S ON A DIFFERENT LEVEL THAN THE REST OF US.
VICTORY!♡
VIC-TORY!♡
STOP!
EVERYONE, GATHER!
HUH? CAPTAIN?
CAPTAIN, HAVE A DRINK!

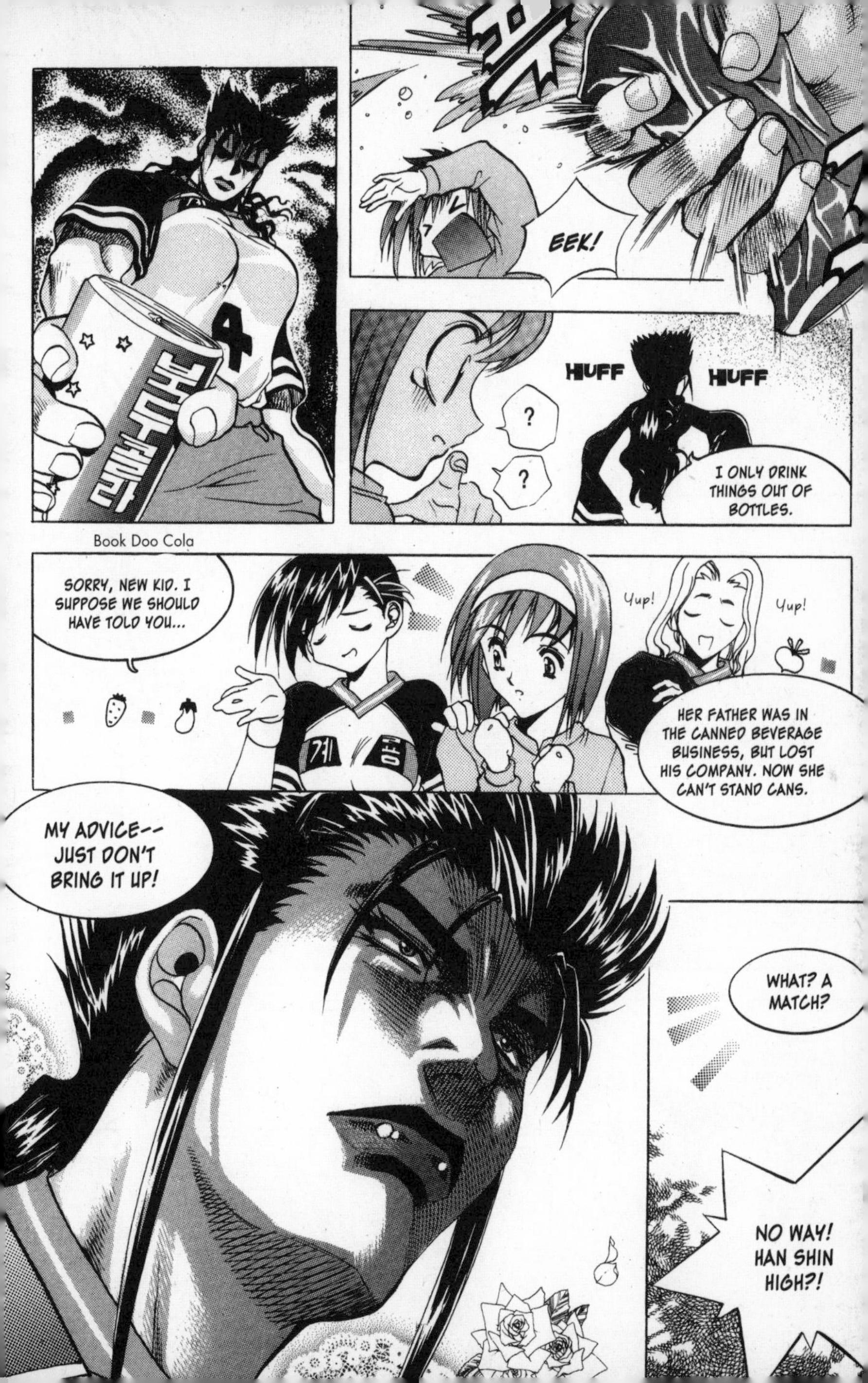
Book Doo Cola
EEK!
?
?
HUFF
HUFF
I ONLY DRINK THINGS OUT OF BOTTLES.
SORRY, NEW KID. I SUPPOSE WE SHOULD HAVE TOLD YOU...
Yup!
Yup!
HER FATHER WAS IN THE CANNED BEVERAGE BUSINESS, BUT LOST HIS COMPANY. NOW SHE CAN'T STAND CANS.
MY ADVICE-- JUST DON'T BRING IT UP!
WHAT? A MATCH?
NO WAY! HAN SHIN HIGH?!

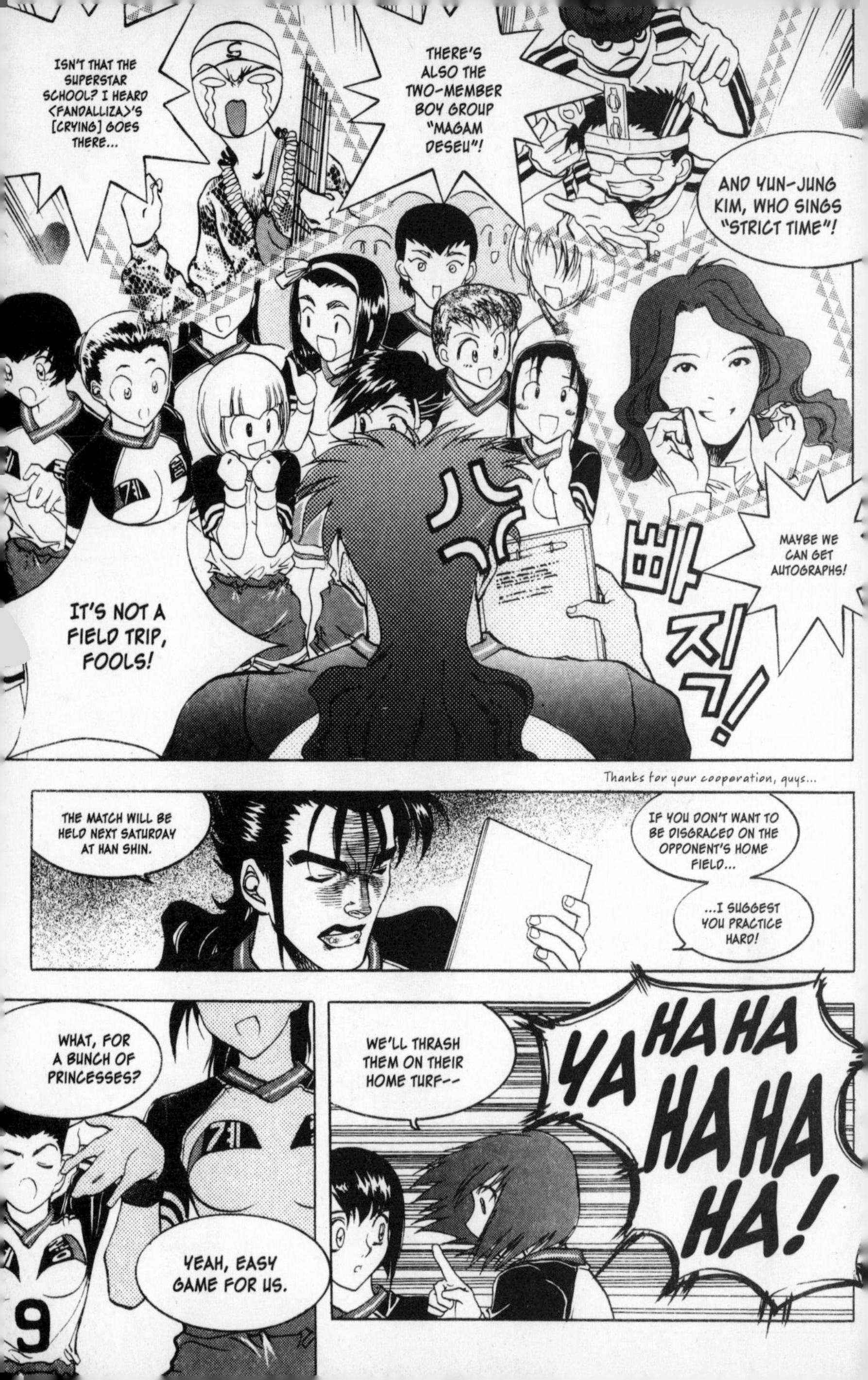

ISN'T THAT THE SUPERSTAR SCHOOL? I HEARD <FANDALLIZA>'S [CRYING] GOES THERE...
THERE'S ALSO THE TWO-MEMBER BOY GROUP "MAGAM DESEU"!
AND YUN-JUNG KIM, WHO SINGS "STRICT TIME"!
MAYBE WE CAN GET AUTOGRAPHS!
IT'S NOT A FIELD TRIP, FOOLS!
빠직!
Thanks for your cooperation, guys...
THE MATCH WILL BE HELD NEXT SATURDAY AT HAN SHIN.
IF YOU DON'T WANT TO BE DISGRACED ON THE OPPONENT'S HOME FIELD...
...I SUGGEST YOU PRACTICE HARD!
WHAT, FOR A BUNCH OF PRINCESSES?
YEAH, EASY GAME FOR US.
WE'LL THRASH THEM ON THEIR HOME TURF--
YAHAHAHAHAHAHAHAHA!

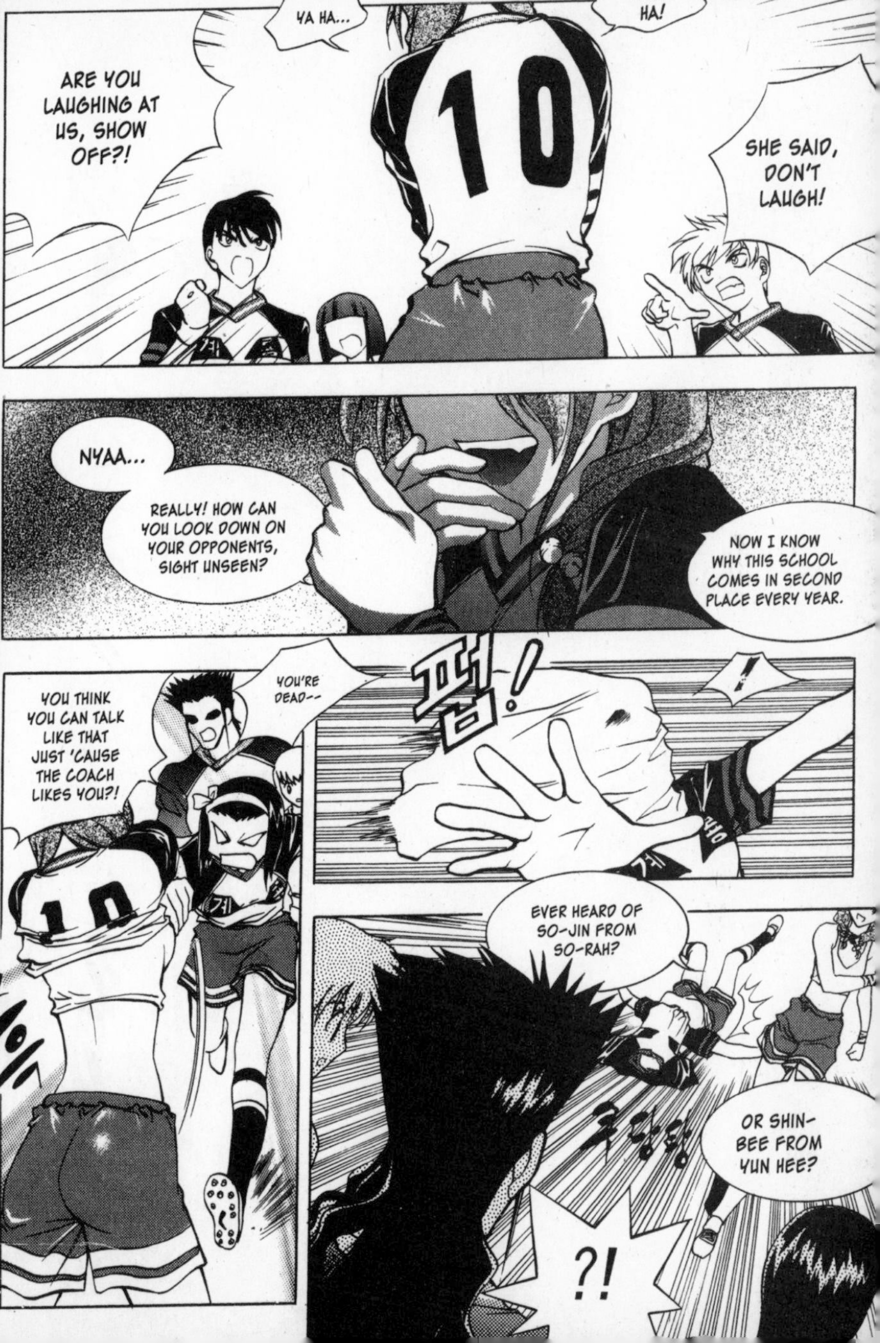
ARE YOU LAUGHING AT US, SHOW OFF?!
YA HA...
HA HA HA!
SHE SAID, DON'T LAUGH!
NYAA...
REALLY! HOW CAN YOU LOOK DOWN ON YOUR OPPONENTS, SIGHT UNSEEN?
NOW I KNOW WHY THIS SCHOOL COMES IN SECOND PLACE EVERY YEAR.
YOU THINK YOU CAN TALK LIKE THAT JUST 'CAUSE THE COACH LIKES YOU?!
YOU'RE DEAD--
퍽!
!
EVER HEARD OF SO-JIN FROM SO-RAH?
OR SHIN-BEE FROM YUN HEE?
?!

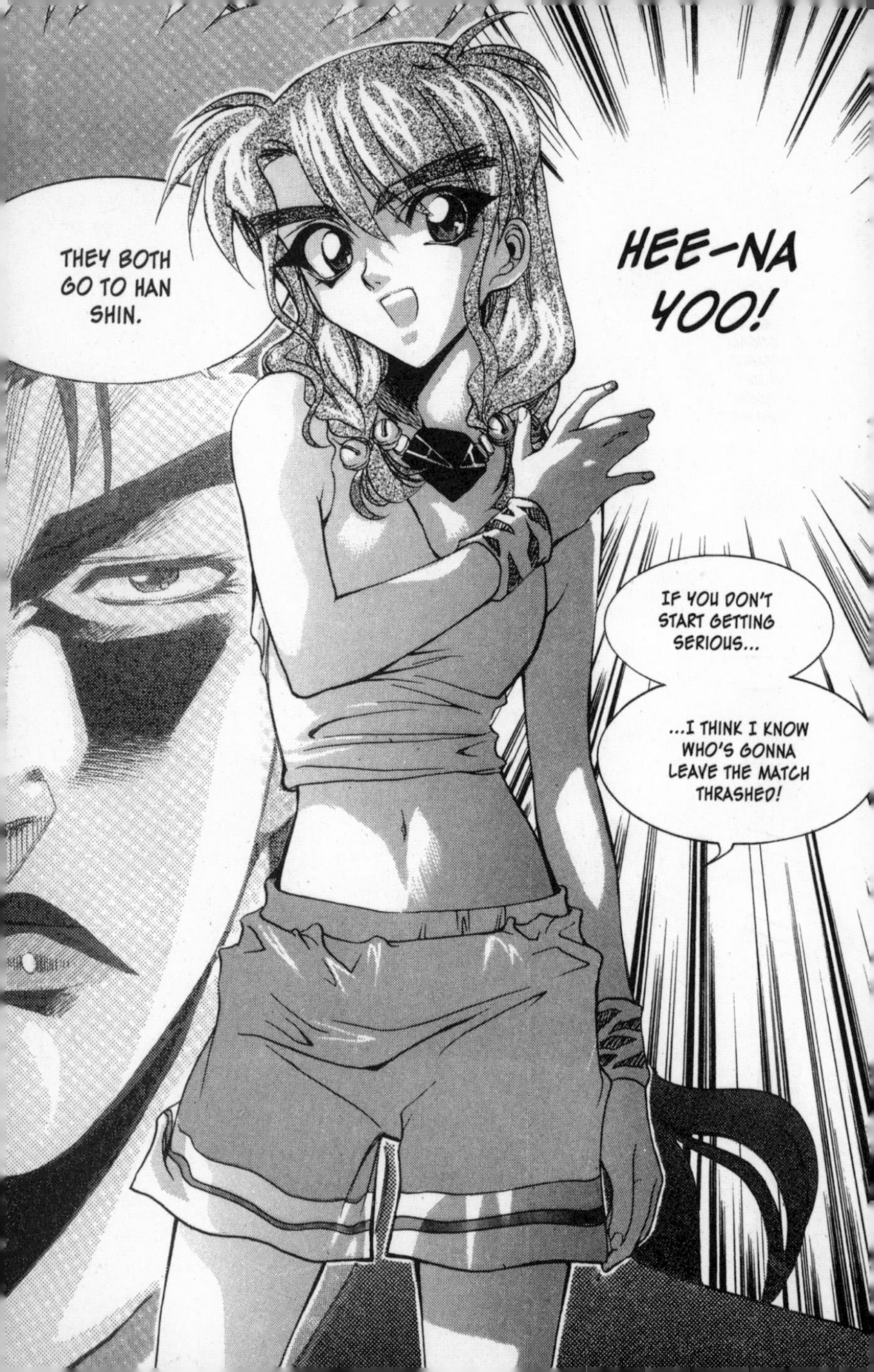
THEY BOTH GO TO HAN SHIN.
HEE-NA YOO!
IF YOU DON'T START GETTING SERIOUS...
...I THINK I KNOW WHO'S GONNA LEAVE THE MATCH THRASHED!

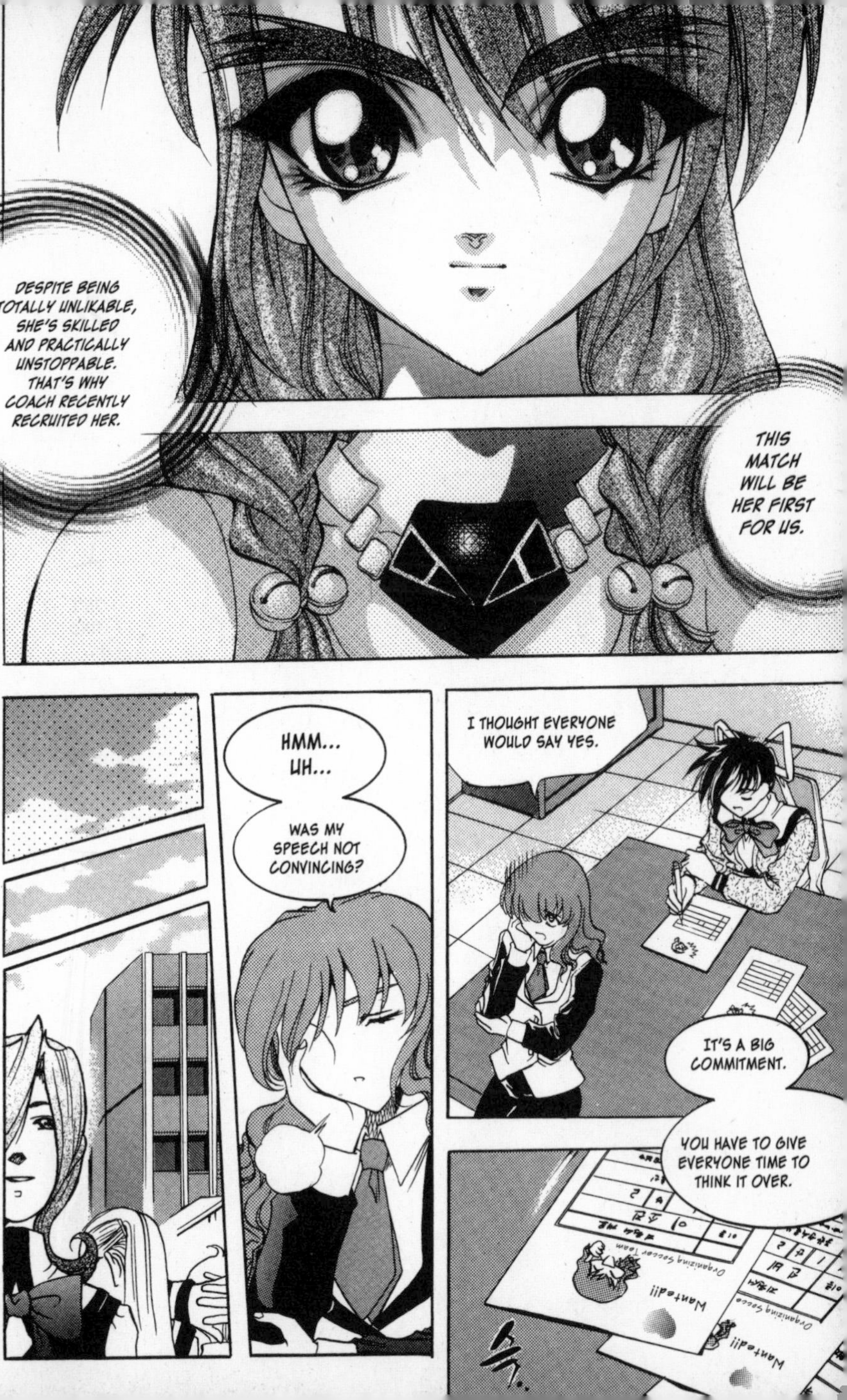
DESPITE BEING TOTALLY UNLIKABLE, SHE'S SKILLED AND PRACTICALLY UNSTOPPABLE. THAT'S WHY COACH RECENTLY RECRUITED HER.
THIS MATCH WILL BE HER FIRST FOR US.
HMM... UH...
WAS MY SPEECH NOT CONVINCING?
I THOUGHT EVERYONE WOULD SAY YES.
IT'S A BIG COMMITMENT.
YOU HAVE TO GIVE EVERYONE TIME TO THINK IT OVER.

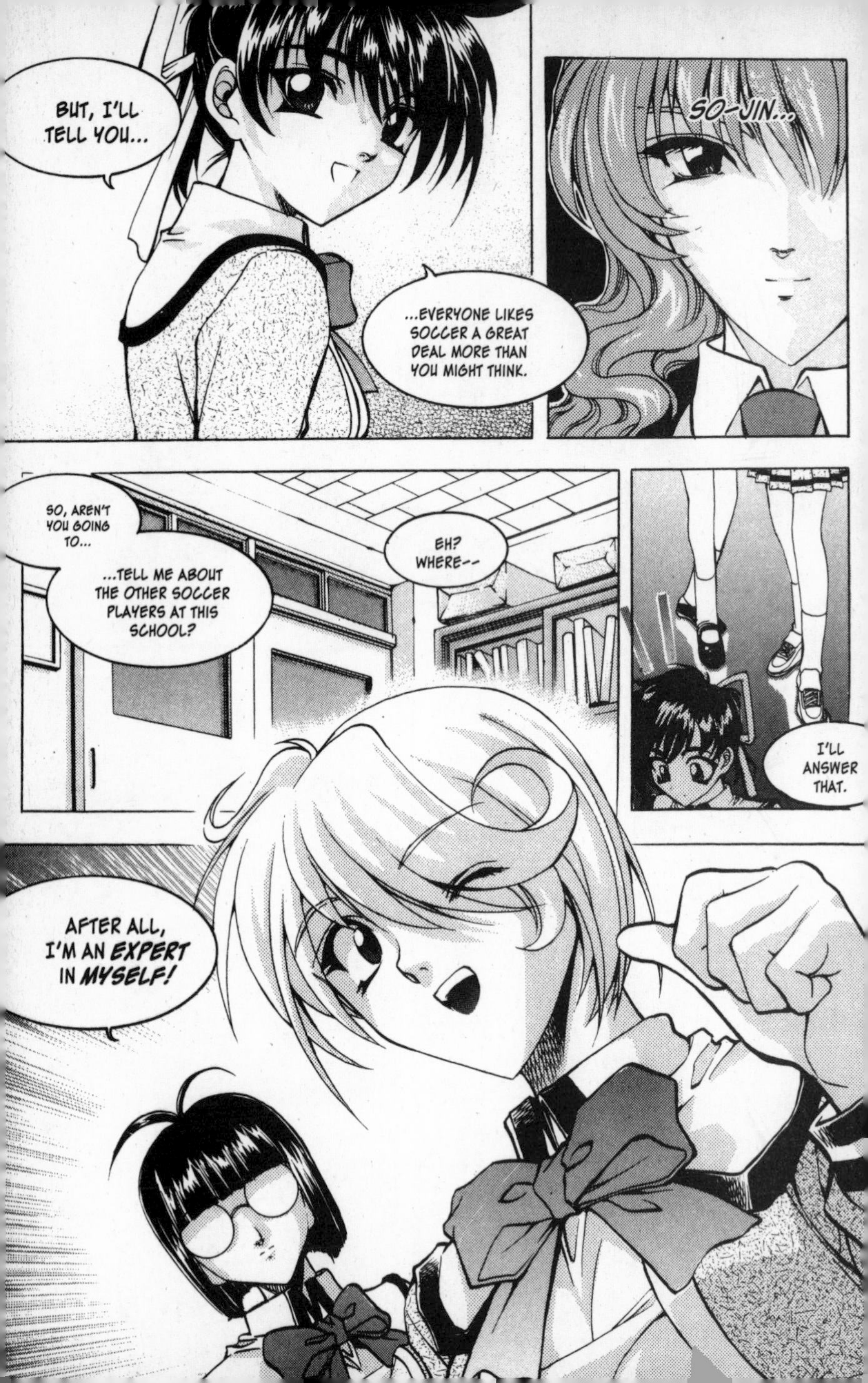
BUT, I'LL TELL YOU...
...EVERYONE LIKES SOCCER A GREAT DEAL MORE THAN YOU MIGHT THINK.
SO-JIN...
SO, AREN'T YOU GOING TO...
...TELL ME ABOUT THE OTHER SOCCER PLAYERS AT THIS SCHOOL?
EH? WHERE--
I'LL ANSWER THAT.
AFTER ALL, I'M AN *EXPERT* IN *MYSELF!*

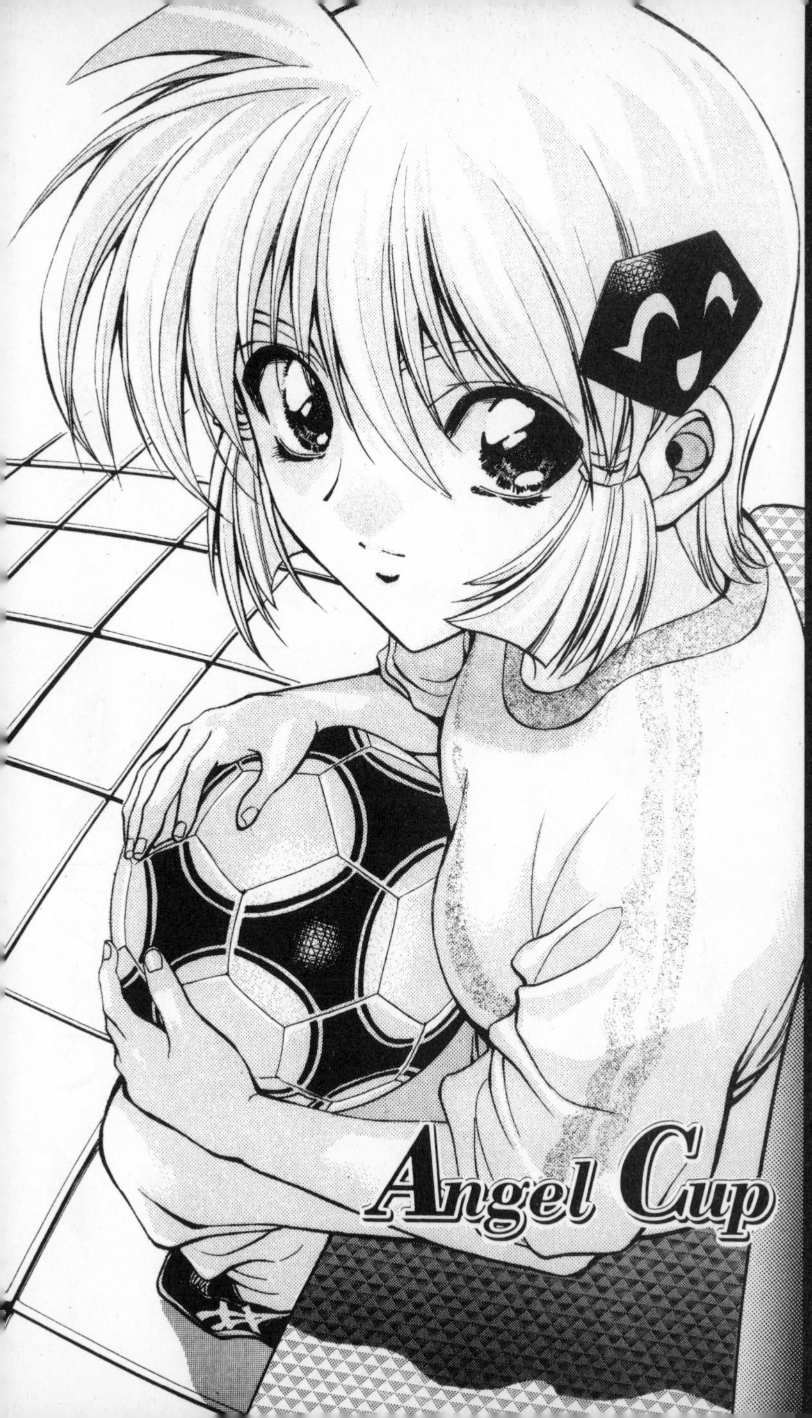
Angel Cup

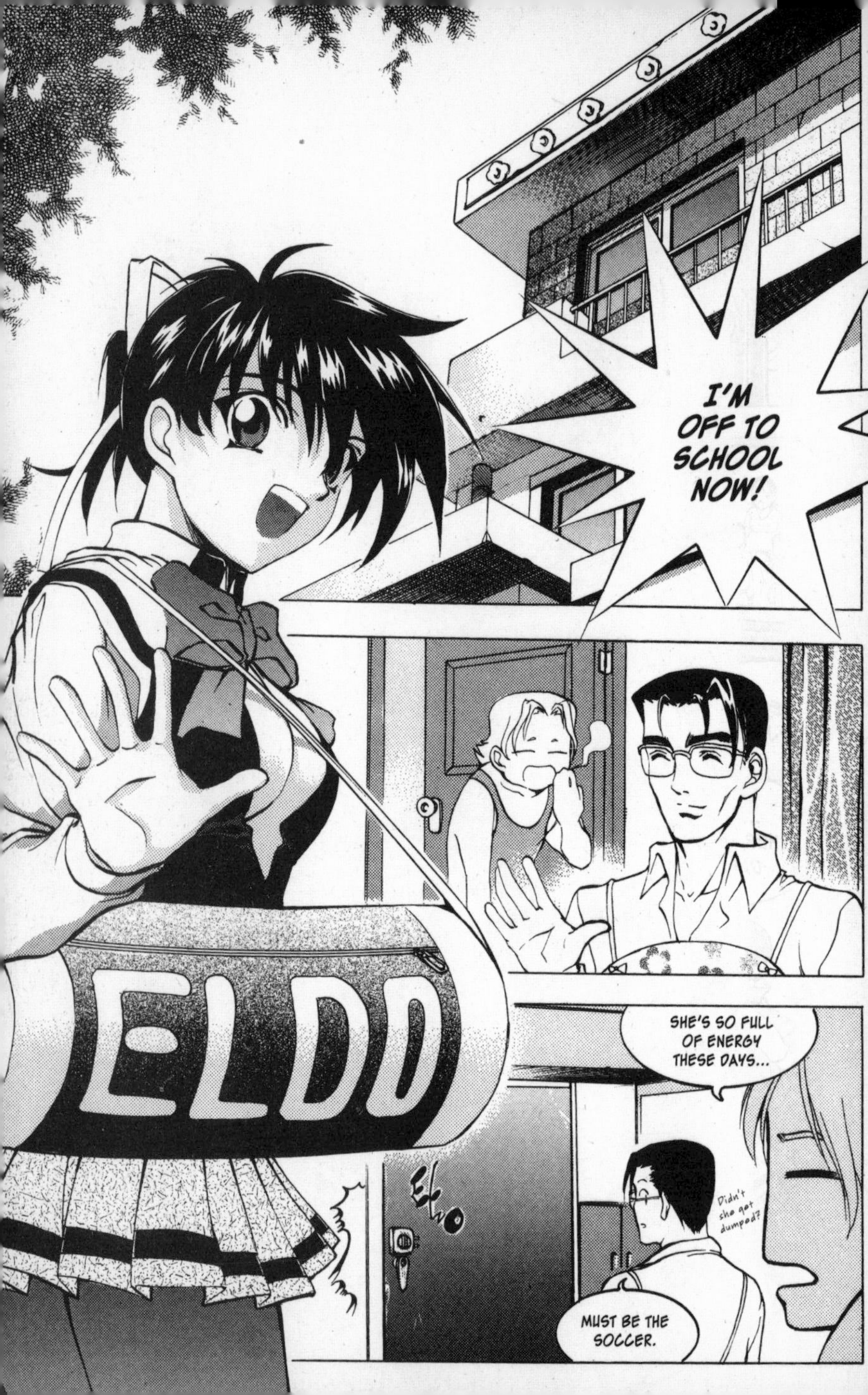
I'M OFF TO SCHOOL NOW!
ELDO
SHE'S SO FULL OF ENERGY THESE DAYS...
Didn't she get dumped?
MUST BE THE SOCCER.

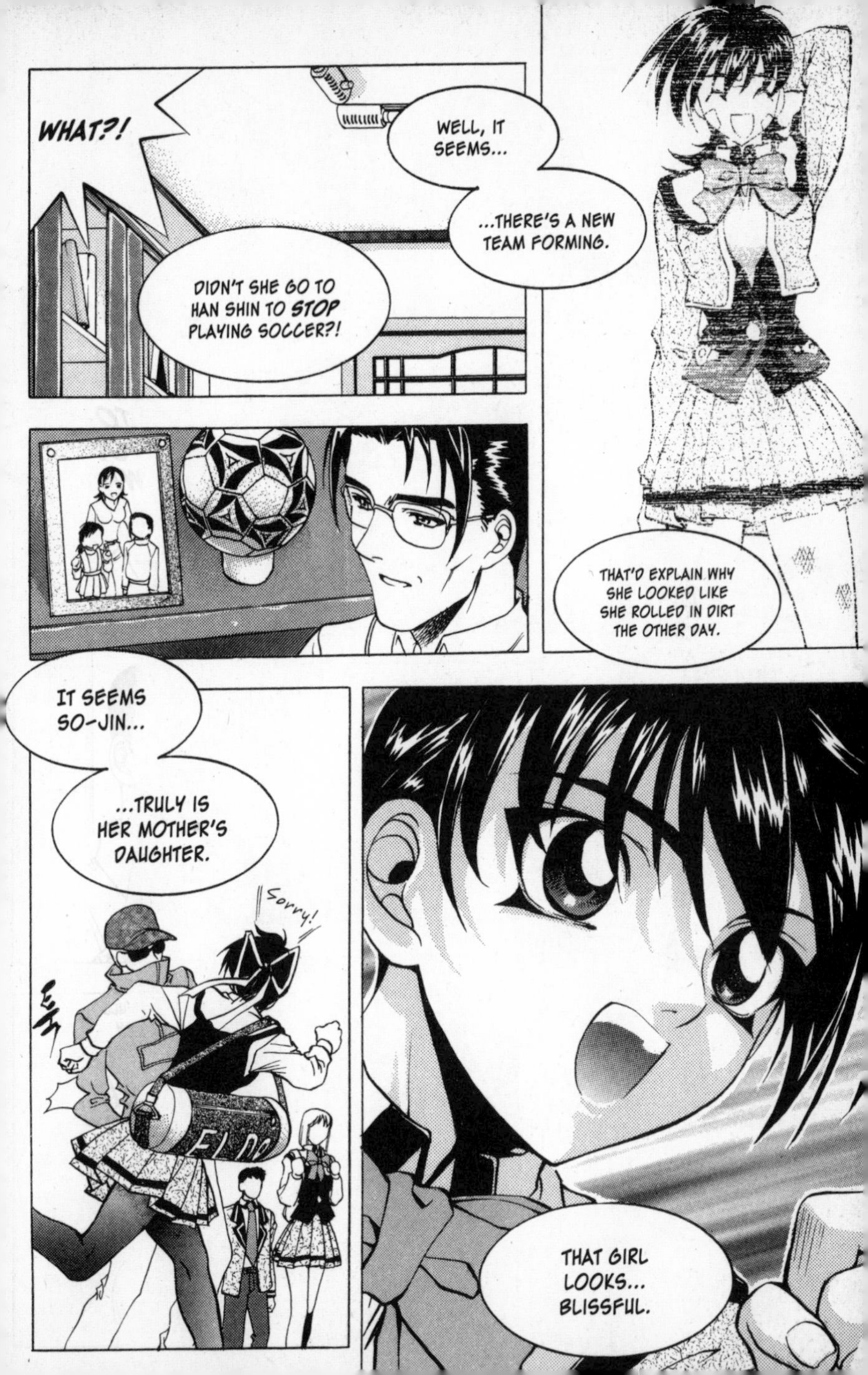
WHAT?!
WELL, IT SEEMS...
...THERE'S A NEW TEAM FORMING.
DIDN'T SHE GO TO HAN SHIN TO STOP PLAYING SOCCER?!
THAT'D EXPLAIN WHY SHE LOOKED LIKE SHE ROLLED IN DIRT THE OTHER DAY.
IT SEEMS SO-JIN...
...TRULY IS HER MOTHER'S DAUGHTER.
Sorry!
THAT GIRL LOOKS... BLISSFUL.

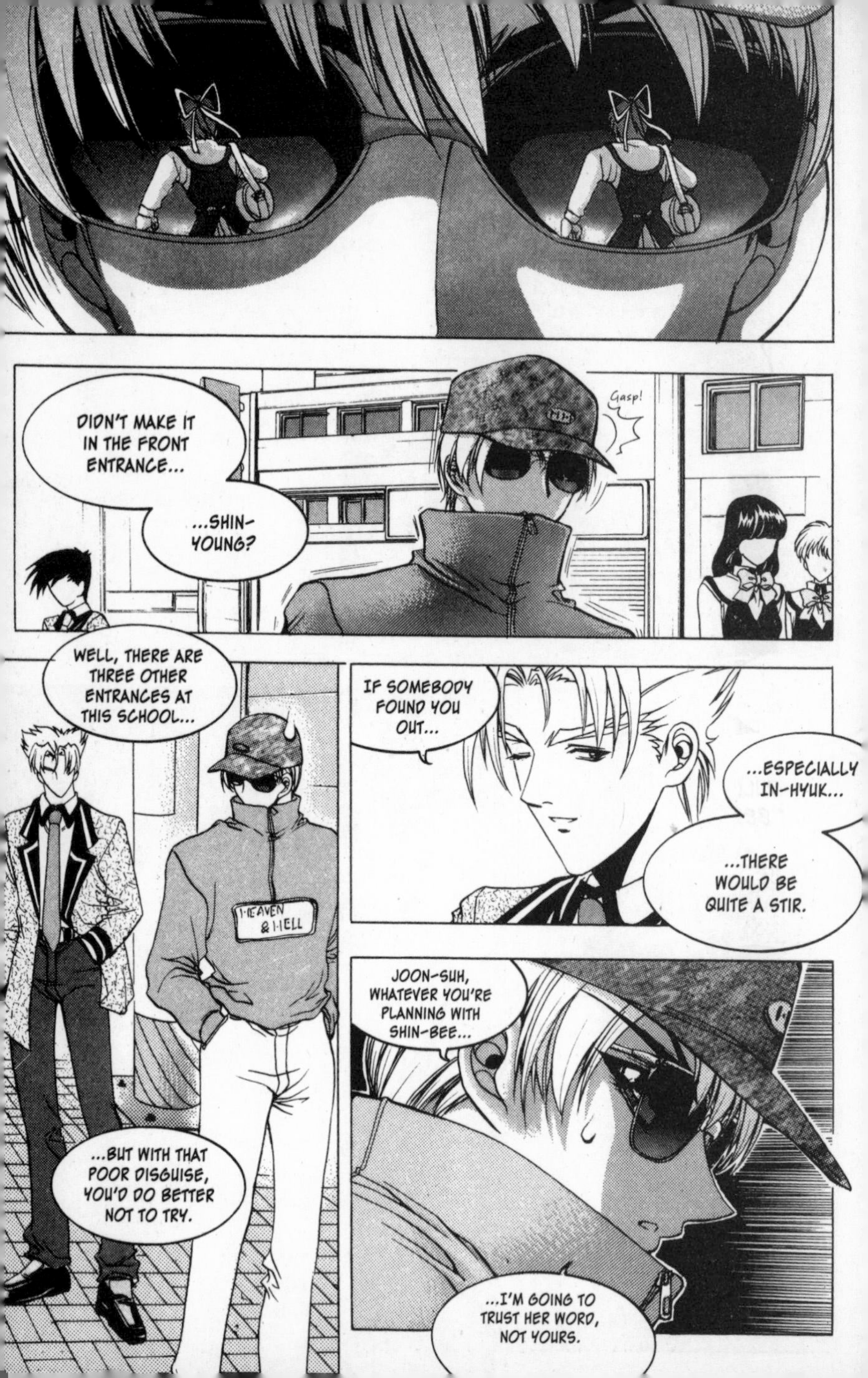
DIDN'T MAKE IT IN THE FRONT ENTRANCE...
...SHIN-YOUNG?
Gasp!
WELL, THERE ARE THREE OTHER ENTRANCES AT THIS SCHOOL...
HEAVEN & HELL
...BUT WITH THAT POOR DISGUISE, YOU'D DO BETTER NOT TO TRY.
IF SOMEBODY FOUND YOU OUT...
...ESPECIALLY IN-HYUK...
...THERE WOULD BE QUITE A STIR.
JOON-SUH, WHATEVER YOU'RE PLANNING WITH SHIN-BEE...
...I'M GOING TO TRUST HER WORD, NOT YOURS.

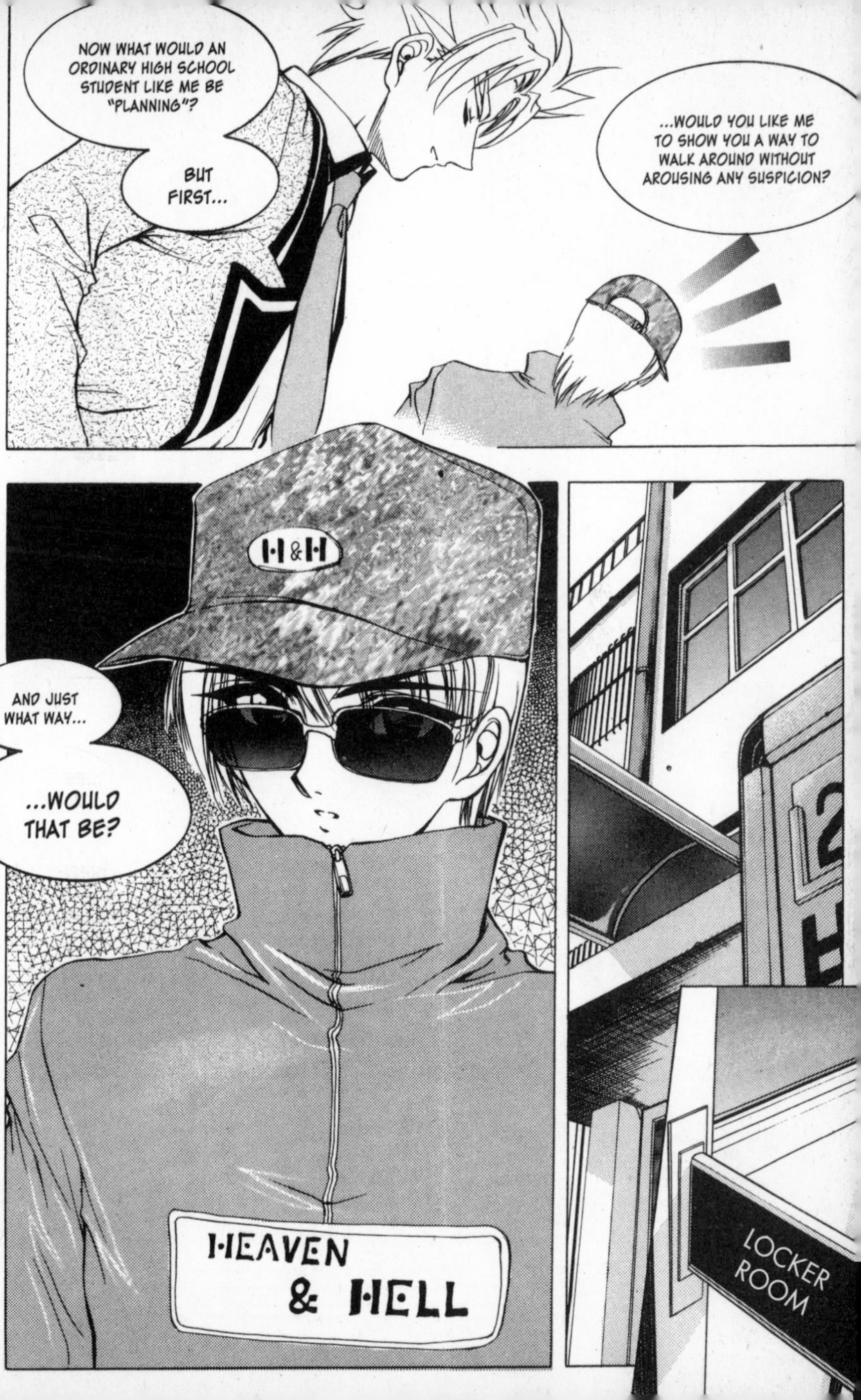
NOW WHAT WOULD AN ORDINARY HIGH SCHOOL STUDENT LIKE ME BE "PLANNING"?
BUT FIRST...
...WOULD YOU LIKE ME TO SHOW YOU A WAY TO WALK AROUND WITHOUT AROUSING ANY SUSPICION?
H&H
AND JUST WHAT WAY...
...WOULD THAT BE?
HEAVEN & HELL
LOCKER ROOM

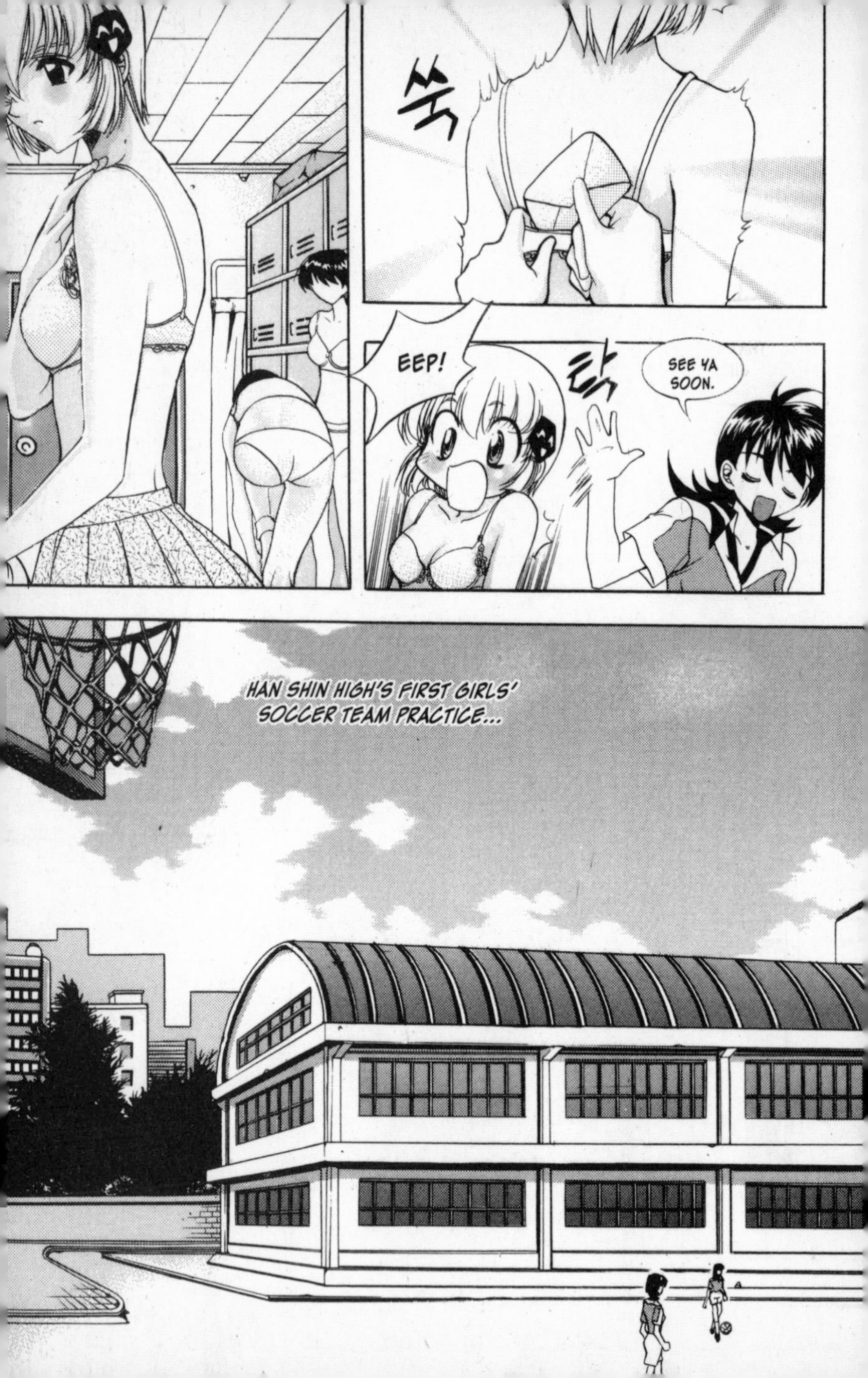
쑥
EEP!
탁
SEE YA SOON.
HAN SHIN HIGH'S FIRST GIRLS' SOCCER TEAM PRACTICE...

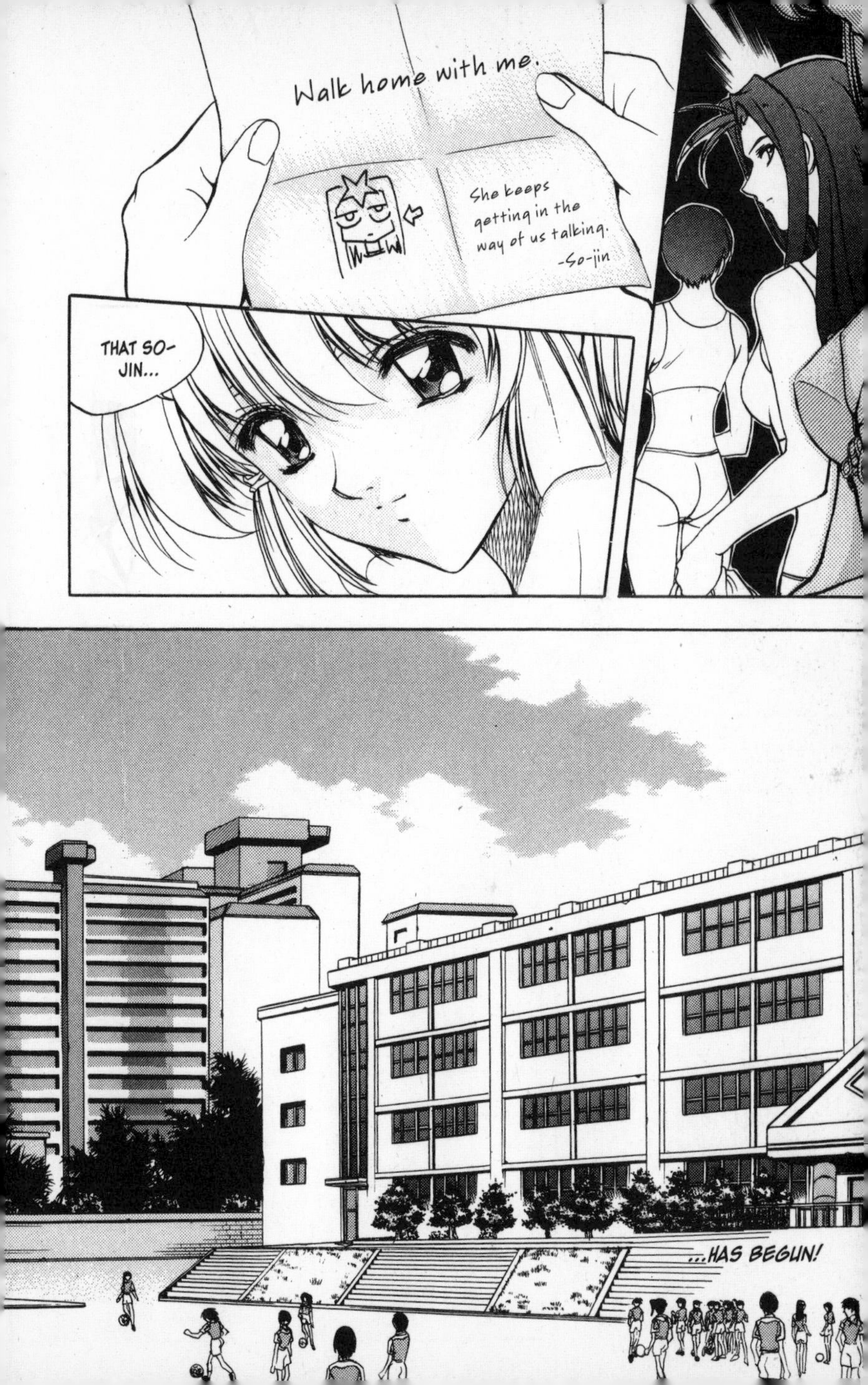
Walk home with me.
She keeps getting in the way of us talking.
-So-jin
THAT SO-JIN...
...HAS BEGUN!

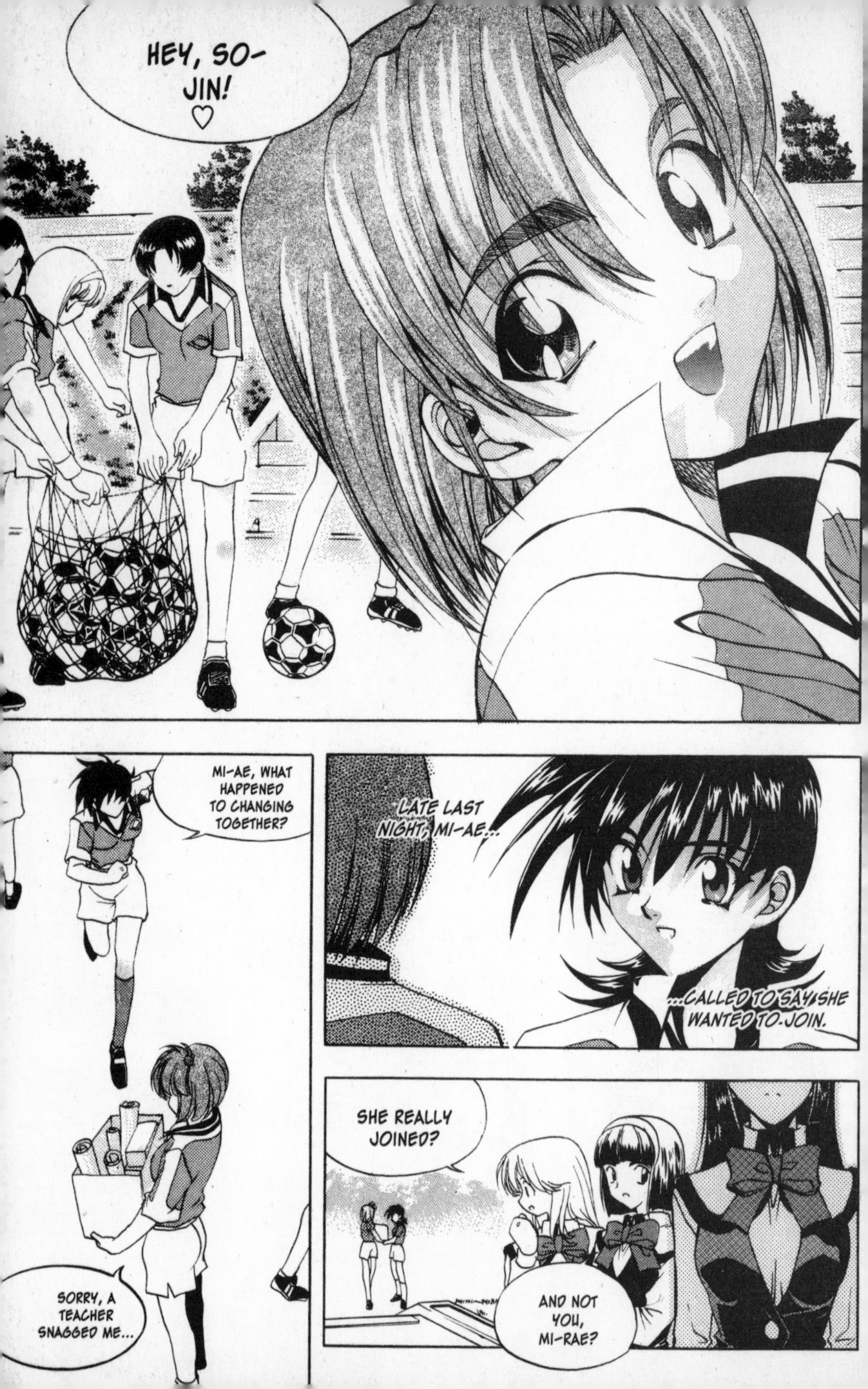

HEY, SO-JIN! ♡
MI-AE, WHAT HAPPENED TO CHANGING TOGETHER?
SORRY, A TEACHER SNAGGED ME...
LATE LAST NIGHT, MI-AE...
...CALLED TO SAY SHE WANTED TO JOIN.
SHE REALLY JOINED?
AND NOT YOU, MI-RAE?

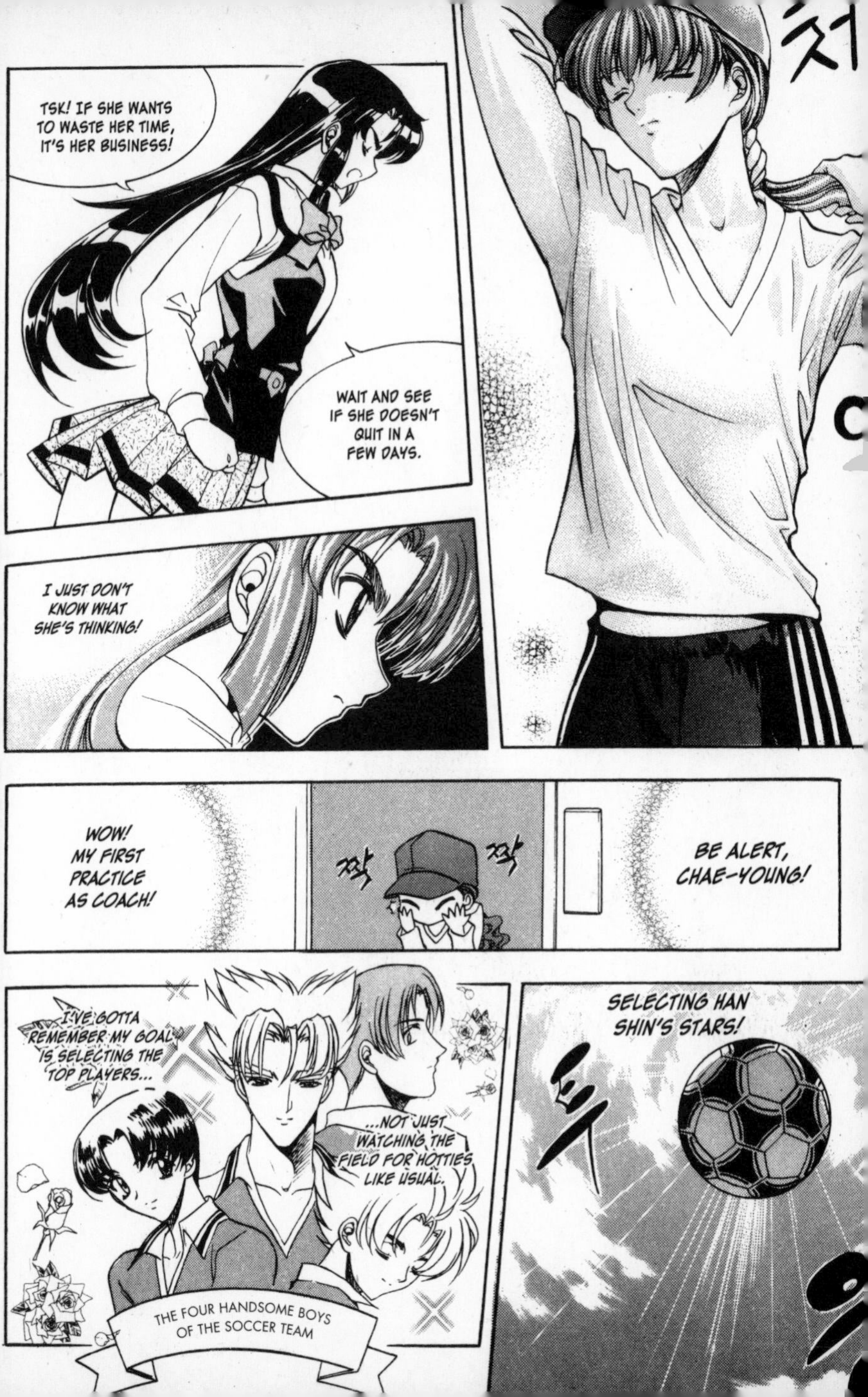
TSK! IF SHE WANTS TO WASTE HER TIME, IT'S HER BUSINESS!
WAIT AND SEE IF SHE DOESN'T QUIT IN A FEW DAYS.
I JUST DON'T KNOW WHAT SHE'S THINKING!
WOW! MY FIRST PRACTICE AS COACH!
BE ALERT, CHAE-YOUNG!
I'VE GOTTA REMEMBER MY GOAL IS SELECTING THE TOP PLAYERS...
...NOT JUST WATCHING THE FIELD FOR HOTTIES LIKE USUAL.
THE FOUR HANDSOME BOYS OF THE SOCCER TEAM
SELECTING HAN SHIN'S STARS!

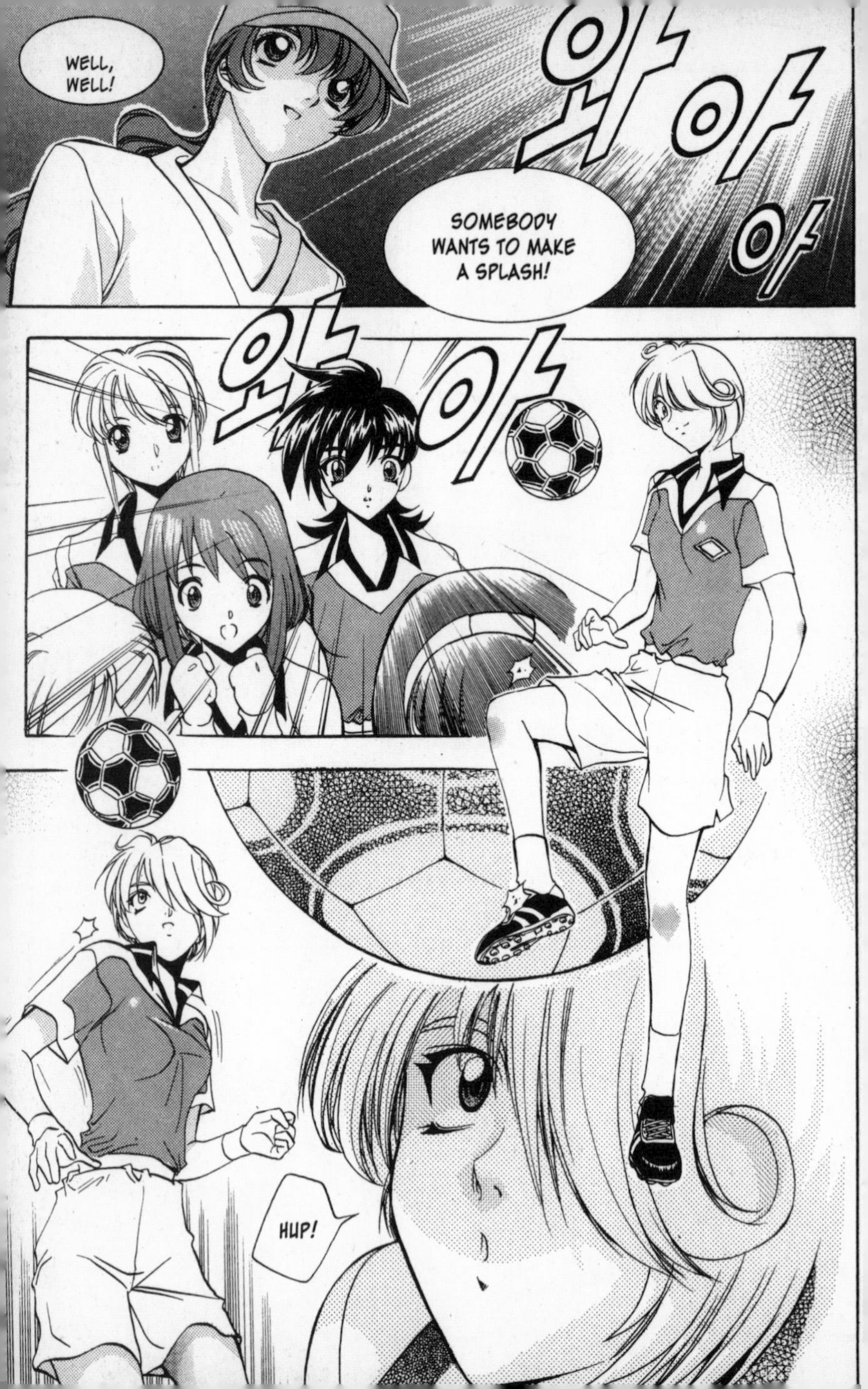
WELL, WELL!
SOMEBODY WANTS TO MAKE A SPLASH!
와아아
와아
HUP!

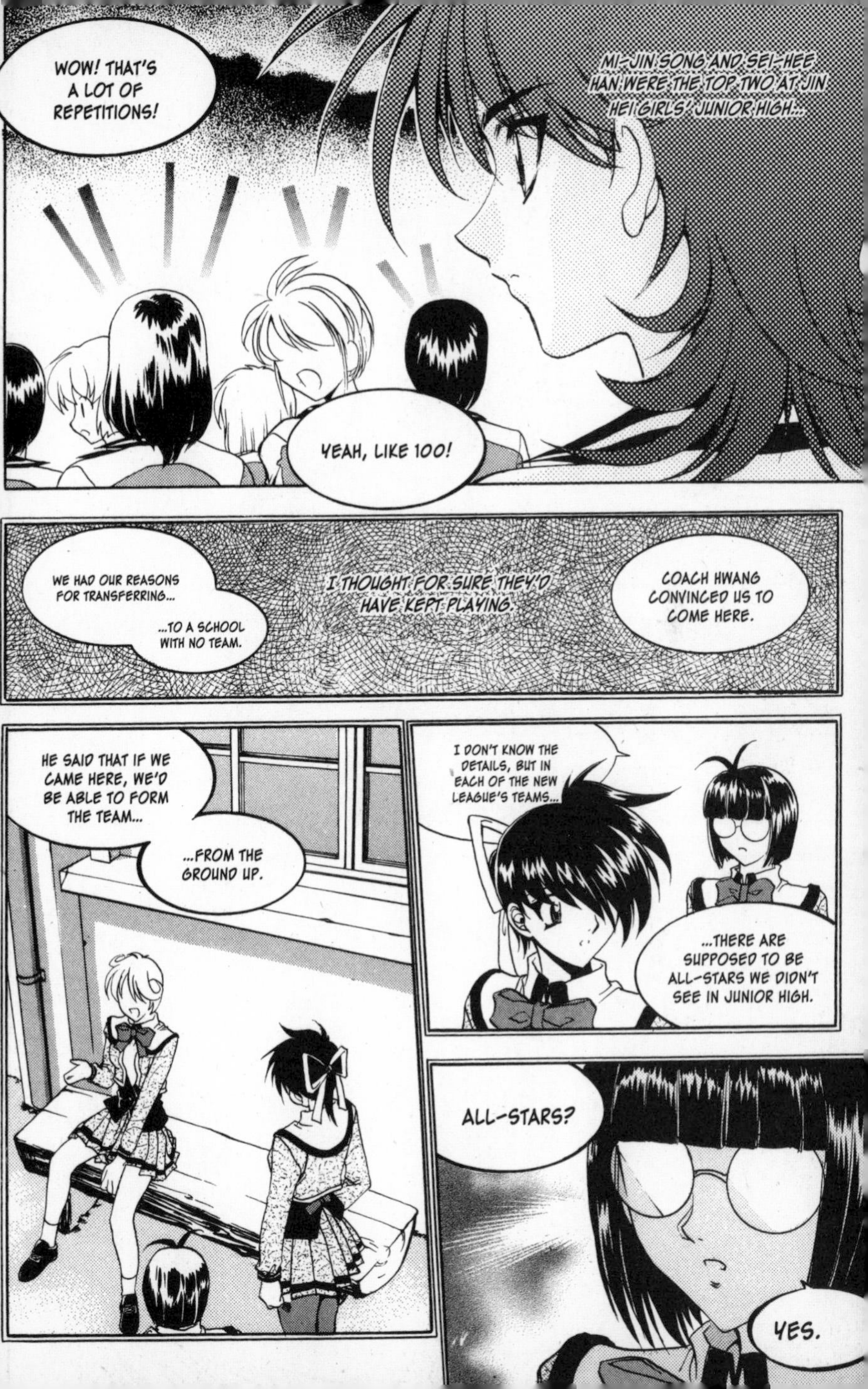
WOW! THAT'S A LOT OF REPETITIONS!
MI-JIN SONG AND SEI-HEE HAN WERE THE TOP TWO AT JIN HEI GIRLS' JUNIOR HIGH...
YEAH, LIKE 100!
WE HAD OUR REASONS FOR TRANSFERRING...
...TO A SCHOOL WITH NO TEAM.
I THOUGHT FOR SURE THEY'D HAVE KEPT PLAYING.
COACH HWANG CONVINCED US TO COME HERE.
HE SAID THAT IF WE CAME HERE, WE'D BE ABLE TO FORM THE TEAM...
...FROM THE GROUND UP.
I DON'T KNOW THE DETAILS, BUT IN EACH OF THE NEW LEAGUE'S TEAMS...
...THERE ARE SUPPOSED TO BE ALL-STARS WE DIDN'T SEE IN JUNIOR HIGH.
ALL-STARS?
YES.

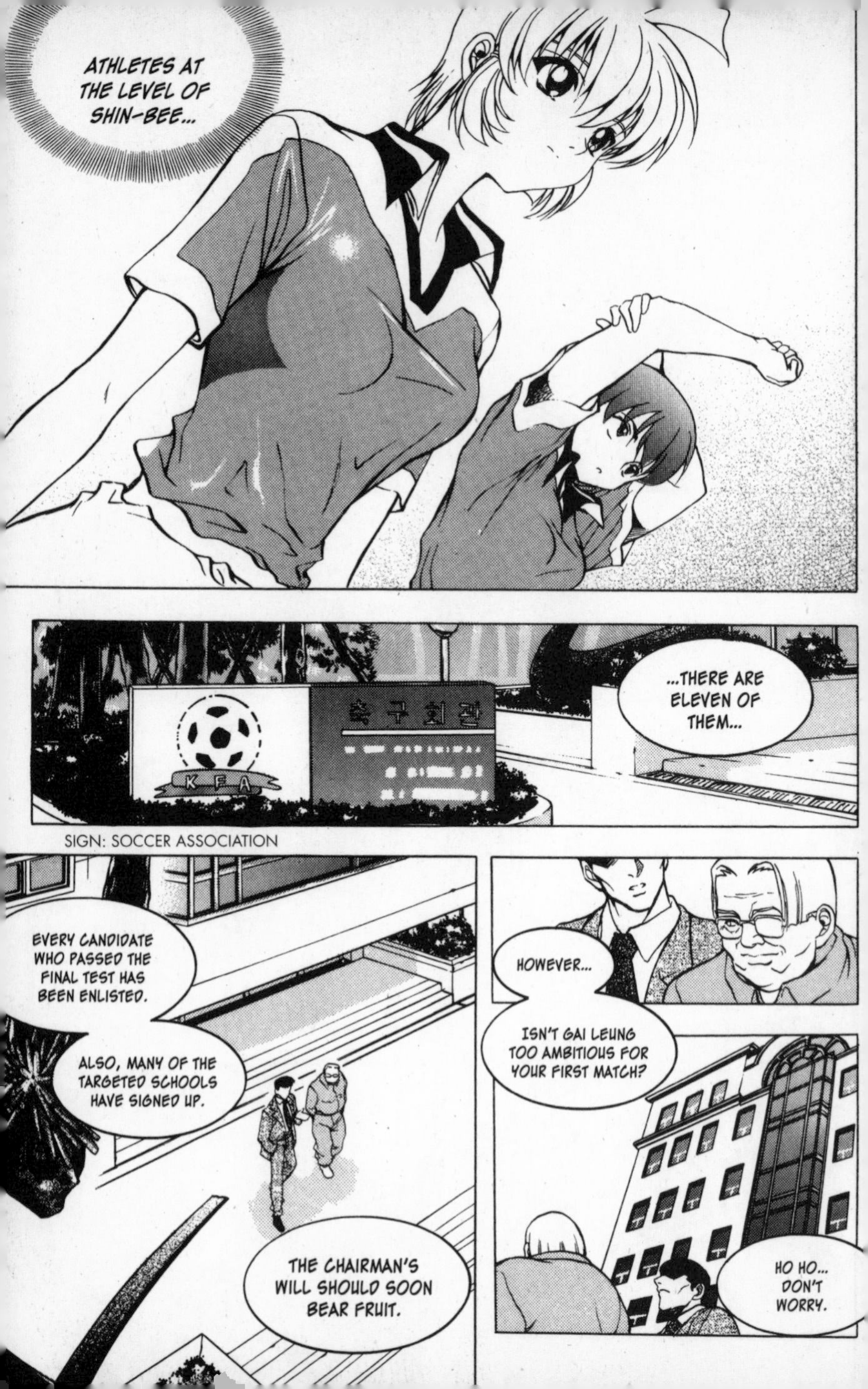
ATHLETES AT THE LEVEL OF SHIN-BEE...
...THERE ARE ELEVEN OF THEM...
K F A
EVERY CANDIDATE WHO PASSED THE FINAL TEST HAS BEEN ENLISTED.
ALSO, MANY OF THE TARGETED SCHOOLS HAVE SIGNED UP.
THE CHAIRMAN'S WILL SHOULD SOON BEAR FRUIT.
HOWEVER...
ISN'T GAI LEUNG TOO AMBITIOUS FOR YOUR FIRST MATCH?
HO HO... DON'T WORRY.
SIGN: SOCCER ASSOCIATION

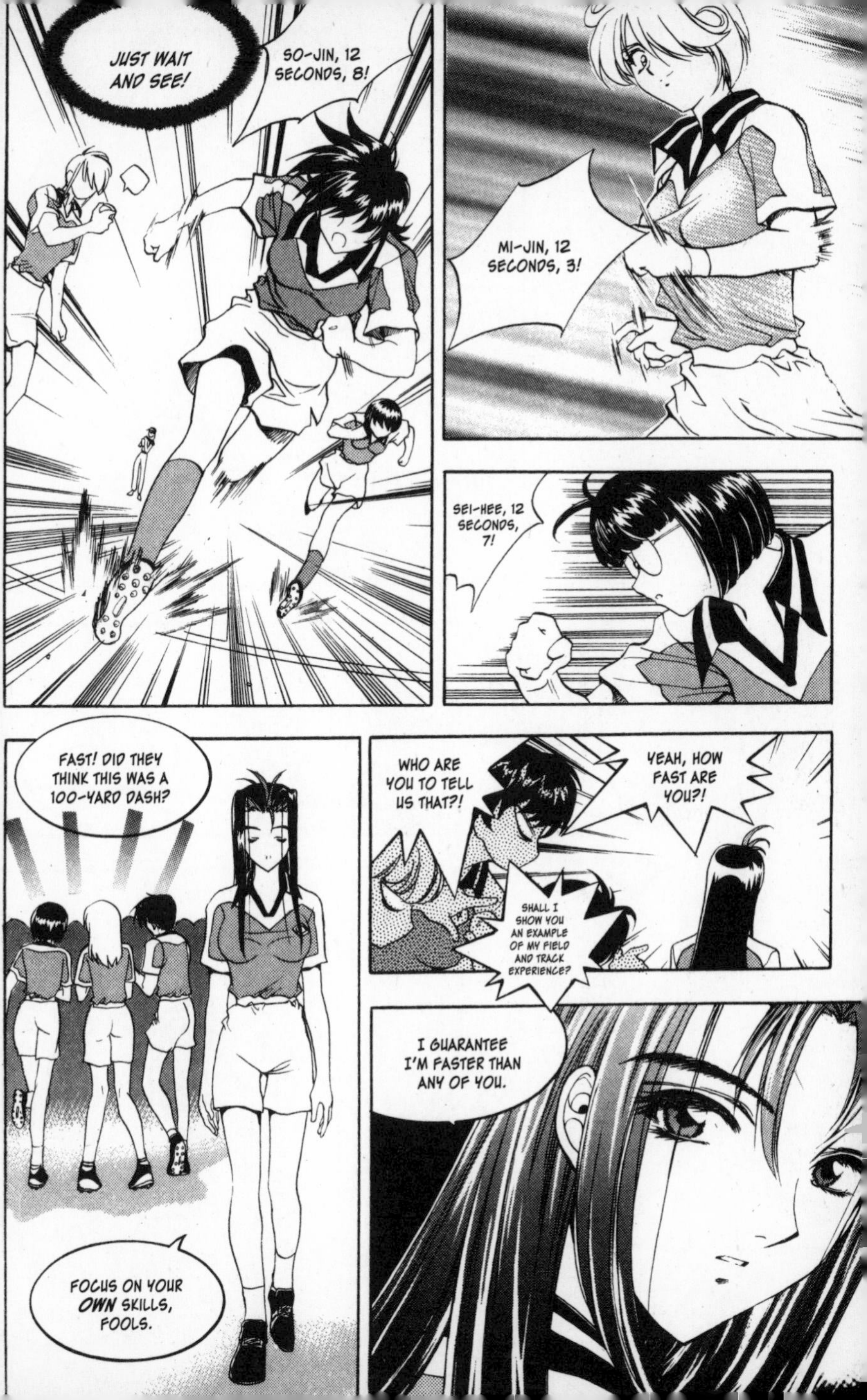
JUST WAIT AND SEE!
SO-JIN, 12 SECONDS, 8!
MI-JIN, 12 SECONDS, 3!
SEI-HEE, 12 SECONDS, 7!
FAST! DID THEY THINK THIS WAS A 100-YARD DASH?
FOCUS ON YOUR OWN SKILLS, FOOLS.
WHO ARE YOU TO TELL US THAT?!
YEAH, HOW FAST ARE YOU?!
SHALL I SHOW YOU AN EXAMPLE OF MY FIELD AND TRACK EXPERIENCE?
I GUARANTEE I'M FASTER THAN ANY OF YOU.

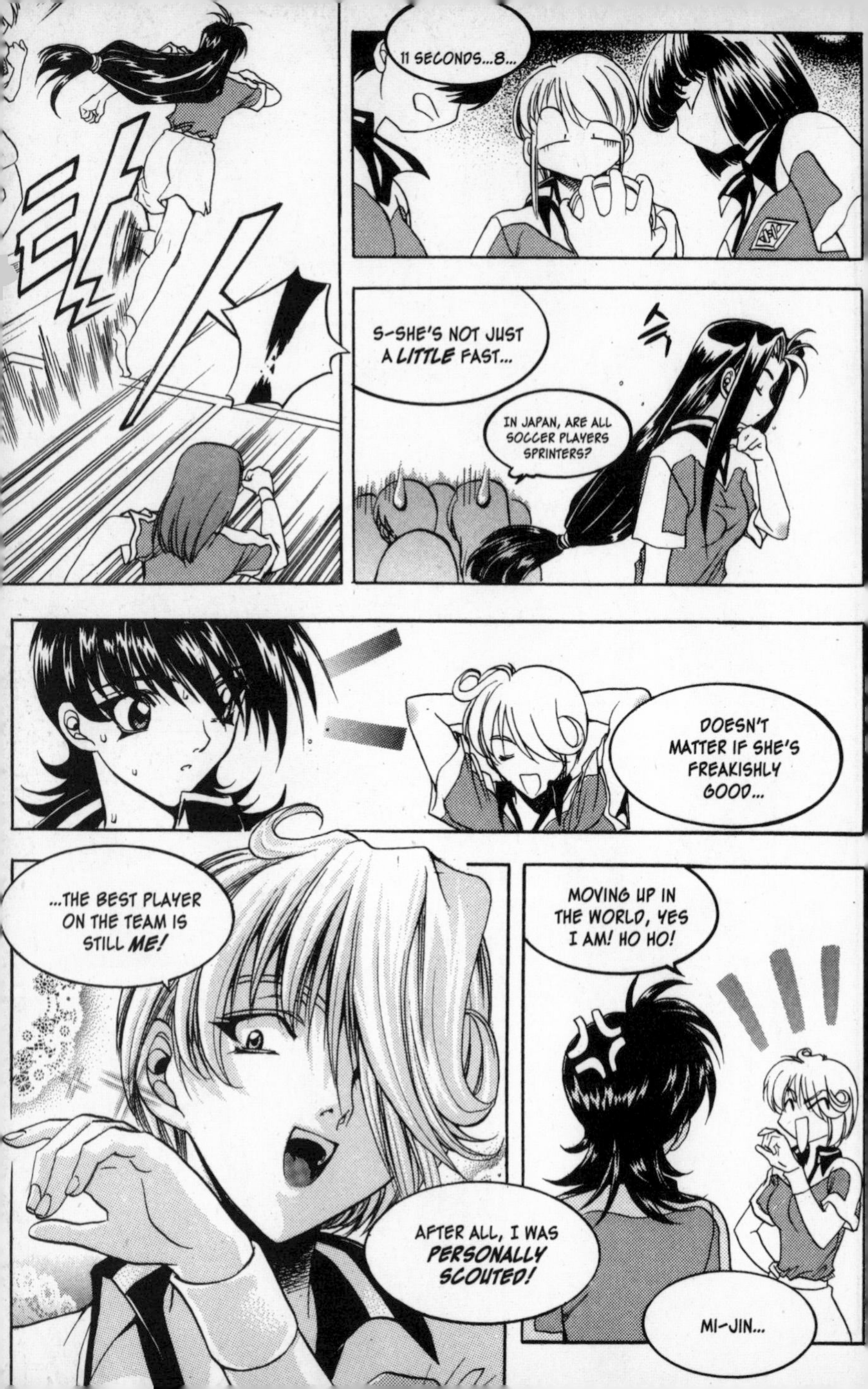
11 SECONDS...8...
S-SHE'S NOT JUST A LITTLE FAST...
스
IN JAPAN, ARE ALL SOCCER PLAYERS SPRINTERS?
DOESN'T MATTER IF SHE'S FREAKISHLY GOOD...
...THE BEST PLAYER ON THE TEAM IS STILL ME!
AFTER ALL, I WAS PERSONALLY SCOUTED!
MOVING UP IN THE WORLD, YES I AM! HO HO!
MI-JIN...

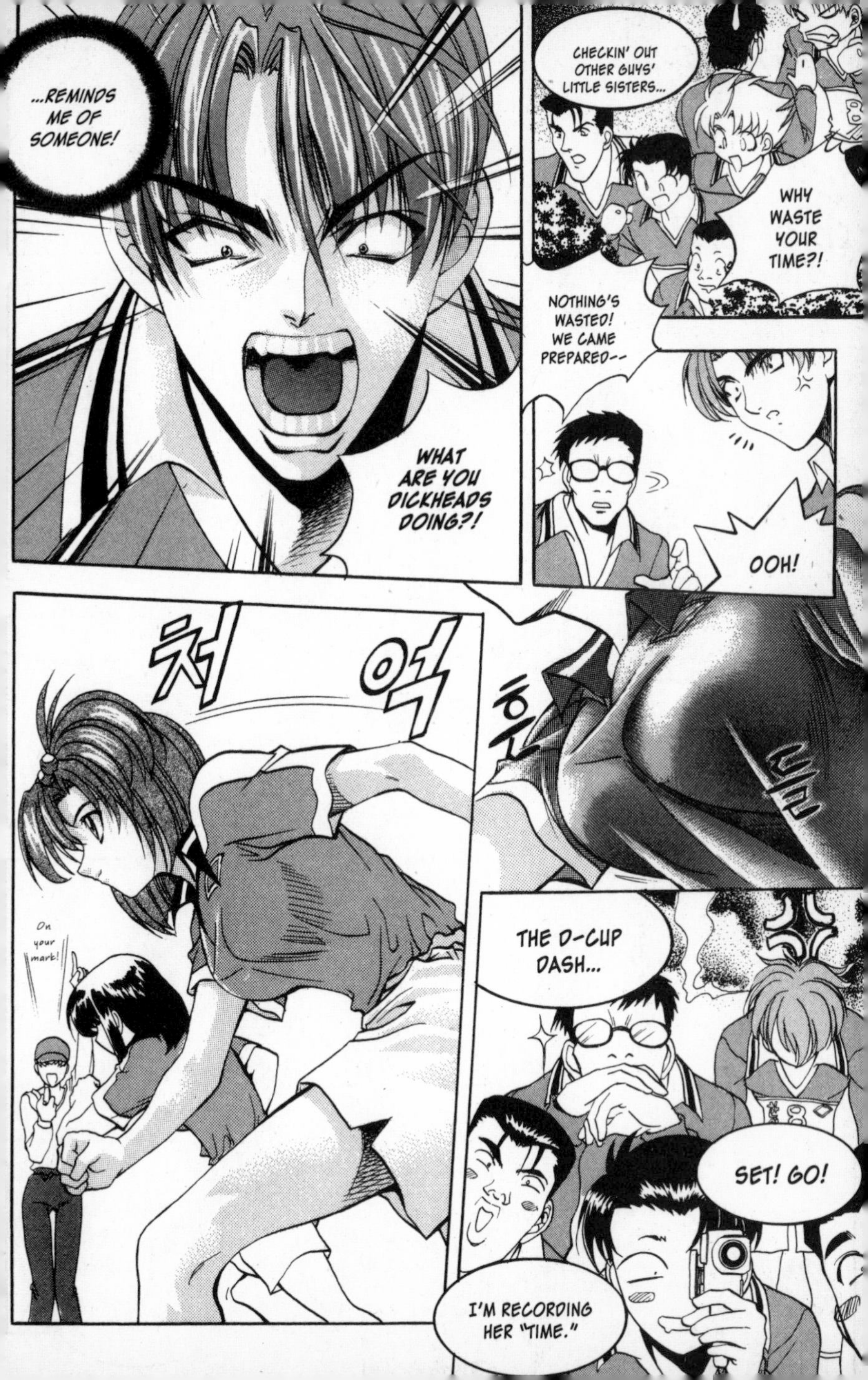
...REMINDS ME OF SOMEONE!
WHAT ARE YOU DICKHEADS DOING?!
CHECKIN' OUT OTHER GUYS' LITTLE SISTERS...
WHY WASTE YOUR TIME?!
NOTHING'S WASTED! WE CAME PREPARED--
OOH!
처 억
On your mark!
THE D-CUP DASH...
SET! GO!
I'M RECORDING HER "TIME."

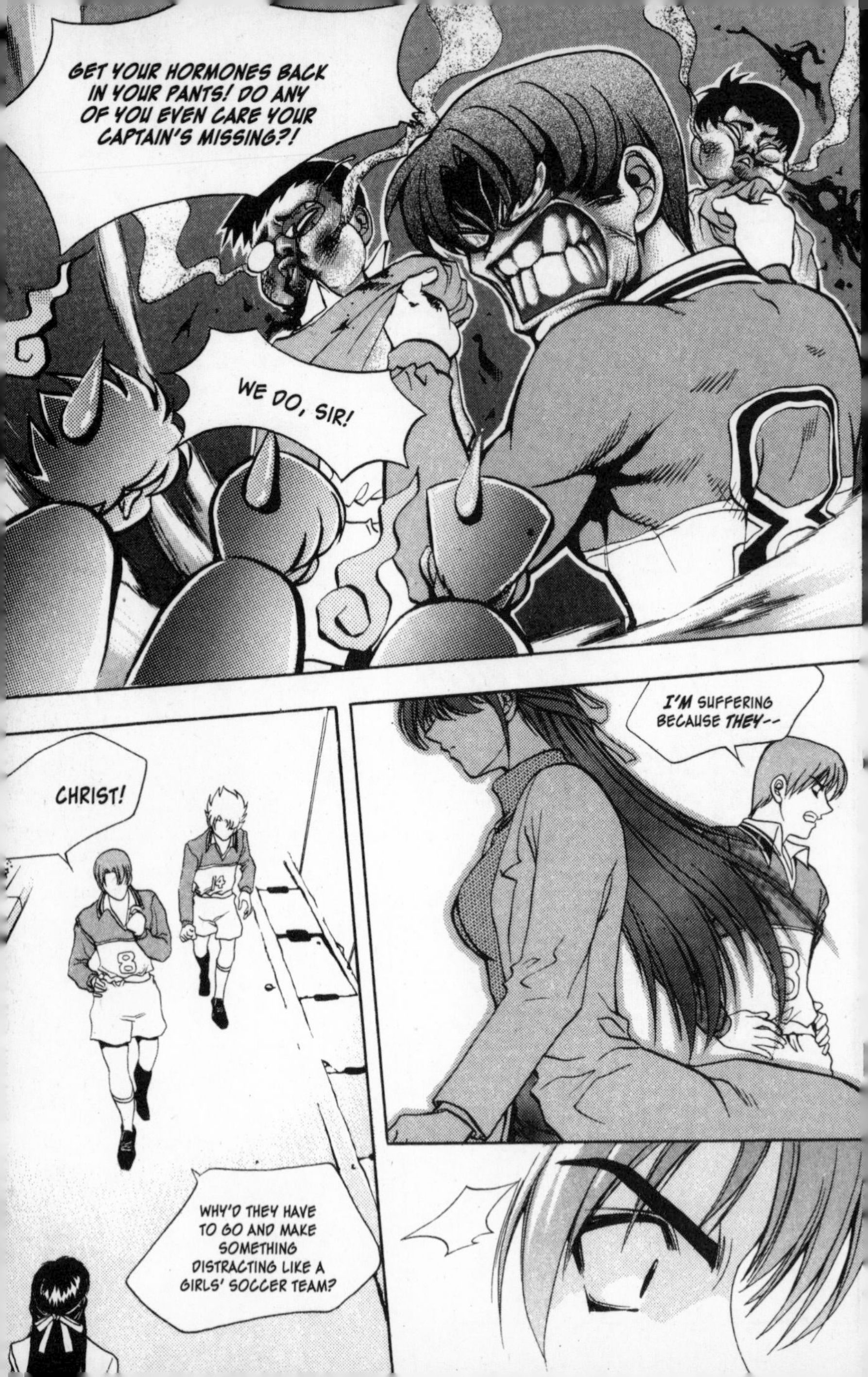
GET YOUR HORMONES BACK IN YOUR PANTS! DO ANY OF YOU EVEN CARE YOUR CAPTAIN'S MISSING?!
WE DO, SIR!
CHRIST!
I'M SUFFERING BECAUSE THEY--
WHY'D THEY HAVE TO GO AND MAKE SOMETHING DISTRACTING LIKE A GIRLS' SOCCER TEAM?

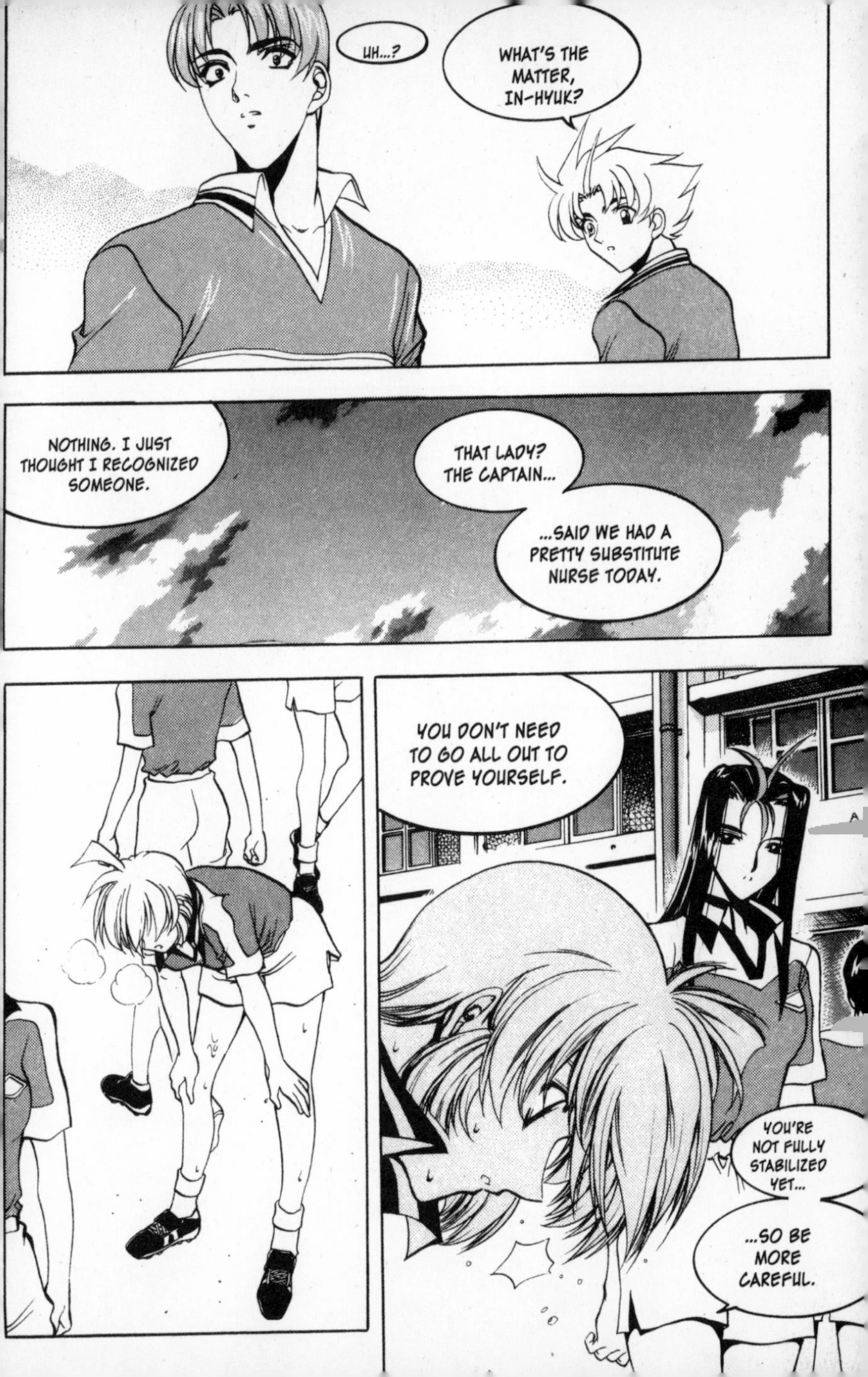
UH...?
WHAT'S THE MATTER, IN-HYUK?
NOTHING. I JUST THOUGHT I RECOGNIZED SOMEONE.
THAT LADY? THE CAPTAIN...
...SAID WE HAD A PRETTY SUBSTITUTE NURSE TODAY.
YOU DON'T NEED TO GO ALL OUT TO PROVE YOURSELF.
YOU'RE NOT FULLY STABILIZED YET...
...SO BE MORE CAREFUL.

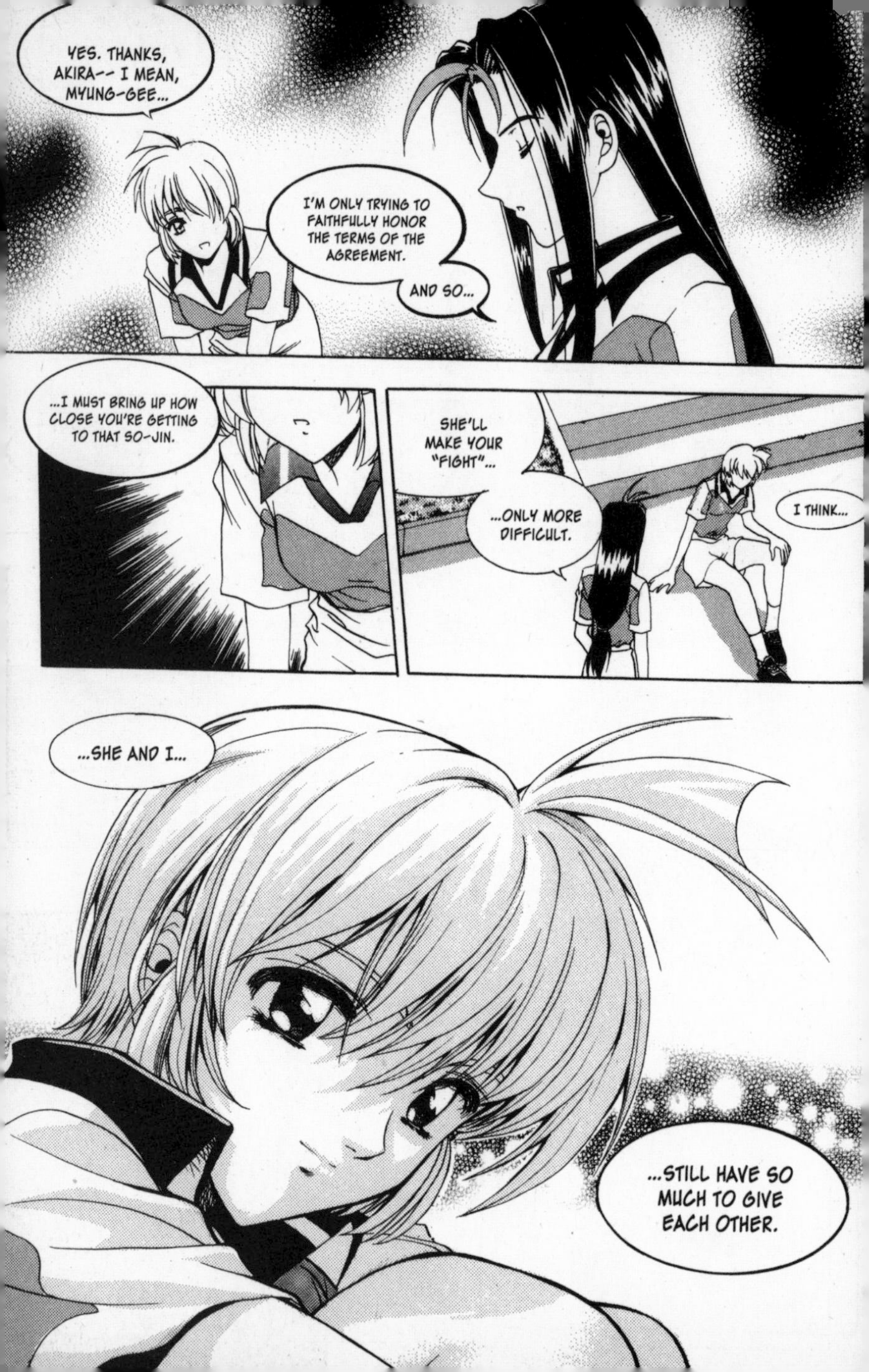
YES. THANKS, AKIRA-- I MEAN, MYUNG-GEE...
I'M ONLY TRYING TO FAITHFULLY HONOR THE TERMS OF THE AGREEMENT.
AND SO...
...I MUST BRING UP HOW CLOSE YOU'RE GETTING TO THAT SO-JIN.
SHE'LL MAKE YOUR "FIGHT"...
...ONLY MORE DIFFICULT.
I THINK...
...SHE AND I...
...STILL HAVE SO MUCH TO GIVE EACH OTHER.

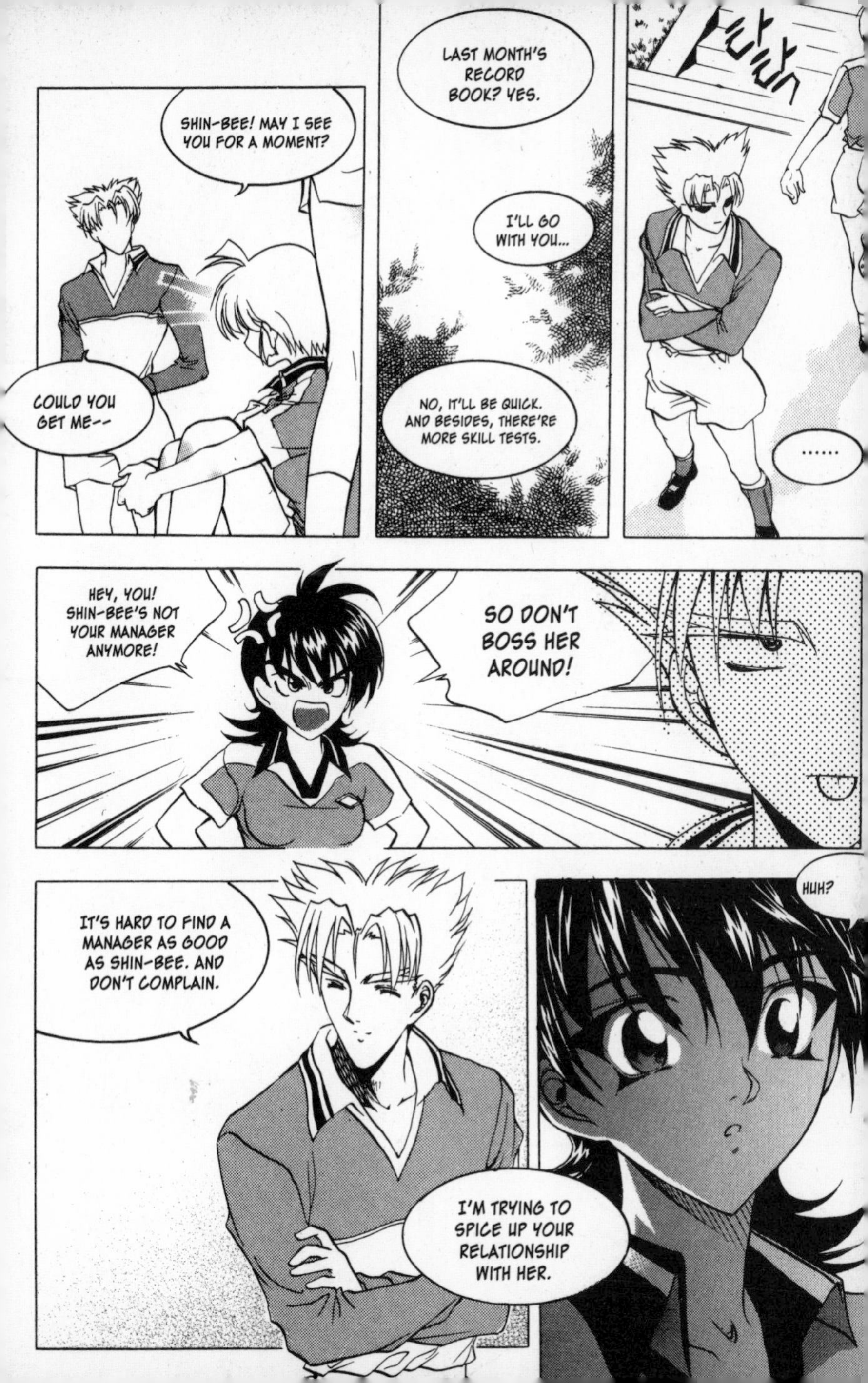
SHIN-BEE! MAY I SEE YOU FOR A MOMENT?
COULD YOU GET ME--
LAST MONTH'S RECORD BOOK? YES.
I'LL GO WITH YOU...
NO, IT'LL BE QUICK. AND BESIDES, THERE'RE MORE SKILL TESTS.
......
HEY, YOU! SHIN-BEE'S NOT YOUR MANAGER ANYMORE!
SO DON'T BOSS HER AROUND!
IT'S HARD TO FIND A MANAGER AS GOOD AS SHIN-BEE. AND DON'T COMPLAIN.
I'M TRYING TO SPICE UP YOUR RELATIONSHIP WITH HER.
HUH?

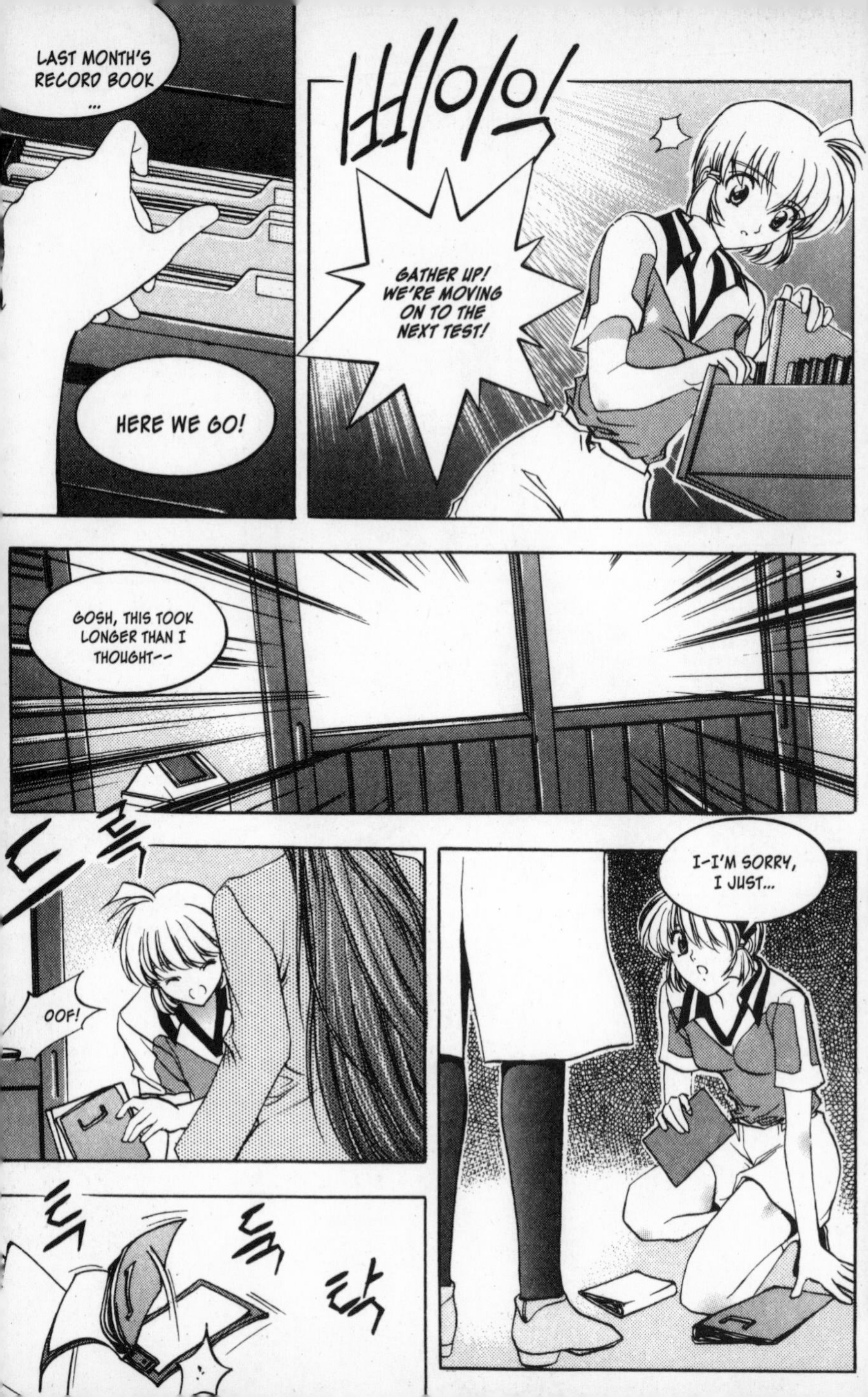
LAST MONTH'S RECORD BOOK ...
HERE WE GO!
GATHER UP! WE'RE MOVING ON TO THE NEXT TEST!
GOSH, THIS TOOK LONGER THAN I THOUGHT--
OOF!
I-I'M SORRY, I JUST...

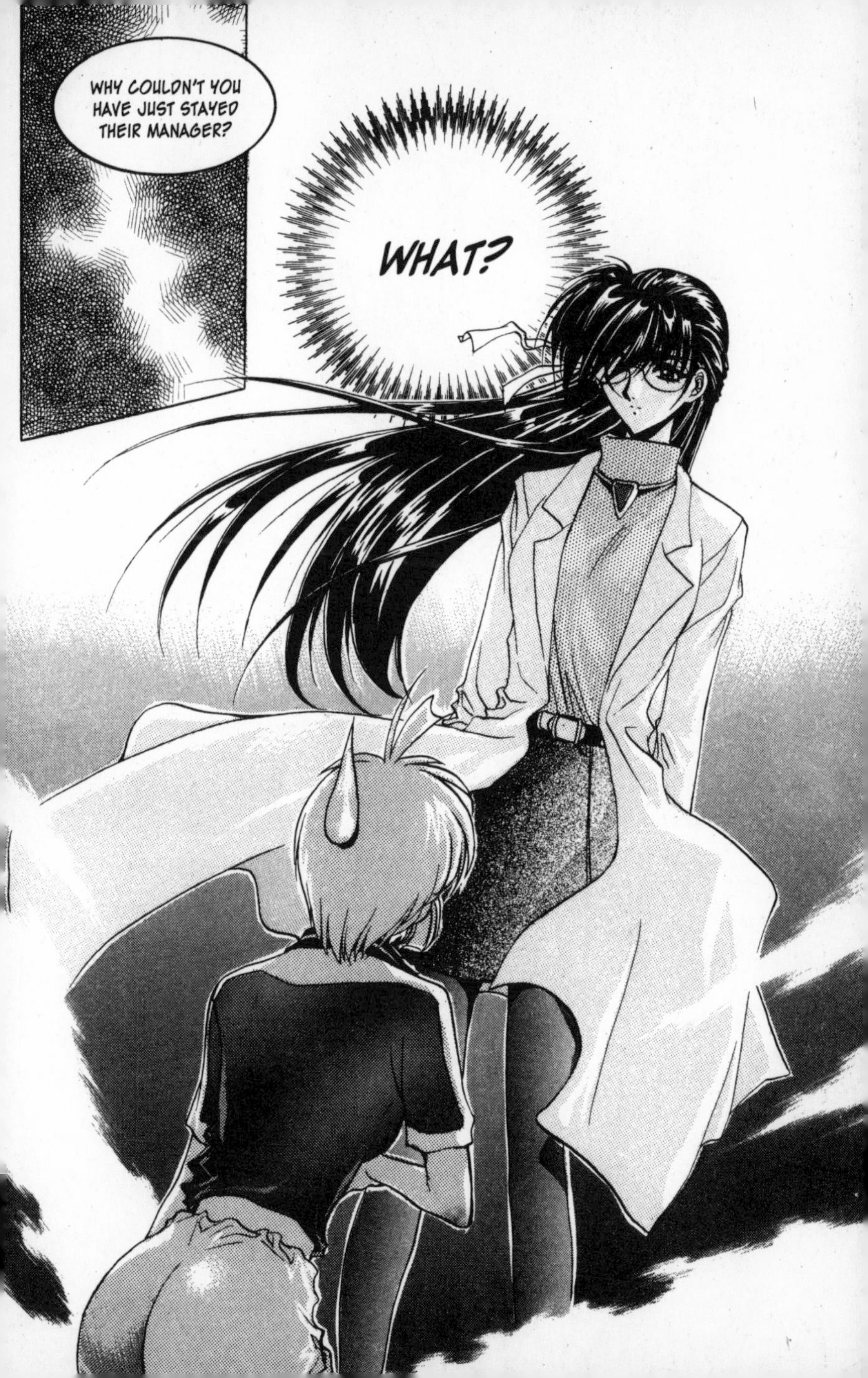
WHY COULDN'T YOU HAVE JUST STAYED THEIR MANAGER?
WHAT?

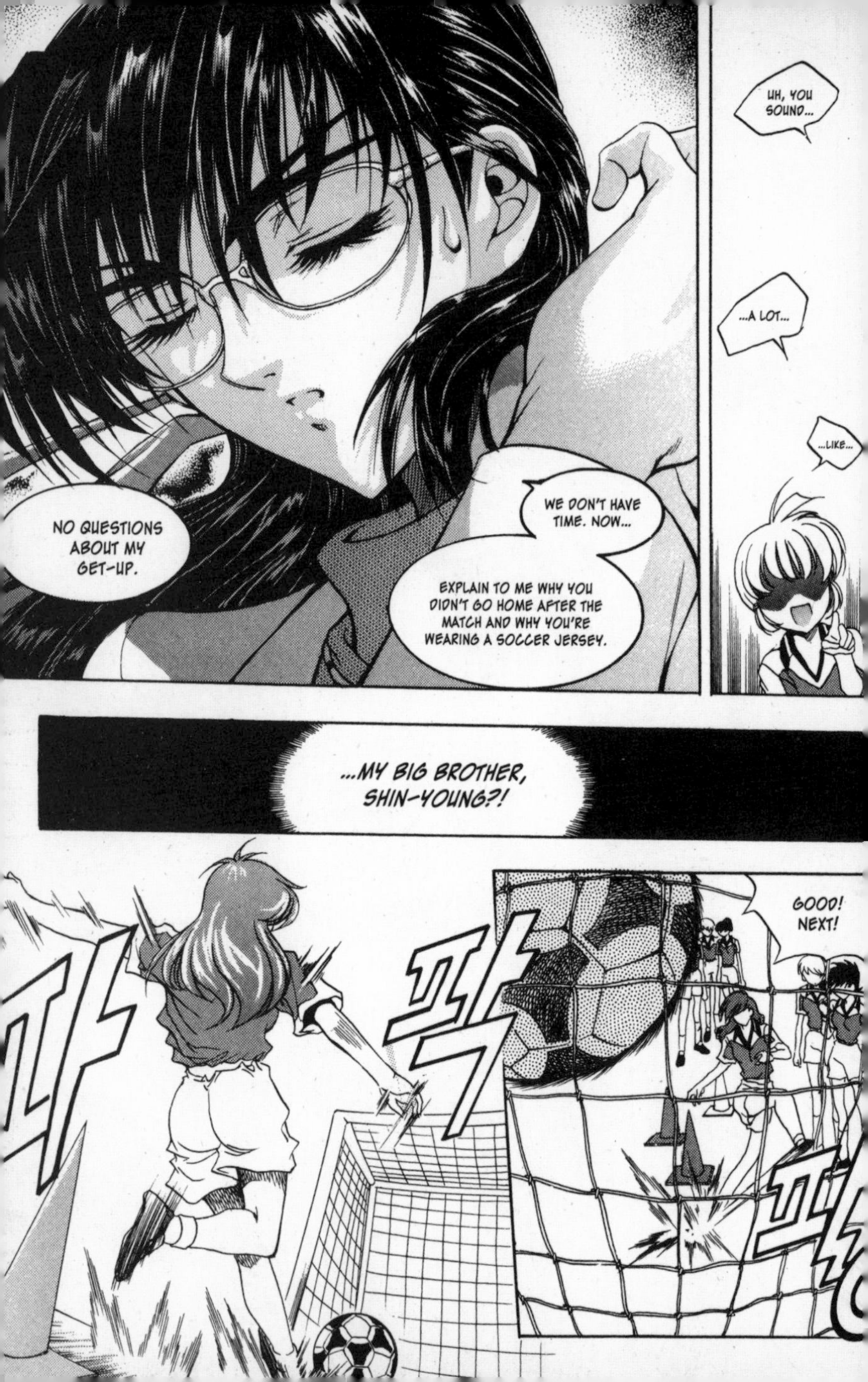
NO QUESTIONS ABOUT MY GET-UP.
WE DON'T HAVE TIME. NOW...
EXPLAIN TO ME WHY YOU DIDN'T GO HOME AFTER THE MATCH AND WHY YOU'RE WEARING A SOCCER JERSEY.
UH, YOU SOUND...
...A LOT...
...LIKE...
...MY BIG BROTHER, SHIN-YOUNG?!
GOOD! NEXT!

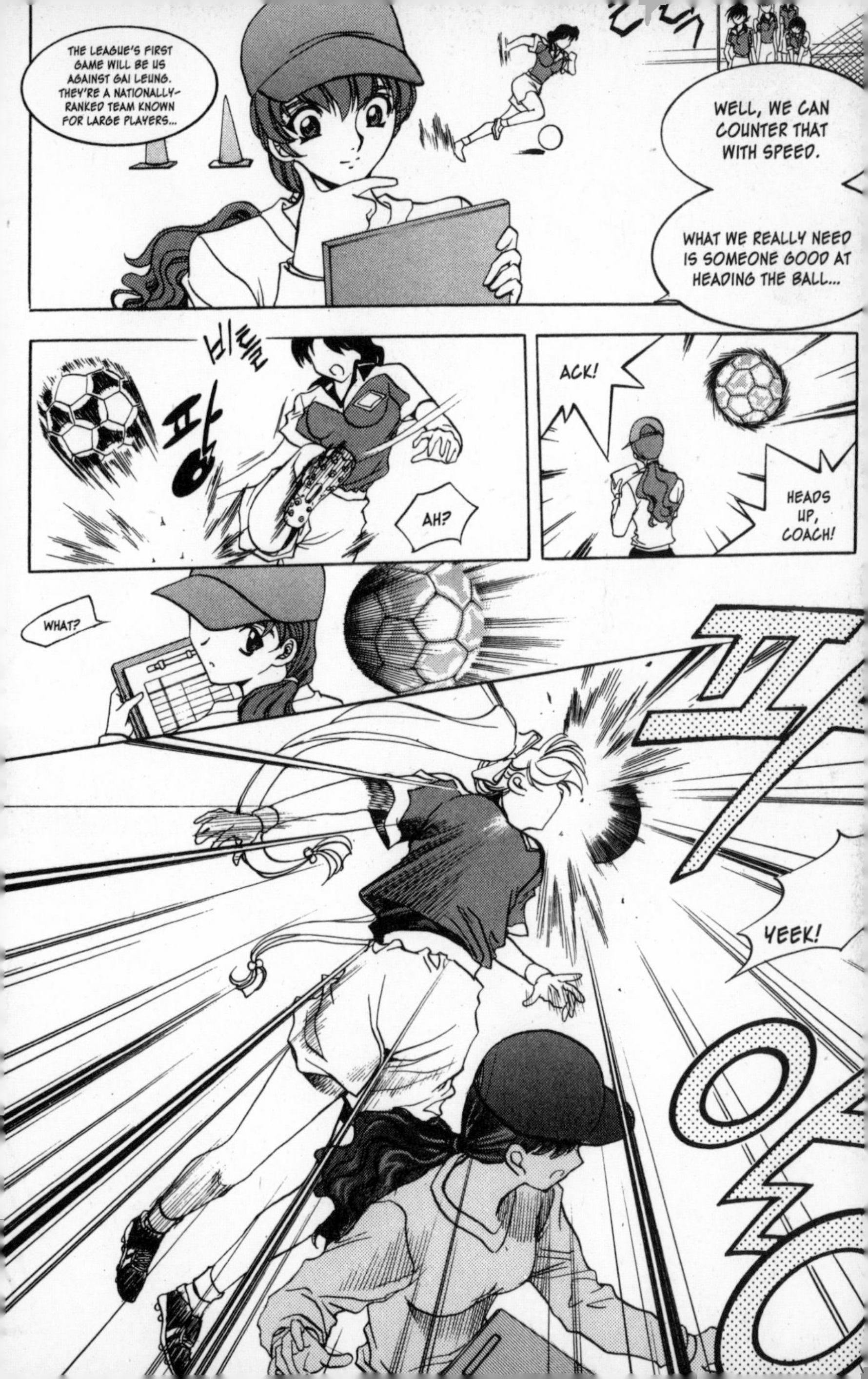
THE LEAGUE'S FIRST GAME WILL BE US AGAINST GAI LEUNG. THEY'RE A NATIONALLY-RANKED TEAM KNOWN FOR LARGE PLAYERS...
WELL, WE CAN COUNTER THAT WITH SPEED.
WHAT WE REALLY NEED IS SOMEONE GOOD AT HEADING THE BALL...
AH?
ACK!
HEADS UP, COACH!
WHAT?
YEEK!

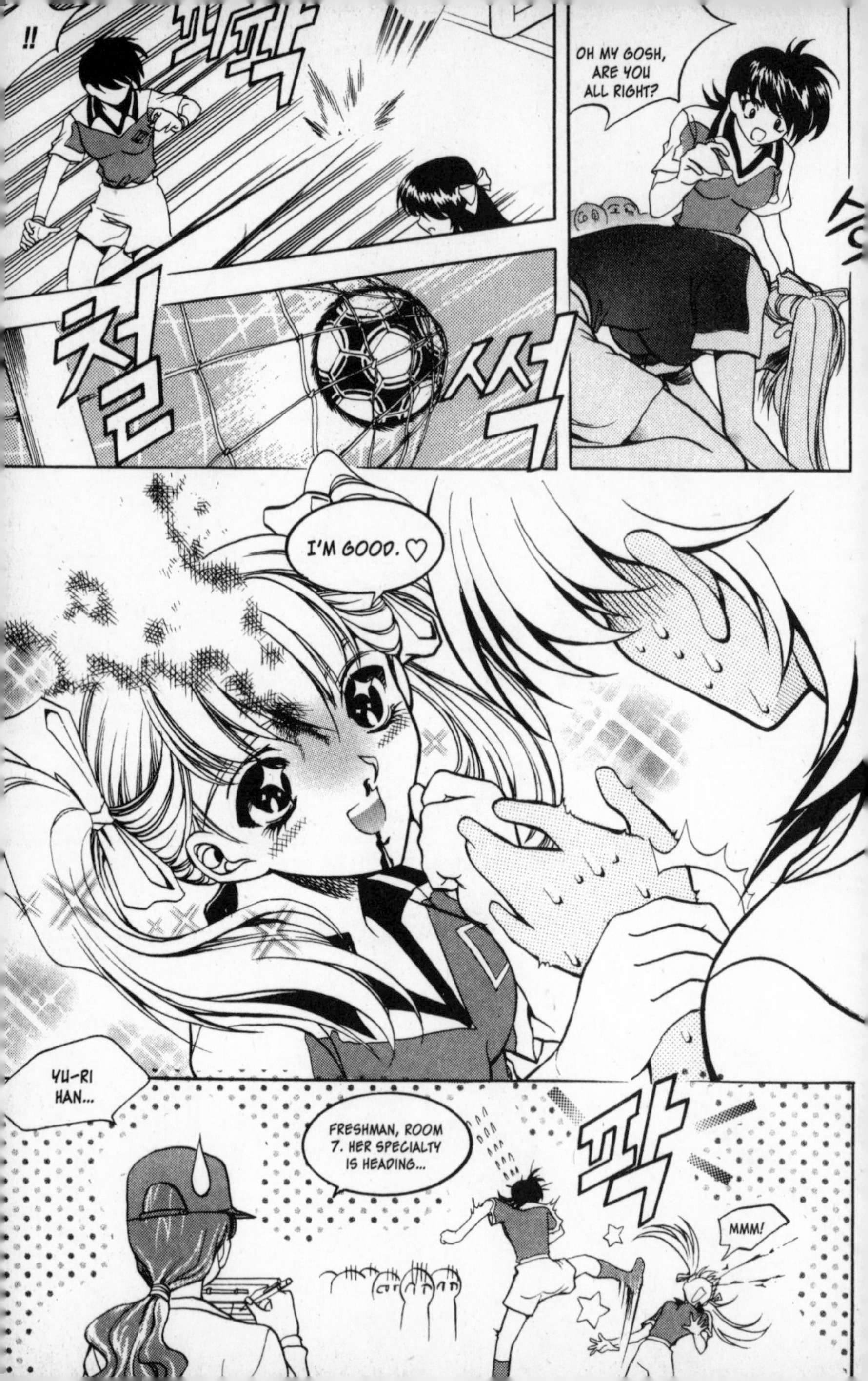
!!
OH MY GOSH, ARE YOU ALL RIGHT?
철썩
I'M GOOD. ♡
YU-RI HAN...
FRESHMAN, ROOM 7. HER SPECIALTY IS HEADING...
팍
MMM!

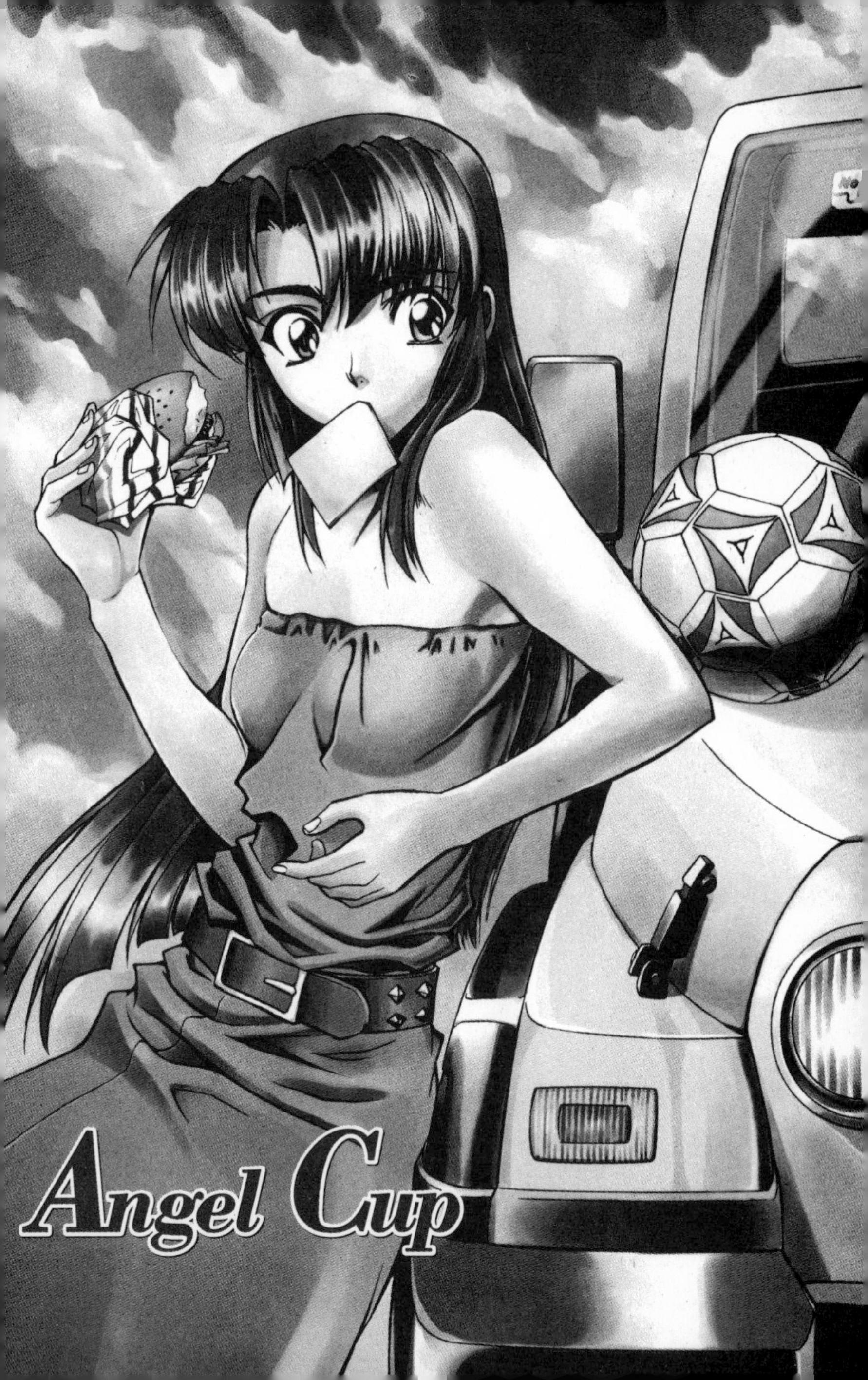
Angel Cup

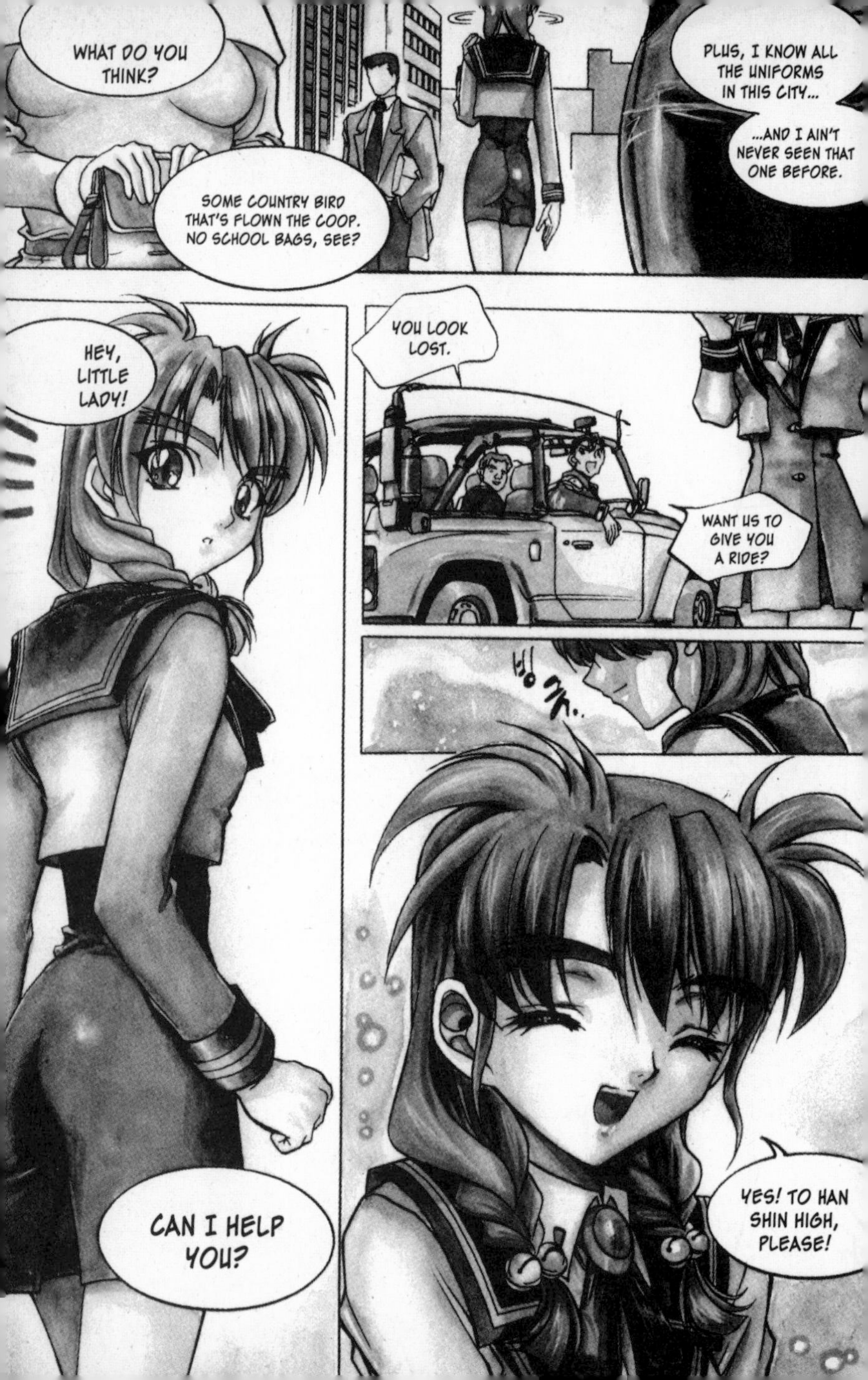

WHAT DO YOU THINK?
SOME COUNTRY BIRD THAT'S FLOWN THE COOP. NO SCHOOL BAGS, SEE?
PLUS, I KNOW ALL THE UNIFORMS IN THIS CITY...
...AND I AIN'T NEVER SEEN THAT ONE BEFORE.
HEY, LITTLE LADY!
CAN I HELP YOU?
YOU LOOK LOST.
WANT US TO GIVE YOU A RIDE?
YES! TO HAN SHIN HIGH, PLEASE!

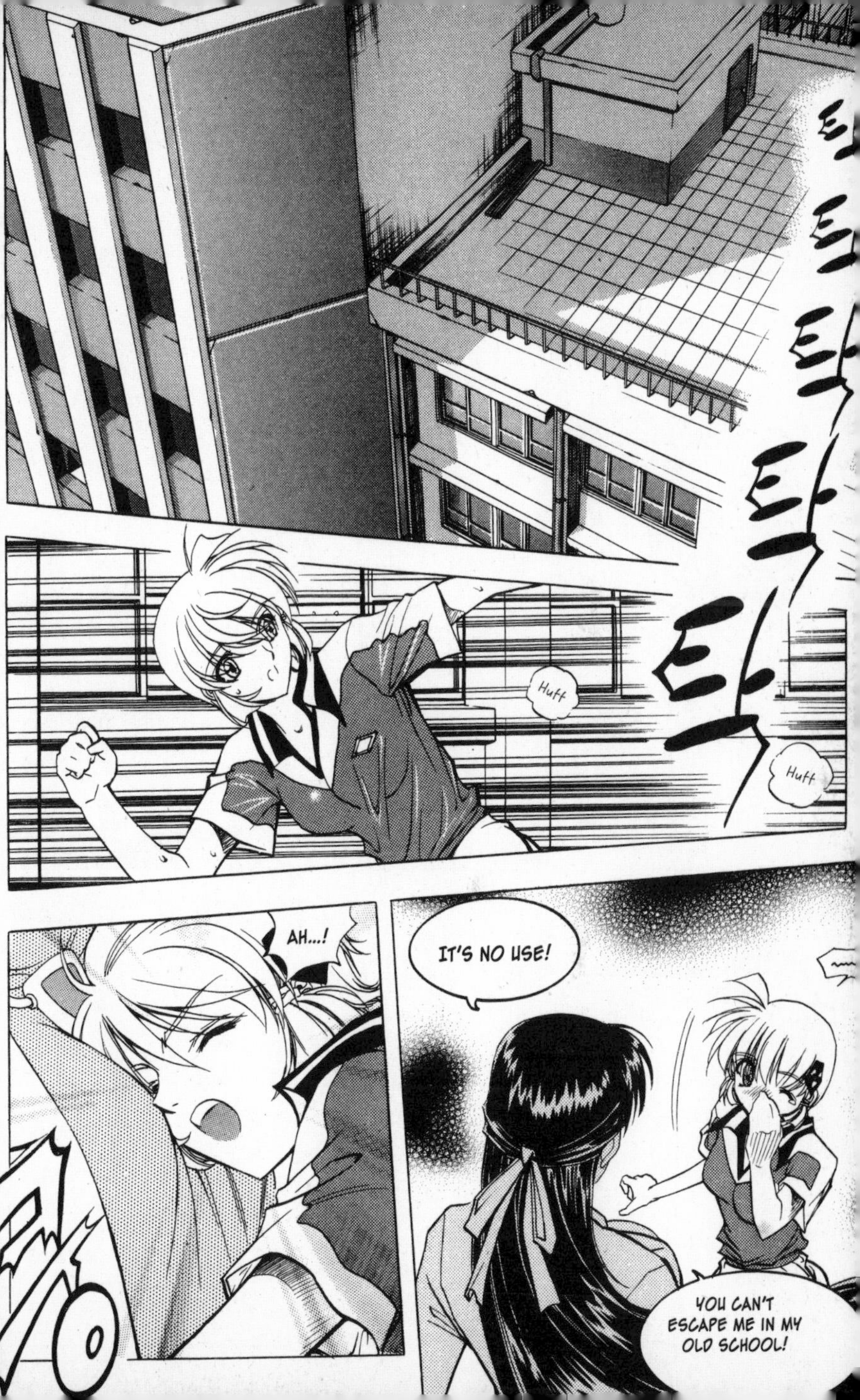
Huff
Huff
AH...!
IT'S NO USE!
YOU CAN'T ESCAPE ME IN MY OLD SCHOOL!

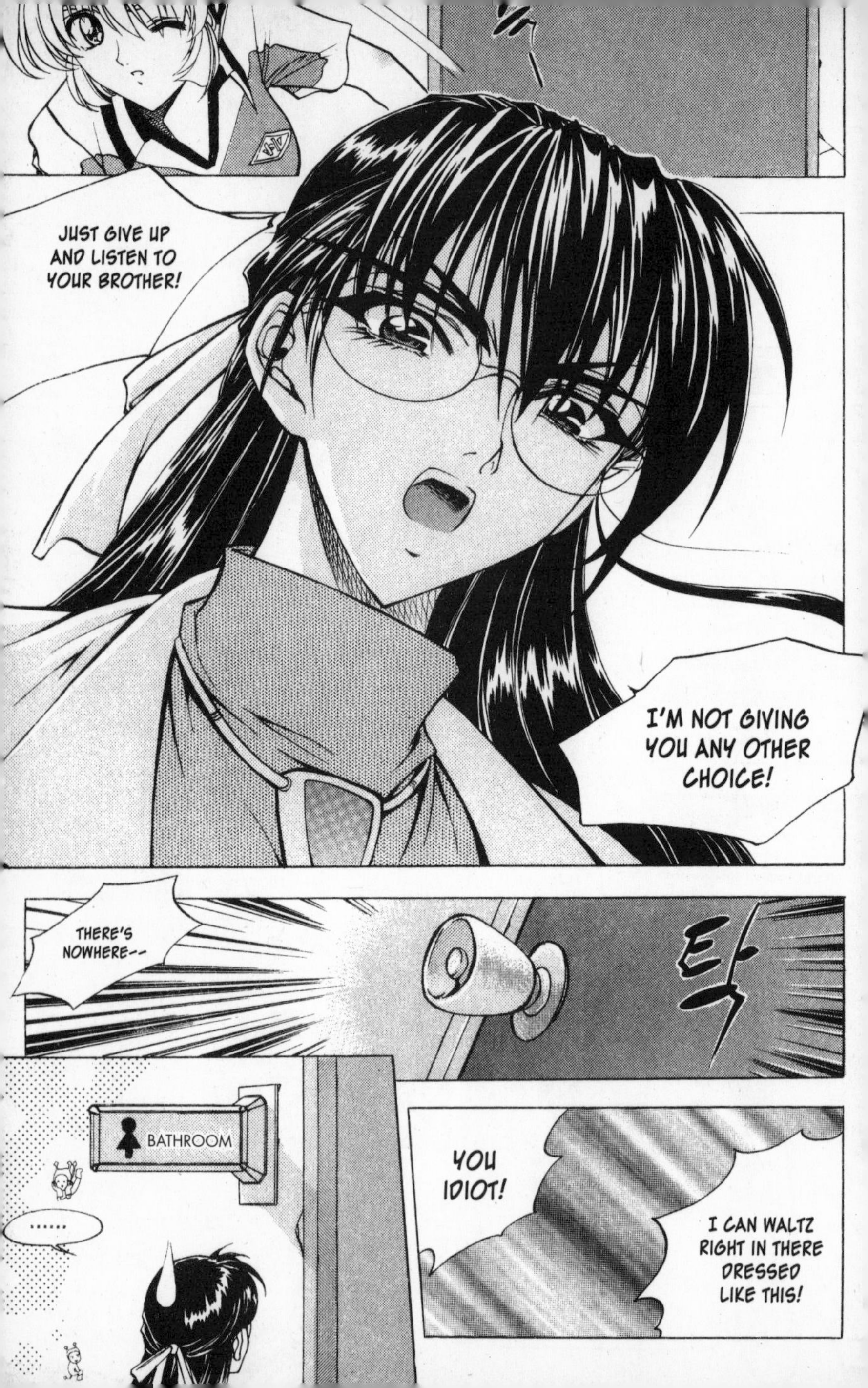

JUST GIVE UP AND LISTEN TO YOUR BROTHER!
I'M NOT GIVING YOU ANY OTHER CHOICE!
THERE'S NOWHERE--
탁
BATHROOM
......
YOU IDIOT!
I CAN WALTZ RIGHT IN THERE DRESSED LIKE THIS!

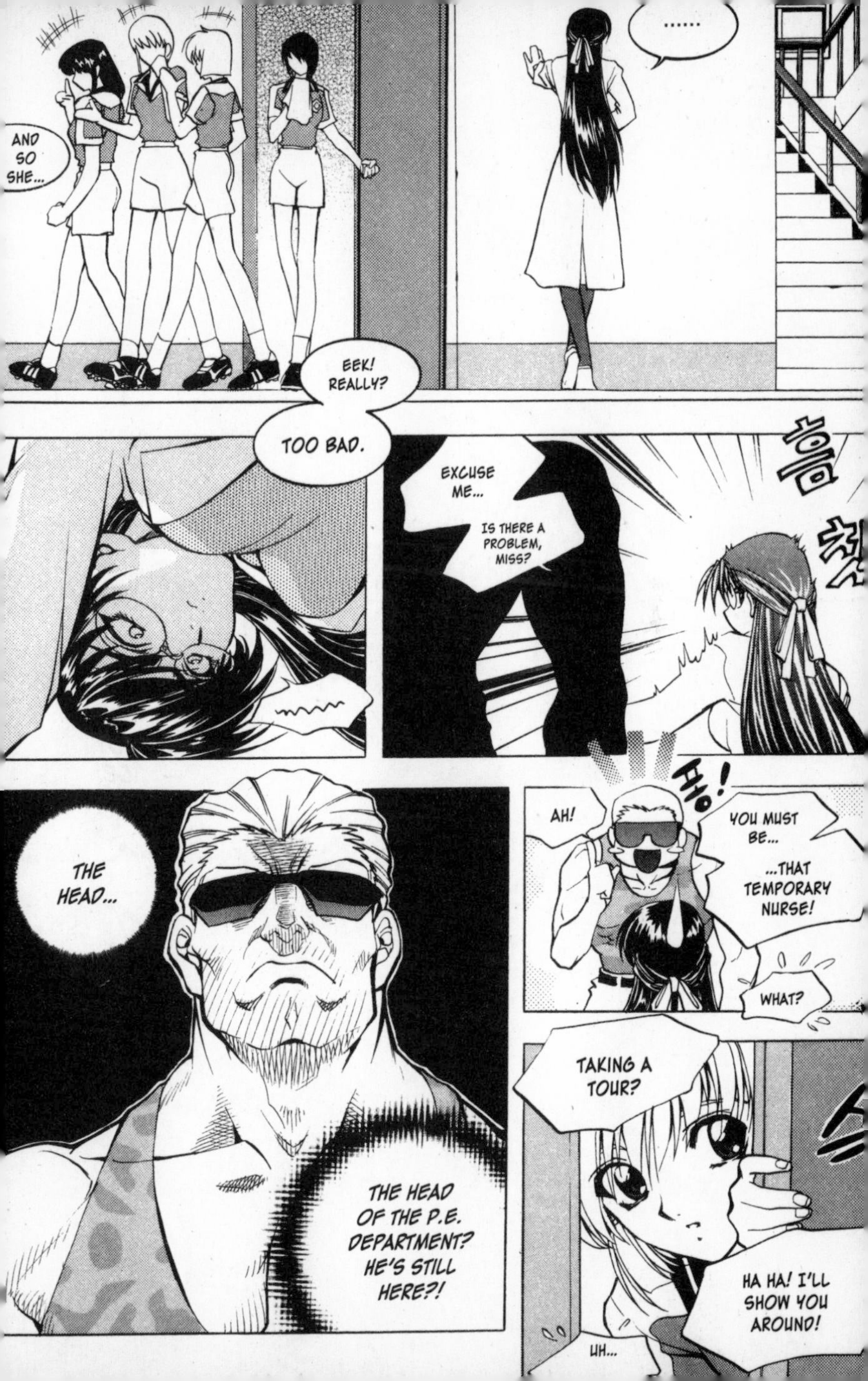
AND SO SHE...
EEK! REALLY?
TOO BAD.
......
EXCUSE ME...
IS THERE A PROBLEM, MISS?
흠칫
THE HEAD...
THE HEAD OF THE P.E. DEPARTMENT? HE'S STILL HERE?!
AH!
YOU MUST BE...
...THAT TEMPORARY NURSE!
WHAT?
TAKING A TOUR?
HA HA! I'LL SHOW YOU AROUND!
UH...

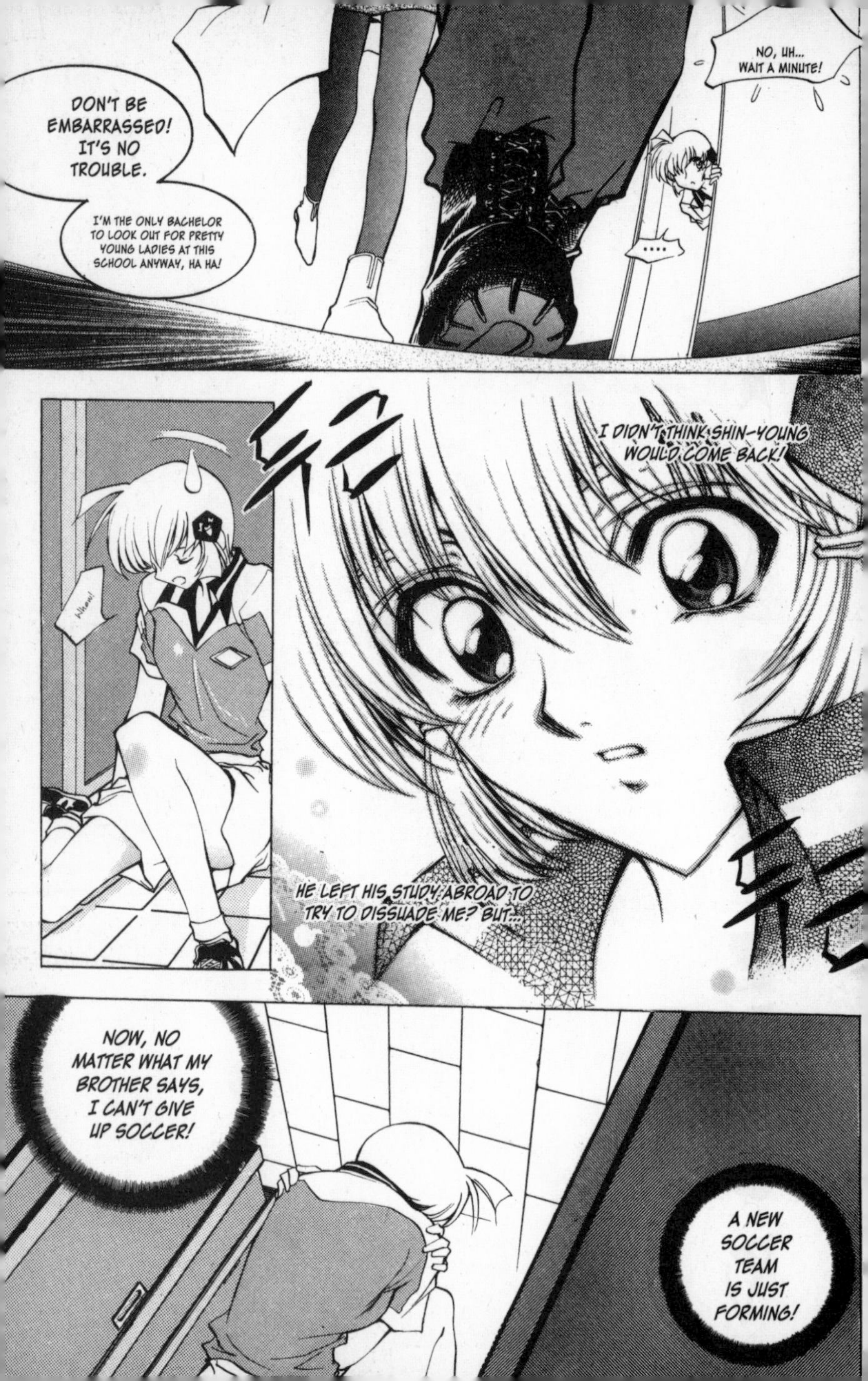
DON'T BE EMBARRASSED! IT'S NO TROUBLE.
I'M THE ONLY BACHELOR TO LOOK OUT FOR PRETTY YOUNG LADIES AT THIS SCHOOL ANYWAY, HA HA!
NO, UH... WAIT A MINUTE!
....
Whew!
I DIDN'T THINK SHIN-YOUNG WOULD COME BACK!
HE LEFT HIS STUDY ABROAD TO TRY TO DISSUADE ME? BUT...
NOW, NO MATTER WHAT MY BROTHER SAYS, I CAN'T GIVE UP SOCCER!
A NEW SOCCER TEAM IS JUST FORMING!

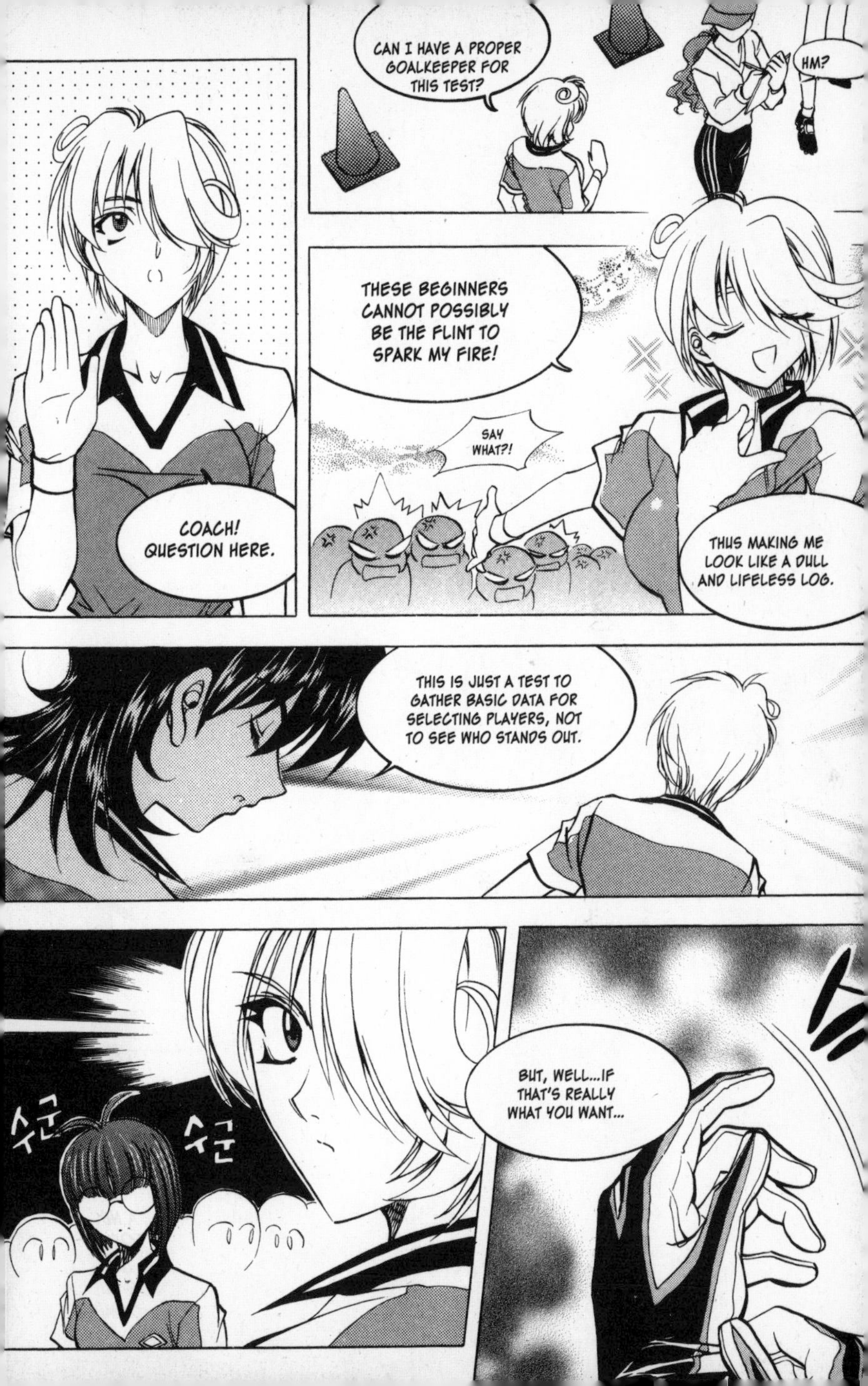
COACH! QUESTION HERE.
CAN I HAVE A PROPER GOALKEEPER FOR THIS TEST?
HM?
THESE BEGINNERS CANNOT POSSIBLY BE THE FLINT TO SPARK MY FIRE!
SAY WHAT?!
THUS MAKING ME LOOK LIKE A DULL AND LIFELESS LOG.
THIS IS JUST A TEST TO GATHER BASIC DATA FOR SELECTING PLAYERS, NOT TO SEE WHO STANDS OUT.
수군
수군
BUT, WELL...IF THAT'S REALLY WHAT YOU WANT...

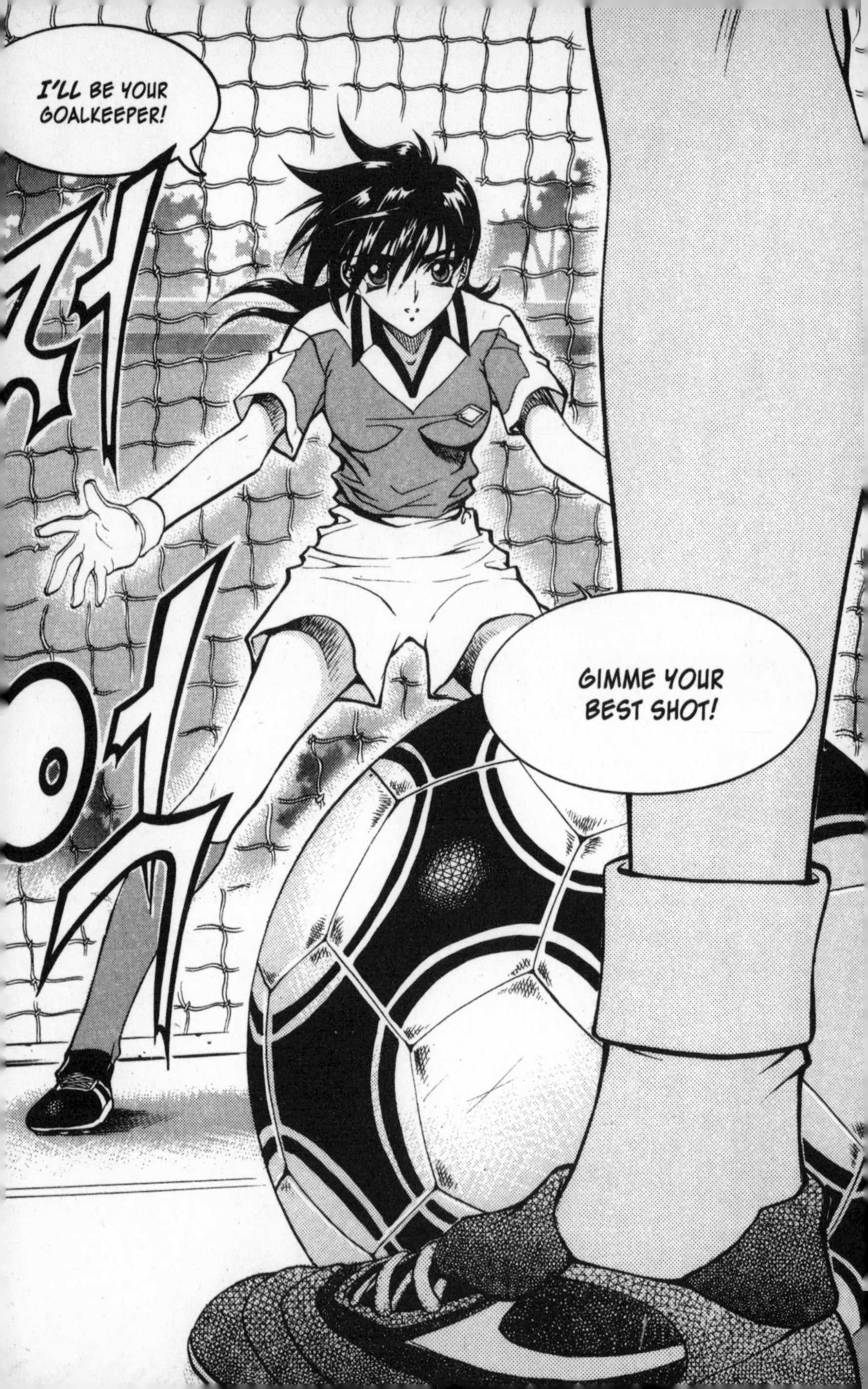
I'LL BE YOUR GOALKEEPER!
GIMME YOUR BEST SHOT!

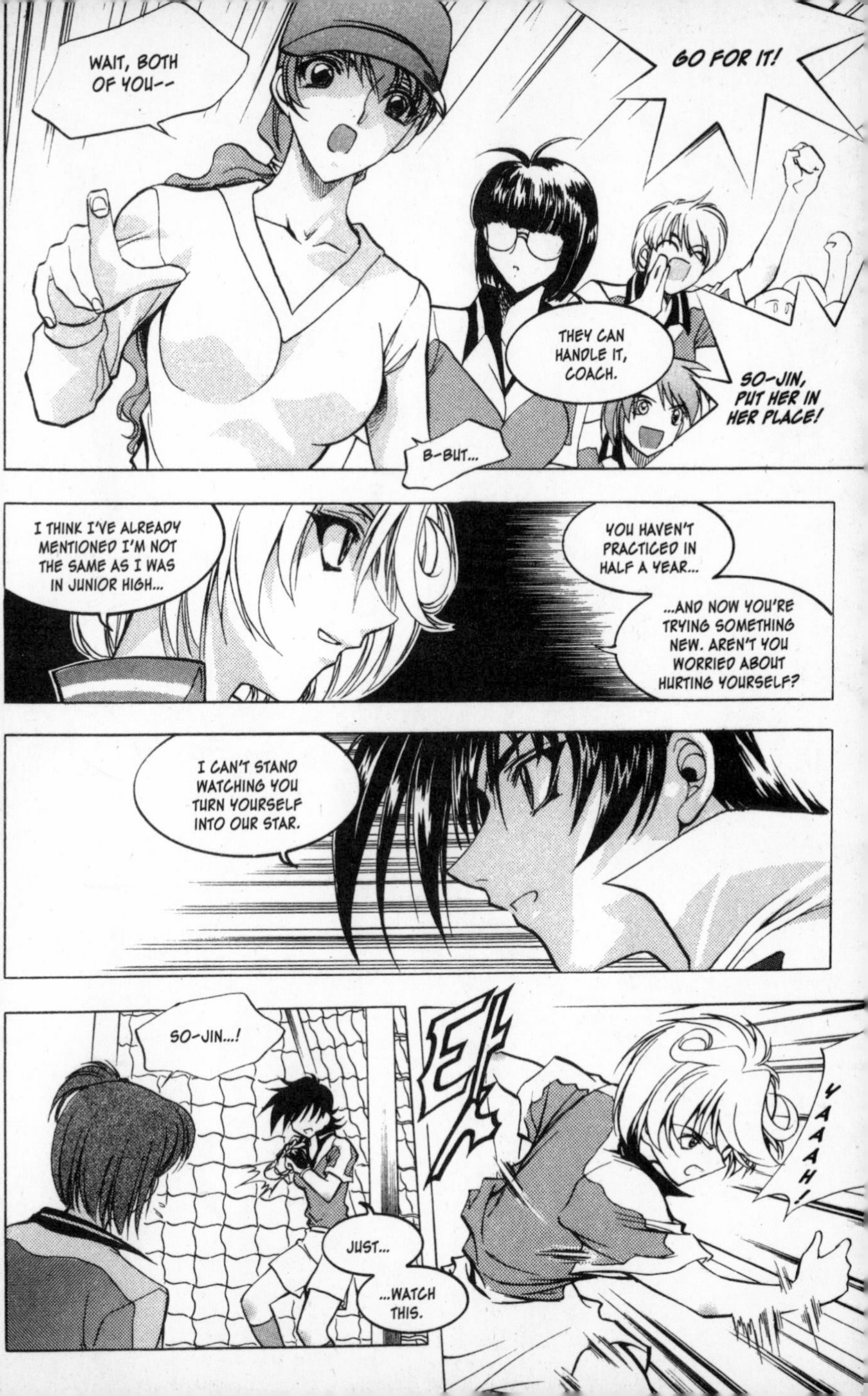
WAIT, BOTH OF YOU--
GO FOR IT!
THEY CAN HANDLE IT, COACH.
SO-JIN, PUT HER IN HER PLACE!
B-BUT...
I THINK I'VE ALREADY MENTIONED I'M NOT THE SAME AS I WAS IN JUNIOR HIGH...
YOU HAVEN'T PRACTICED IN HALF A YEAR...
...AND NOW YOU'RE TRYING SOMETHING NEW. AREN'T YOU WORRIED ABOUT HURTING YOURSELF?
I CAN'T STAND WATCHING YOU TURN YOURSELF INTO OUR STAR.
SO-JIN...!
JUST...
...WATCH THIS.
YAAAAH!

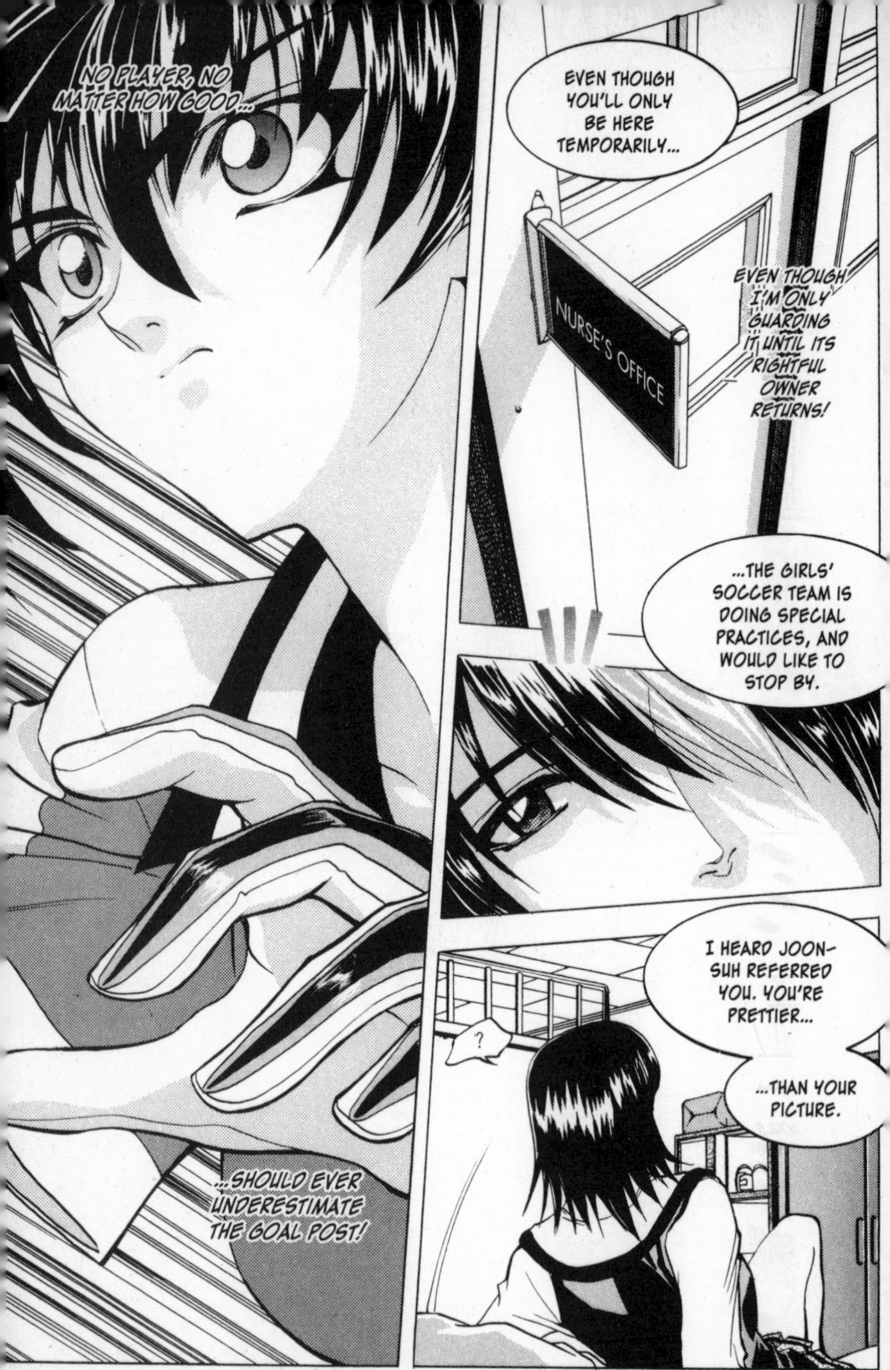
NO PLAYER, NO MATTER HOW GOOD...
...SHOULD EVER UNDERESTIMATE THE GOAL POST!
EVEN THOUGH YOU'LL ONLY BE HERE TEMPORARILY...
NURSE'S OFFICE
EVEN THOUGH I'M ONLY GUARDING IT UNTIL ITS RIGHTFUL OWNER RETURNS!
...THE GIRLS' SOCCER TEAM IS DOING SPECIAL PRACTICES, AND WOULD LIKE TO STOP BY.
I HEARD JOON-SUH REFERRED YOU. YOU'RE PRETTIER...
?
...THAN YOUR PICTURE.

↑ Fell asleep while skipping class.

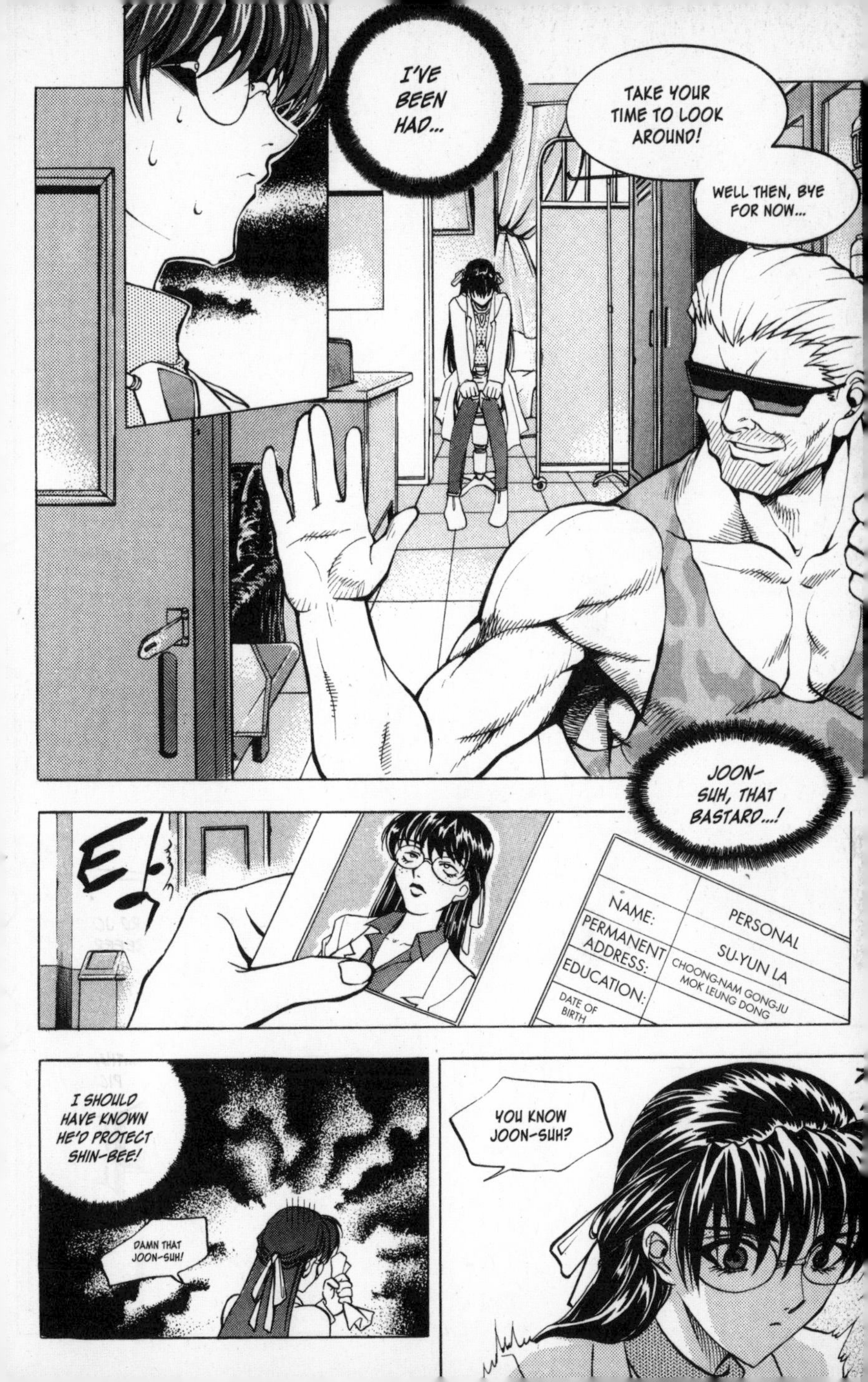
I'VE BEEN HAD...
TAKE YOUR TIME TO LOOK AROUND!
WELL THEN, BYE FOR NOW...
JOON-SUH, THAT BASTARD...!
PERSONAL
NAME:
SU-YUN LA
PERMANENT ADDRESS:
CHOONG-NAM GONG-JU MOK LEUNG DONG
EDUCATION:
DATE OF BIRTH
I SHOULD HAVE KNOWN HE'D PROTECT SHIN-BEE!
DAMN THAT JOON-SUH!
YOU KNOW JOON-SUH?

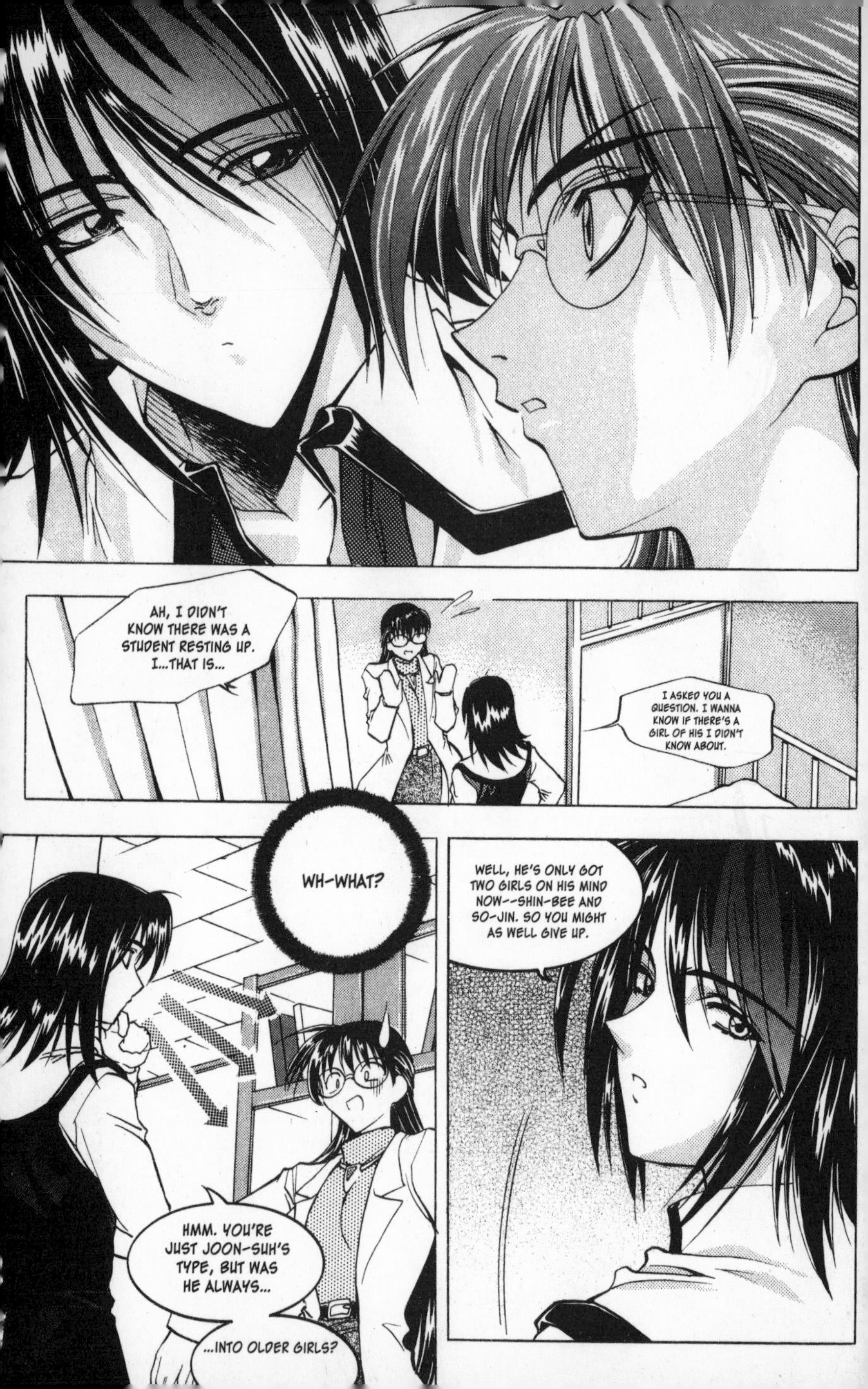
AH, I DIDN'T KNOW THERE WAS A STUDENT RESTING UP. I...THAT IS...
I ASKED YOU A QUESTION. I WANNA KNOW IF THERE'S A GIRL OF HIS I DIDN'T KNOW ABOUT.
WH-WHAT?
HMM. YOU'RE JUST JOON-SUH'S TYPE, BUT WAS HE ALWAYS...
...INTO OLDER GIRLS?
WELL, HE'S ONLY GOT TWO GIRLS ON HIS MIND NOW--SHIN-BEE AND SO-JIN. SO YOU MIGHT AS WELL GIVE UP.

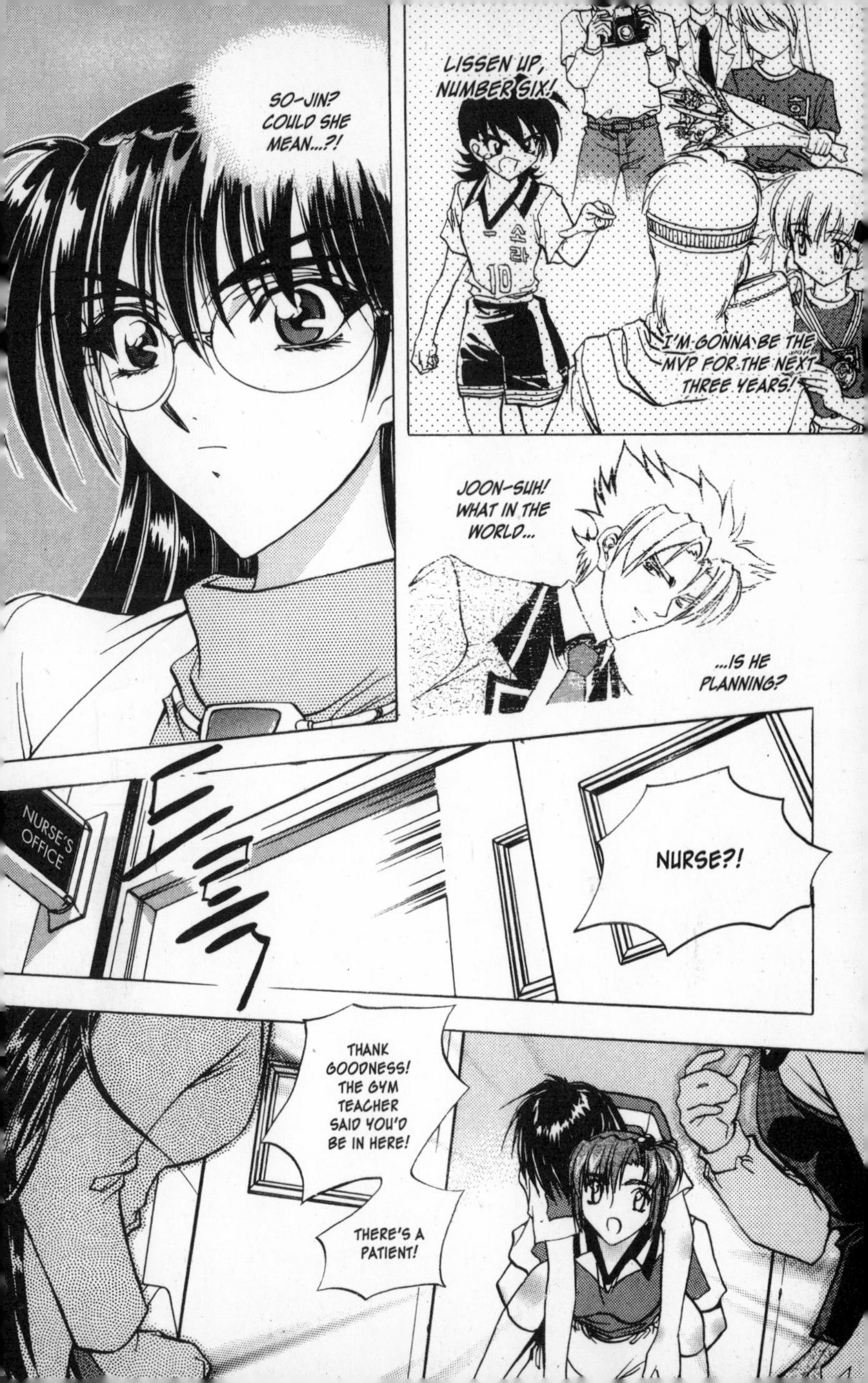
SO-JIN? COULD SHE MEAN...?!
LISSEN UP, NUMBER SIX!
10
I'M GONNA BE THE MVP FOR THE NEXT THREE YEARS!
JOON-SUH! WHAT IN THE WORLD...
...IS HE PLANNING?
NURSE'S OFFICE
NURSE?!
THANK GOODNESS! THE GYM TEACHER SAID YOU'D BE IN HERE!
THERE'S A PATIENT!

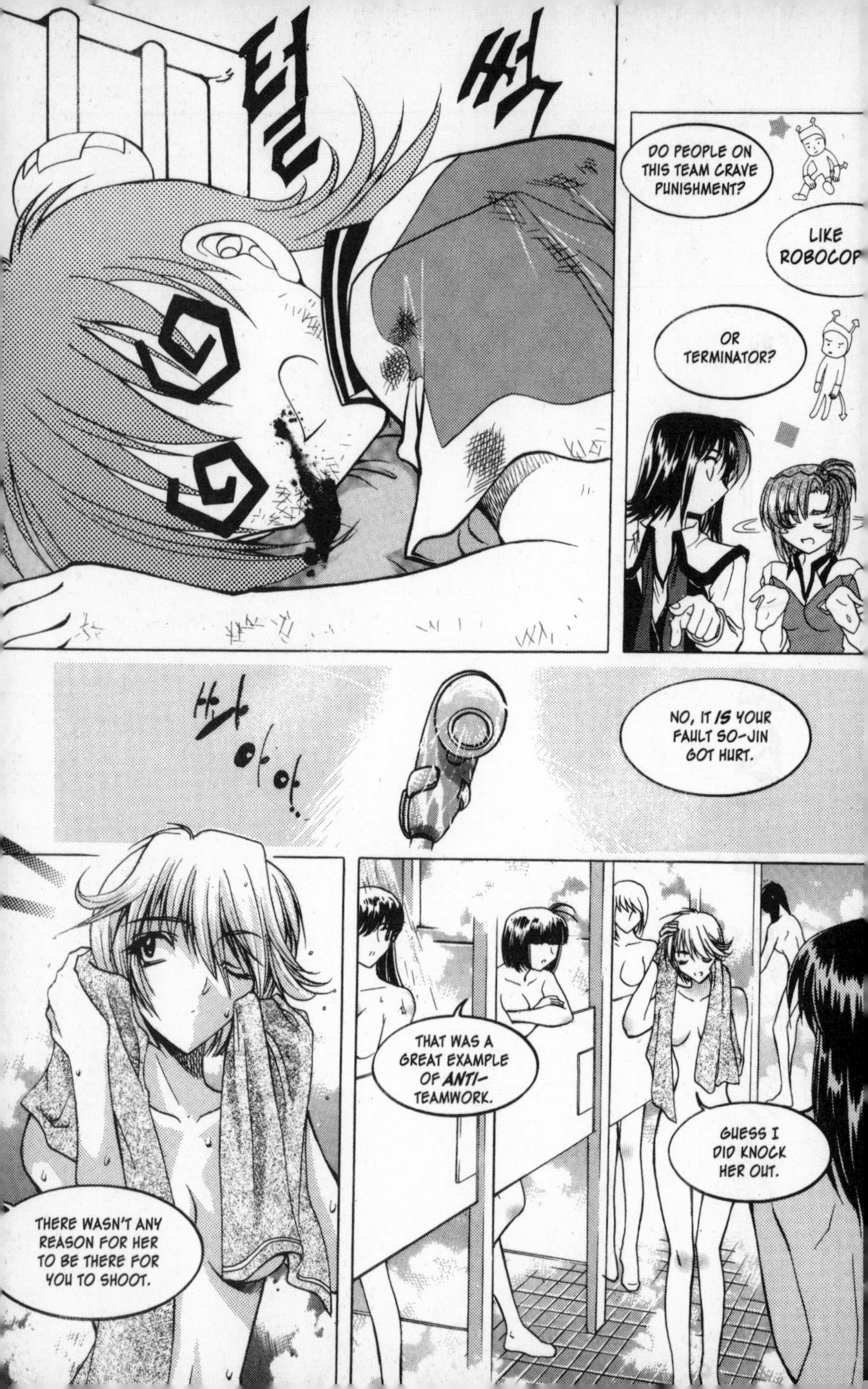
털썩
DO PEOPLE ON THIS TEAM CRAVE PUNISHMENT?
LIKE ROBOCOP
OR TERMINATOR?
쏴아아...
NO, IT *IS* YOUR FAULT SO-JIN GOT HURT.
THERE WASN'T ANY REASON FOR HER TO BE THERE FOR YOU TO SHOOT.
THAT WAS A GREAT EXAMPLE OF *ANTI*-TEAMWORK.
GUESS I DID KNOCK HER OUT.

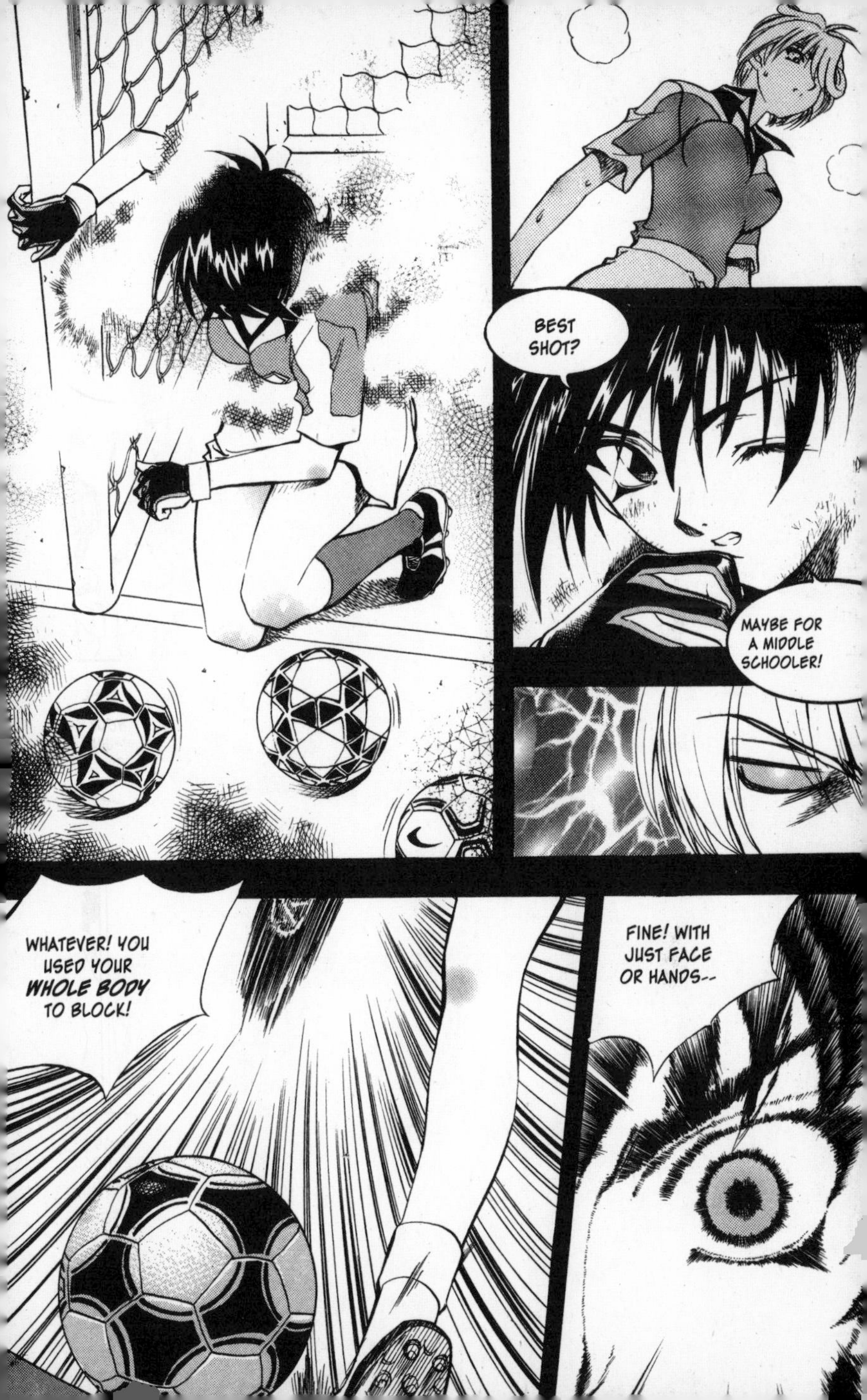
BEST SHOT?
MAYBE FOR A MIDDLE SCHOOLER!
WHATEVER! YOU USED YOUR ***WHOLE BODY*** TO BLOCK!
FINE! WITH JUST FACE OR HANDS--

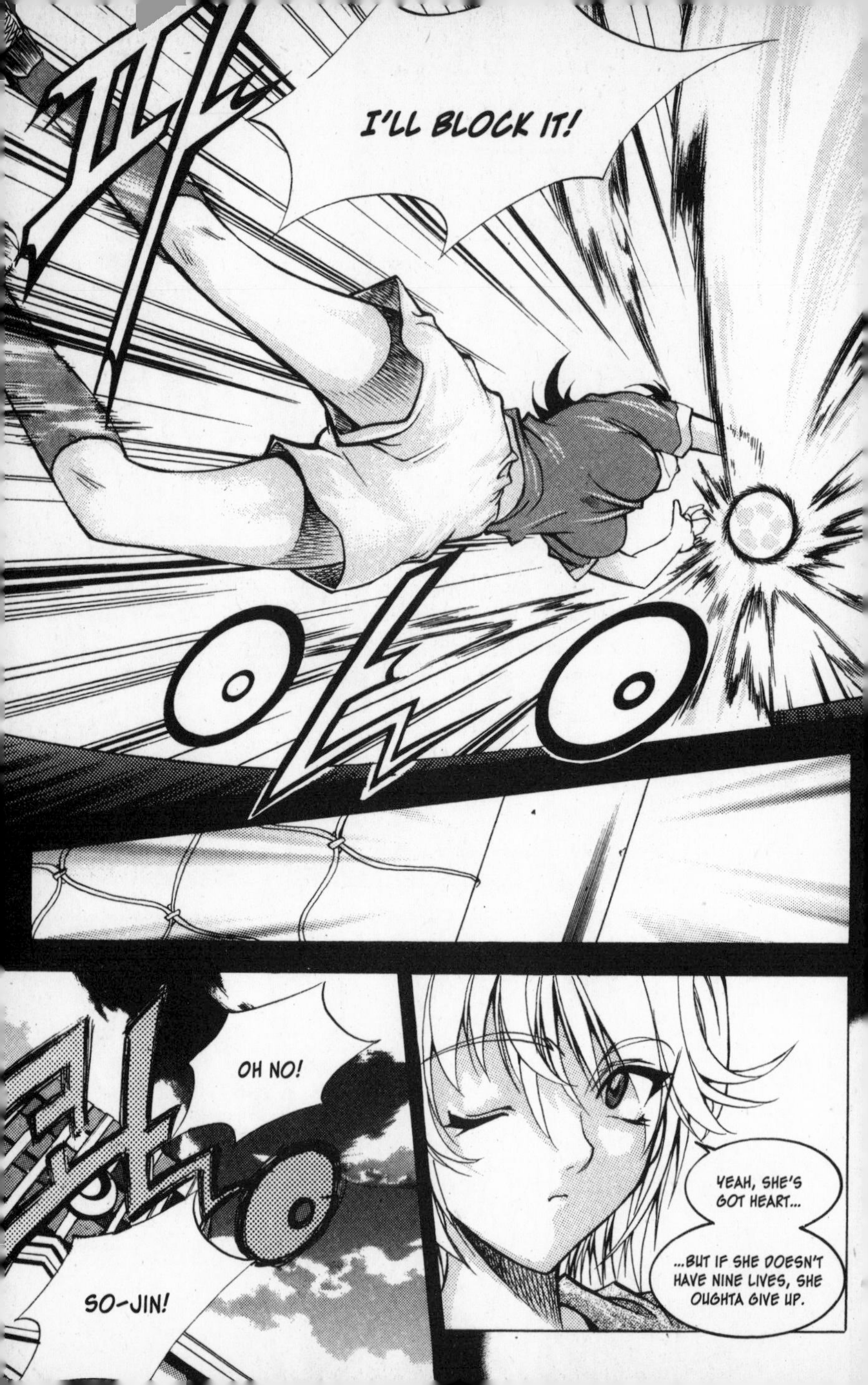
I'LL BLOCK IT!
OH NO!
SO-JIN!
YEAH, SHE'S GOT HEART...
...BUT IF SHE DOESN'T HAVE NINE LIVES, SHE OUGHTA GIVE UP.

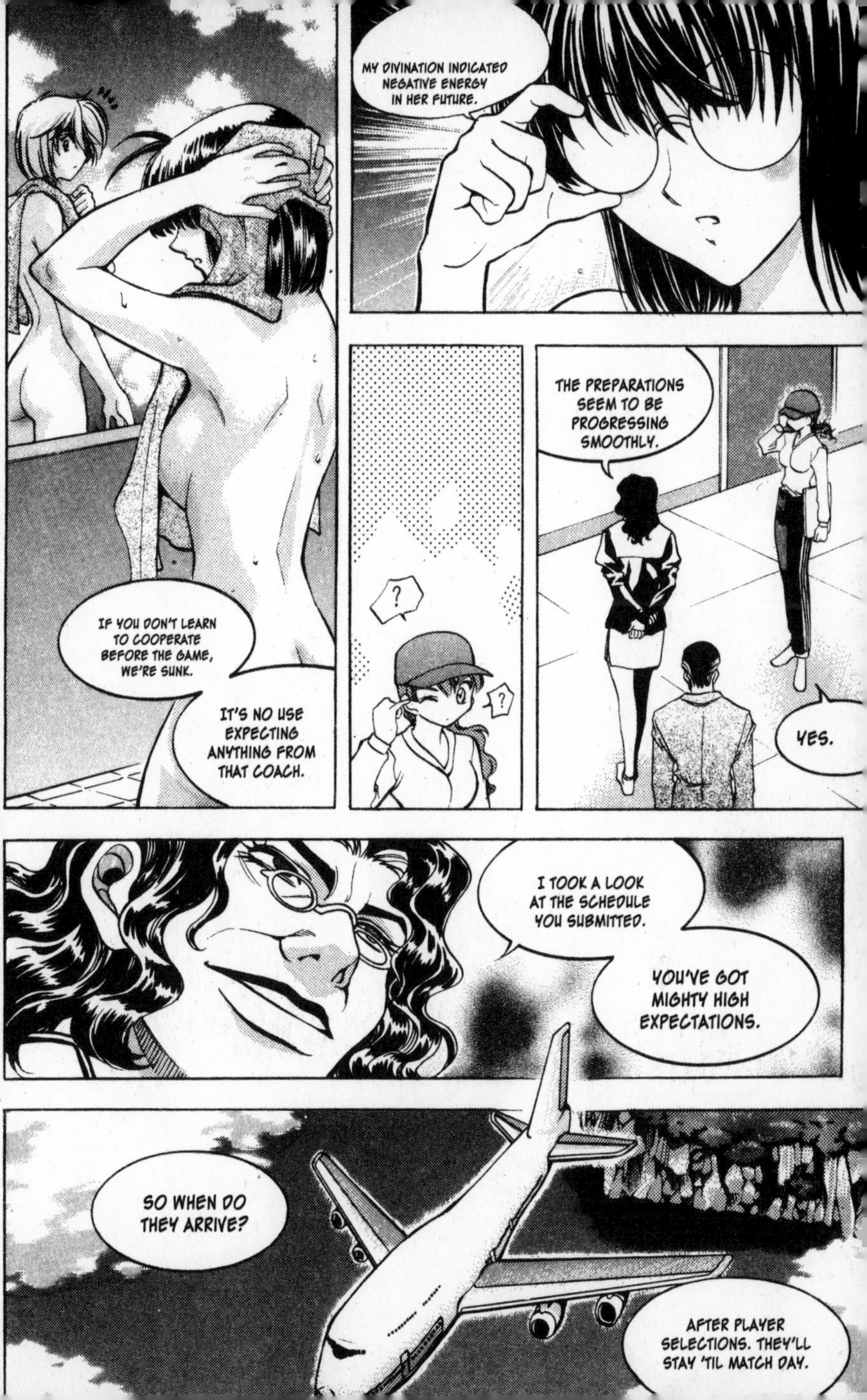
IF YOU DON'T LEARN TO COOPERATE BEFORE THE GAME, WE'RE SUNK.
IT'S NO USE EXPECTING ANYTHING FROM THAT COACH.
MY DIVINATION INDICATED NEGATIVE ENERGY IN HER FUTURE.
?
?
THE PREPARATIONS SEEM TO BE PROGRESSING SMOOTHLY.
YES.
I TOOK A LOOK AT THE SCHEDULE YOU SUBMITTED.
YOU'VE GOT MIGHTY HIGH EXPECTATIONS.
SO WHEN DO THEY ARRIVE?
AFTER PLAYER SELECTIONS. THEY'LL STAY 'TIL MATCH DAY.

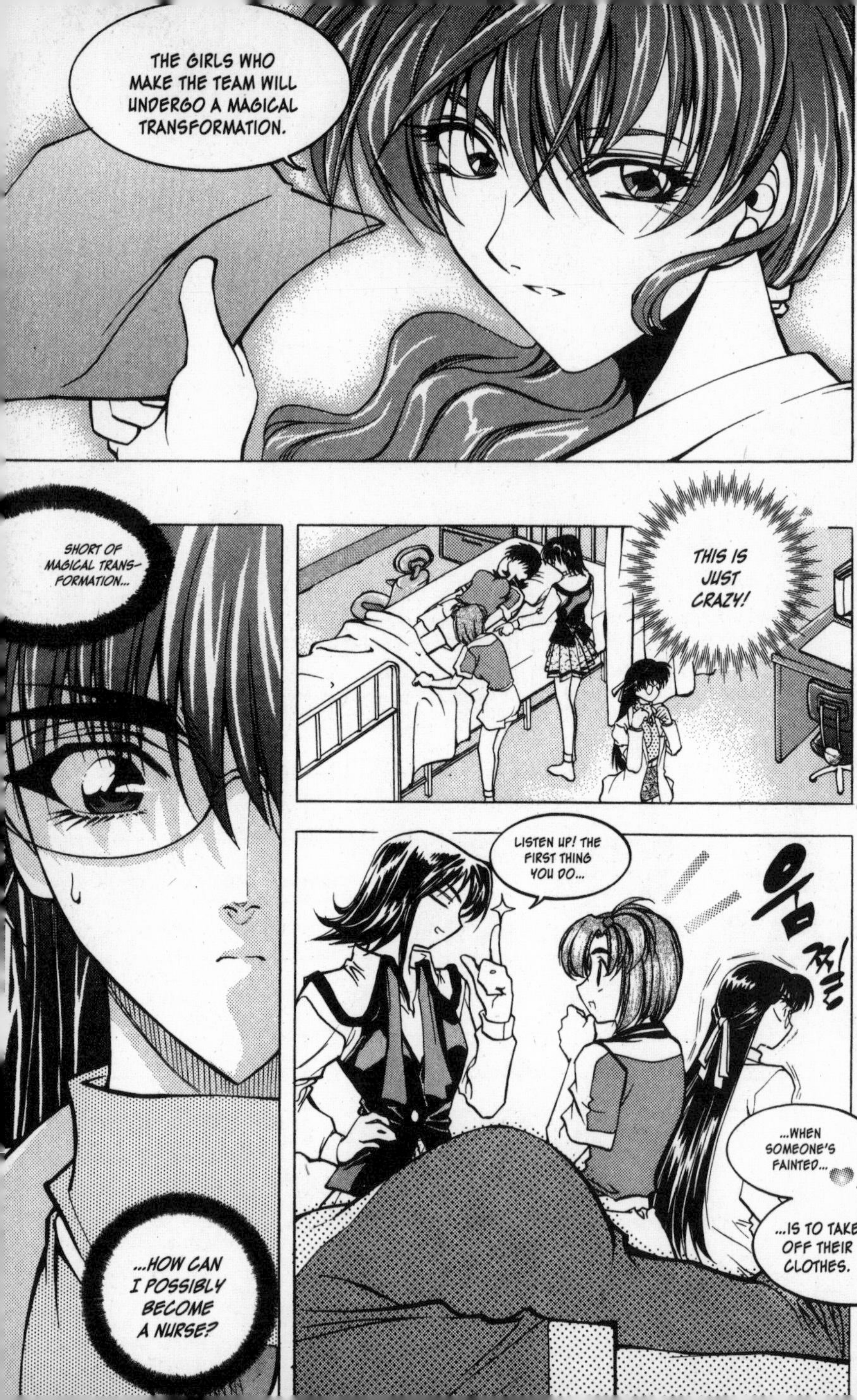
THE GIRLS WHO MAKE THE TEAM WILL UNDERGO A MAGICAL TRANSFORMATION.
SHORT OF MAGICAL TRANS-FORMATION...
...HOW CAN I POSSIBLY BECOME A NURSE?
THIS IS JUST CRAZY!
LISTEN UP! THE FIRST THING YOU DO...
움찔
...WHEN SOMEONE'S FAINTED...
...IS TO TAKE OFF THEIR CLOTHES.

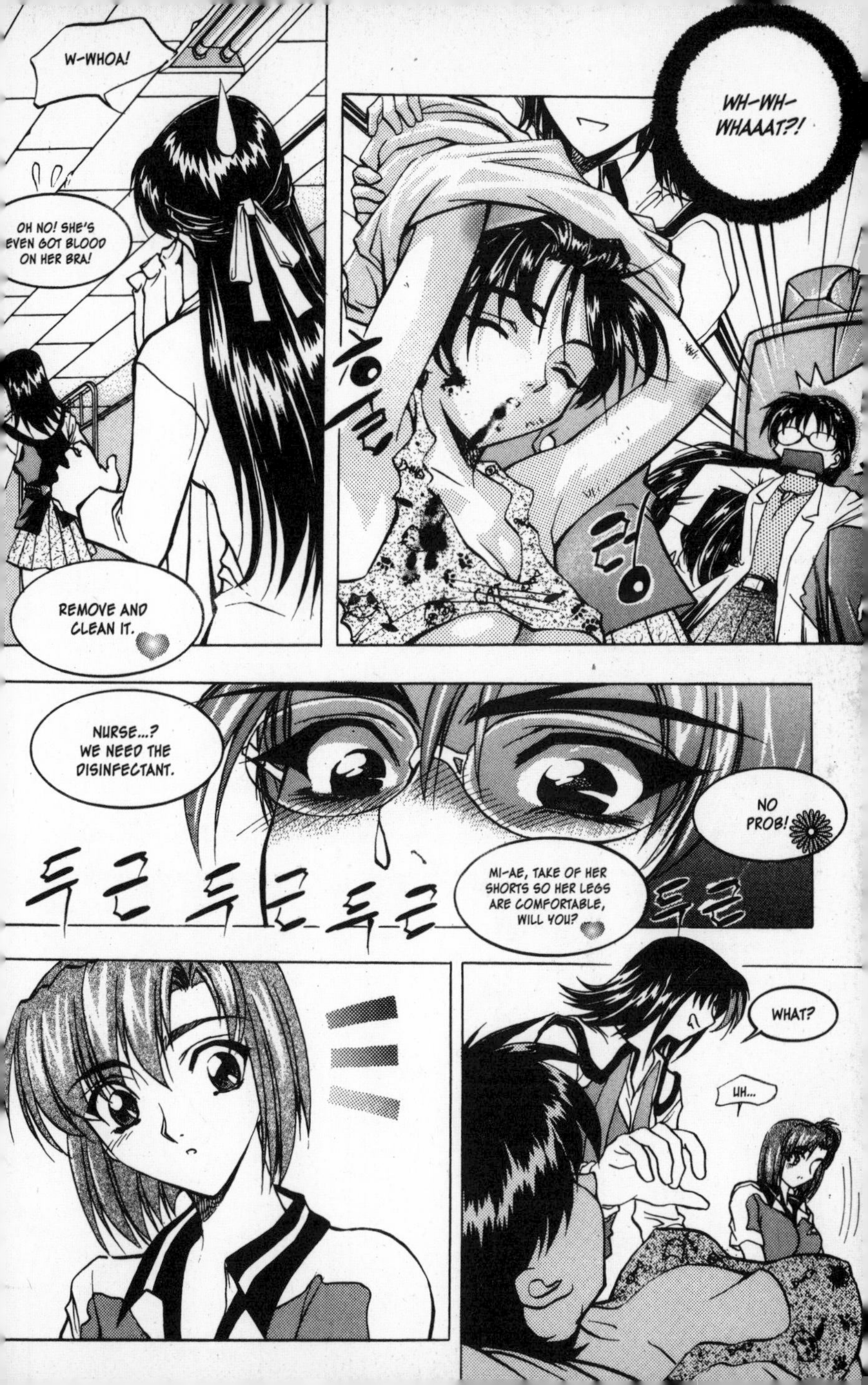
W-WHOA!
OH NO! SHE'S EVEN GOT BLOOD ON HER BRA!
REMOVE AND CLEAN IT.
WH-WH-WHAAAT?!
NURSE...? WE NEED THE DISINFECTANT.
두근 두근 두근
NO PROB!
MI-AE, TAKE OF HER SHORTS SO HER LEGS ARE COMFORTABLE, WILL YOU?
두근
WHAT?
UH...

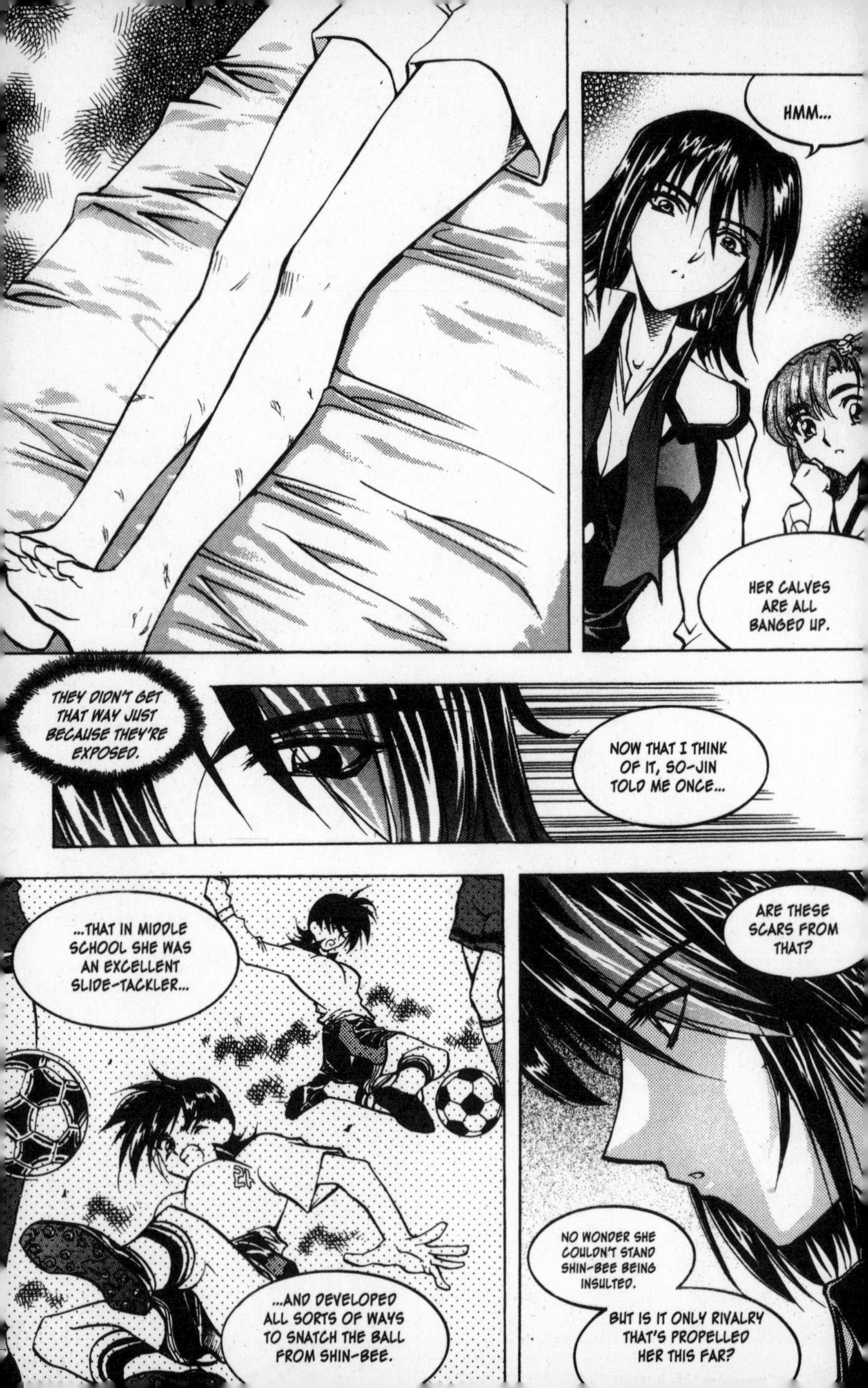
HMM...
HER CALVES ARE ALL BANGED UP.
THEY DIDN'T GET THAT WAY JUST BECAUSE THEY'RE EXPOSED.
NOW THAT I THINK OF IT, SO-JIN TOLD ME ONCE...
...THAT IN MIDDLE SCHOOL SHE WAS AN EXCELLENT SLIDE-TACKLER...
...AND DEVELOPED ALL SORTS OF WAYS TO SNATCH THE BALL FROM SHIN-BEE.
ARE THESE SCARS FROM THAT?
NO WONDER SHE COULDN'T STAND SHIN-BEE BEING INSULTED.
BUT IS IT ONLY RIVALRY THAT'S PROPELLED HER THIS FAR?

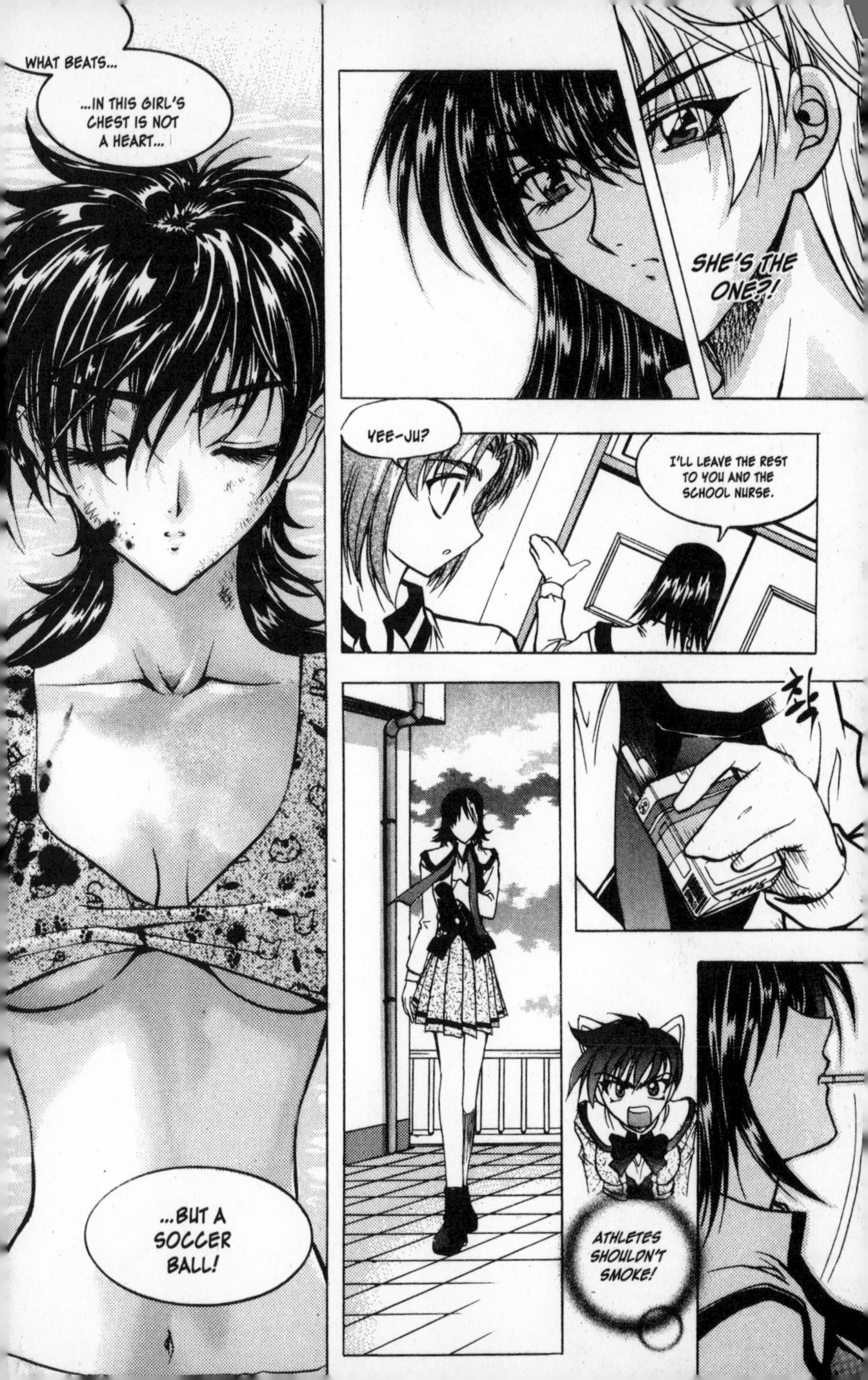
WHAT BEATS...
...IN THIS GIRL'S CHEST IS NOT A HEART...
...BUT A SOCCER BALL!
SHE'S THE ONE?!
YEE-JU?
I'LL LEAVE THE REST TO YOU AND THE SCHOOL NURSE.
ATHLETES SHOULDN'T SMOKE!

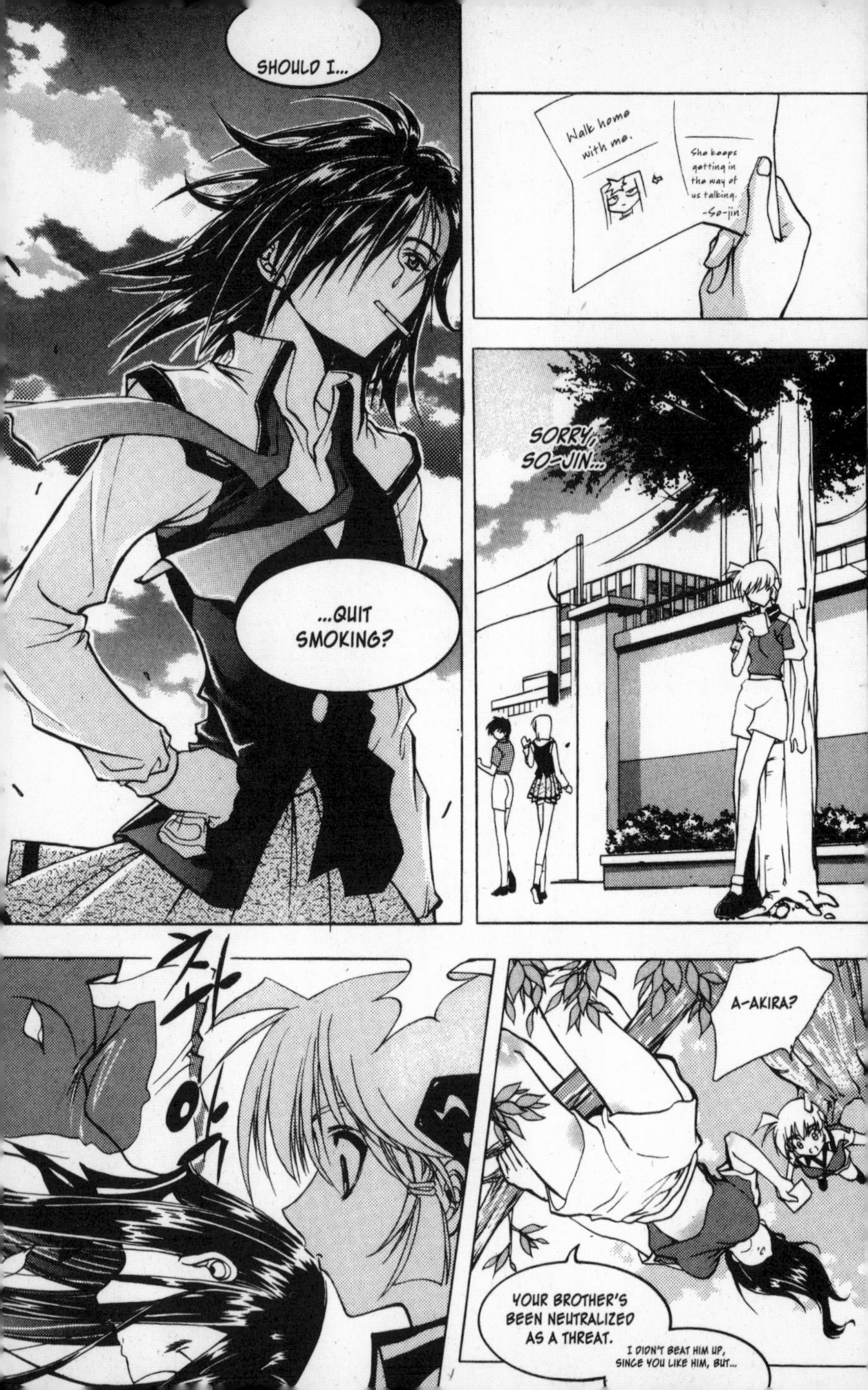
SHOULD I...
...QUIT SMOKING?
Walk home with me.
She keeps getting in the way of us talking.
-So-jin
SORRY, SO-JIN...
A-AKIRA?
YOUR BROTHER'S BEEN NEUTRALIZED AS A THREAT.
I DIDN'T BEAT HIM UP, SINCE YOU LIKE HIM, BUT...

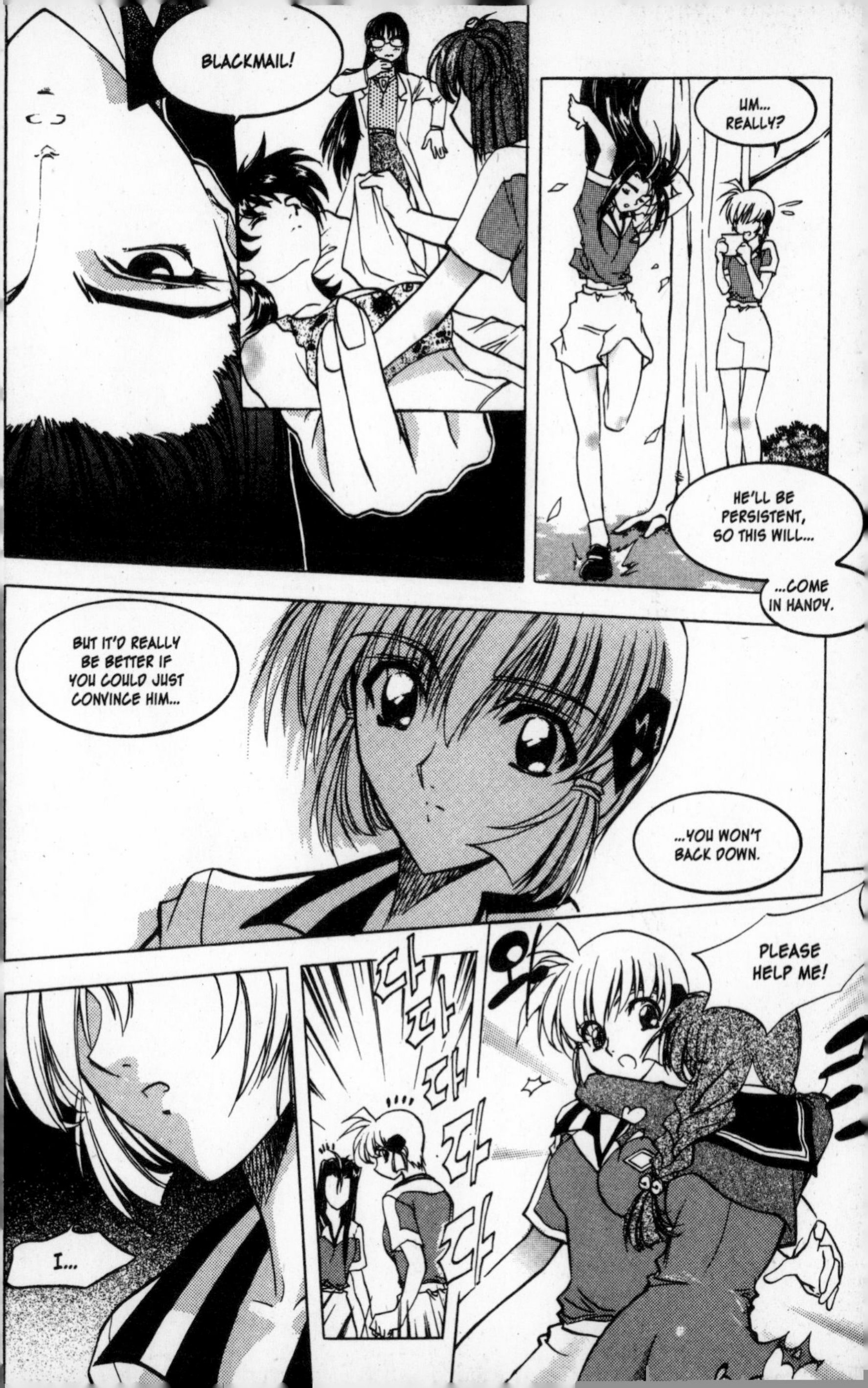
BLACKMAIL!
UM... REALLY?
HE'LL BE PERSISTENT, SO THIS WILL...
...COME IN HANDY.
BUT IT'D REALLY BE BETTER IF YOU COULD JUST CONVINCE HIM...
...YOU WON'T BACK DOWN.
I...
PLEASE HELP ME!

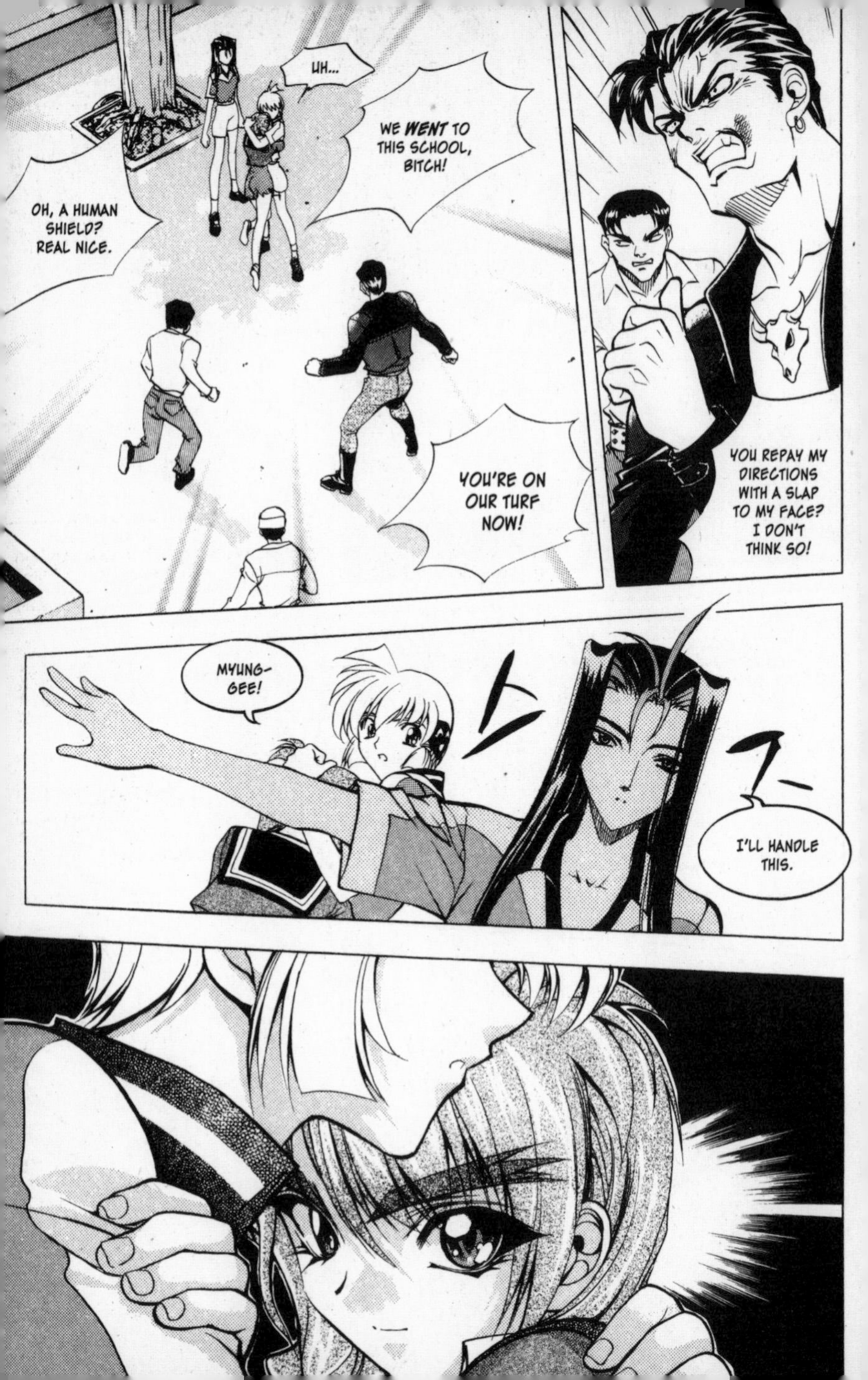

UH...
OH, A HUMAN SHIELD? REAL NICE.
WE WENT TO THIS SCHOOL, BITCH!
YOU'RE ON OUR TURF NOW!
YOU REPAY MY DIRECTIONS WITH A SLAP TO MY FACE? I DON'T THINK SO!
MYUNG-GEE!
I'LL HANDLE THIS.

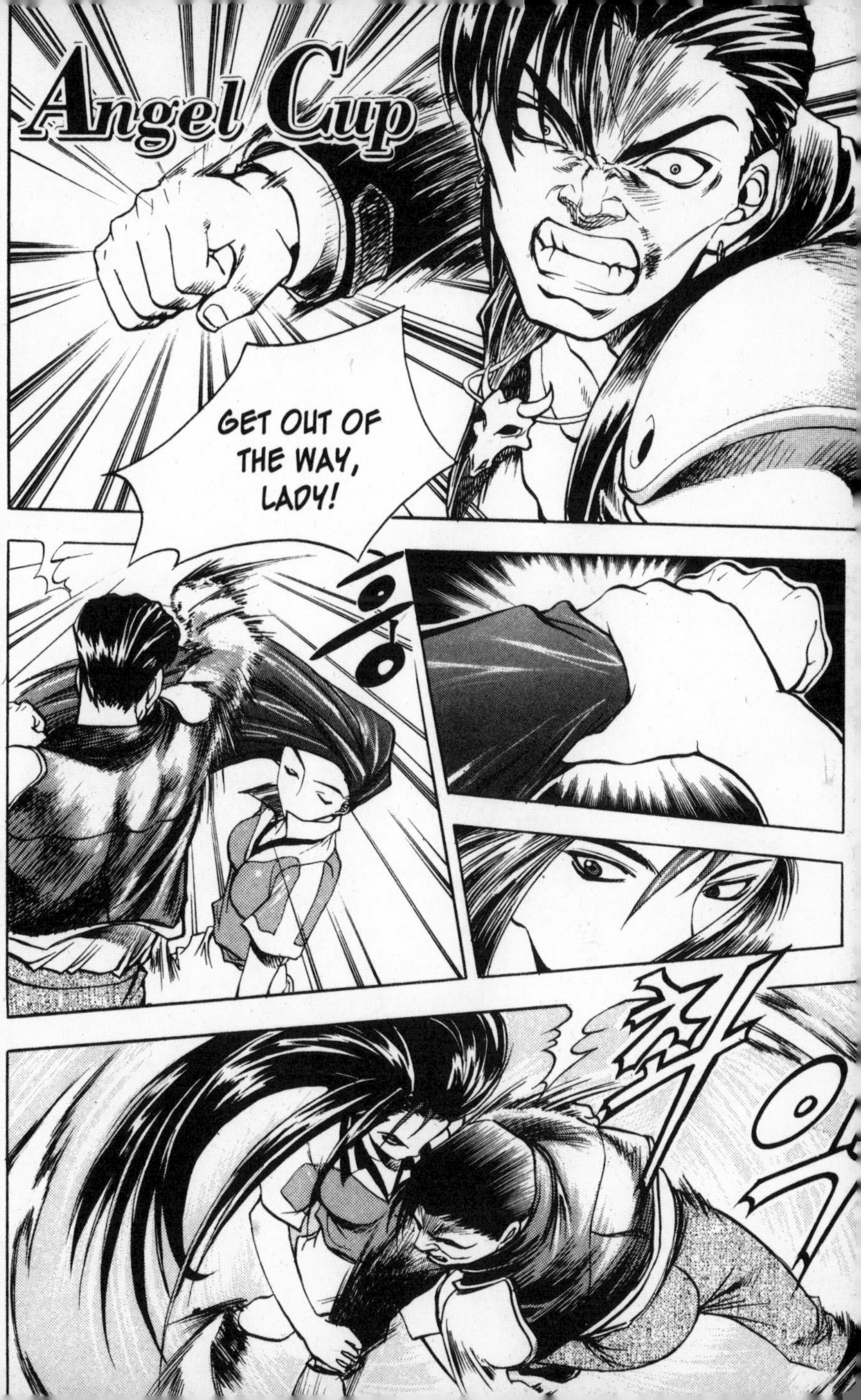
Angel Cup
GET OUT OF THE WAY, LADY!

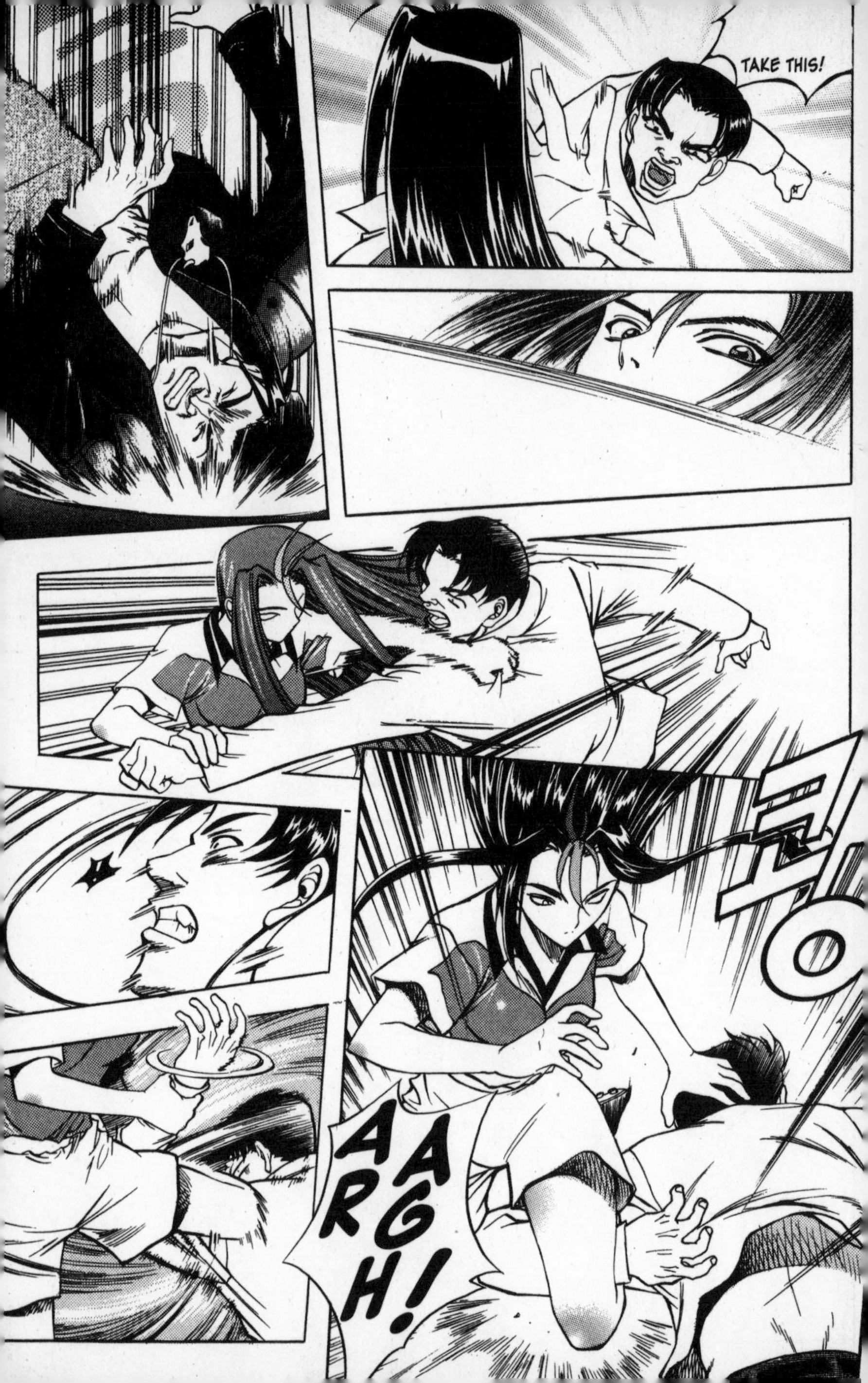
TAKE THIS!
AARGH!

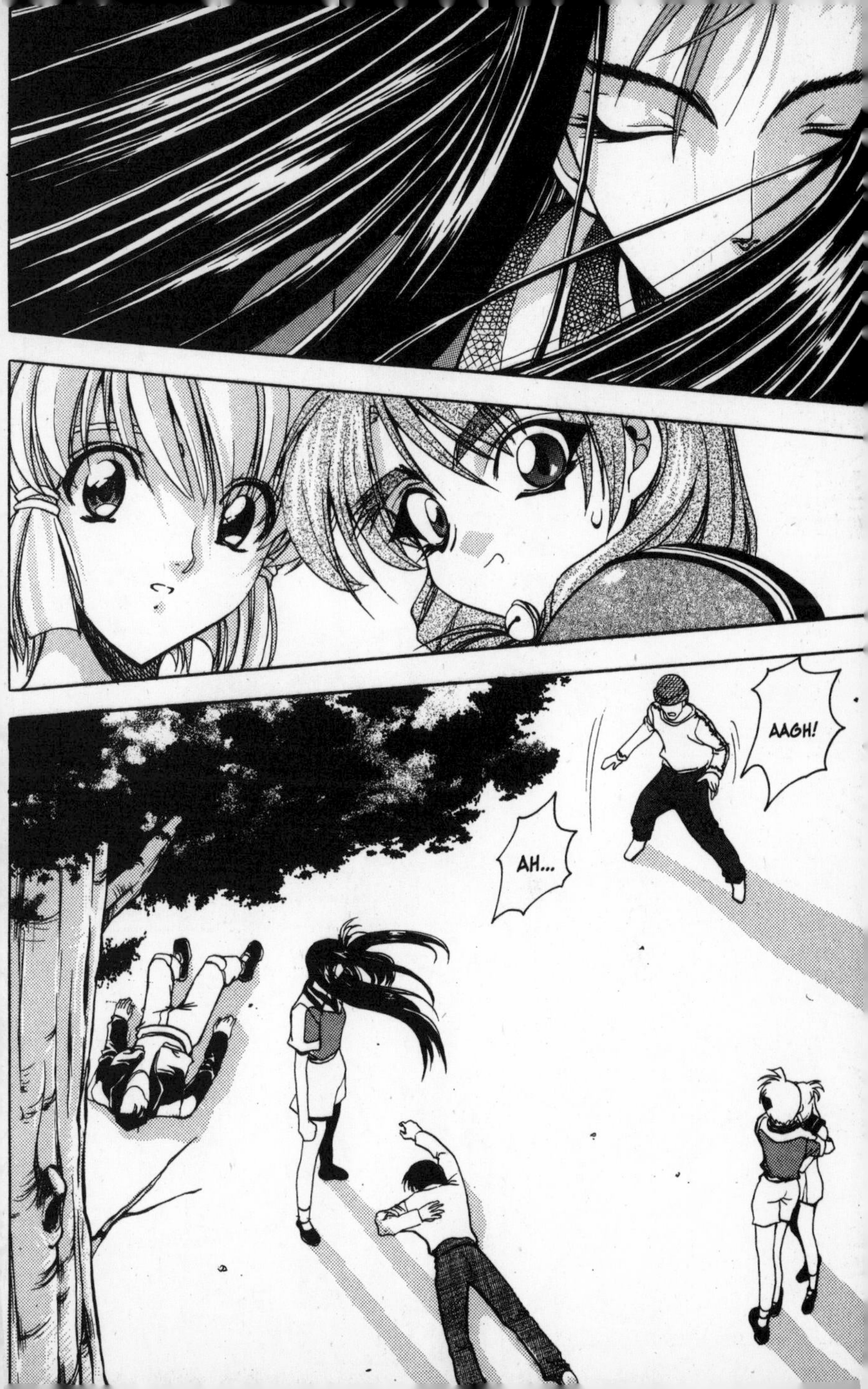
AAGH!
AH...

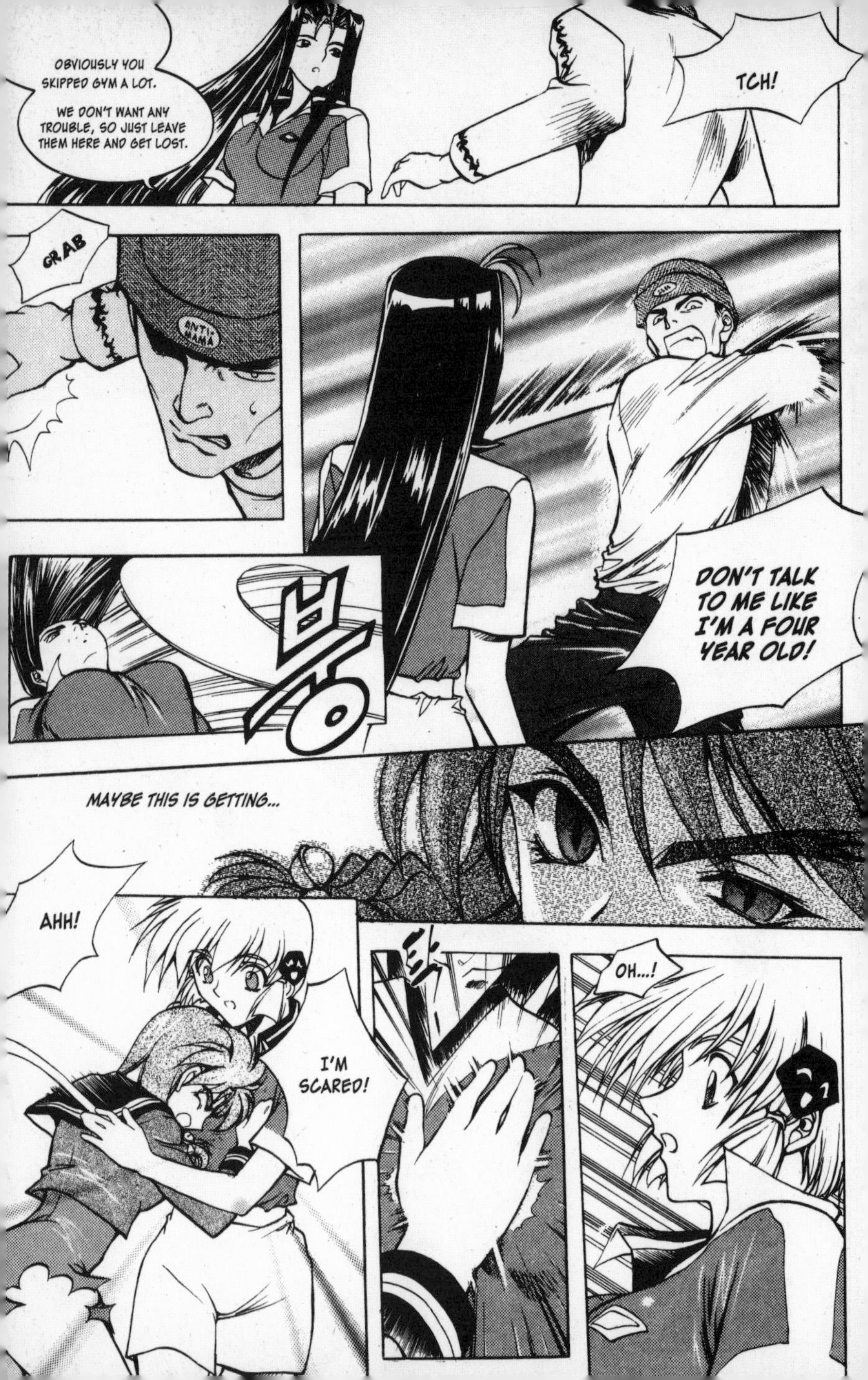
OBVIOUSLY YOU SKIPPED GYM A LOT.
WE DON'T WANT ANY TROUBLE, SO JUST LEAVE THEM HERE AND GET LOST.
TCH!
GRAB
ANTI-MAMA
DON'T TALK TO ME LIKE I'M A FOUR YEAR OLD!
MAYBE THIS IS GETTING...
AHH!
I'M SCARED!
OH...!

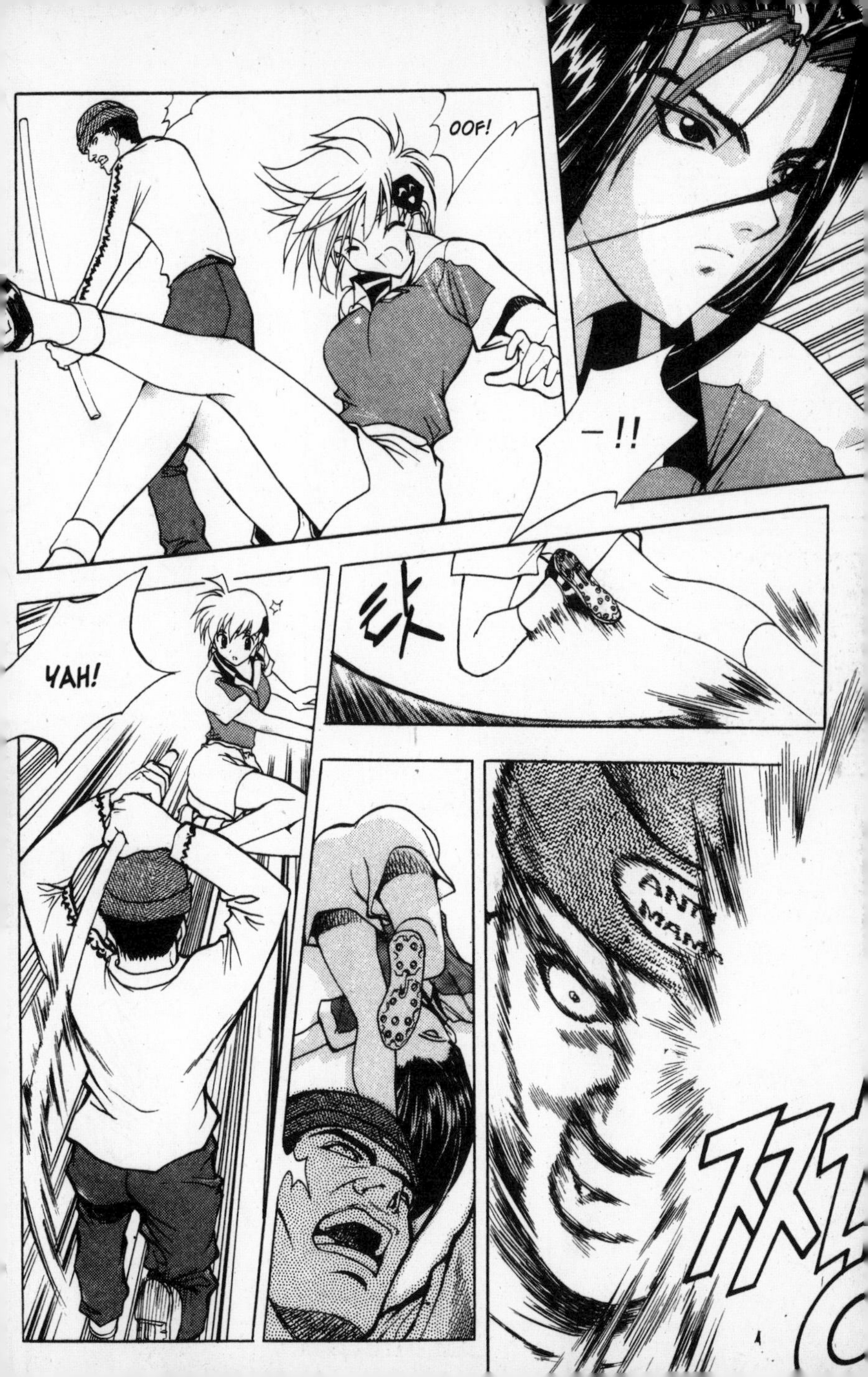
OOF!
—!!
YAH!

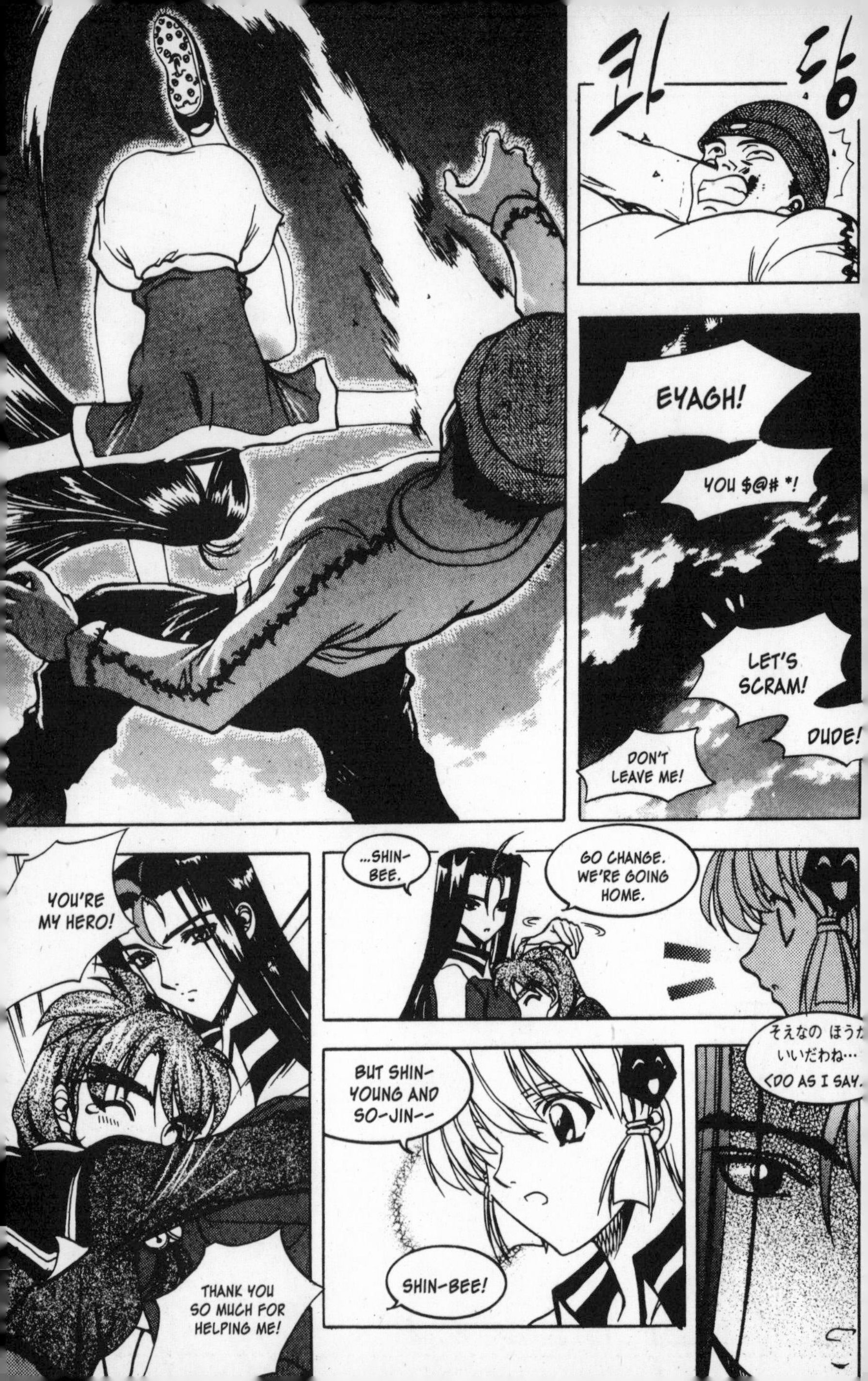
콰 당
EYAGH!
YOU $@# *!
LET'S SCRAM!
DUDE!
DON'T LEAVE ME!
YOU'RE MY HERO!
THANK YOU SO MUCH FOR HELPING ME!
...SHIN-BEE.
GO CHANGE. WE'RE GOING HOME.
BUT SHIN-YOUNG AND SO-JIN--
SHIN-BEE!
そえなの ほうか いいだわね…
<DO AS I SAY.

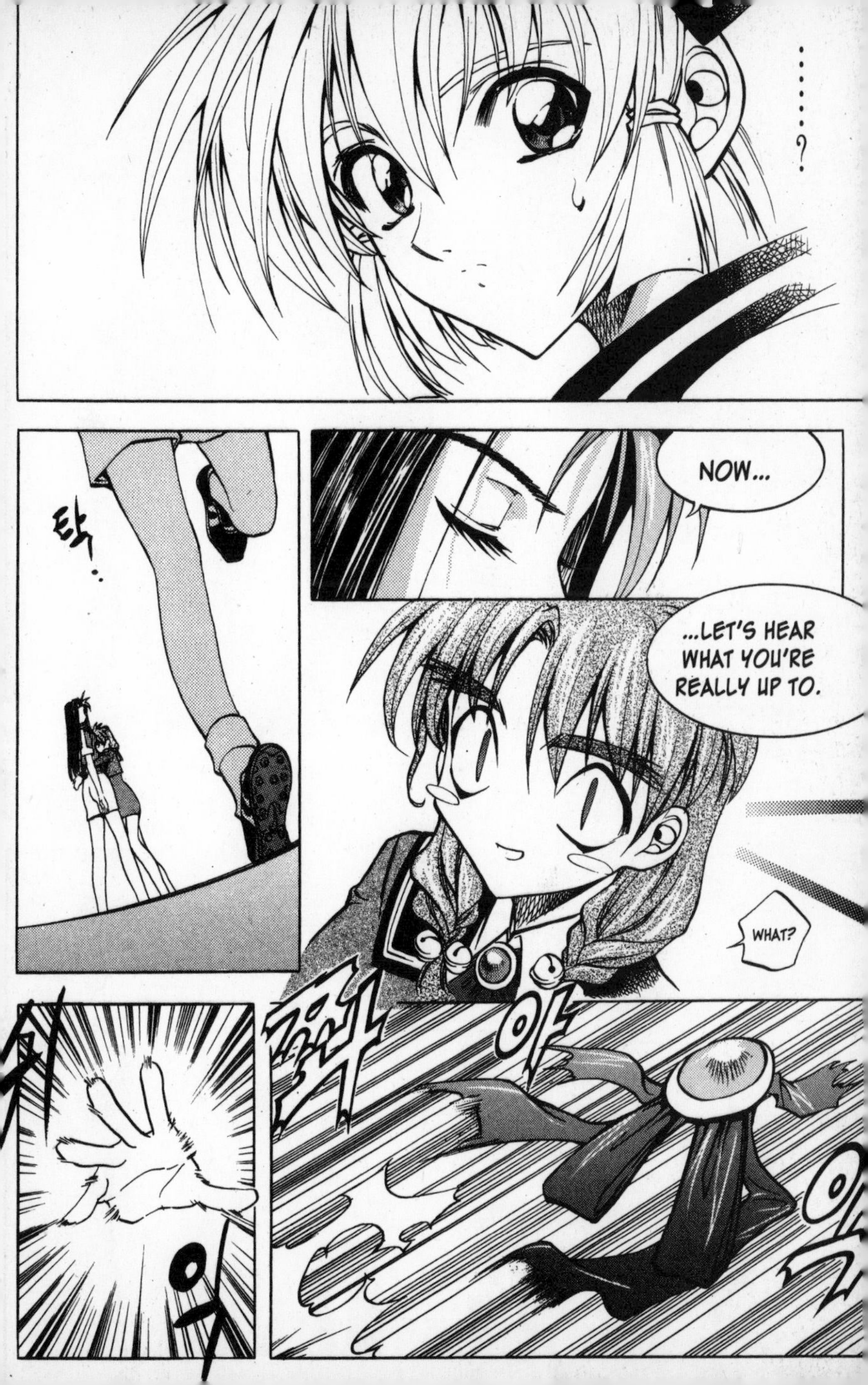
....?
탁..
NOW...
...LET'S HEAR WHAT YOU'RE REALLY UP TO.
WHAT?

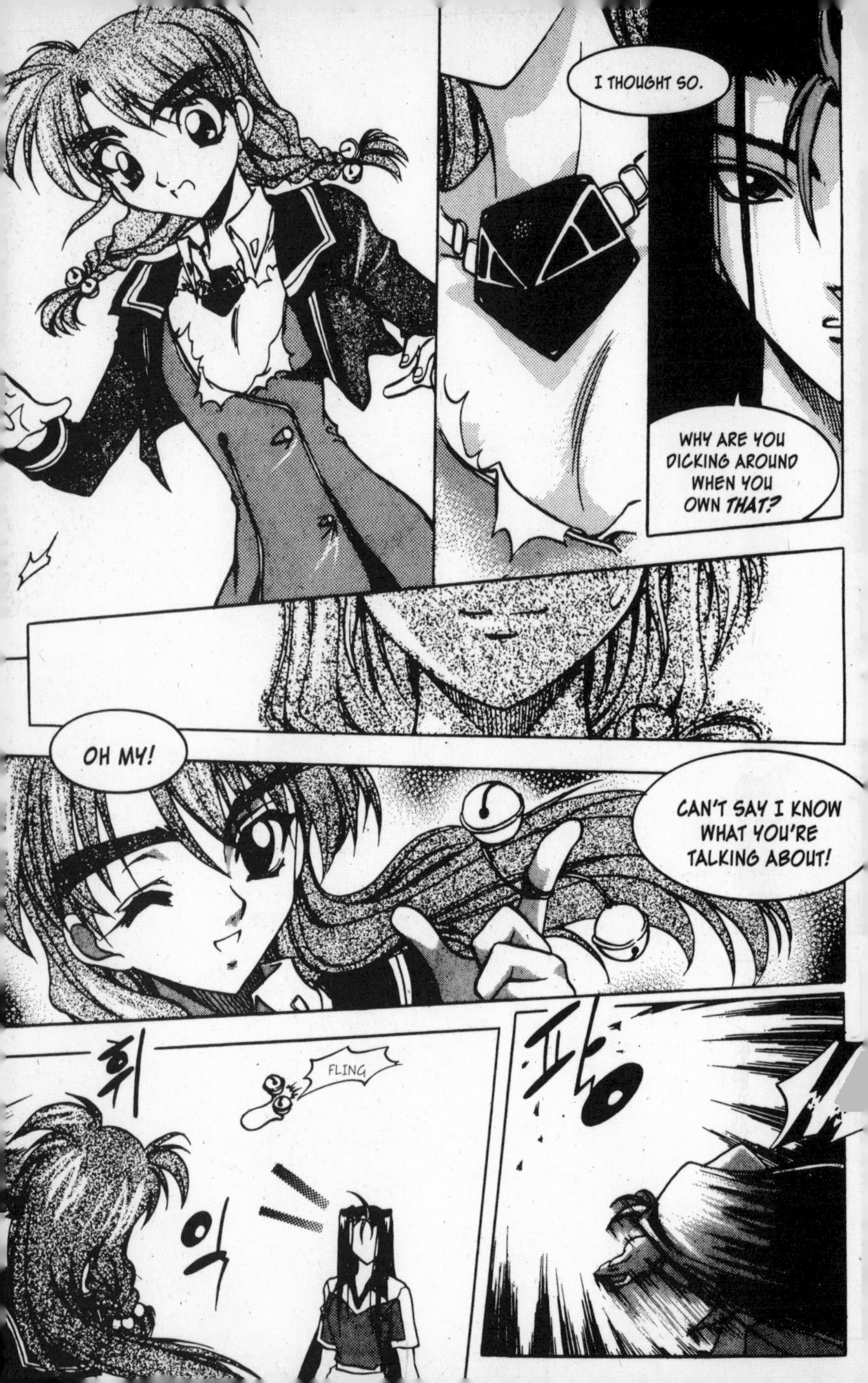
I THOUGHT SO.
WHY ARE YOU DICKING AROUND WHEN YOU OWN THAT?
OH MY!
CAN'T SAY I KNOW WHAT YOU'RE TALKING ABOUT!
휘
FLING
익
팡

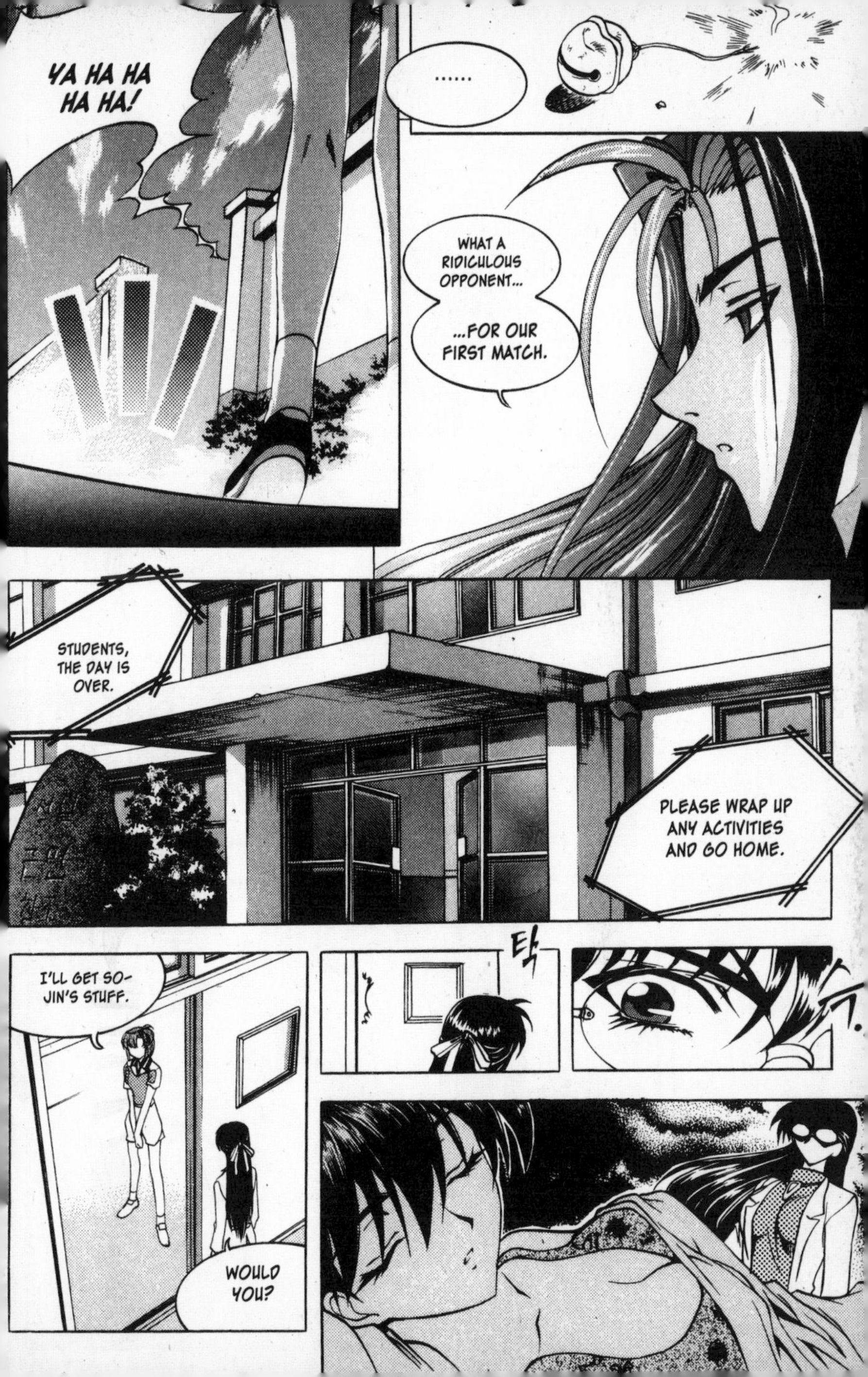
YA HA HA HA HA!
......
WHAT A RIDICULOUS OPPONENT...
...FOR OUR FIRST MATCH.
STUDENTS, THE DAY IS OVER.
PLEASE WRAP UP ANY ACTIVITIES AND GO HOME.
I'LL GET SO-JIN'S STUFF.
WOULD YOU?

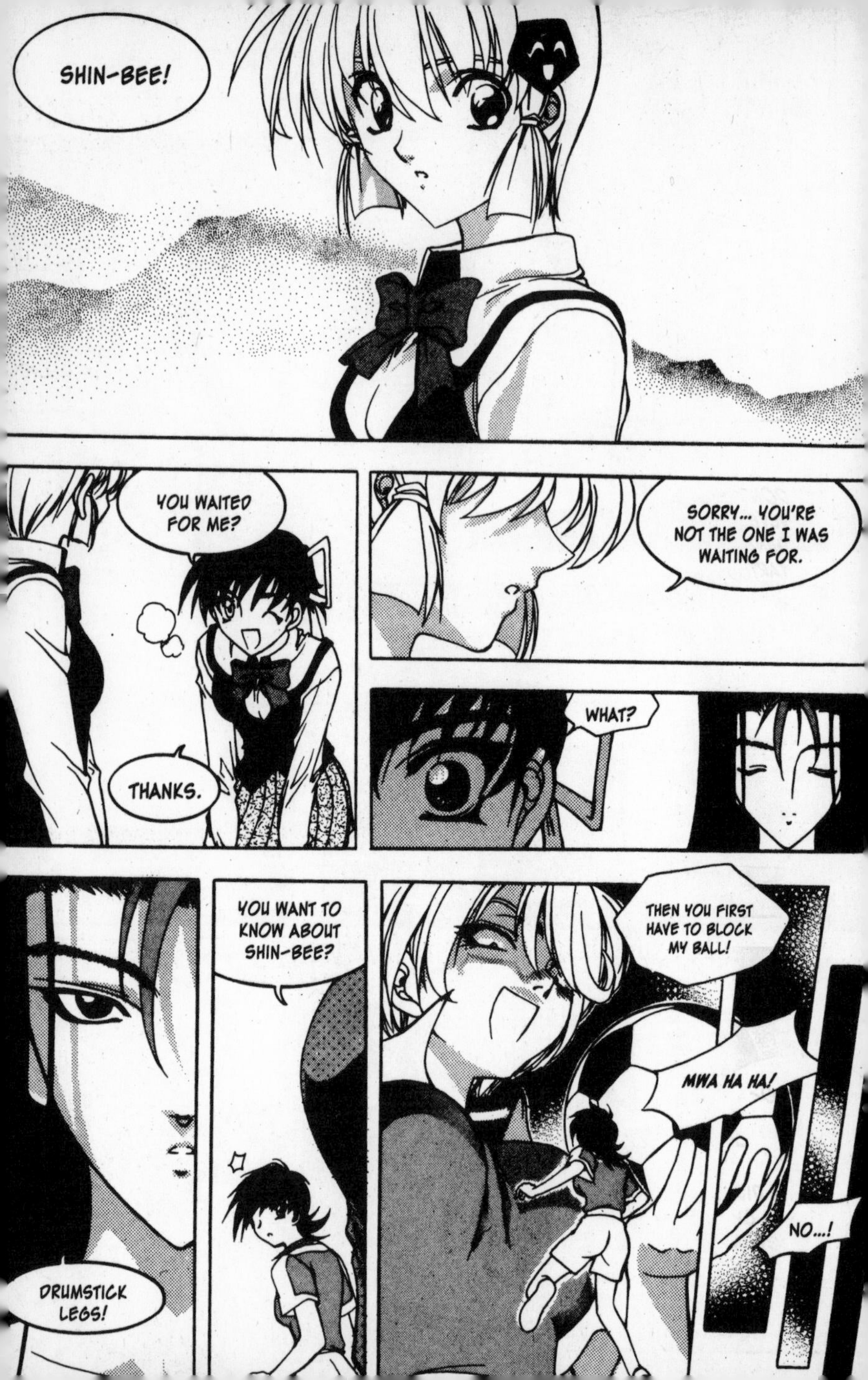
SHIN-BEE!
YOU WAITED FOR ME?
THANKS.
SORRY... YOU'RE NOT THE ONE I WAS WAITING FOR.
WHAT?
DRUMSTICK LEGS!
YOU WANT TO KNOW ABOUT SHIN-BEE?
THEN YOU FIRST HAVE TO BLOCK MY BALL!
MWA HA HA!
NO...!

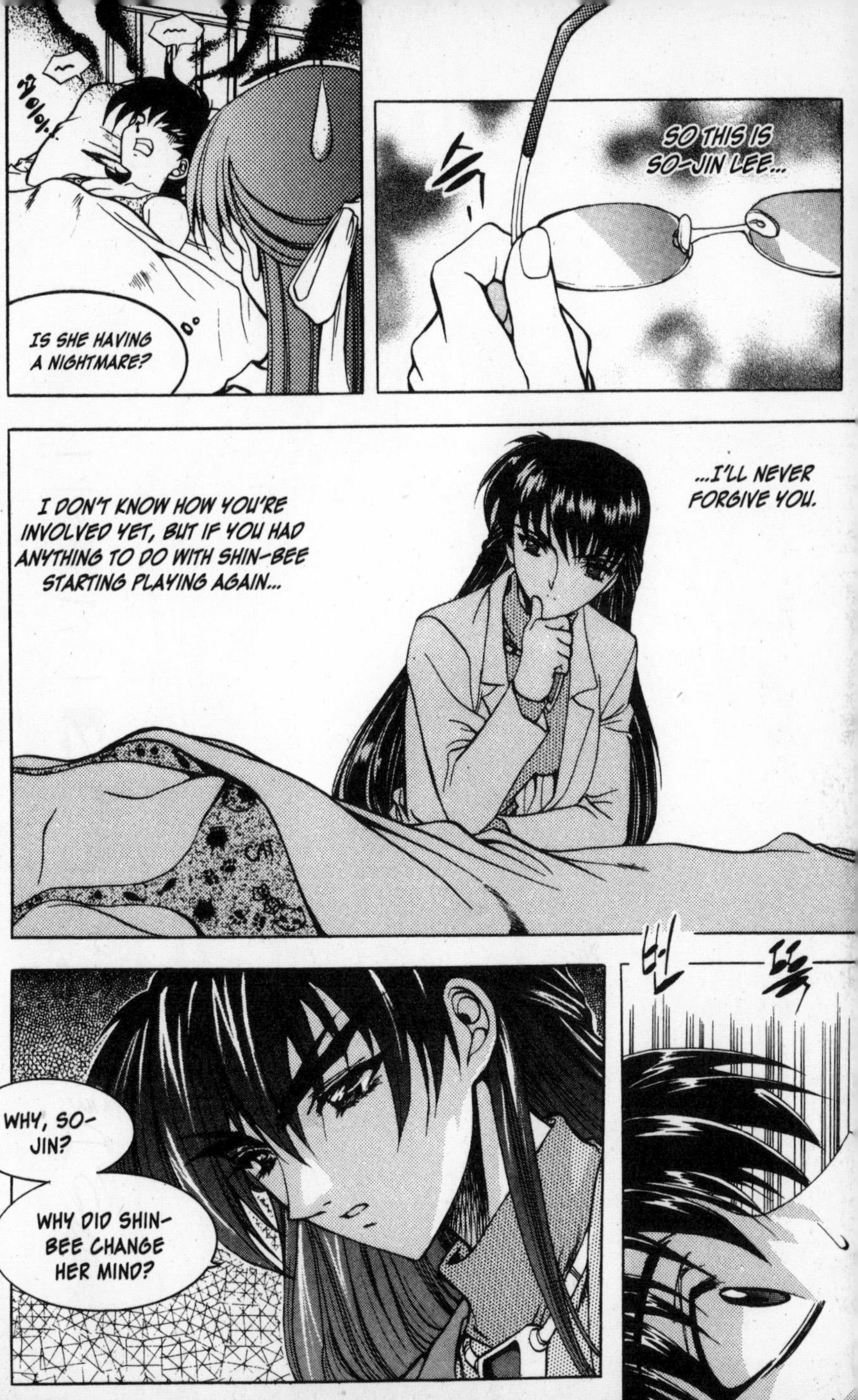
~
~
끙이이..
IS SHE HAVING A NIGHTMARE?
SO THIS IS SO-JIN LEE...
I DON'T KNOW HOW YOU'RE INVOLVED YET, BUT IF YOU HAD ANYTHING TO DO WITH SHIN-BEE STARTING PLAYING AGAIN...
...I'LL NEVER FORGIVE YOU.
WHY, SO-JIN?
WHY DID SHIN-BEE CHANGE HER MIND?
번 뜩

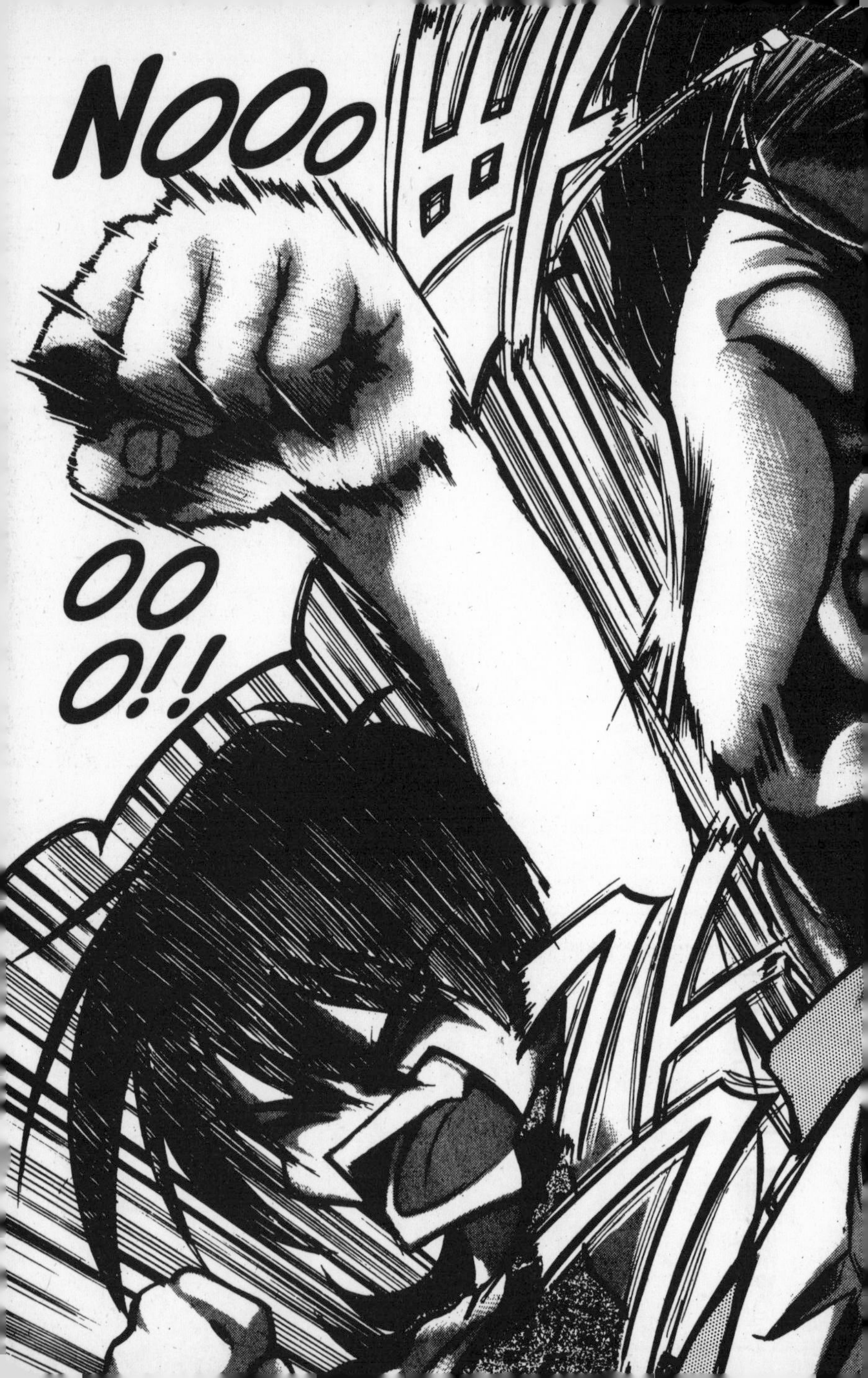
NOOoo!!
OO
O!!

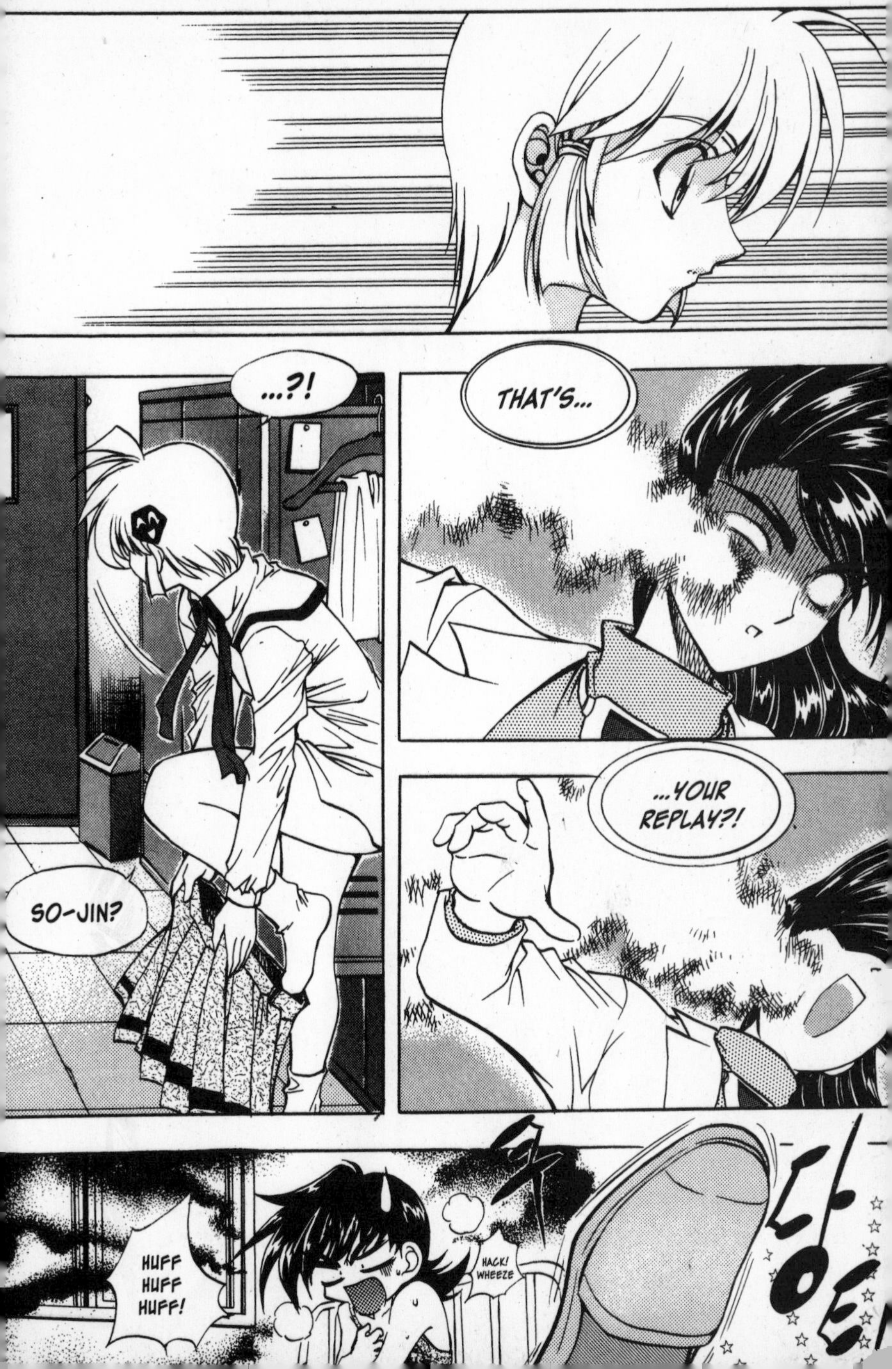
...?!
SO-JIN?
THAT'S...
...YOUR REPLAY?!
HUFF HUFF HUFF!
HACK! WHEEZE

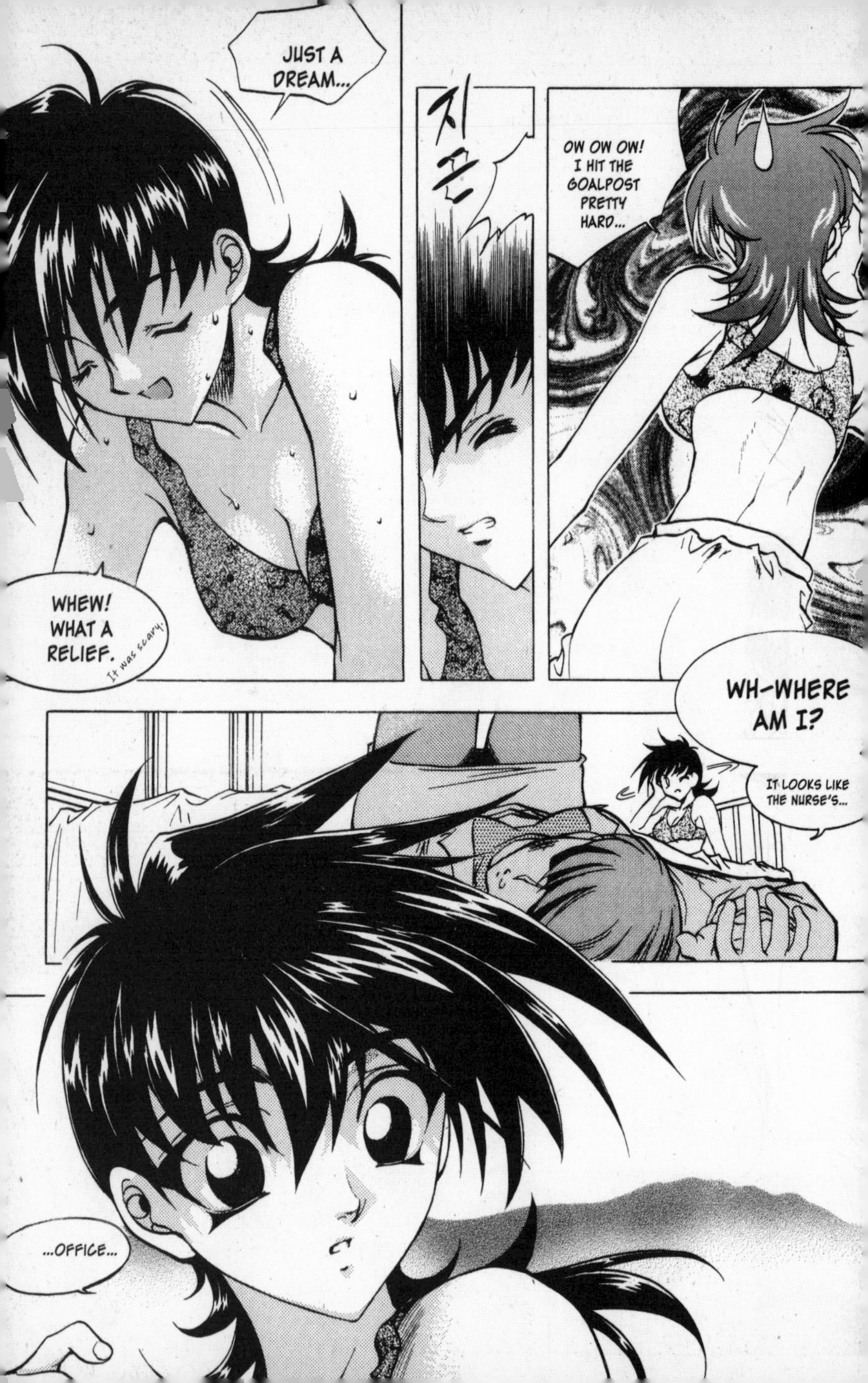
JUST A DREAM...
WHEW! WHAT A RELIEF.
It was scary.
지끈
OW OW OW! I HIT THE GOALPOST PRETTY HARD...
WH-WHERE AM I?
IT LOOKS LIKE THE NURSE'S...
...OFFICE...

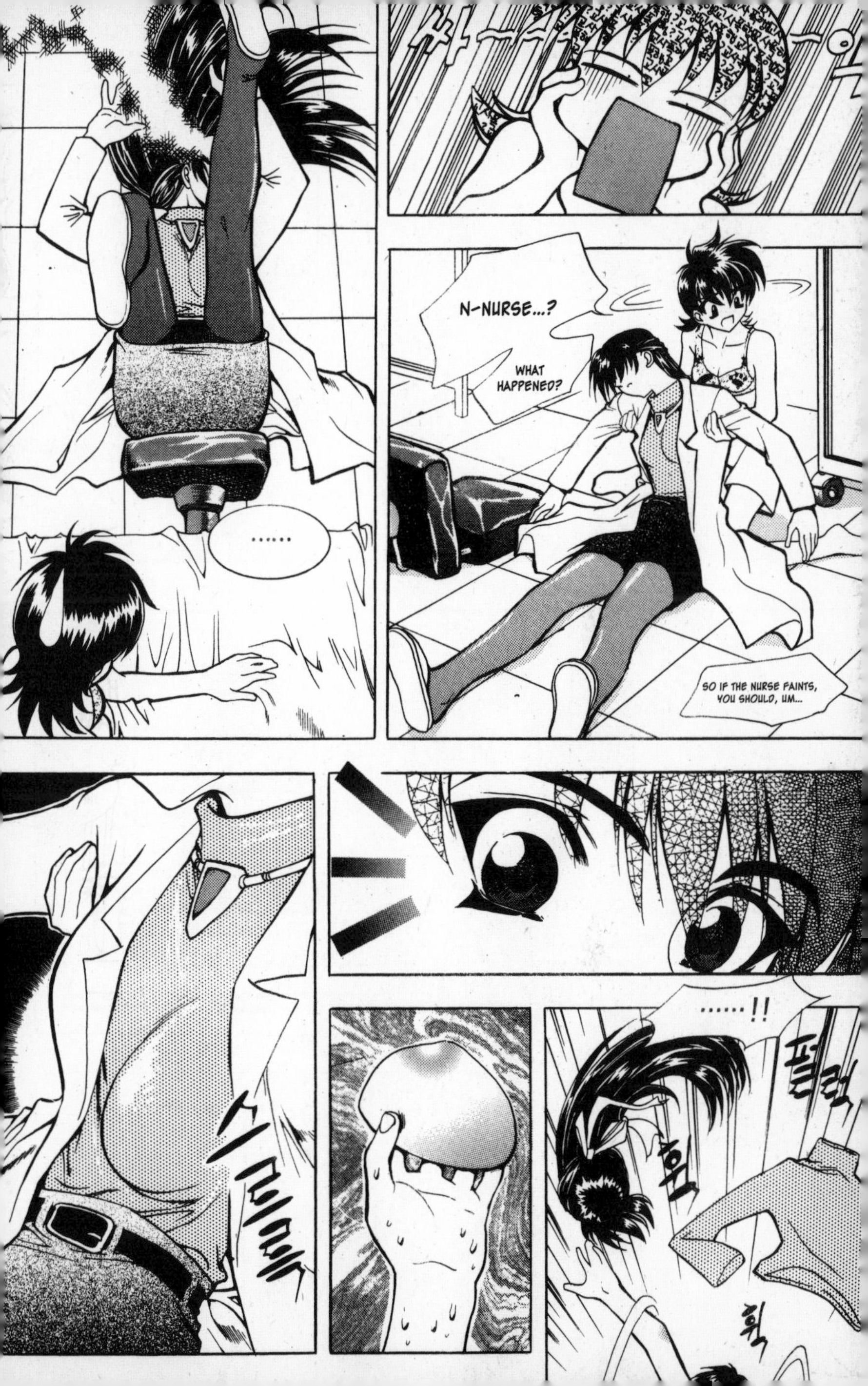
......
N-NURSE...?
WHAT HAPPENED?
SO IF THE NURSE FAINTS, YOU SHOULD, UM...
......!!

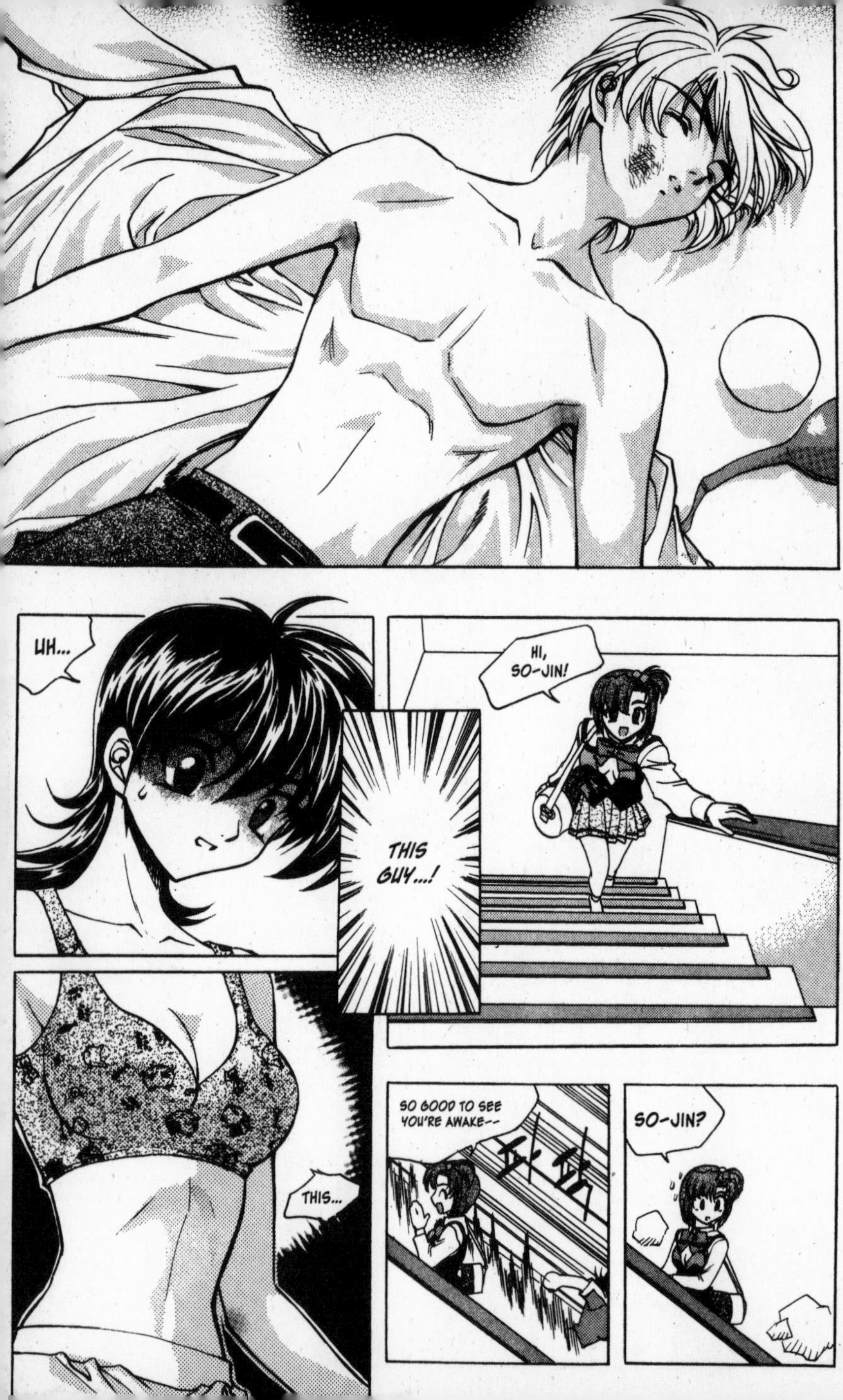
UH...
THIS GUY...!
HI, SO-JIN!
THIS...
SO GOOD TO SEE YOU'RE AWAKE--
SO-JIN?

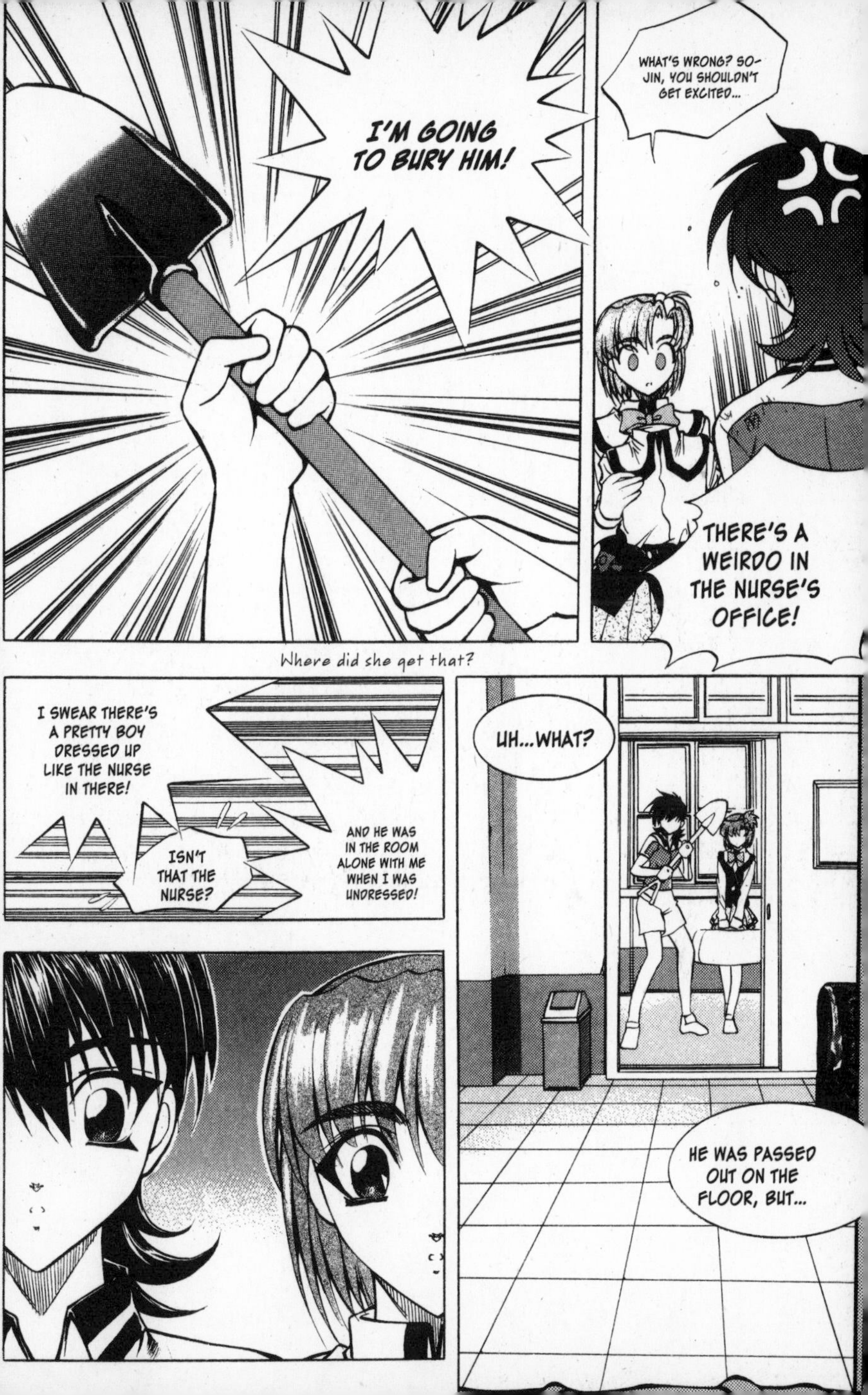
I'M GOING TO BURY HIM!
WHAT'S WRONG? SO-JIN, YOU SHOULDN'T GET EXCITED...
THERE'S A WEIRDO IN THE NURSE'S OFFICE!
Where did she get that?
I SWEAR THERE'S A PRETTY BOY DRESSED UP LIKE THE NURSE IN THERE!
ISN'T THAT THE NURSE?
AND HE WAS IN THE ROOM ALONE WITH ME WHEN I WAS UNDRESSED!
UH...WHAT?
HE WAS PASSED OUT ON THE FLOOR, BUT...

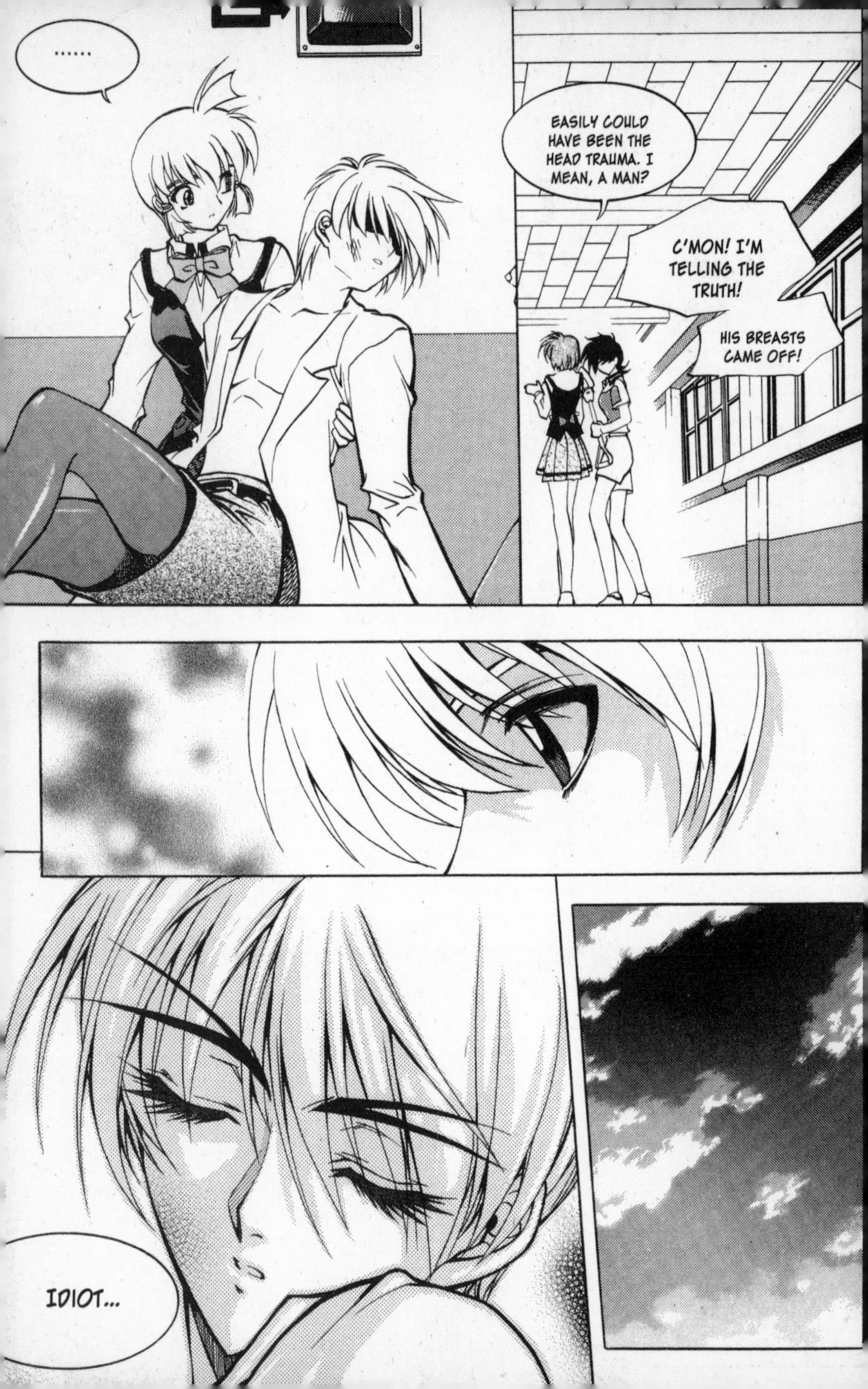
......
EASILY COULD HAVE BEEN THE HEAD TRAUMA. I MEAN, A MAN?
C'MON! I'M TELLING THE TRUTH!
HIS BREASTS CAME OFF!
IDIOT...

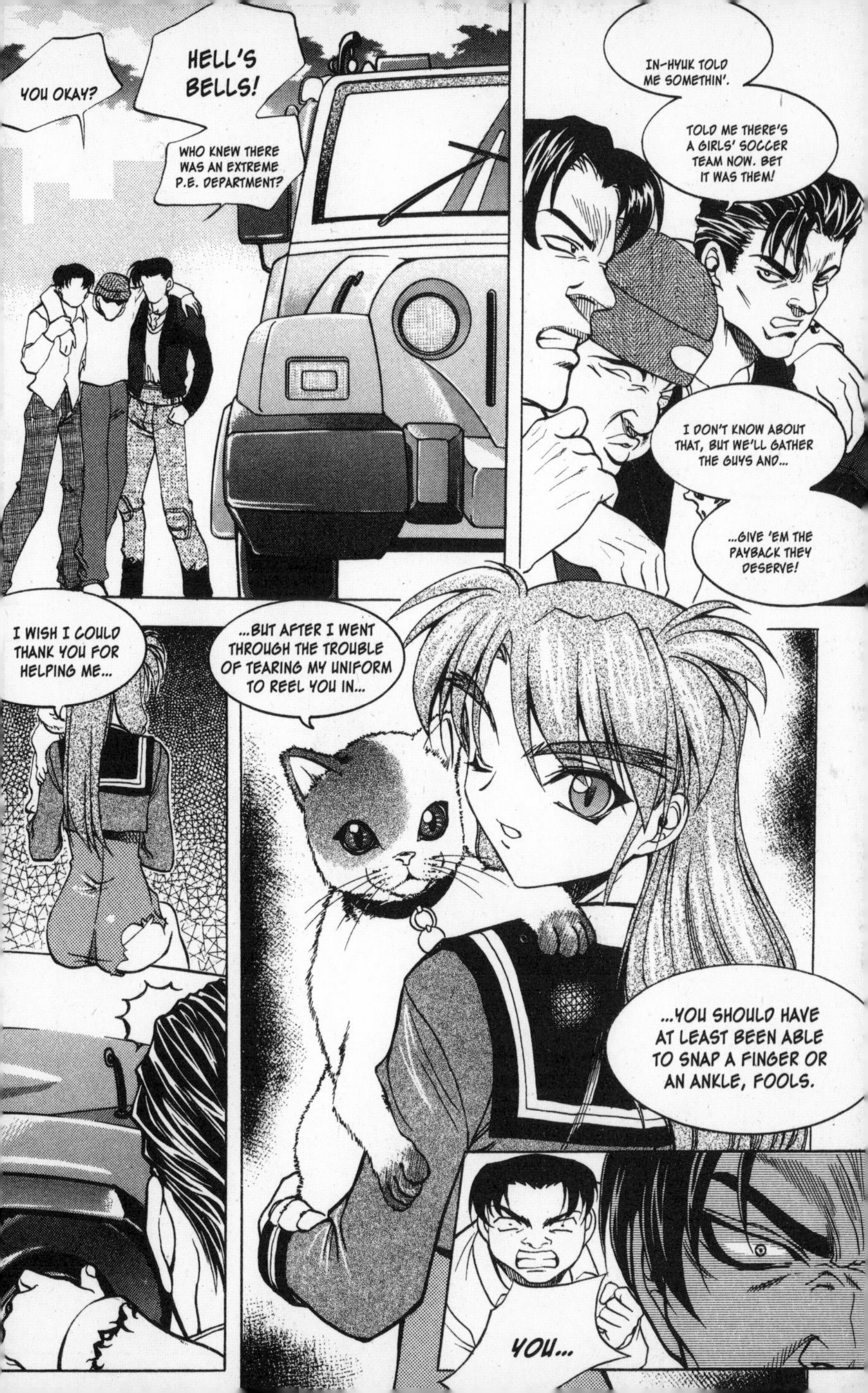
YOU OKAY?
HELL'S BELLS!
WHO KNEW THERE WAS AN EXTREME P.E. DEPARTMENT?
IN-HYUK TOLD ME SOMETHIN'.
TOLD ME THERE'S A GIRLS' SOCCER TEAM NOW. BET IT WAS THEM!
I DON'T KNOW ABOUT THAT, BUT WE'LL GATHER THE GUYS AND...
...GIVE 'EM THE PAYBACK THEY DESERVE!
I WISH I COULD THANK YOU FOR HELPING ME...
...BUT AFTER I WENT THROUGH THE TROUBLE OF TEARING MY UNIFORM TO REEL YOU IN...
...YOU SHOULD HAVE AT LEAST BEEN ABLE TO SNAP A FINGER OR AN ANKLE, FOOLS.
YOU...

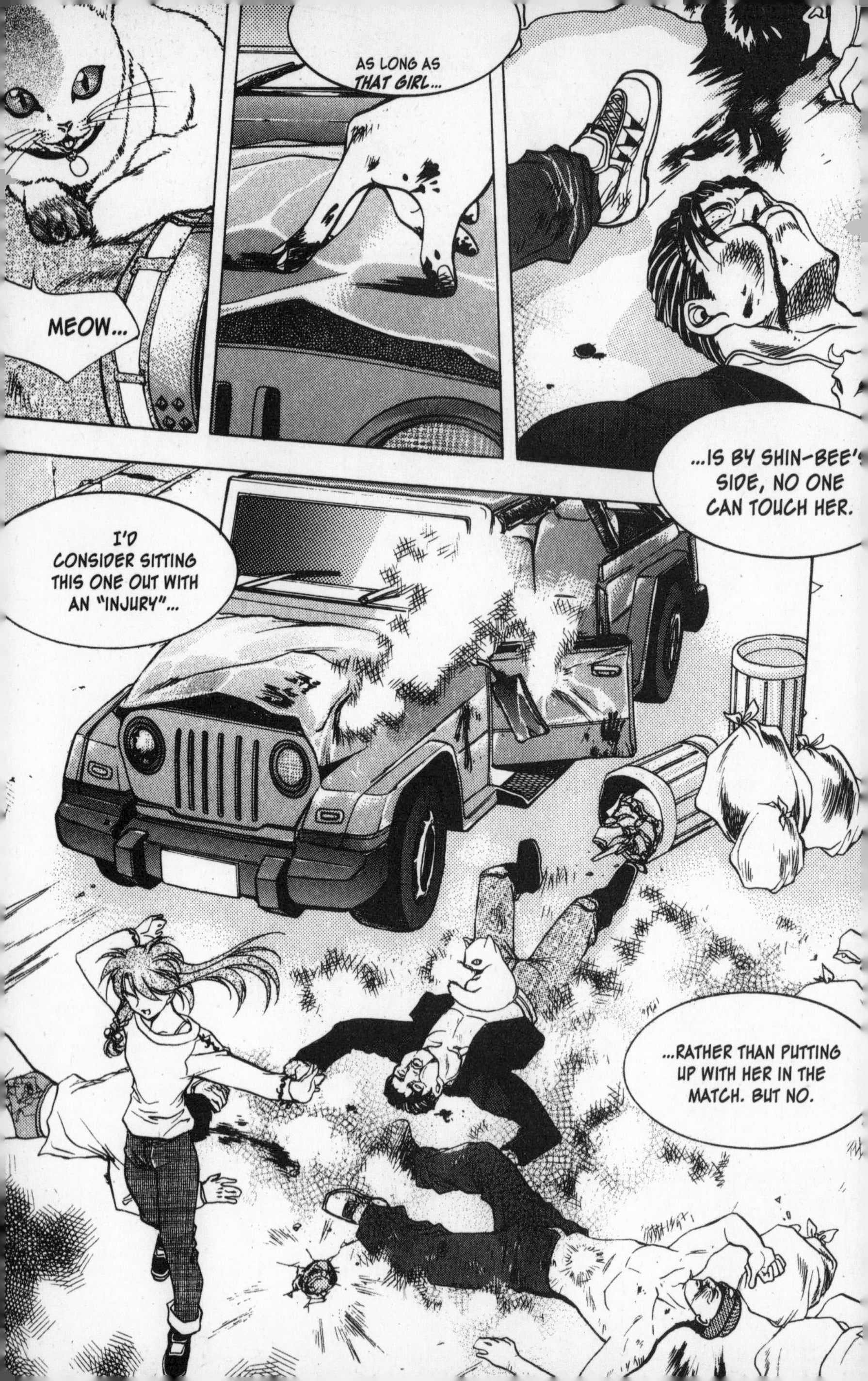
MEOW...
AS LONG AS THAT GIRL...
...IS BY SHIN-BEE'S SIDE, NO ONE CAN TOUCH HER.
I'D CONSIDER SITTING THIS ONE OUT WITH AN "INJURY"...
...RATHER THAN PUTTING UP WITH HER IN THE MATCH. BUT NO.

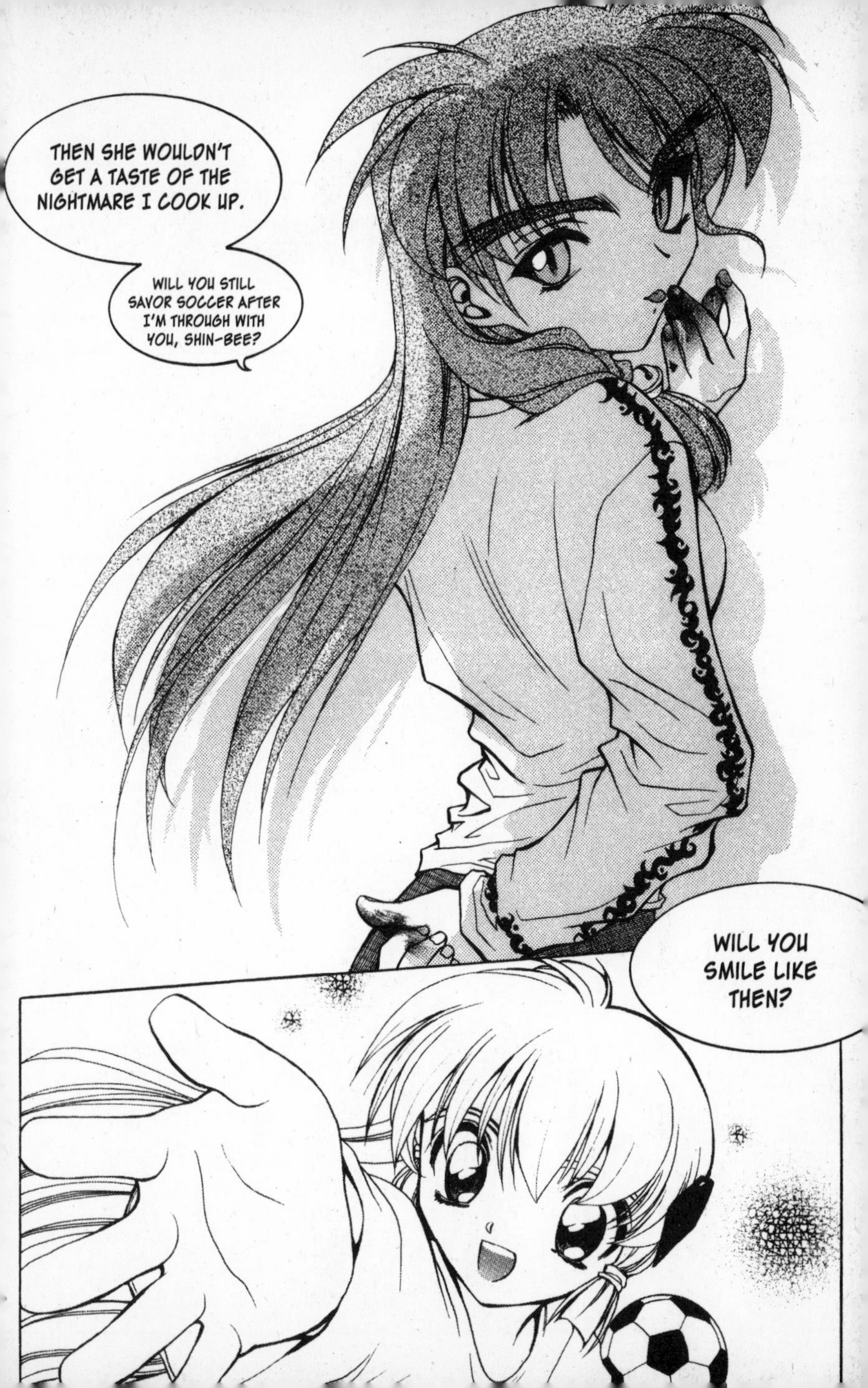
THEN SHE WOULDN'T GET A TASTE OF THE NIGHTMARE I COOK UP.
WILL YOU STILL SAVOR SOCCER AFTER I'M THROUGH WITH YOU, SHIN-BEE?
WILL YOU SMILE LIKE THEN?

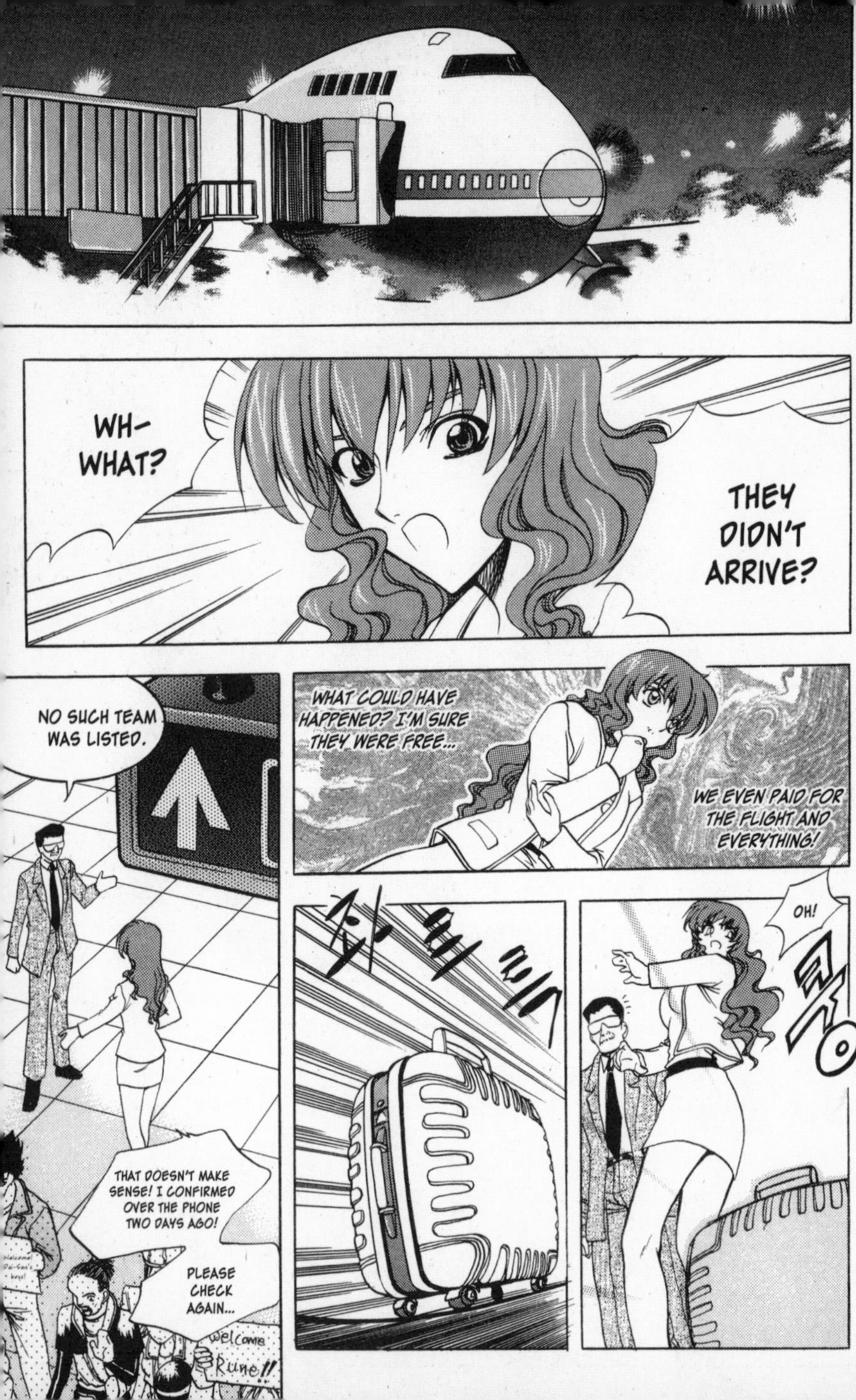
WH- WHAT?
THEY DIDN'T ARRIVE?
NO SUCH TEAM WAS LISTED.
THAT DOESN'T MAKE SENSE! I CONFIRMED OVER THE PHONE TWO DAYS AGO!
PLEASE CHECK AGAIN...
Welcome! Dai-San's boys!
Welcome Rune!!
WHAT COULD HAVE HAPPENED? I'M SURE THEY WERE FREE...
WE EVEN PAID FOR THE FLIGHT AND EVERYTHING!
OH!

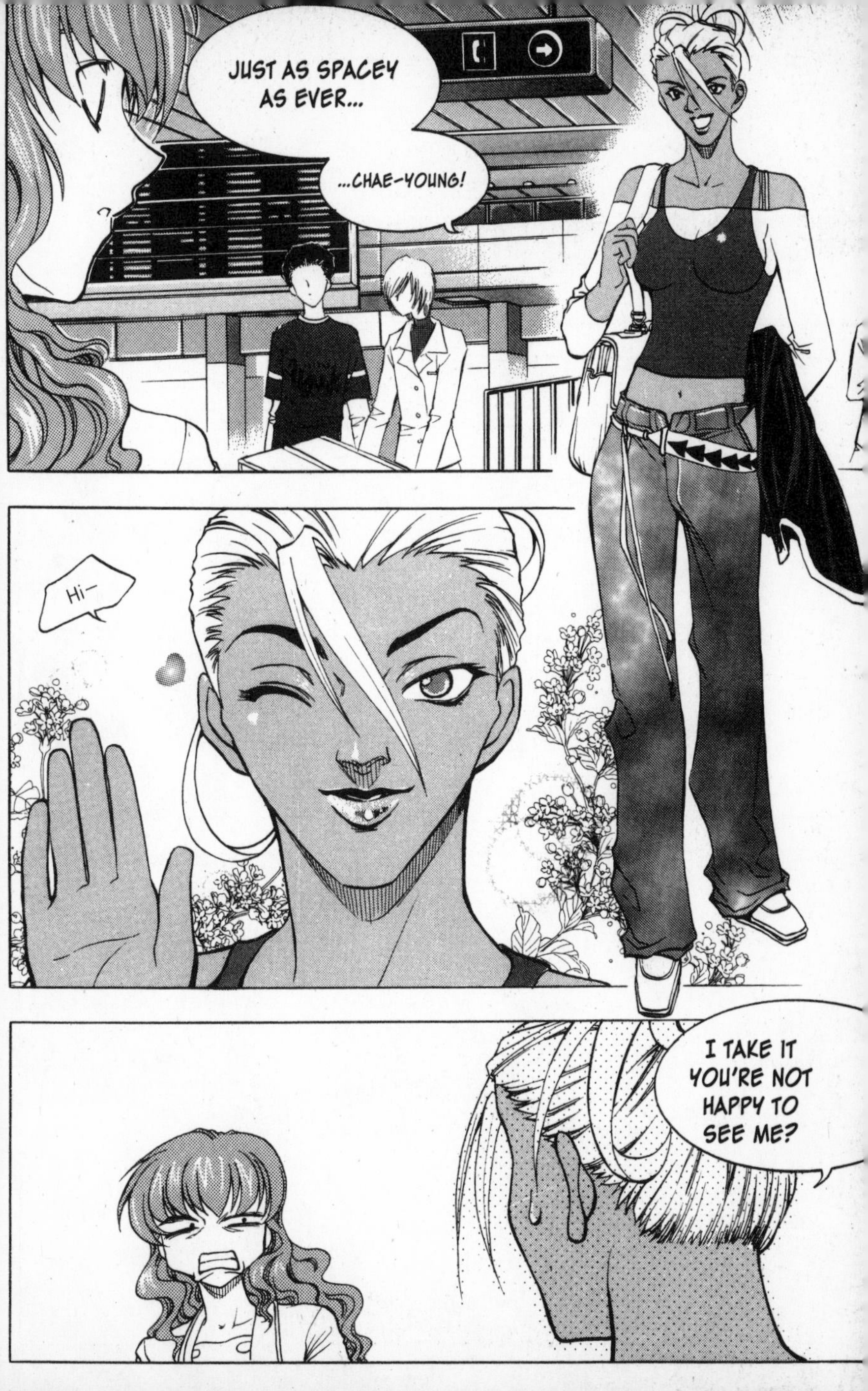
JUST AS SPACEY AS EVER...
...CHAE-YOUNG!
Hi-
I TAKE IT YOU'RE NOT HAPPY TO SEE ME?

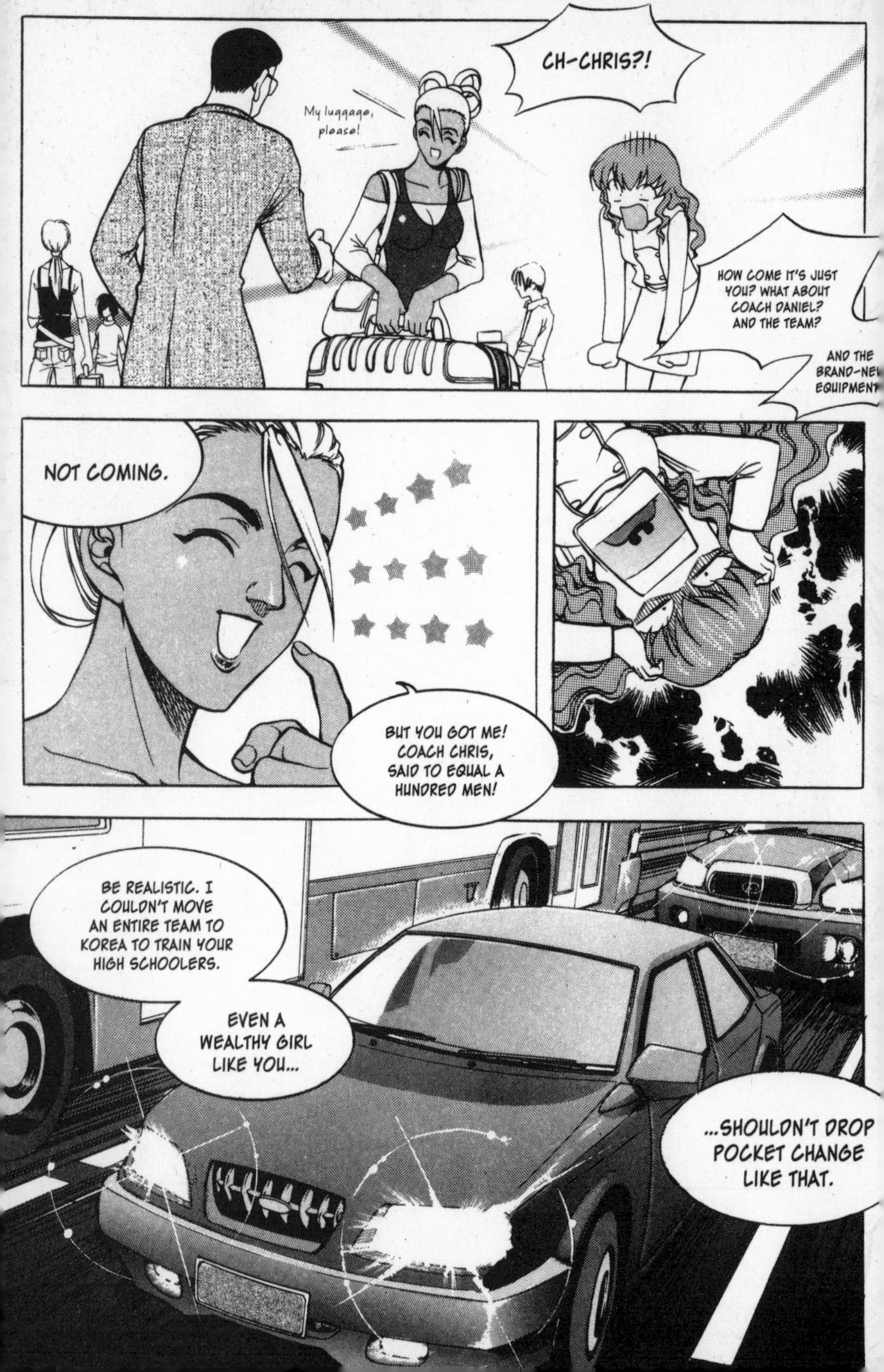
My luggage, please!
CH-CHRIS?!
HOW COME IT'S JUST YOU? WHAT ABOUT COACH DANIEL? AND THE TEAM?
AND THE BRAND-NEW EQUIPMENT
NOT COMING.
BUT YOU GOT ME! COACH CHRIS, SAID TO EQUAL A HUNDRED MEN!
BE REALISTIC. I COULDN'T MOVE AN ENTIRE TEAM TO KOREA TO TRAIN YOUR HIGH SCHOOLERS.
EVEN A WEALTHY GIRL LIKE YOU...
...SHOULDN'T DROP POCKET CHANGE LIKE THAT.

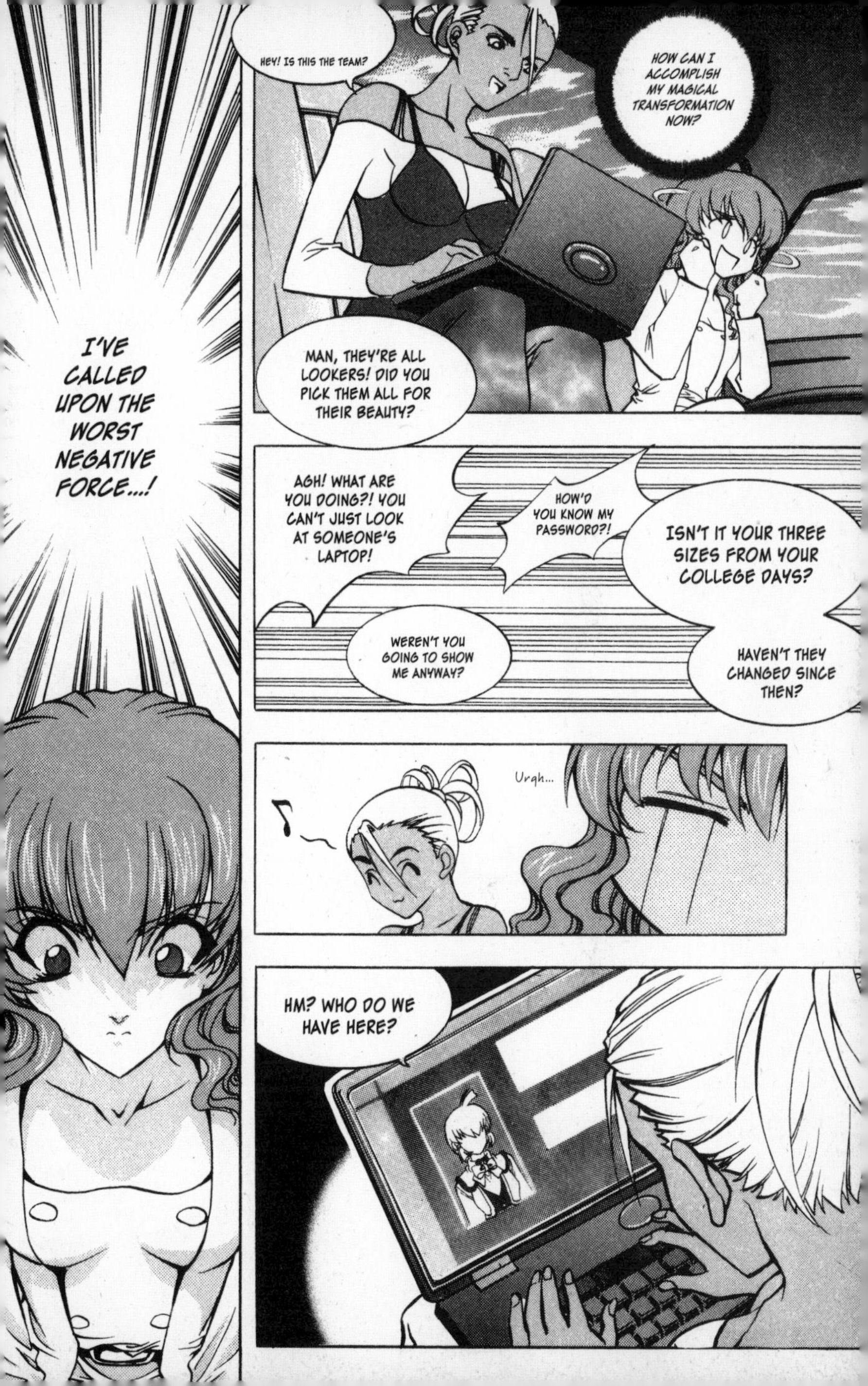
I'VE CALLED UPON THE WORST NEGATIVE FORCE...!
HEY! IS THIS THE TEAM?
HOW CAN I ACCOMPLISH MY MAGICAL TRANSFORMATION NOW?
MAN, THEY'RE ALL LOOKERS! DID YOU PICK THEM ALL FOR THEIR BEAUTY?
AGH! WHAT ARE YOU DOING?! YOU CAN'T JUST LOOK AT SOMEONE'S LAPTOP!
HOW'D YOU KNOW MY PASSWORD?!
ISN'T IT YOUR THREE SIZES FROM YOUR COLLEGE DAYS?
WEREN'T YOU GOING TO SHOW ME ANYWAY?
HAVEN'T THEY CHANGED SINCE THEN?
Urgh...
HM? WHO DO WE HAVE HERE?

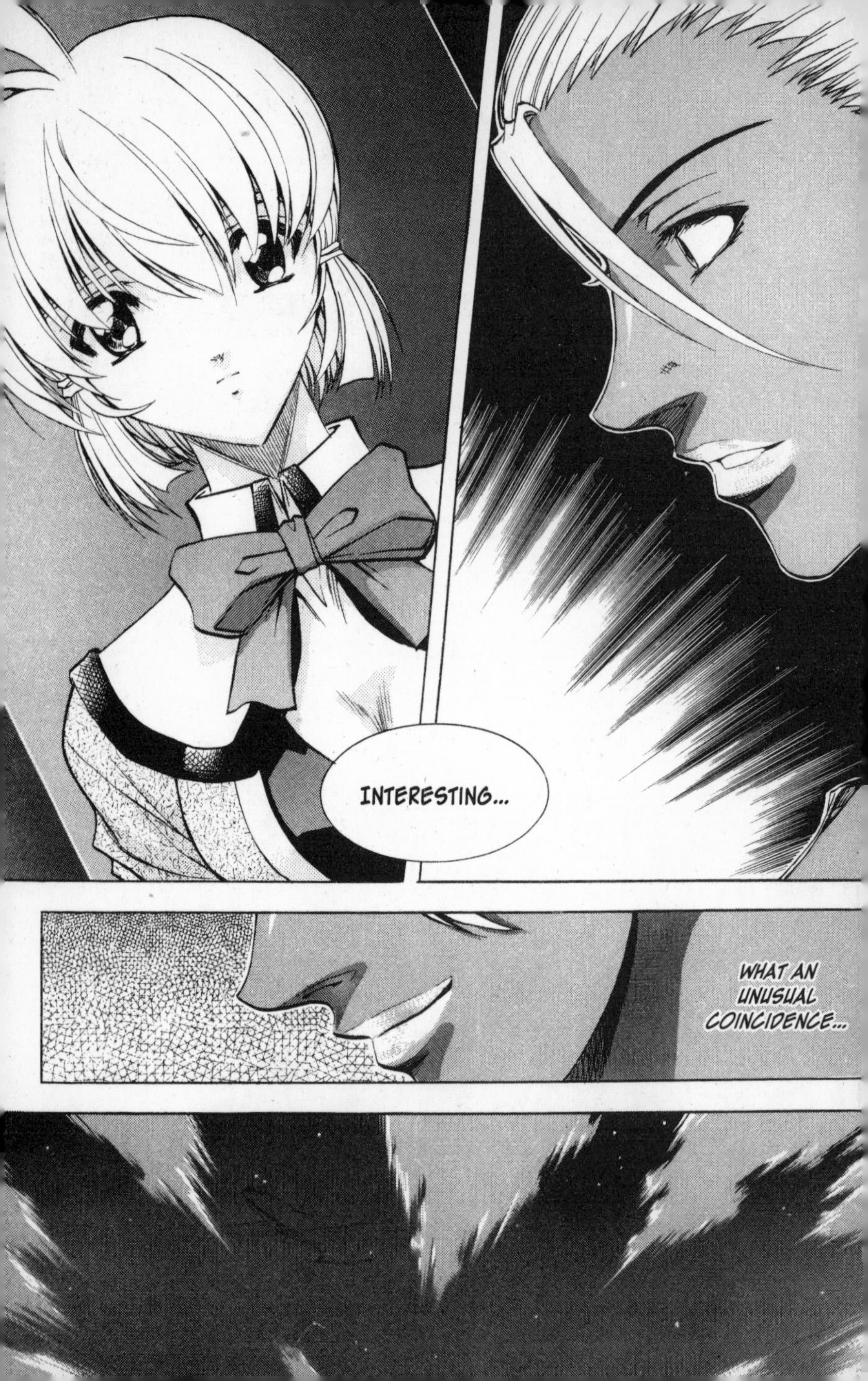
INTERESTING...
WHAT AN UNUSUAL COINCIDENCE...

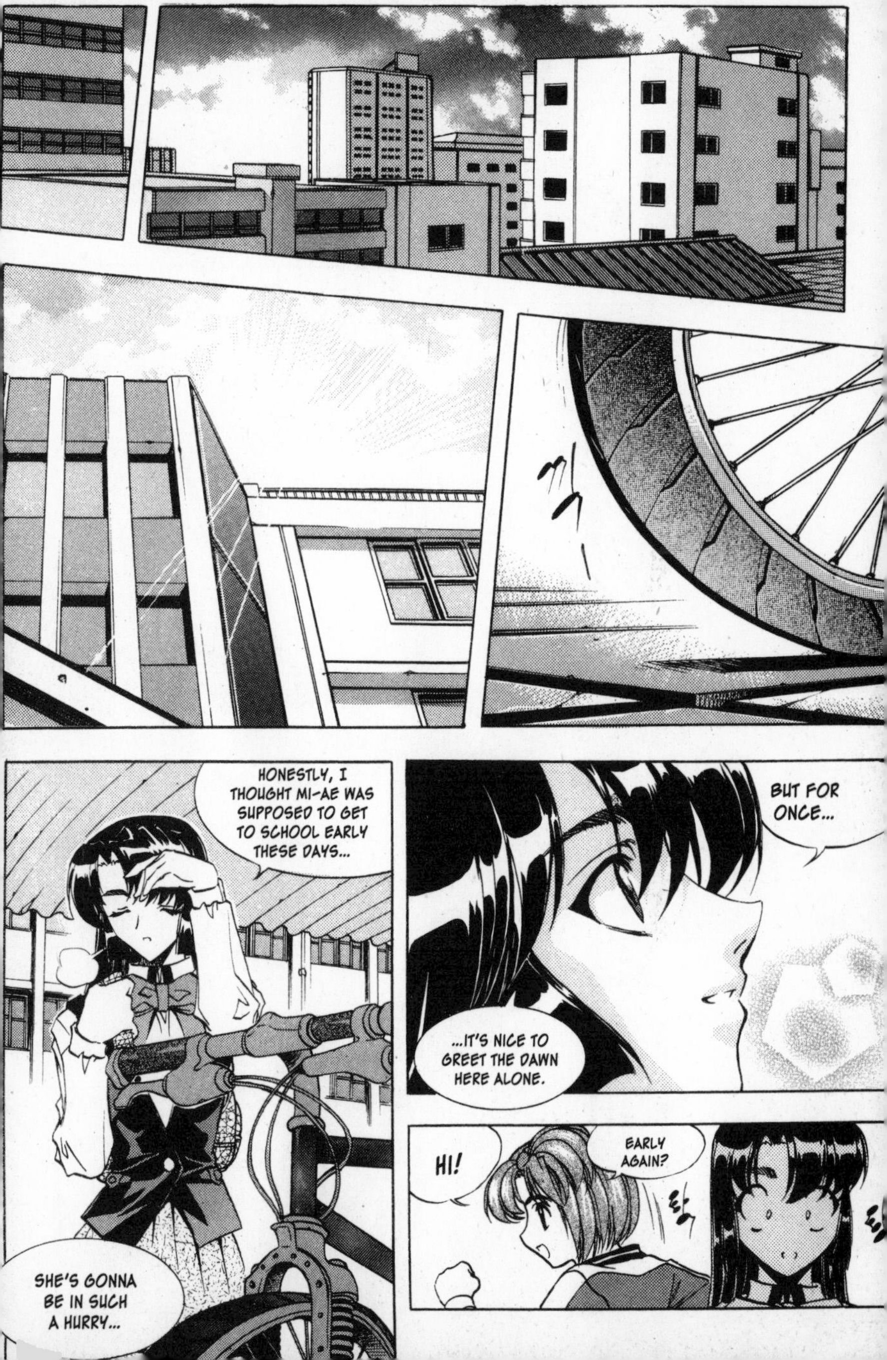
HONESTLY, I THOUGHT MI-AE WAS SUPPOSED TO GET TO SCHOOL EARLY THESE DAYS...
SHE'S GONNA BE IN SUCH A HURRY...
BUT FOR ONCE...
...IT'S NICE TO GREET THE DAWN HERE ALONE.
HI!
EARLY AGAIN?

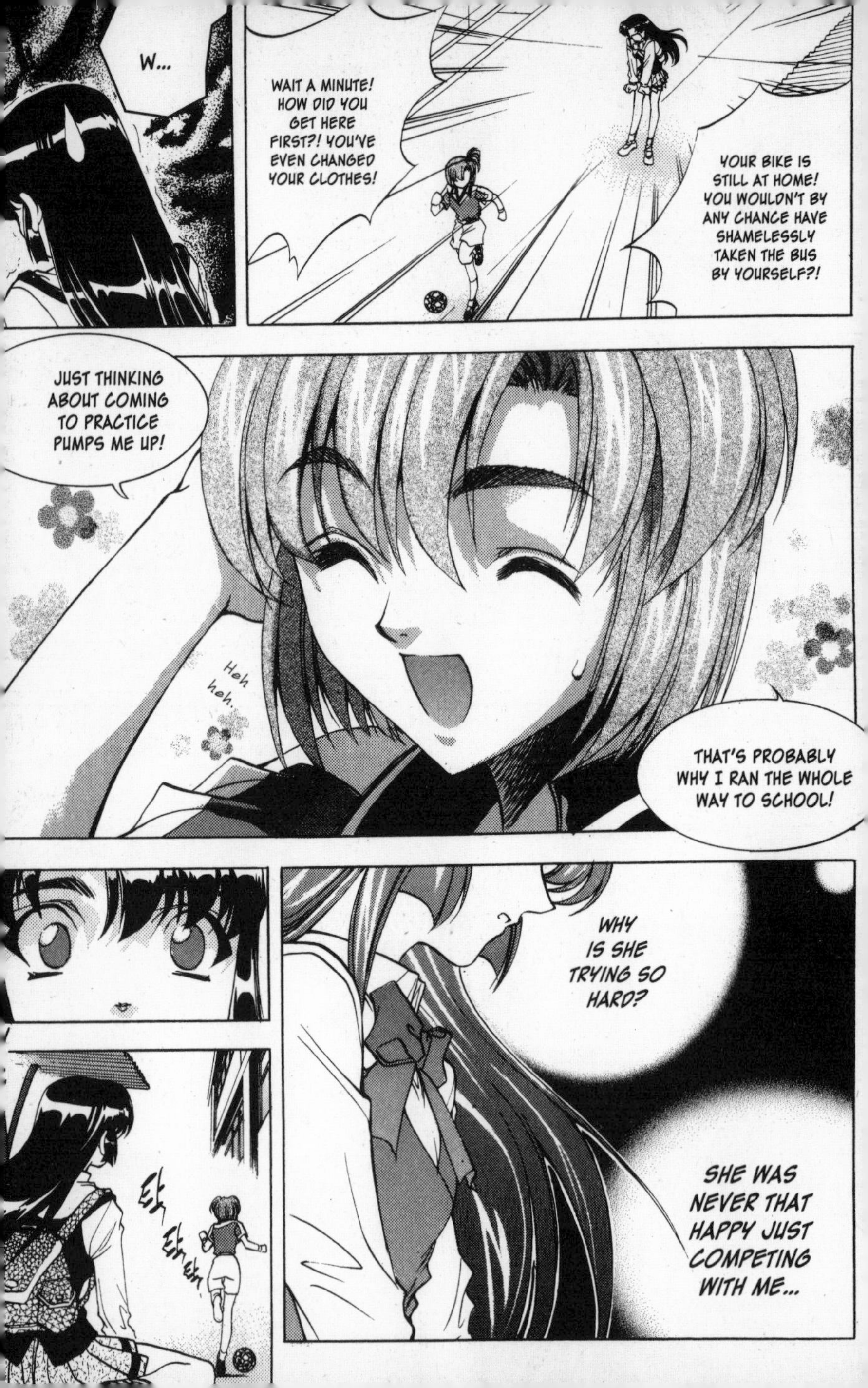
W...
WAIT A MINUTE! HOW DID YOU GET HERE FIRST?! YOU'VE EVEN CHANGED YOUR CLOTHES!
YOUR BIKE IS STILL AT HOME! YOU WOULDN'T BY ANY CHANCE HAVE SHAMELESSLY TAKEN THE BUS BY YOURSELF?!
JUST THINKING ABOUT COMING TO PRACTICE PUMPS ME UP!
Heh heh.
THAT'S PROBABLY WHY I RAN THE WHOLE WAY TO SCHOOL!
WHY IS SHE TRYING SO HARD?
SHE WAS NEVER THAT HAPPY JUST COMPETING WITH ME...

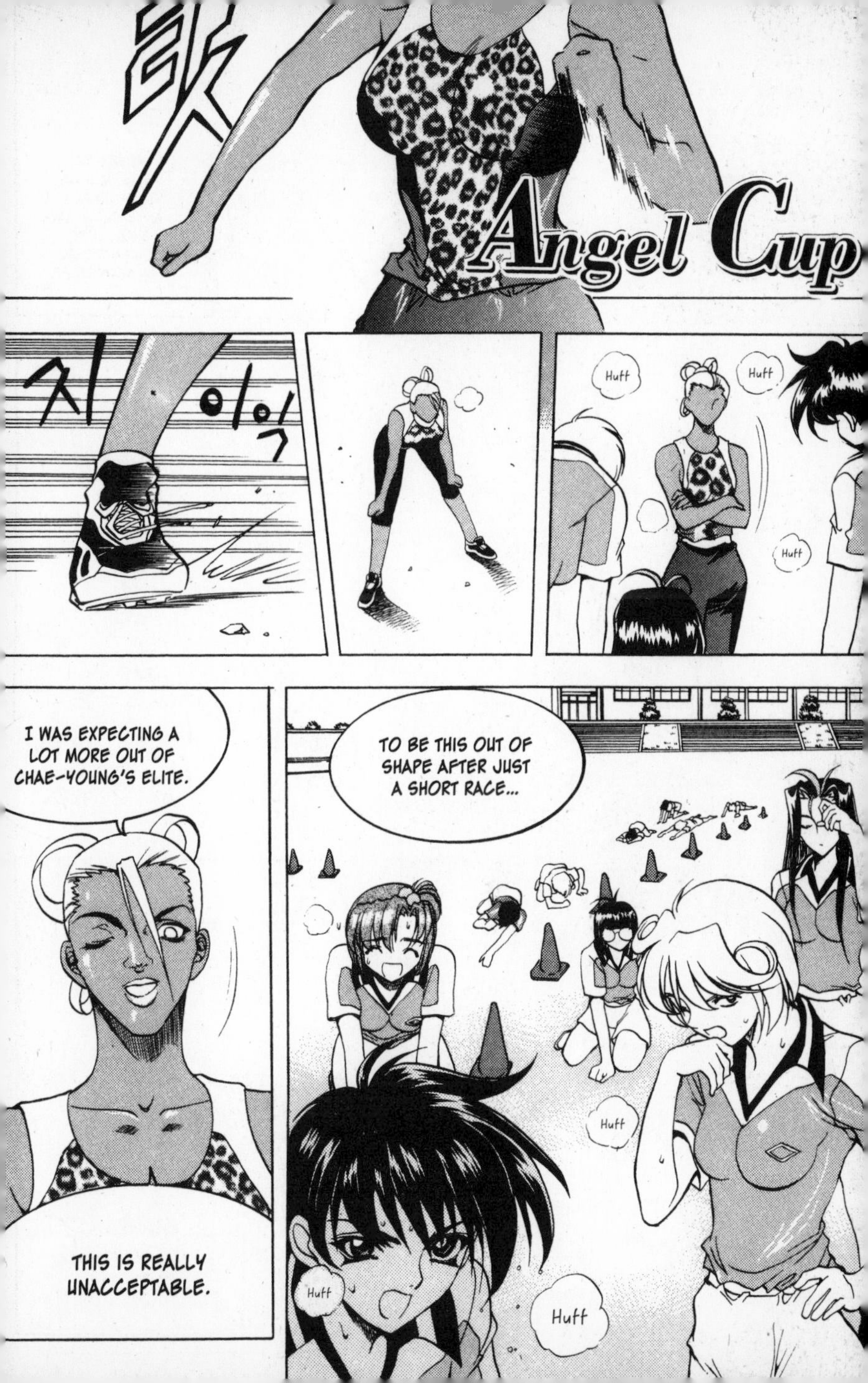
Angel Cup
지이익
Huff
Huff
Huff
I WAS EXPECTING A LOT MORE OUT OF CHAE-YOUNG'S ELITE.
THIS IS REALLY UNACCEPTABLE.
TO BE THIS OUT OF SHAPE AFTER JUST A SHORT RACE...
Huff
Huff
Huff

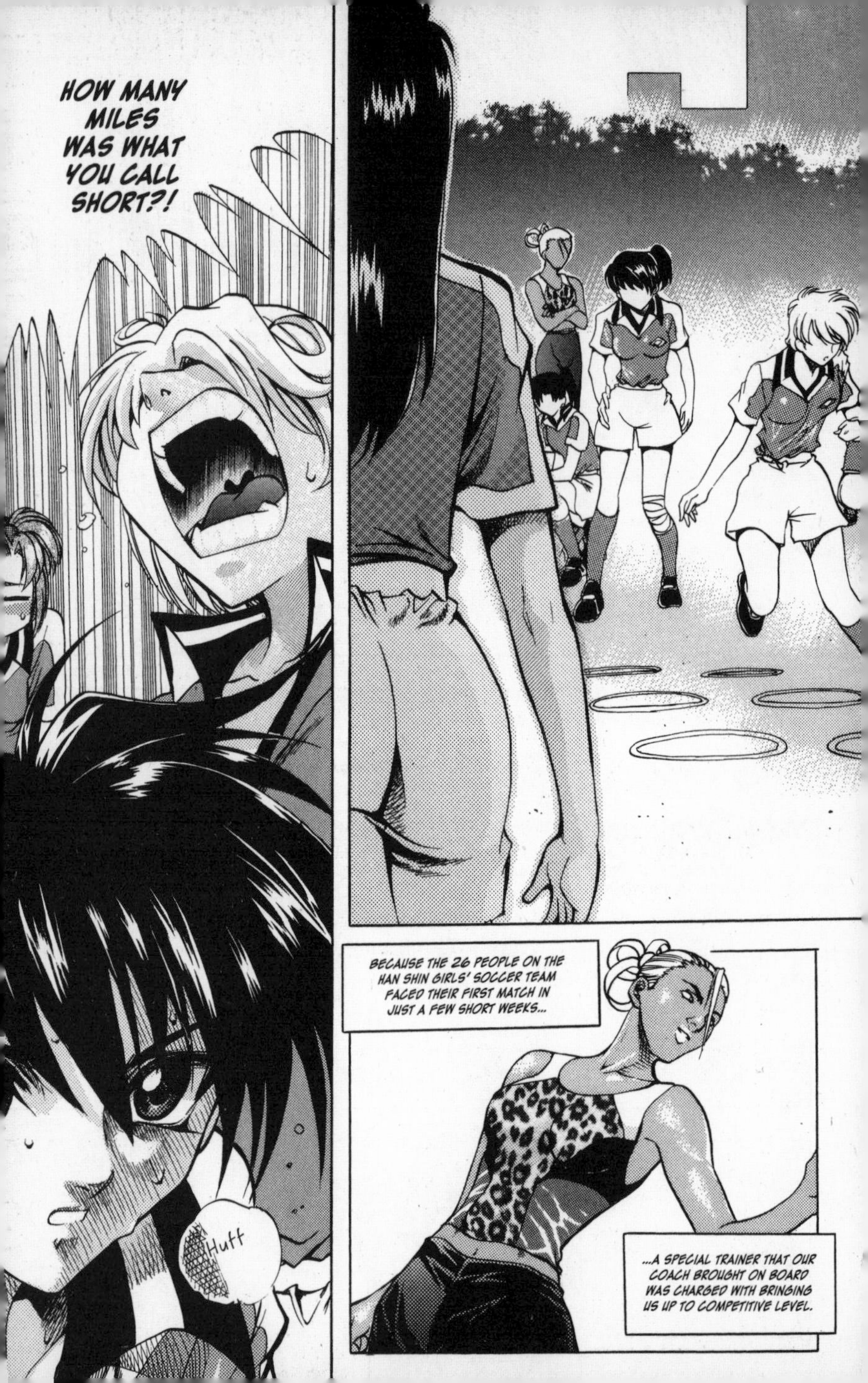
HOW MANY MILES WAS WHAT YOU CALL SHORT?!
Huff
BECAUSE THE 26 PEOPLE ON THE HAN SHIN GIRLS' SOCCER TEAM FACED THEIR FIRST MATCH IN JUST A FEW SHORT WEEKS...
...A SPECIAL TRAINER THAT OUR COACH BROUGHT ON BOARD WAS CHARGED WITH BRINGING US UP TO COMPETITIVE LEVEL.

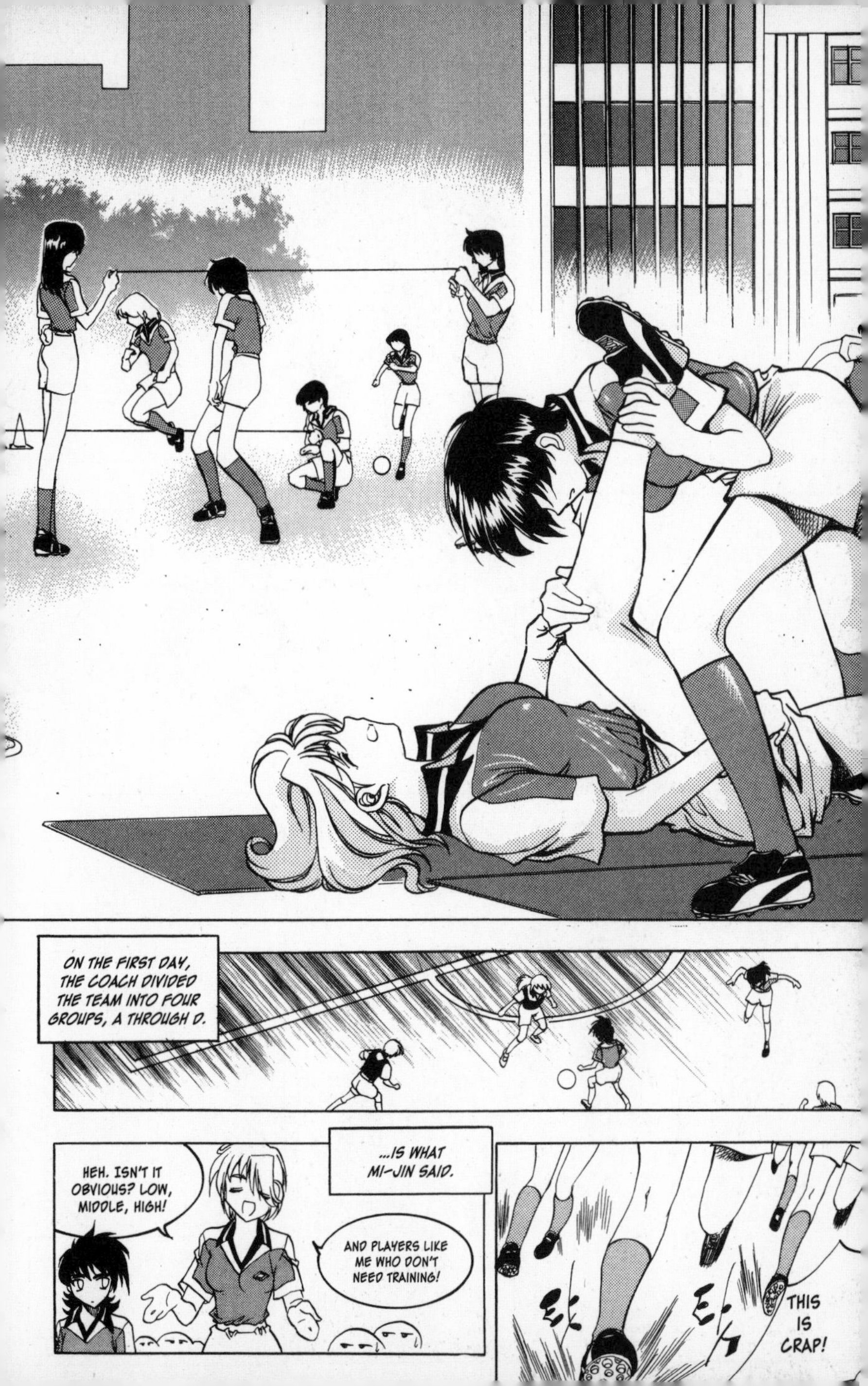
ON THE FIRST DAY, THE COACH DIVIDED THE TEAM INTO FOUR GROUPS, A THROUGH D.
HEH. ISN'T IT OBVIOUS? LOW, MIDDLE, HIGH!
AND PLAYERS LIKE ME WHO DON'T NEED TRAINING!
...IS WHAT MI-JIN SAID.
THIS IS CRAP!

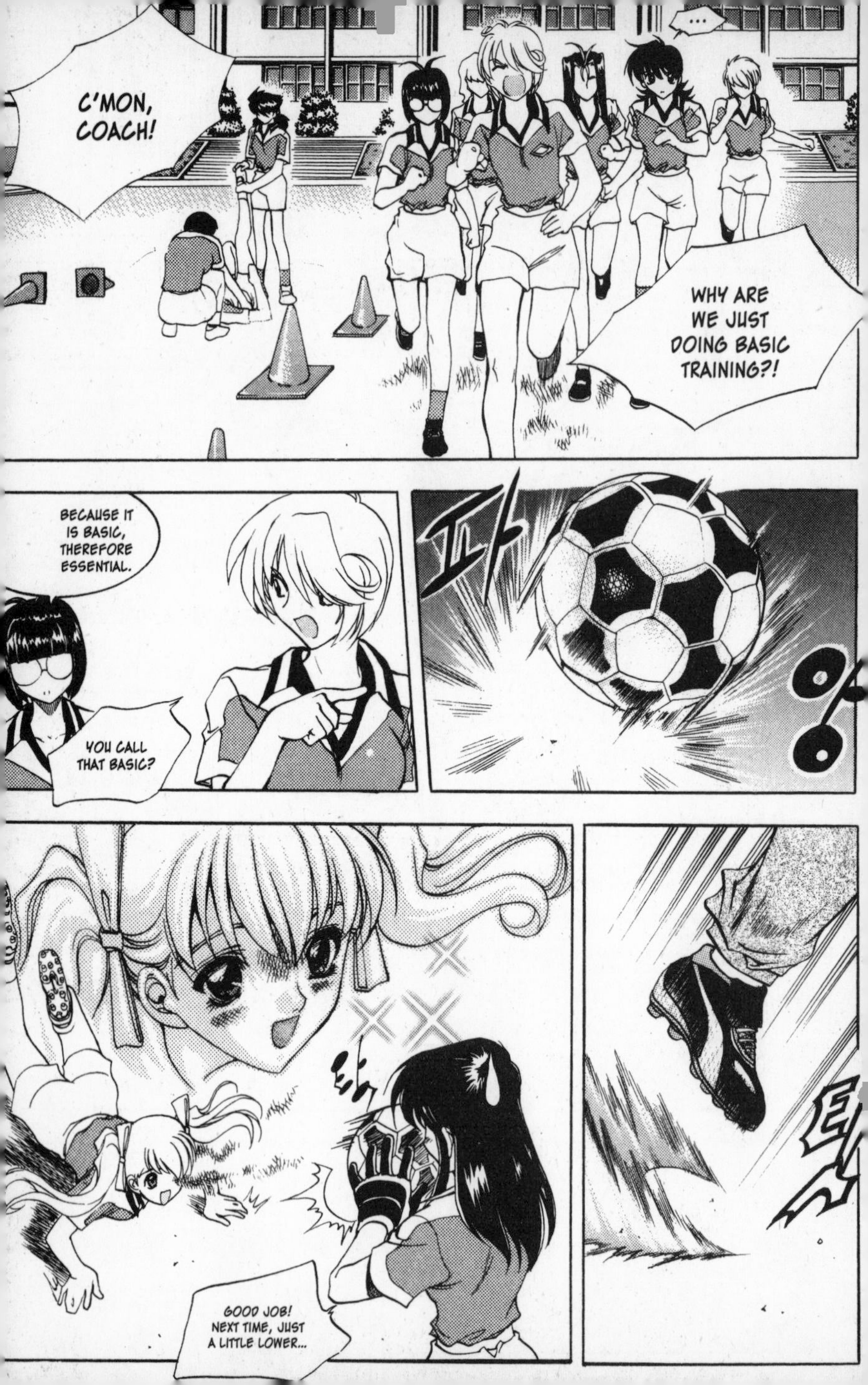
C'MON, COACH!
...
WHY ARE WE JUST DOING BASIC TRAINING?!
BECAUSE IT IS BASIC, THEREFORE ESSENTIAL.
YOU CALL THAT BASIC?
GOOD JOB! NEXT TIME, JUST A LITTLE LOWER...

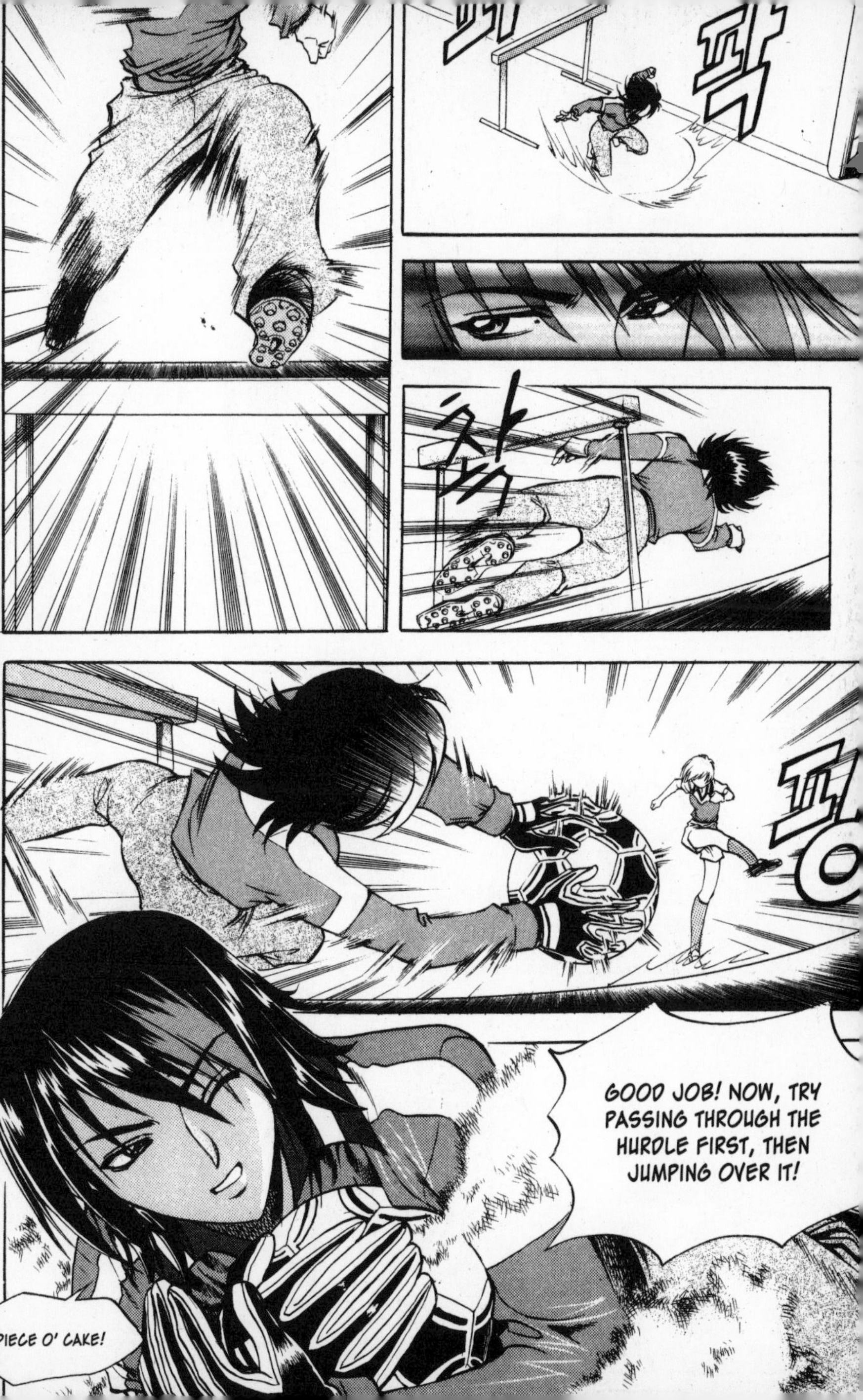
GOOD JOB! NOW, TRY PASSING THROUGH THE HURDLE FIRST, THEN JUMPING OVER IT!
PIECE O' CAKE!

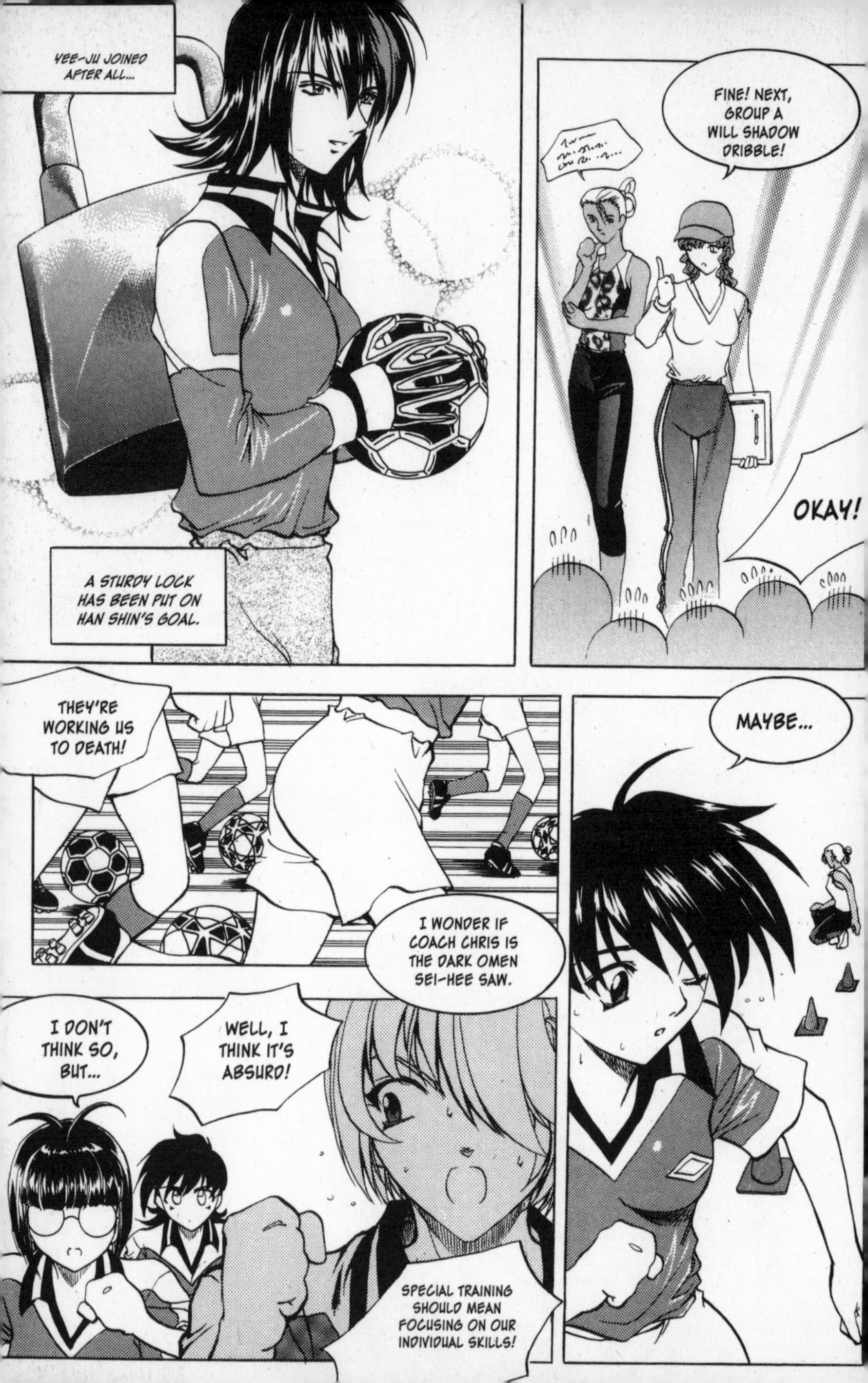
YEE-JU JOINED AFTER ALL...
A STURDY LOCK HAS BEEN PUT ON HAN SHIN'S GOAL.
FINE! NEXT, GROUP A WILL SHADOW DRIBBLE!
OKAY!
THEY'RE WORKING US TO DEATH!
I WONDER IF COACH CHRIS IS THE DARK OMEN SEI-HEE SAW.
I DON'T THINK SO, BUT...
WELL, I THINK IT'S ABSURD!
SPECIAL TRAINING SHOULD MEAN FOCUSING ON OUR INDIVIDUAL SKILLS!
MAYBE...

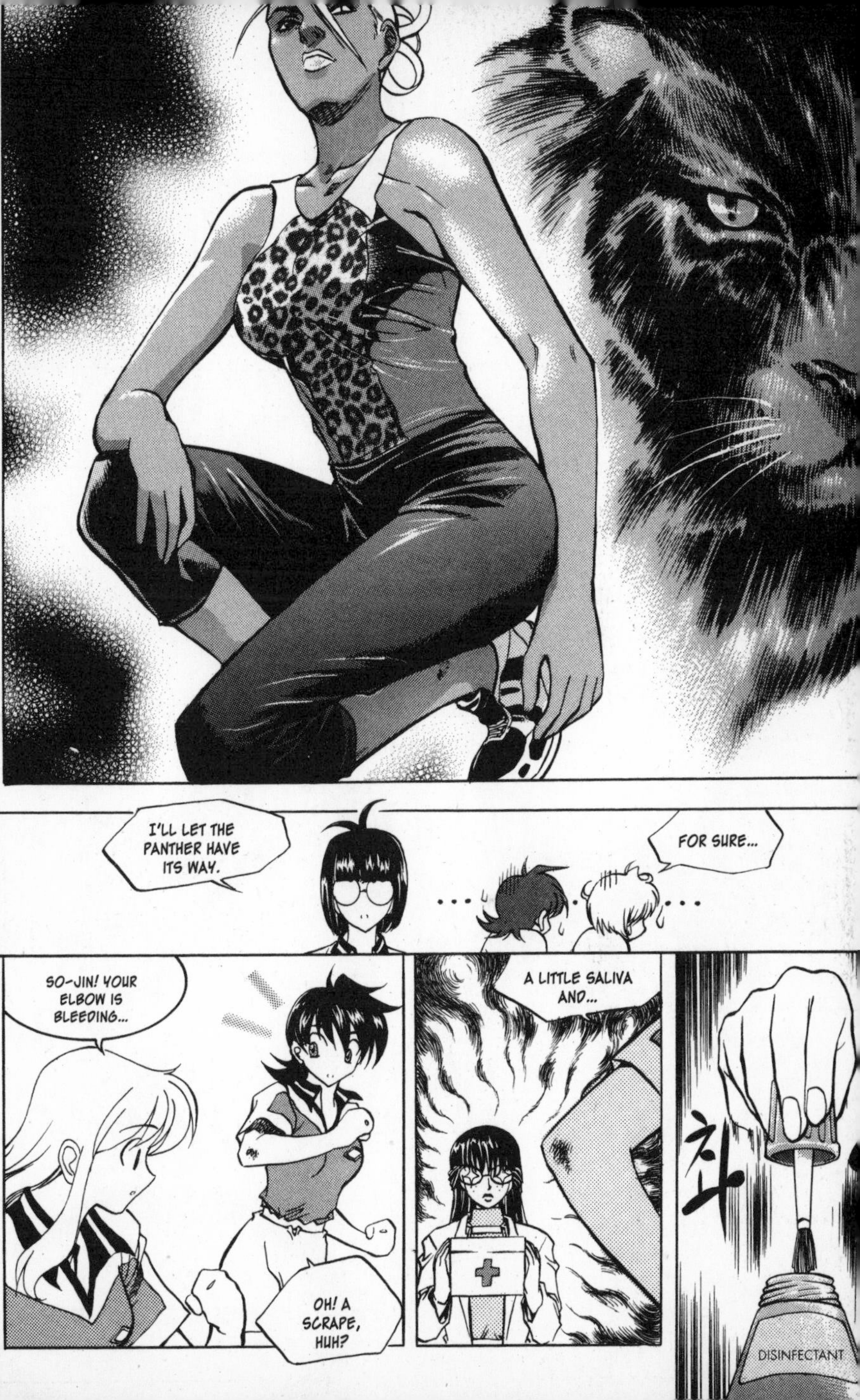
I'LL LET THE PANTHER HAVE ITS WAY.
. . . . . .
FOR SURE...
SO-JIN! YOUR ELBOW IS BLEEDING...
OH! A SCRAPE, HUH?
A LITTLE SALIVA AND...
촤
DISINFECTANT

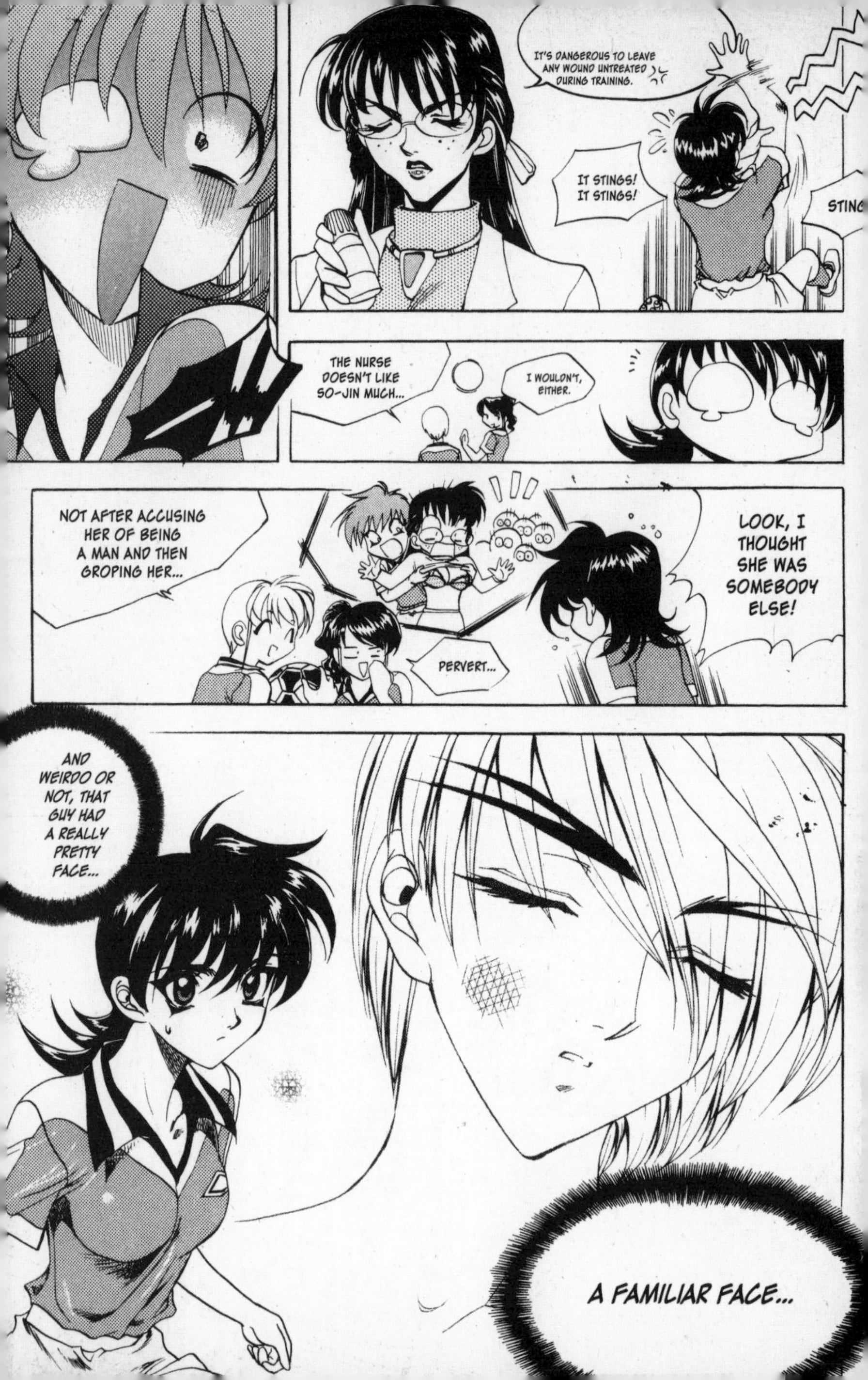
IT'S DANGEROUS TO LEAVE ANY WOUND UNTREATED DURING TRAINING.
IT STINGS! IT STINGS!
STING
THE NURSE DOESN'T LIKE SO-JIN MUCH...
I WOULDN'T, EITHER.
NOT AFTER ACCUSING HER OF BEING A MAN AND THEN GROPING HER...
PERVERT...
LOOK, I THOUGHT SHE WAS SOMEBODY ELSE!
AND WEIRDO OR NOT, THAT GUY HAD A REALLY PRETTY FACE...
A FAMILIAR FACE...

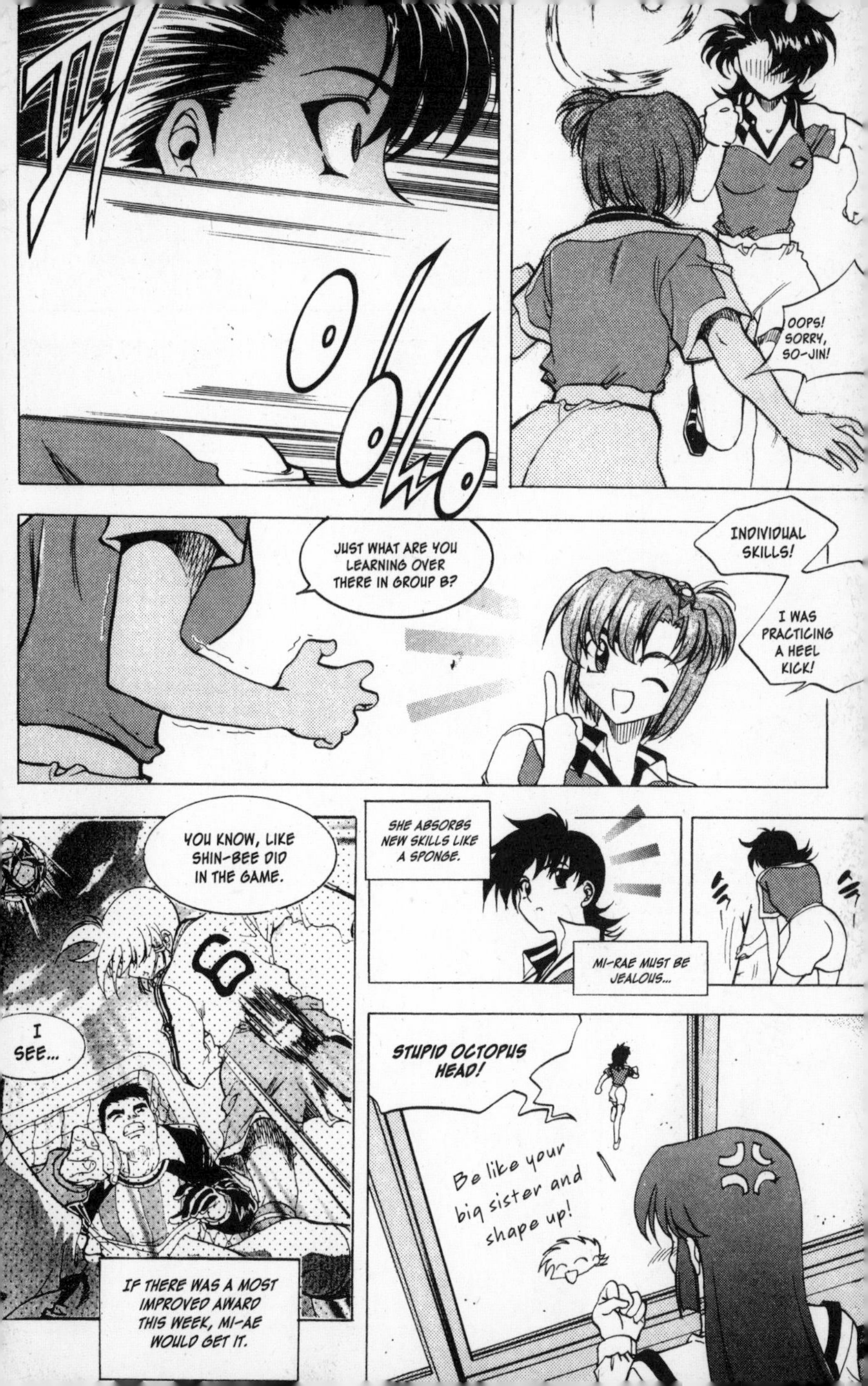
OOPS! SORRY, SO-JIN!
JUST WHAT ARE YOU LEARNING OVER THERE IN GROUP B?
INDIVIDUAL SKILLS!
I WAS PRACTICING A HEEL KICK!
YOU KNOW, LIKE SHIN-BEE DID IN THE GAME.
I SEE...
IF THERE WAS A MOST IMPROVED AWARD THIS WEEK, MI-AE WOULD GET IT.
SHE ABSORBS NEW SKILLS LIKE A SPONGE.
MI-RAE MUST BE JEALOUS...
STUPID OCTOPUS HEAD!
Be like your big sister and shape up!

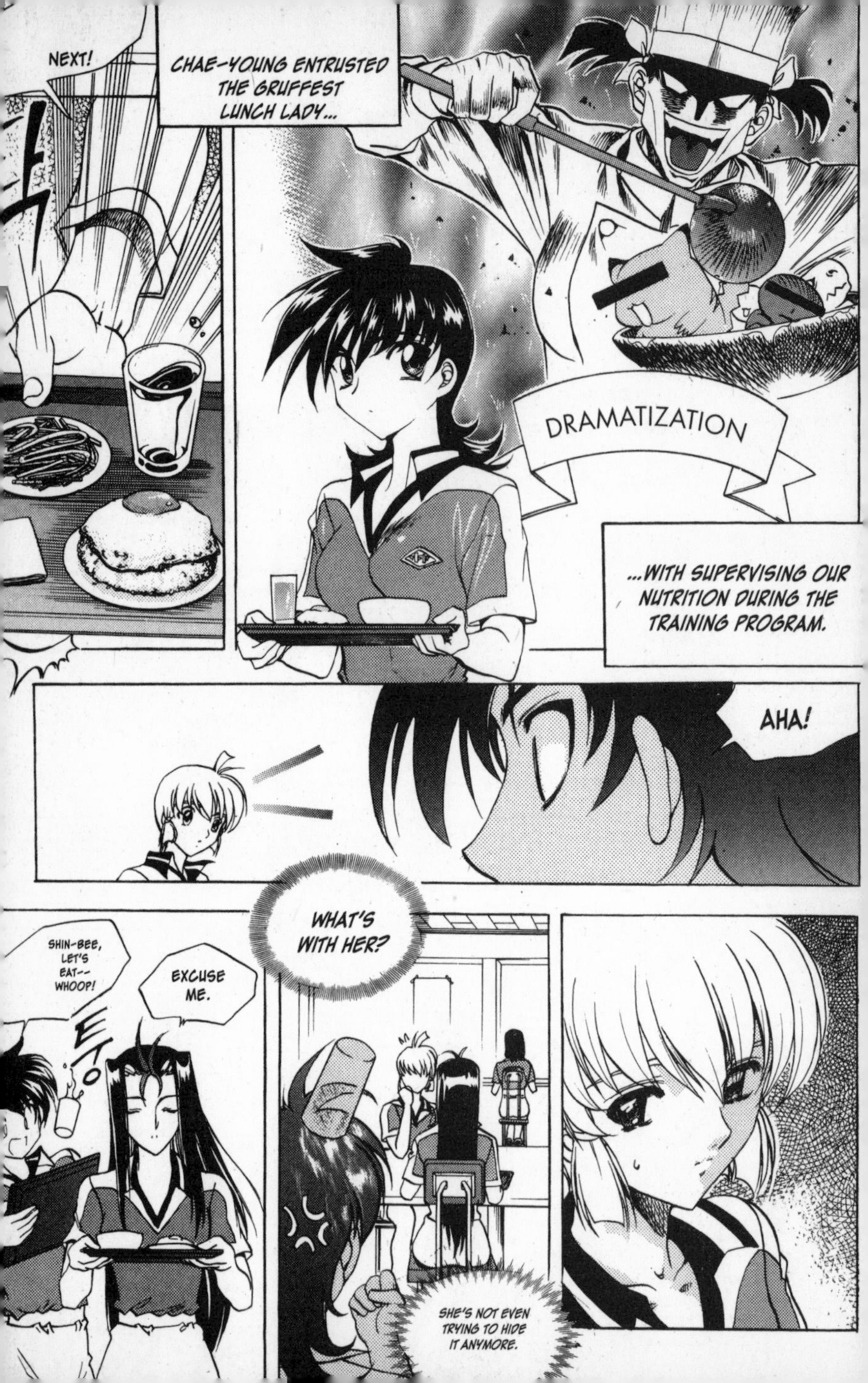
NEXT!
CHAE-YOUNG ENTRUSTED THE GRUFFEST LUNCH LADY...
DRAMATIZATION
...WITH SUPERVISING OUR NUTRITION DURING THE TRAINING PROGRAM.
AHA!
SHIN-BEE, LET'S EAT-- WHOOP!
EXCUSE ME.
WHAT'S WITH HER?
SHE'S NOT EVEN TRYING TO HIDE IT ANYMORE.

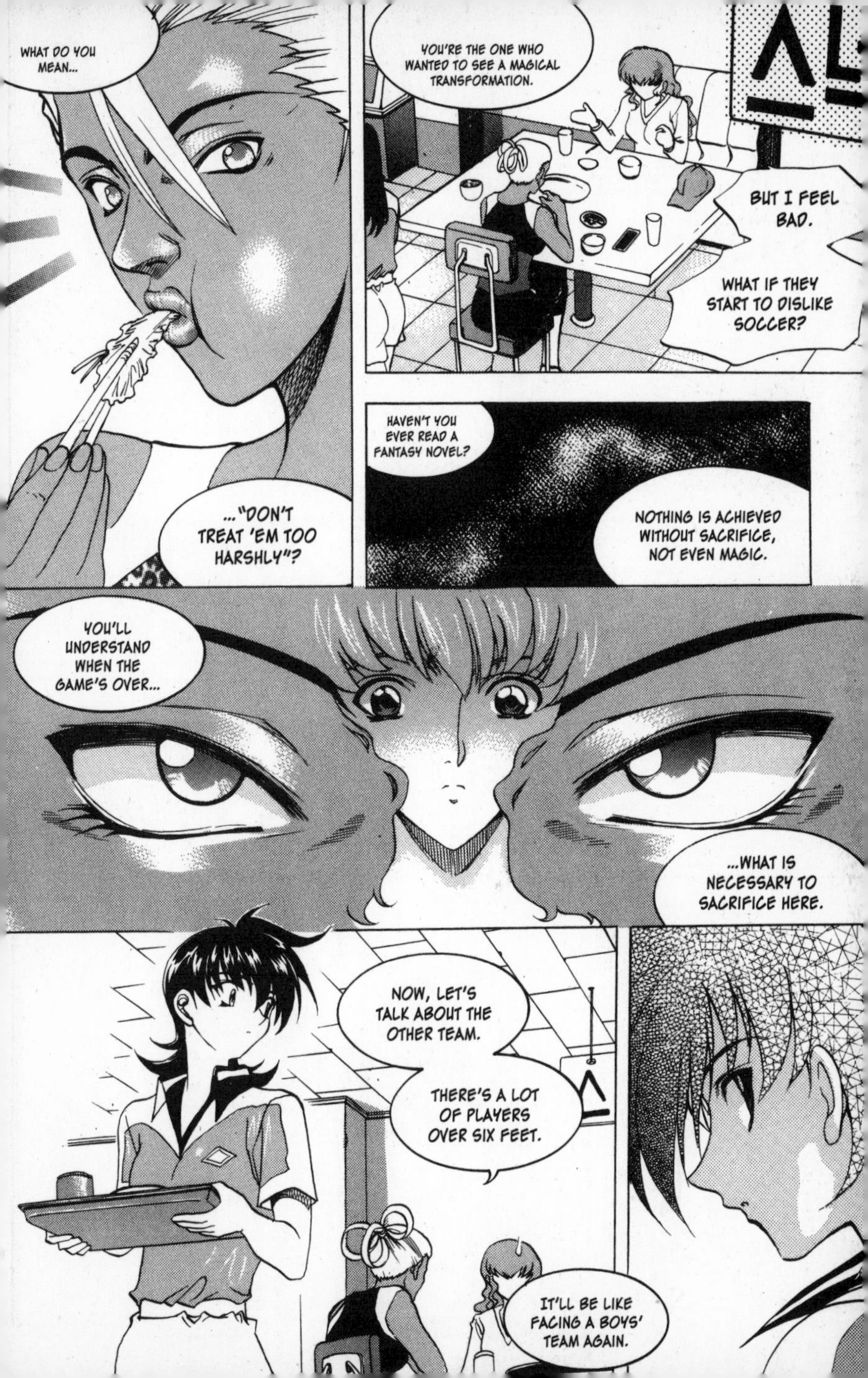
WHAT DO YOU MEAN...
..."DON'T TREAT 'EM TOO HARSHLY"?
YOU'RE THE ONE WHO WANTED TO SEE A MAGICAL TRANSFORMATION.
BUT I FEEL BAD.
WHAT IF THEY START TO DISLIKE SOCCER?
HAVEN'T YOU EVER READ A FANTASY NOVEL?
NOTHING IS ACHIEVED WITHOUT SACRIFICE, NOT EVEN MAGIC.
YOU'LL UNDERSTAND WHEN THE GAME'S OVER...
...WHAT IS NECESSARY TO SACRIFICE HERE.
NOW, LET'S TALK ABOUT THE OTHER TEAM.
THERE'S A LOT OF PLAYERS OVER SIX FEET.
IT'LL BE LIKE FACING A BOYS' TEAM AGAIN.

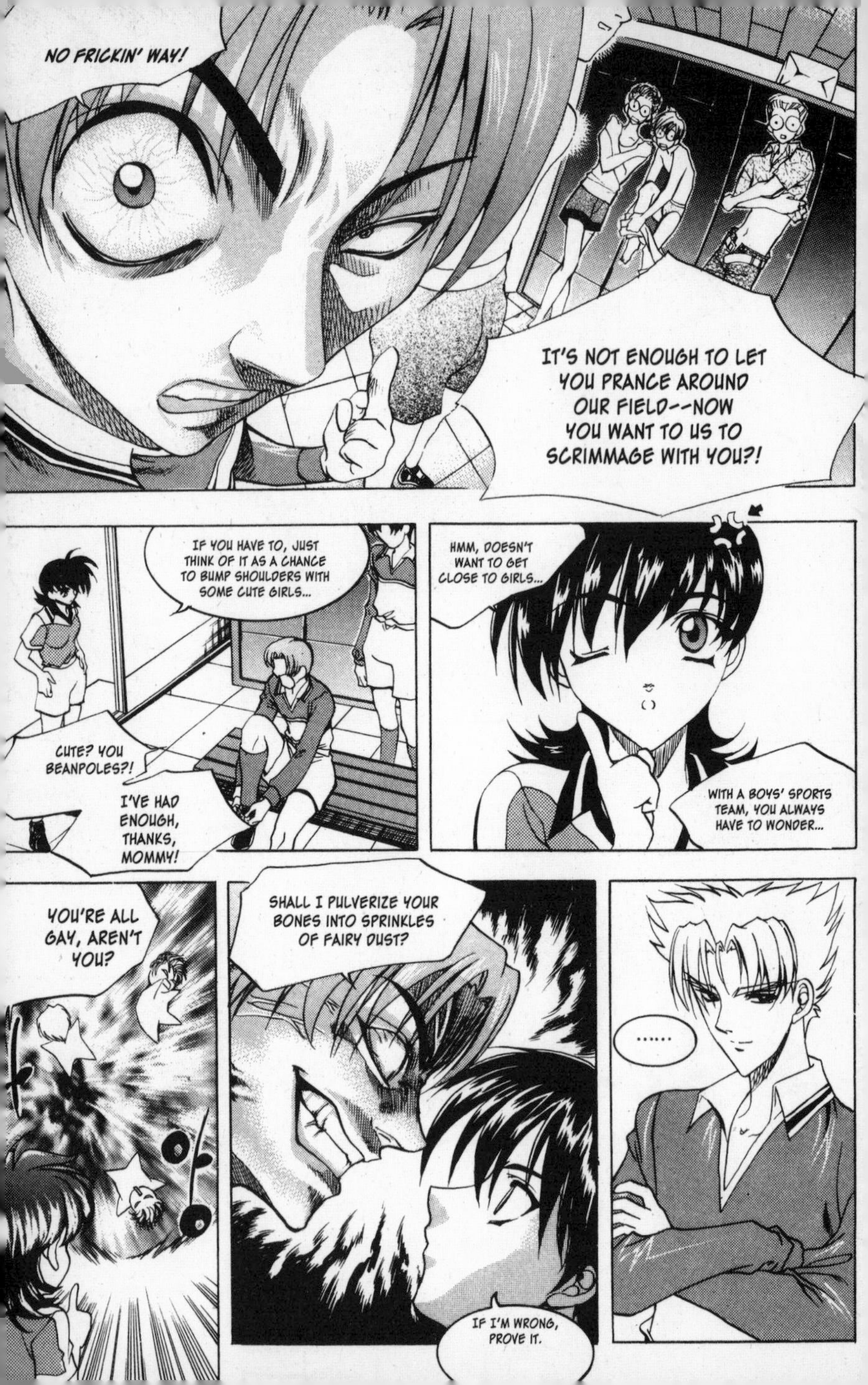
NO FRICKIN' WAY!
IT'S NOT ENOUGH TO LET YOU PRANCE AROUND OUR FIELD--NOW YOU WANT TO US TO SCRIMMAGE WITH YOU?!
IF YOU HAVE TO, JUST THINK OF IT AS A CHANCE TO BUMP SHOULDERS WITH SOME CUTE GIRLS...
CUTE? YOU BEANPOLES?!
I'VE HAD ENOUGH, THANKS, MOMMY!
HMM, DOESN'T WANT TO GET CLOSE TO GIRLS...
WITH A BOYS' SPORTS TEAM, YOU ALWAYS HAVE TO WONDER...
YOU'RE ALL GAY, AREN'T YOU?
SHALL I PULVERIZE YOUR BONES INTO SPRINKLES OF FAIRY DUST?
IF I'M WRONG, PROVE IT.
......

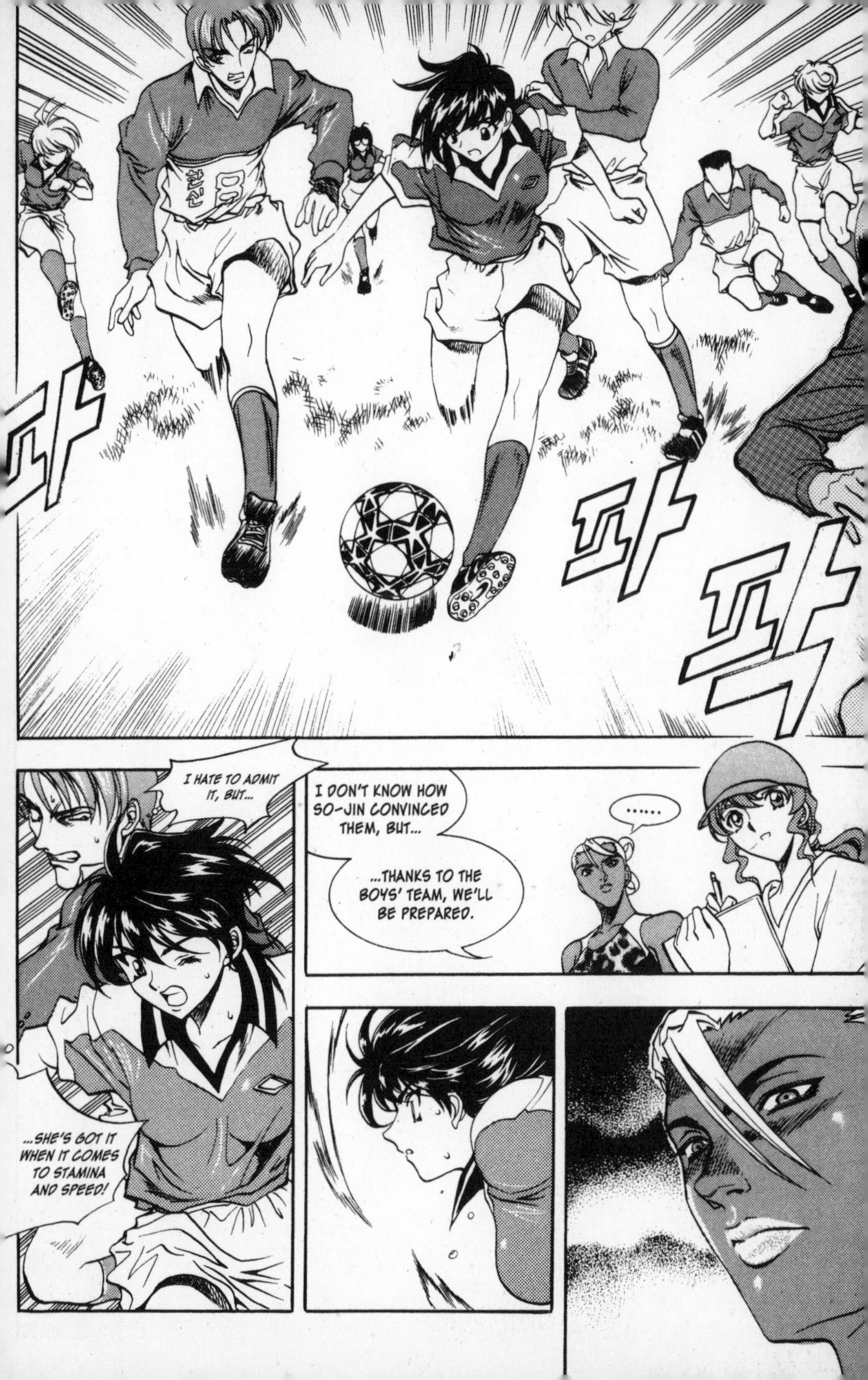
I HATE TO ADMIT IT, BUT...
...SHE'S GOT IT WHEN IT COMES TO STAMINA AND SPEED!
I DON'T KNOW HOW SO-JIN CONVINCED THEM, BUT...
...THANKS TO THE BOYS' TEAM, WE'LL BE PREPARED.
......

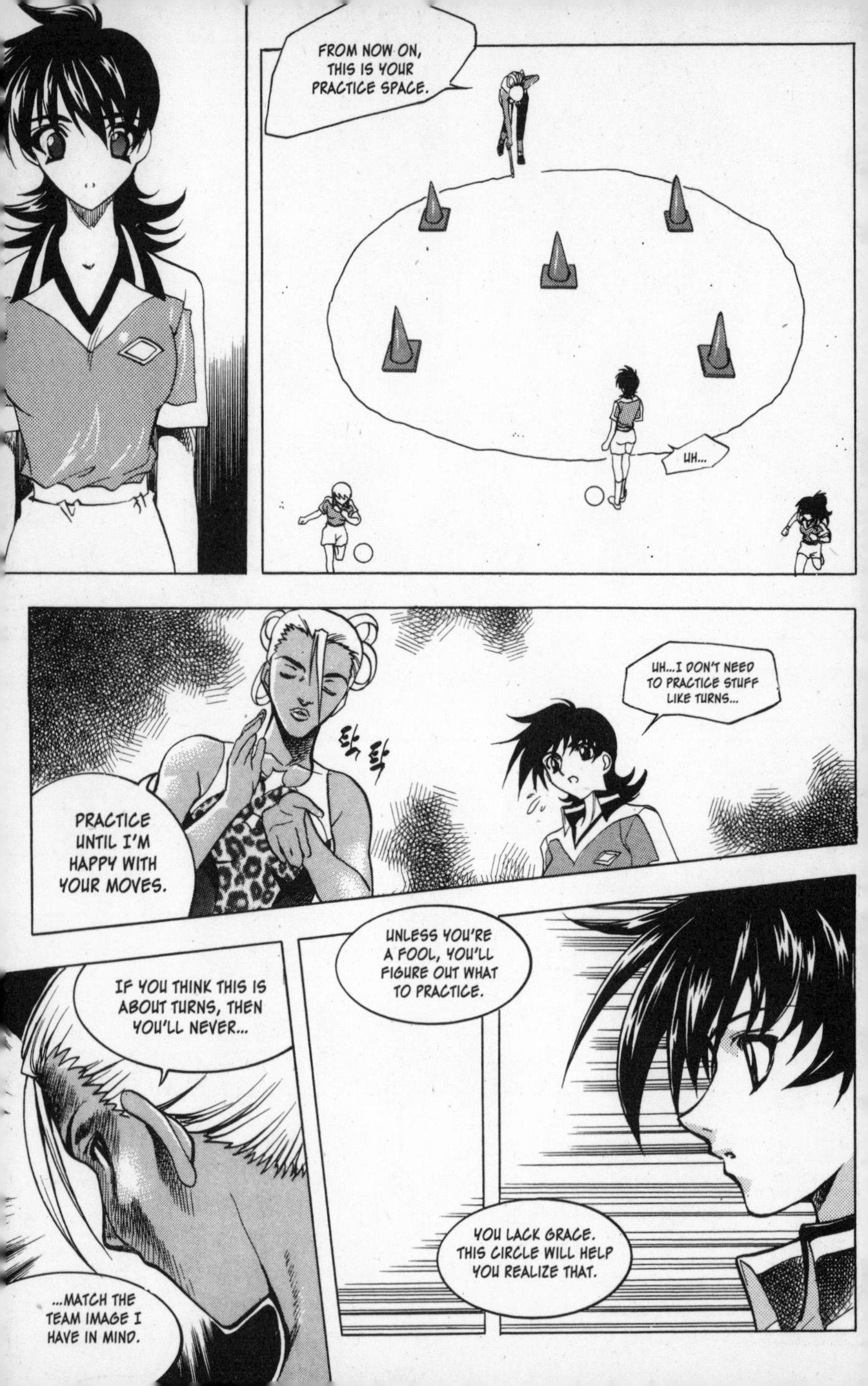
FROM NOW ON, THIS IS YOUR PRACTICE SPACE.
UH...
PRACTICE UNTIL I'M HAPPY WITH YOUR MOVES.
탁 탁
UH...I DON'T NEED TO PRACTICE STUFF LIKE TURNS...
IF YOU THINK THIS IS ABOUT TURNS, THEN YOU'LL NEVER...
...MATCH THE TEAM IMAGE I HAVE IN MIND.
UNLESS YOU'RE A FOOL, YOU'LL FIGURE OUT WHAT TO PRACTICE.
YOU LACK GRACE. THIS CIRCLE WILL HELP YOU REALIZE THAT.

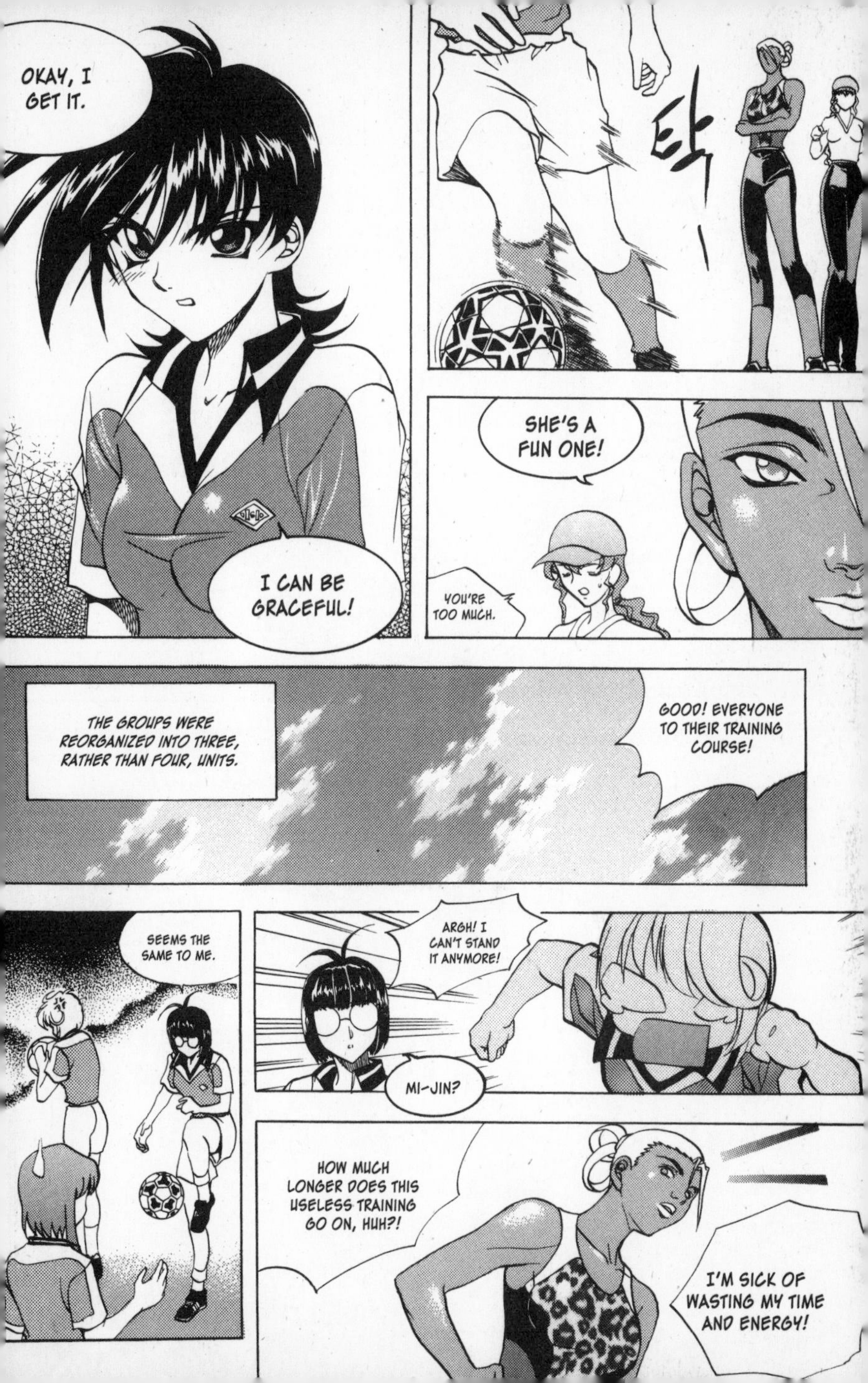
OKAY, I GET IT.
I CAN BE GRACEFUL!
탁
SHE'S A FUN ONE!
YOU'RE TOO MUCH.
THE GROUPS WERE REORGANIZED INTO THREE, RATHER THAN FOUR, UNITS.
GOOD! EVERYONE TO THEIR TRAINING COURSE!
SEEMS THE SAME TO ME.
ARGH! I CAN'T STAND IT ANYMORE!
MI-JIN?
HOW MUCH LONGER DOES THIS USELESS TRAINING GO ON, HUH?!
I'M SICK OF WASTING MY TIME AND ENERGY!

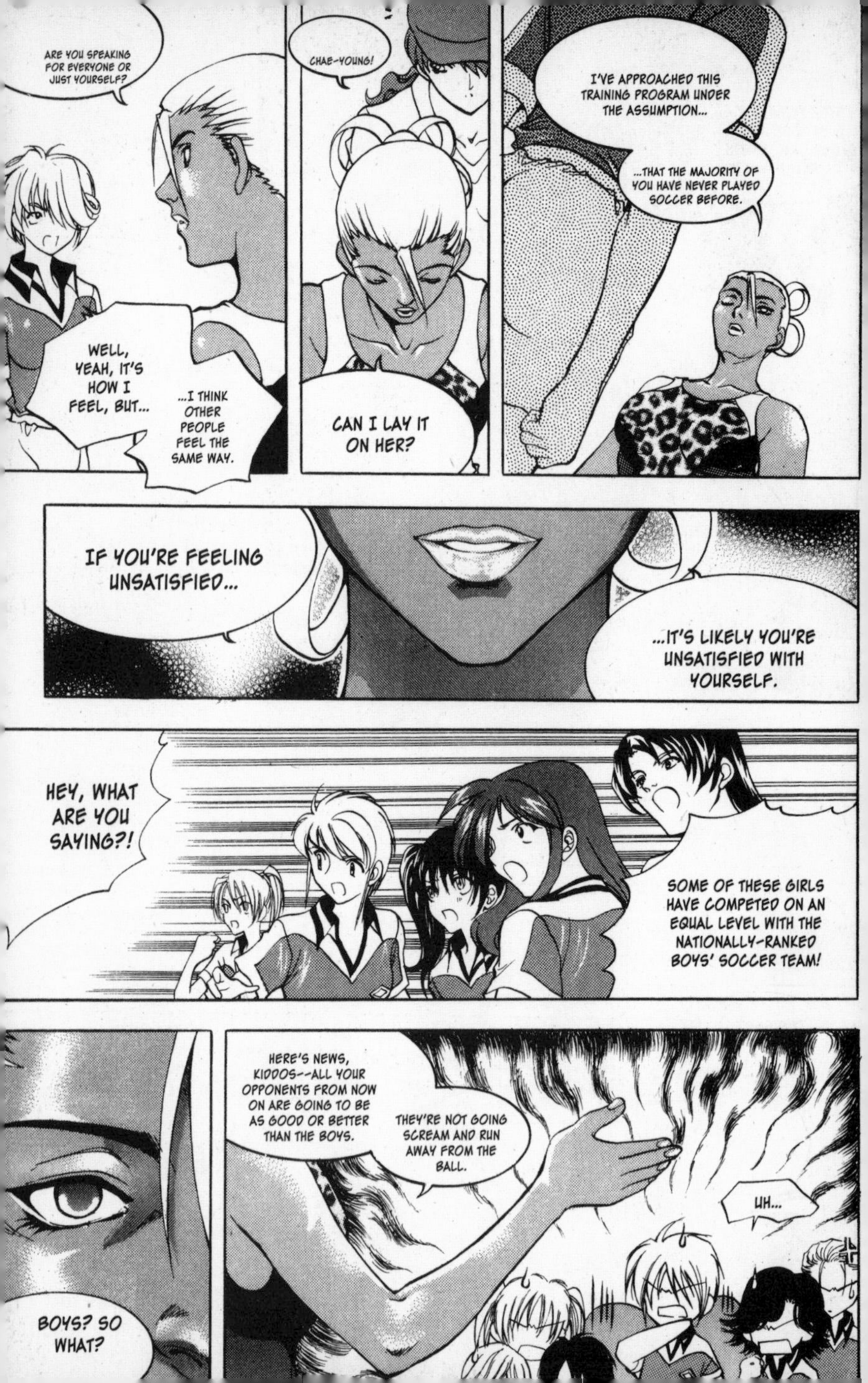

ARE YOU SPEAKING FOR EVERYONE OR JUST YOURSELF?
WELL, YEAH, IT'S HOW I FEEL, BUT...
...I THINK OTHER PEOPLE FEEL THE SAME WAY.
CHAE-YOUNG!
CAN I LAY IT ON HER?
I'VE APPROACHED THIS TRAINING PROGRAM UNDER THE ASSUMPTION...
...THAT THE MAJORITY OF YOU HAVE NEVER PLAYED SOCCER BEFORE.
IF YOU'RE FEELING UNSATISFIED...
...IT'S LIKELY YOU'RE UNSATISFIED WITH YOURSELF.
HEY, WHAT ARE YOU SAYING?!
SOME OF THESE GIRLS HAVE COMPETED ON AN EQUAL LEVEL WITH THE NATIONALLY-RANKED BOYS' SOCCER TEAM!
BOYS? SO WHAT?
HERE'S NEWS, KIDDOS--ALL YOUR OPPONENTS FROM NOW ON ARE GOING TO BE AS GOOD OR BETTER THAN THE BOYS.
THEY'RE NOT GOING SCREAM AND RUN AWAY FROM THE BALL.
UH...

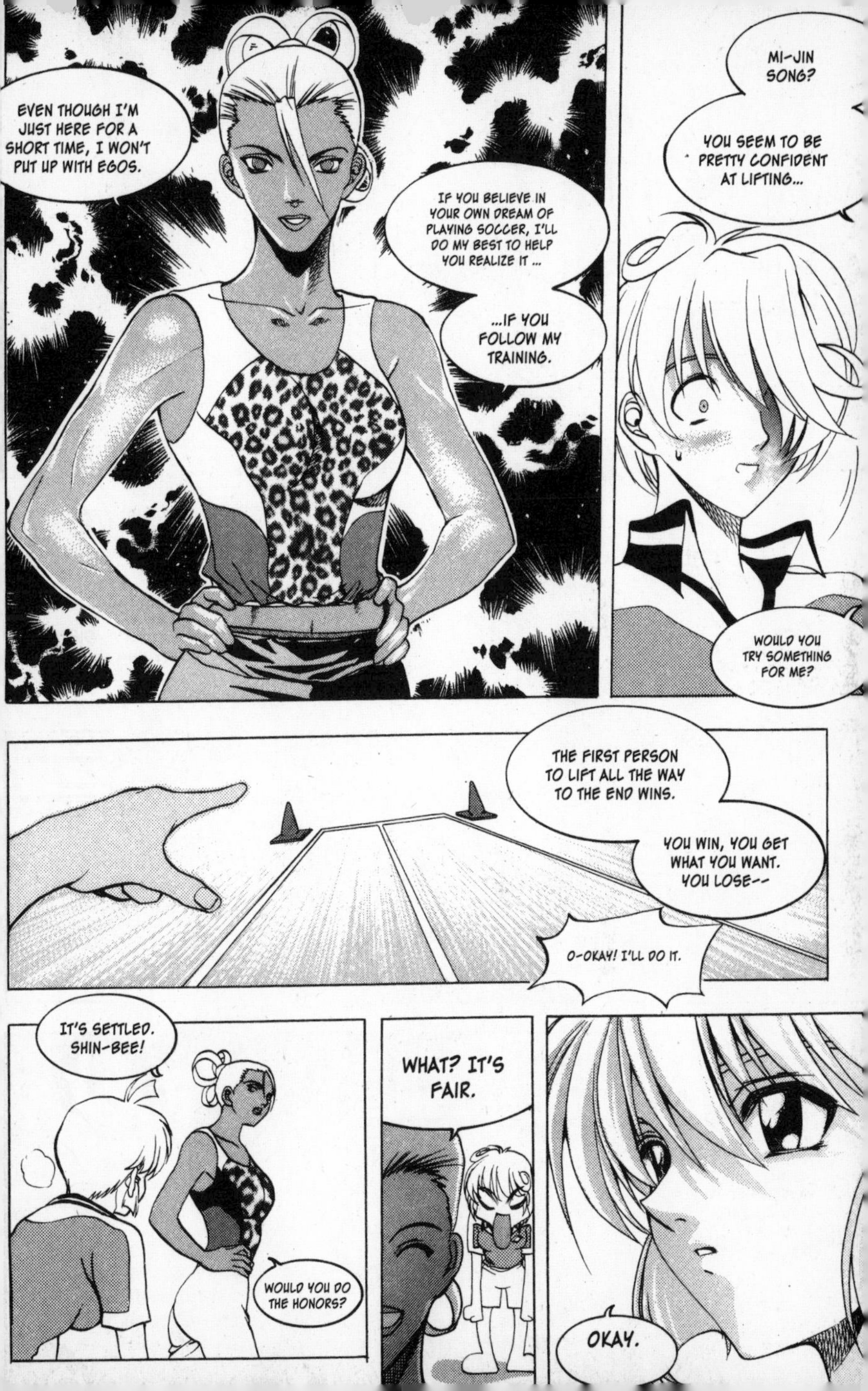

EVEN THOUGH I'M JUST HERE FOR A SHORT TIME, I WON'T PUT UP WITH EGOS.
IF YOU BELIEVE IN YOUR OWN DREAM OF PLAYING SOCCER, I'LL DO MY BEST TO HELP YOU REALIZE IT ...
...IF YOU FOLLOW MY TRAINING.
MI-JIN SONG?
YOU SEEM TO BE PRETTY CONFIDENT AT LIFTING...
WOULD YOU TRY SOMETHING FOR ME?
THE FIRST PERSON TO LIFT ALL THE WAY TO THE END WINS.
YOU WIN, YOU GET WHAT YOU WANT. YOU LOSE--
O-OKAY! I'LL DO IT.
IT'S SETTLED. SHIN-BEE!
WOULD YOU DO THE HONORS?
WHAT? IT'S FAIR.
OKAY.

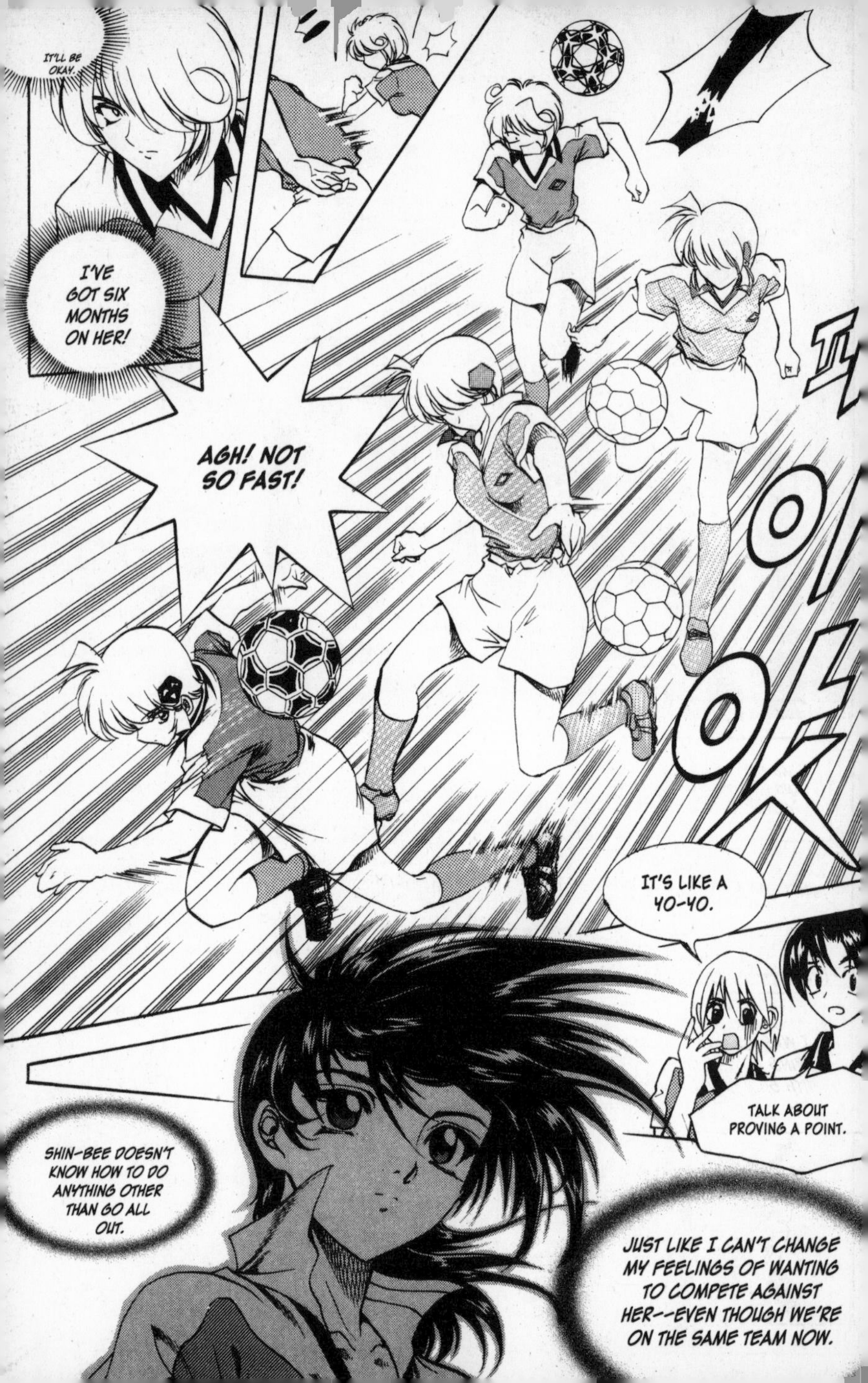
IT'LL BE OKAY.
I'VE GOT SIX MONTHS ON HER!
!
AGH! NOT SO FAST!
IT'S LIKE A YO-YO.
TALK ABOUT PROVING A POINT.
SHIN-BEE DOESN'T KNOW HOW TO DO ANYTHING OTHER THAN GO ALL OUT.
JUST LIKE I CAN'T CHANGE MY FEELINGS OF WANTING TO COMPETE AGAINST HER--EVEN THOUGH WE'RE ON THE SAME TEAM NOW.

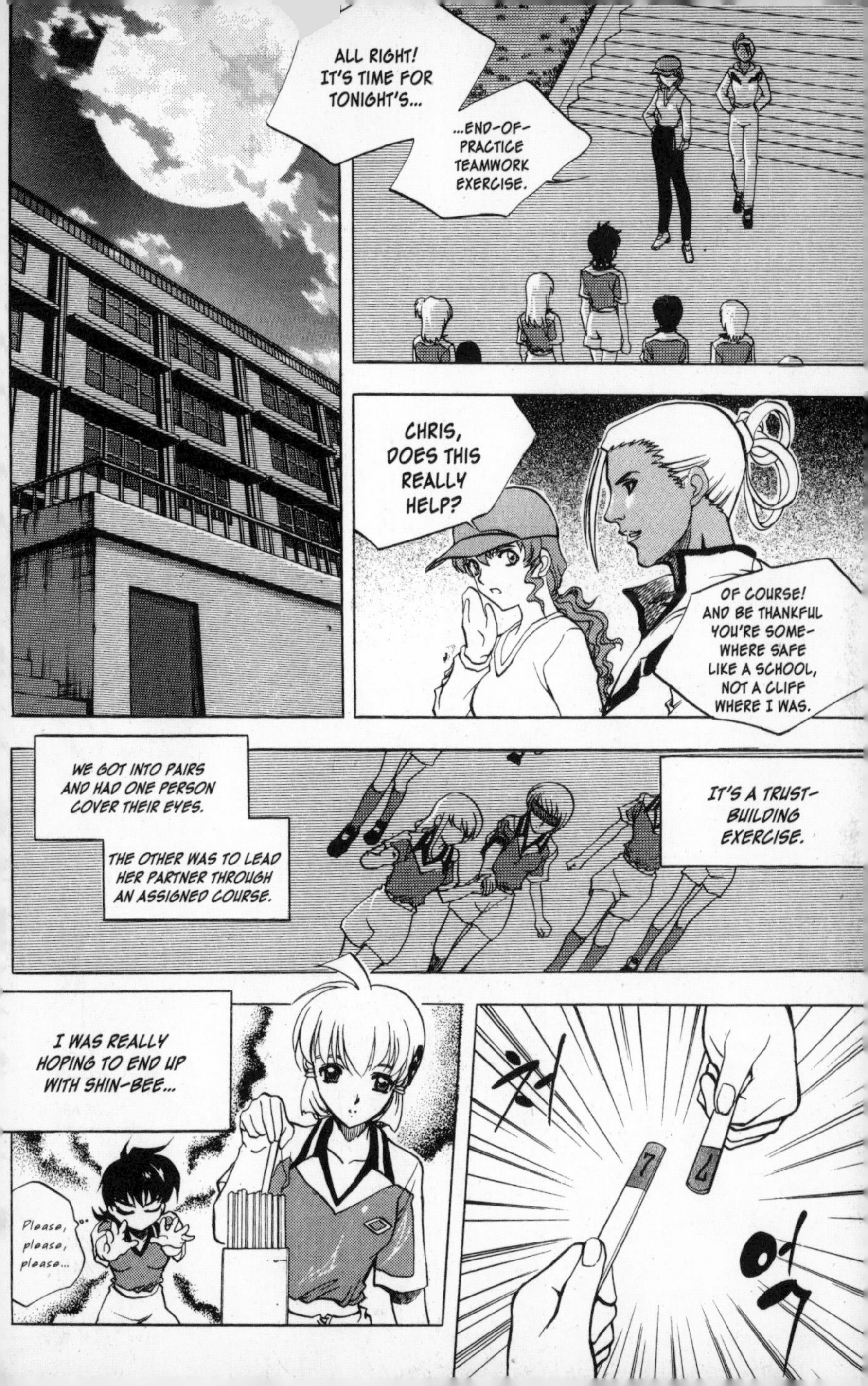
ALL RIGHT! IT'S TIME FOR TONIGHT'S...
...END-OF-PRACTICE TEAMWORK EXERCISE.
CHRIS, DOES THIS REALLY HELP?
OF COURSE! AND BE THANKFUL YOU'RE SOME-WHERE SAFE LIKE A SCHOOL, NOT A CLIFF WHERE I WAS.
WE GOT INTO PAIRS AND HAD ONE PERSON COVER THEIR EYES.
THE OTHER WAS TO LEAD HER PARTNER THROUGH AN ASSIGNED COURSE.
IT'S A TRUST-BUILDING EXERCISE.
I WAS REALLY HOPING TO END UP WITH SHIN-BEE...
Please, please, please...
7
7
억

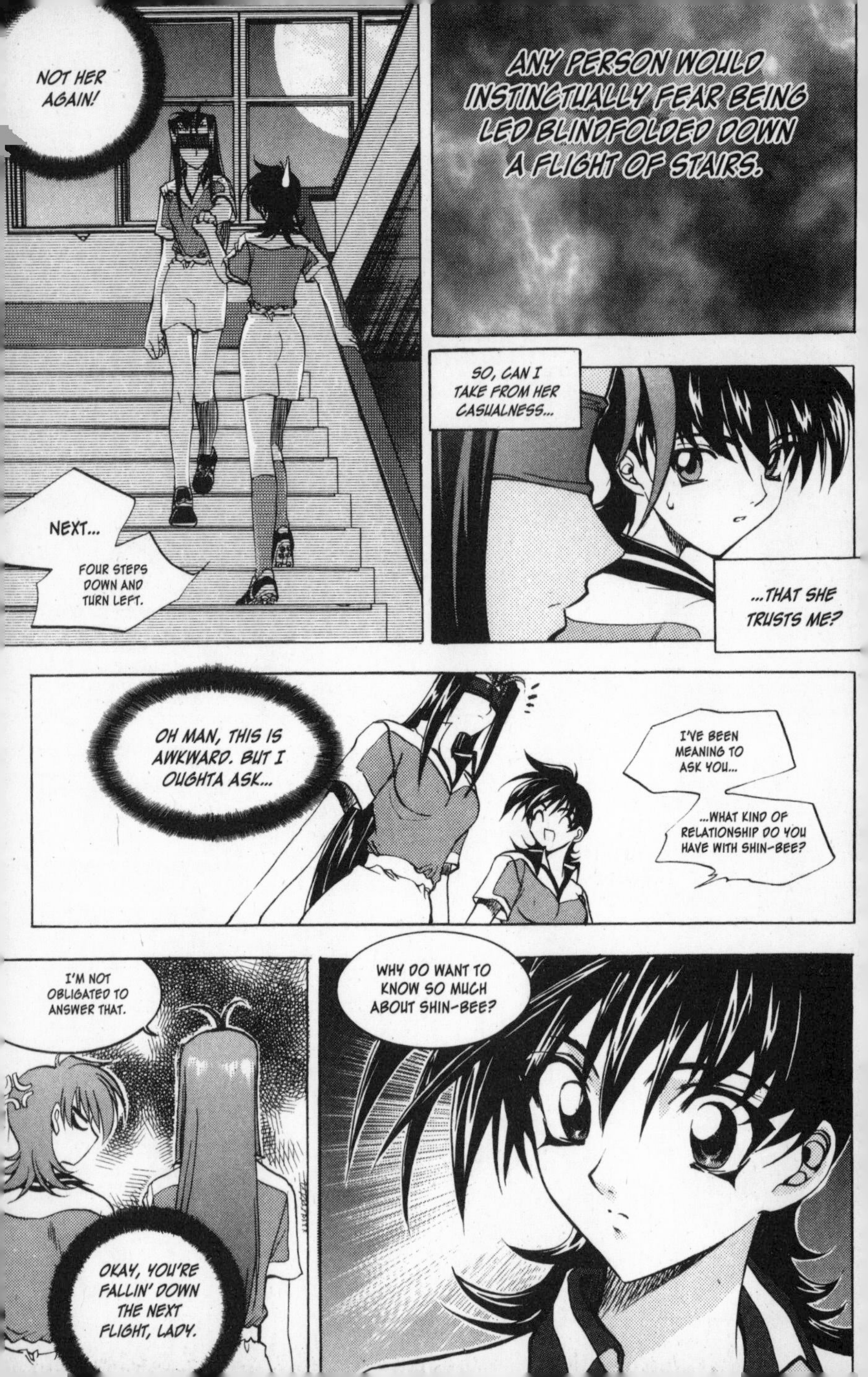
NOT HER AGAIN!
NEXT...
FOUR STEPS DOWN AND TURN LEFT.
ANY PERSON WOULD INSTINCTUALLY FEAR BEING LED BLINDFOLDED DOWN A FLIGHT OF STAIRS.
SO, CAN I TAKE FROM HER CASUALNESS...
...THAT SHE TRUSTS ME?
OH MAN, THIS IS AWKWARD. BUT I OUGHTA ASK...
I'VE BEEN MEANING TO ASK YOU...
...WHAT KIND OF RELATIONSHIP DO YOU HAVE WITH SHIN-BEE?
I'M NOT OBLIGATED TO ANSWER THAT.
OKAY, YOU'RE FALLIN' DOWN THE NEXT FLIGHT, LADY.
WHY DO WANT TO KNOW SO MUCH ABOUT SHIN-BEE?

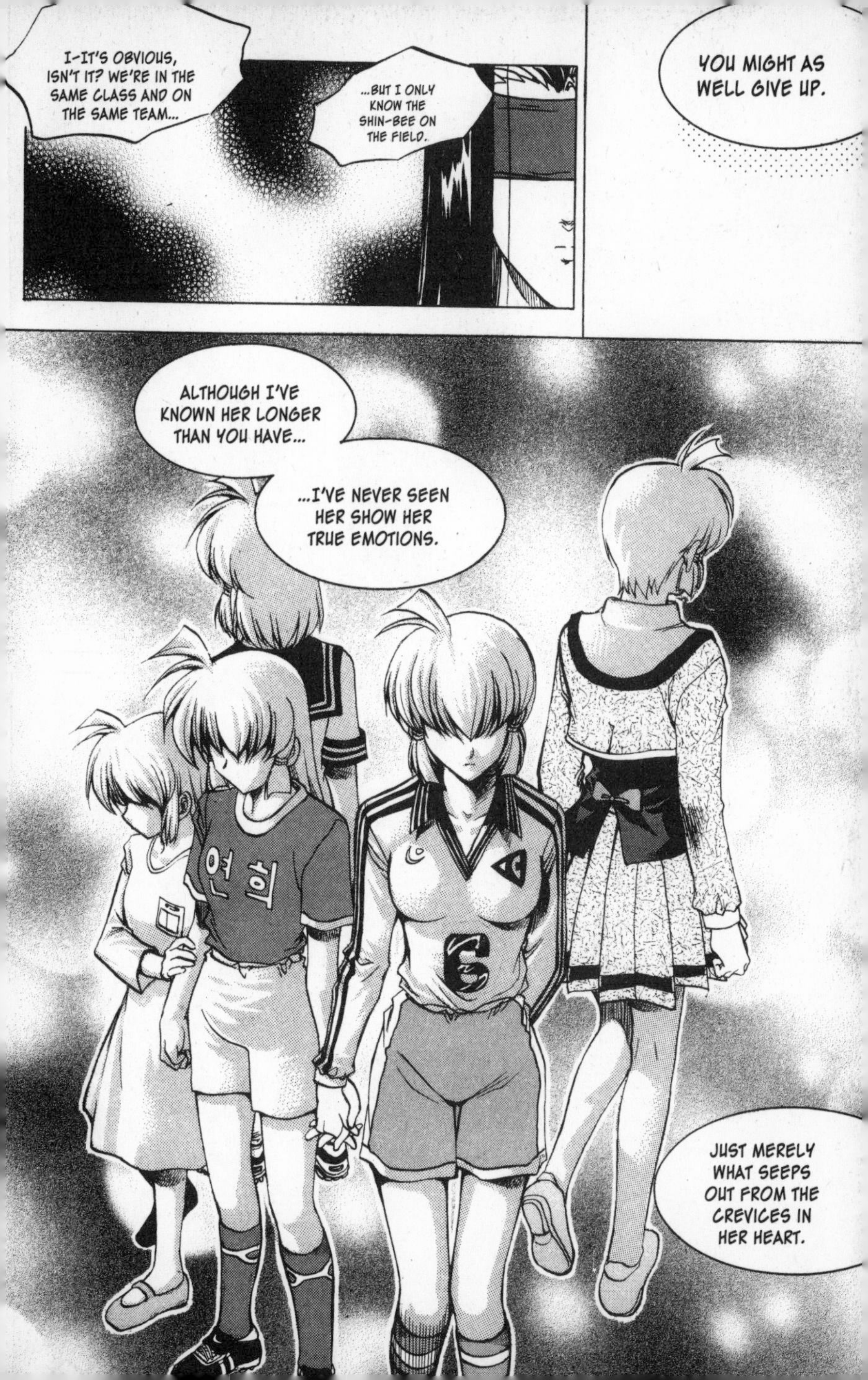
I-IT'S OBVIOUS, ISN'T IT? WE'RE IN THE SAME CLASS AND ON THE SAME TEAM...
...BUT I ONLY KNOW THE SHIN-BEE ON THE FIELD.
YOU MIGHT AS WELL GIVE UP.
ALTHOUGH I'VE KNOWN HER LONGER THAN YOU HAVE...
...I'VE NEVER SEEN HER SHOW HER TRUE EMOTIONS.
연희
6
JUST MERELY WHAT SEEPS OUT FROM THE CREVICES IN HER HEART.

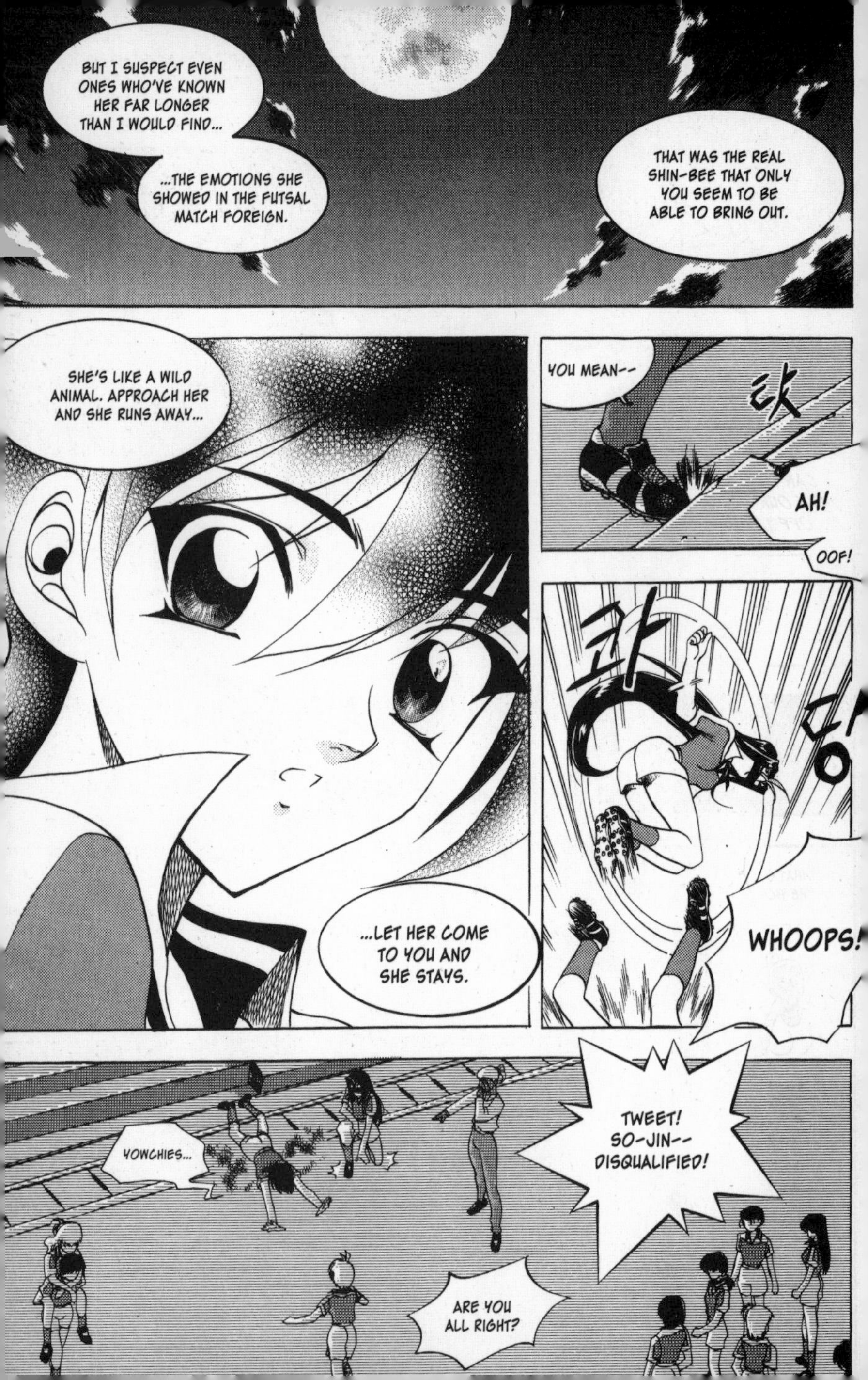
BUT I SUSPECT EVEN ONES WHO'VE KNOWN HER FAR LONGER THAN I WOULD FIND...
...THE EMOTIONS SHE SHOWED IN THE FUTSAL MATCH FOREIGN.
THAT WAS THE REAL SHIN-BEE THAT ONLY YOU SEEM TO BE ABLE TO BRING OUT.
SHE'S LIKE A WILD ANIMAL. APPROACH HER AND SHE RUNS AWAY...
...LET HER COME TO YOU AND SHE STAYS.
YOU MEAN--
AH!
OOF!
WHOOPS!
YOWCHIES...
TWEET! SO-JIN--DISQUALIFIED!
ARE YOU ALL RIGHT?

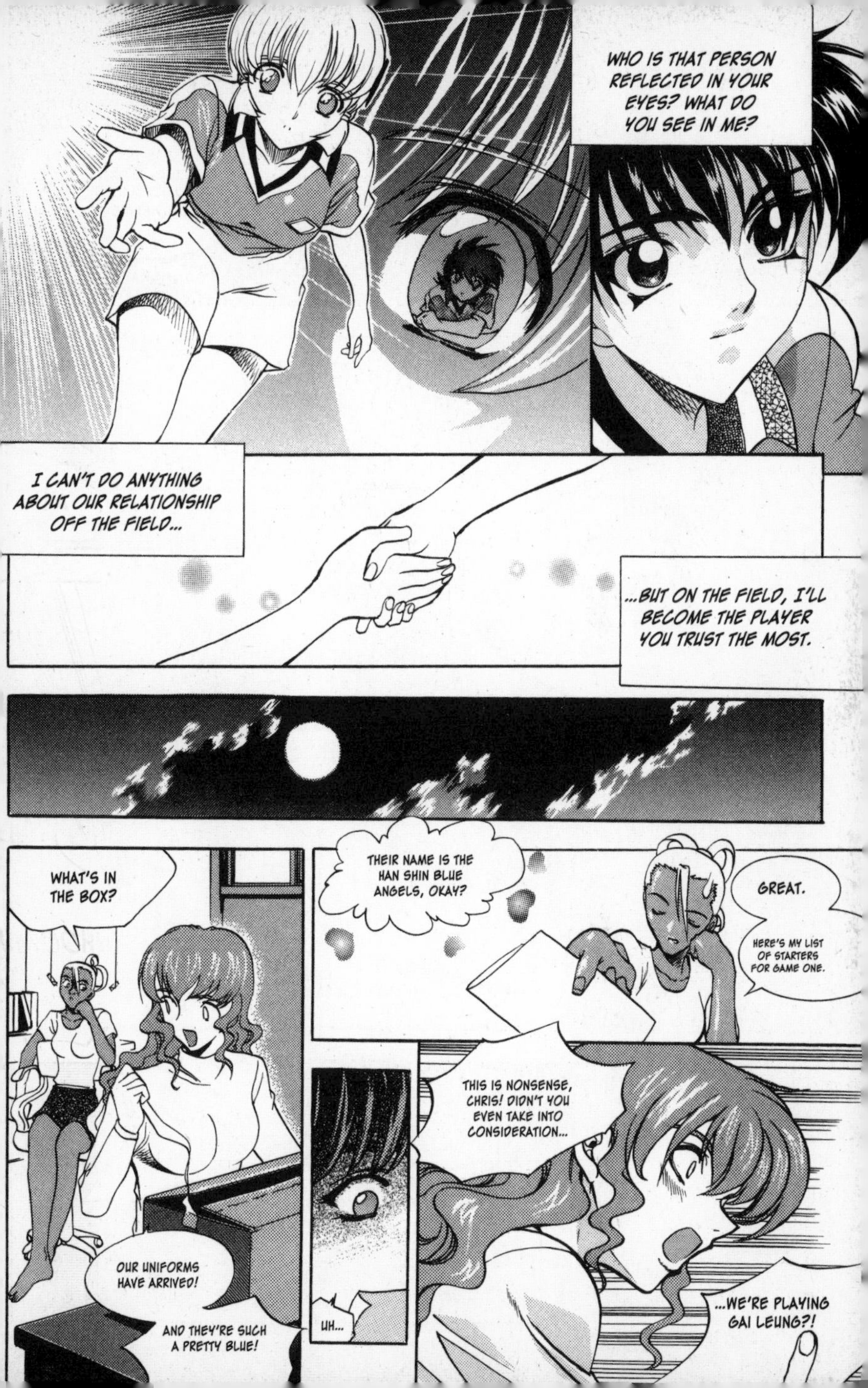
WHO IS THAT PERSON REFLECTED IN YOUR EYES? WHAT DO YOU SEE IN ME?
I CAN'T DO ANYTHING ABOUT OUR RELATIONSHIP OFF THE FIELD...
...BUT ON THE FIELD, I'LL BECOME THE PLAYER YOU TRUST THE MOST.
WHAT'S IN THE BOX?
OUR UNIFORMS HAVE ARRIVED!
AND THEY'RE SUCH A PRETTY BLUE!
THEIR NAME IS THE HAN SHIN BLUE ANGELS, OKAY?
GREAT.
HERE'S MY LIST OF STARTERS FOR GAME ONE.
UH...
THIS IS NONSENSE, CHRIS! DIDN'T YOU EVEN TAKE INTO CONSIDERATION...
...WE'RE PLAYING GAI LEUNG?!

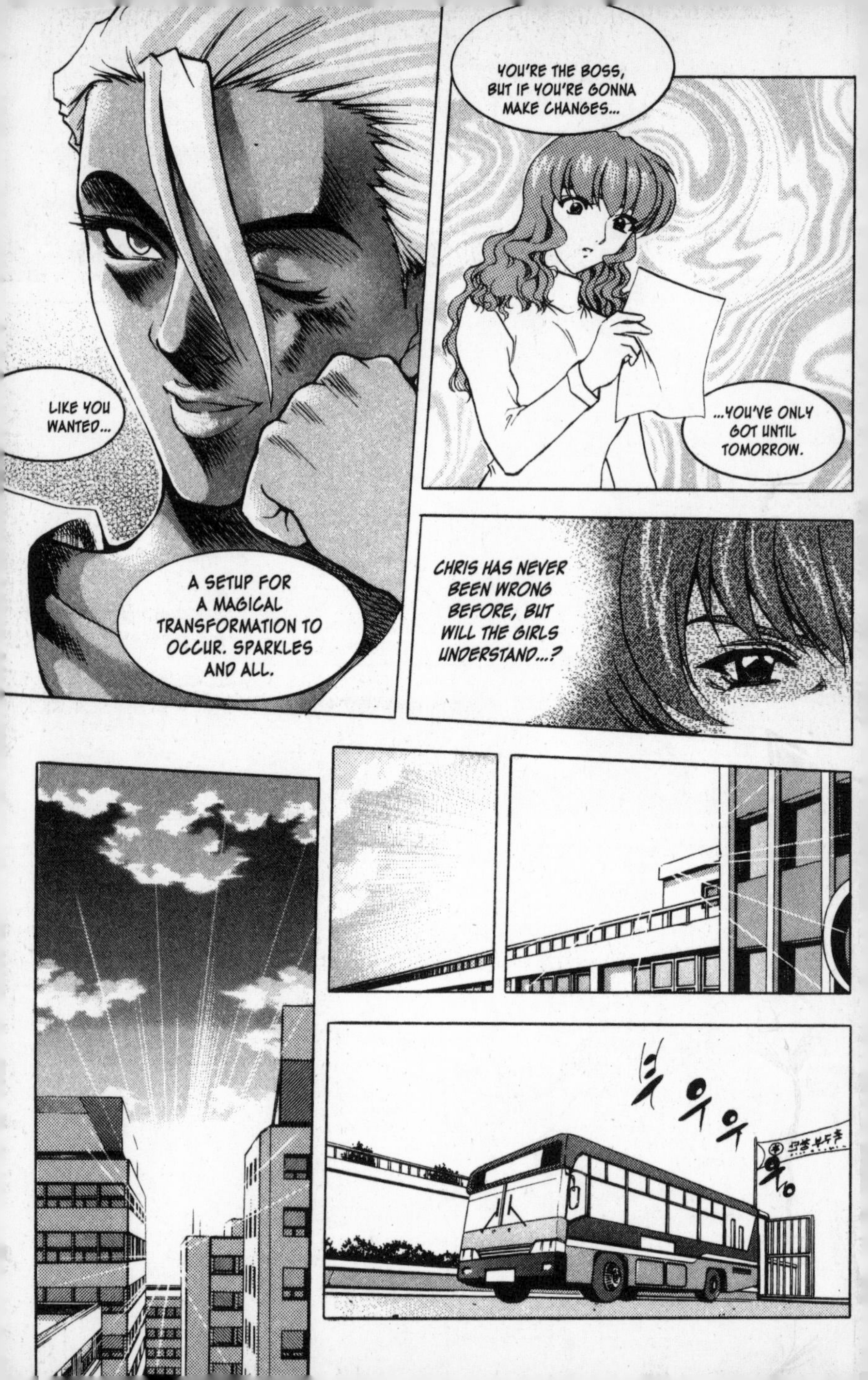
LIKE YOU WANTED...
A SETUP FOR A MAGICAL TRANSFORMATION TO OCCUR. SPARKLES AND ALL.
YOU'RE THE BOSS, BUT IF YOU'RE GONNA MAKE CHANGES...
...YOU'VE ONLY GOT UNTIL TOMORROW.
CHRIS HAS NEVER BEEN WRONG BEFORE, BUT WILL THE GIRLS UNDERSTAND...?
부우우웅

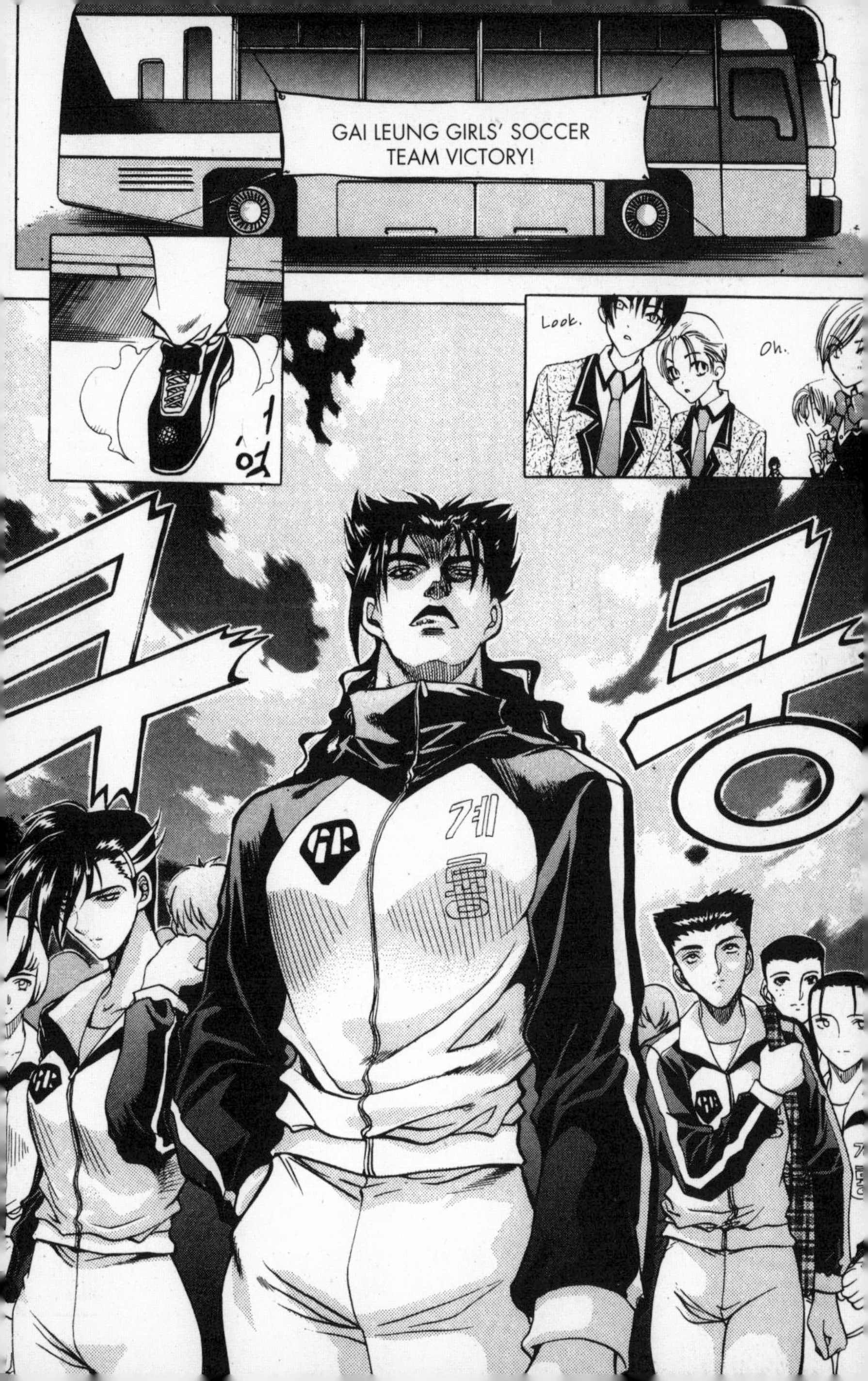
GAI LEUNG GIRLS' SOCCER
TEAM VICTORY!
Look.
Oh.

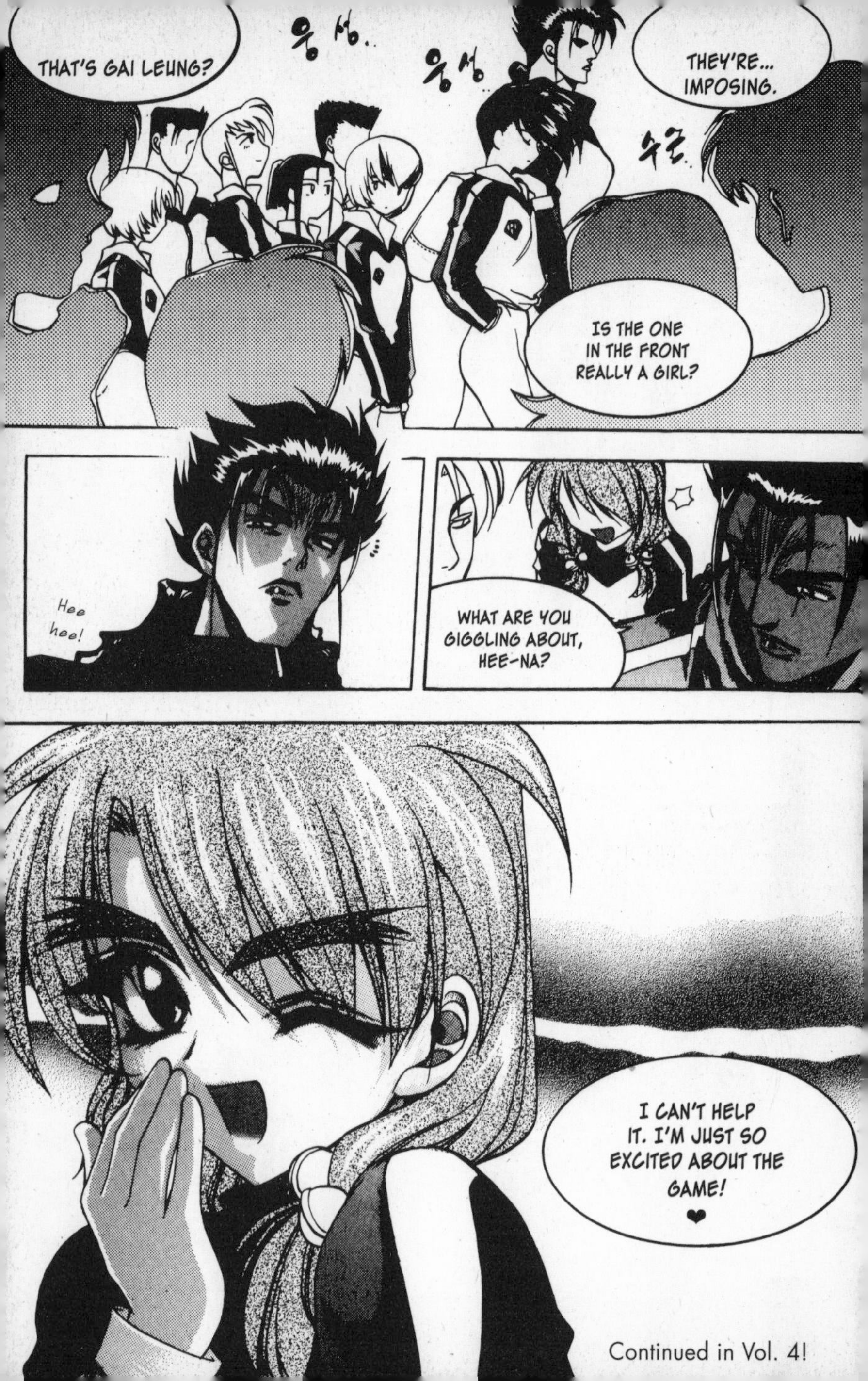
THAT'S GAI LEUNG?
웅성..
웅성..
THEY'RE... IMPOSING.
수군..
IS THE ONE IN THE FRONT REALLY A GIRL?
Hee hee!
WHAT ARE YOU GIGGLING ABOUT, HEE-NA?
I CAN'T HELP IT. I'M JUST SO EXCITED ABOUT THE GAME! ❤
Continued in Vol. 4!

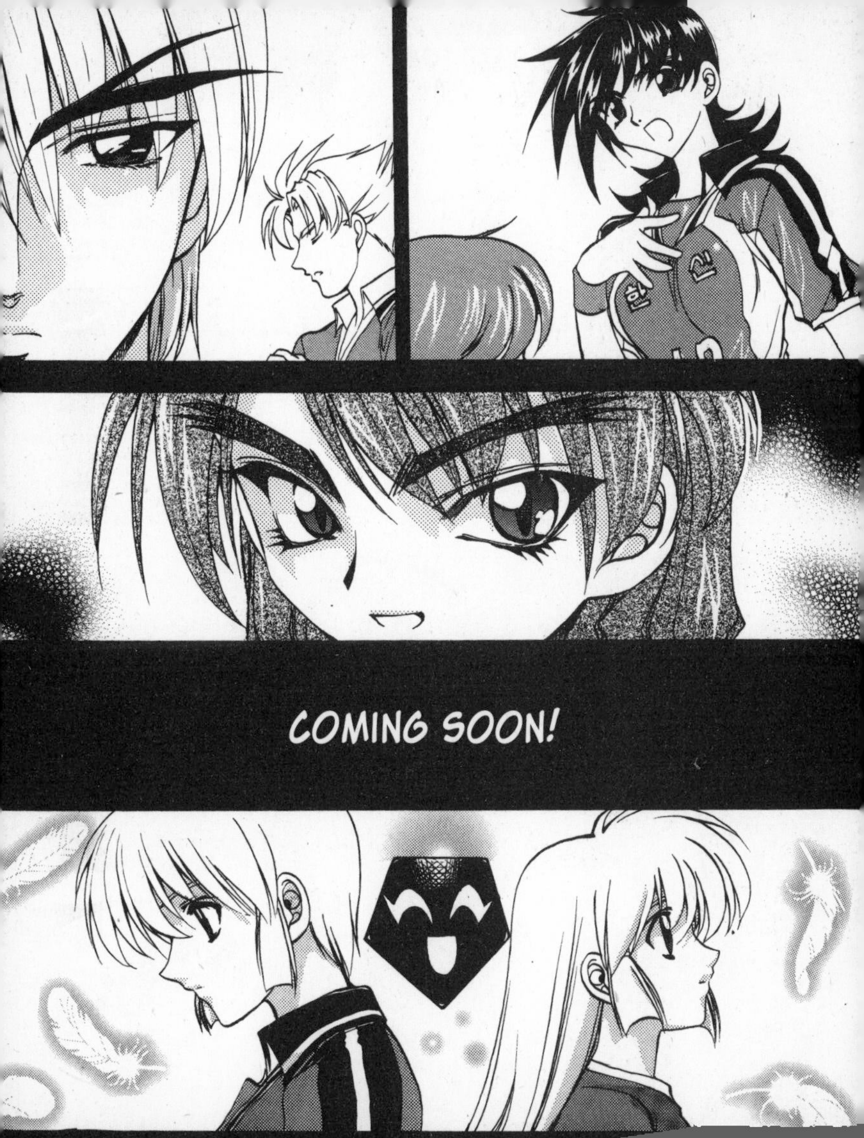
COMING SOON!

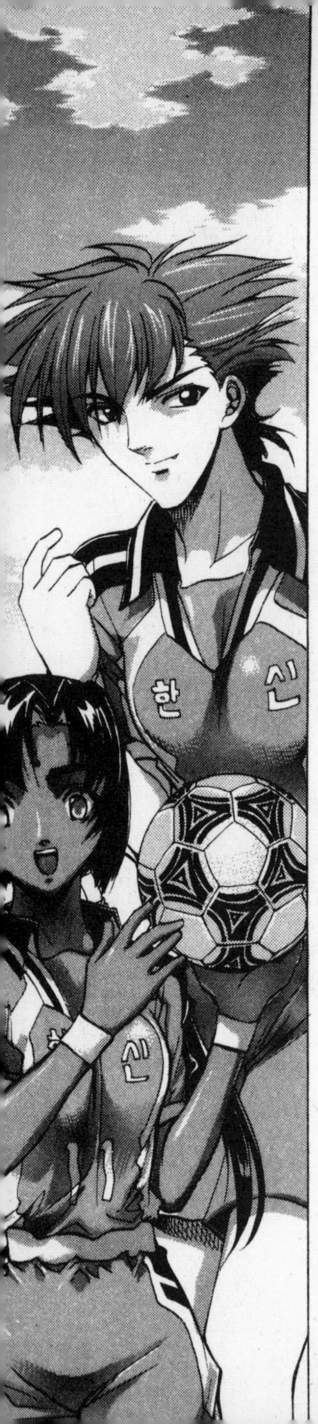

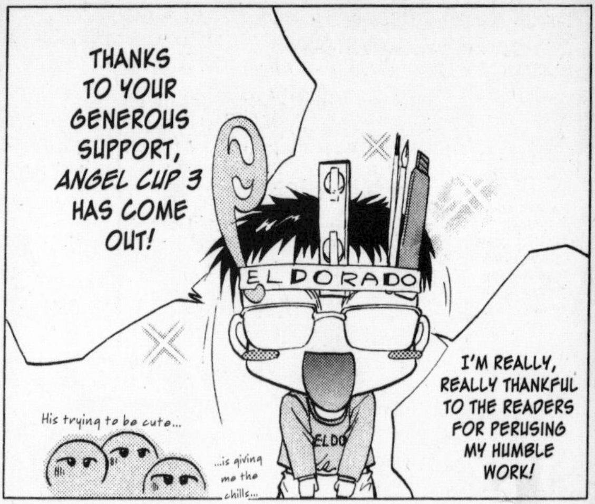
THANKS TO YOUR GENEROUS SUPPORT, ANGEL CUP 3 HAS COME OUT!
ELDORADO
I'M REALLY, REALLY THANKFUL TO THE READERS FOR PERUSING MY HUMBLE WORK!
His trying to be cute...
...is giving me the chills...
ELDO

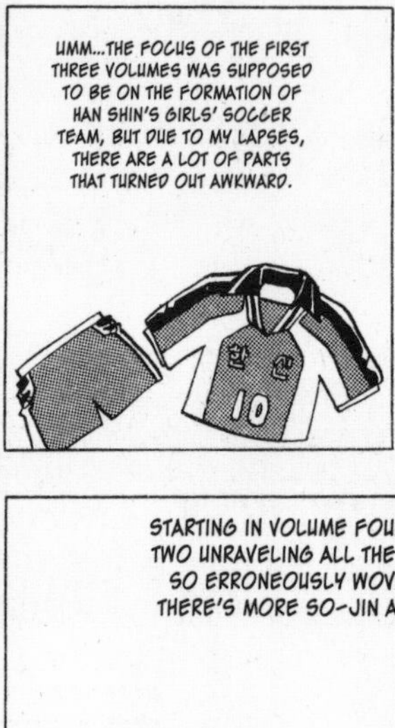
UMM...THE FOCUS OF THE FIRST THREE VOLUMES WAS SUPPOSED TO BE ON THE FORMATION OF HAN SHIN'S GIRLS' SOCCER TEAM, BUT DUE TO MY LAPSES, THERE ARE A LOT OF PARTS THAT TURNED OUT AWKWARD.
10

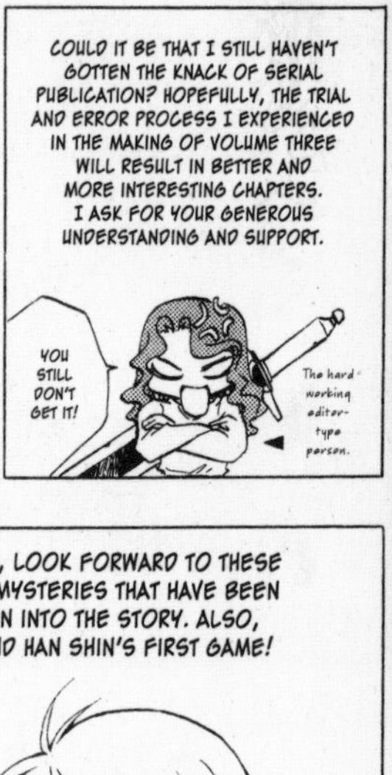
COULD IT BE THAT I STILL HAVEN'T GOTTEN THE KNACK OF SERIAL PUBLICATION? HOPEFULLY, THE TRIAL AND ERROR PROCESS I EXPERIENCED IN THE MAKING OF VOLUME THREE WILL RESULT IN BETTER AND MORE INTERESTING CHAPTERS. I ASK FOR YOUR GENEROUS UNDERSTANDING AND SUPPORT.
YOU STILL DON'T GET IT!
The hard working editor-type person.

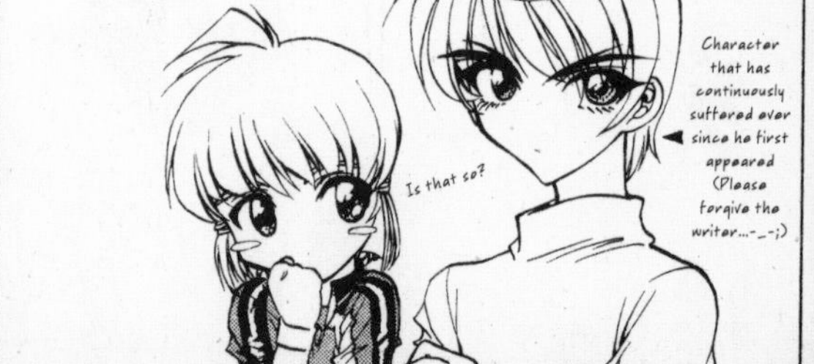
STARTING IN VOLUME FOUR, LOOK FORWARD TO THESE TWO UNRAVELING ALL THE MYSTERIES THAT HAVE BEEN SO ERRONEOUSLY WOVEN INTO THE STORY. ALSO, THERE'S MORE SO-JIN AND HAN SHIN'S FIRST GAME!
Is that so?
Character that has continuously suffered ever since he first appeared (Please forgive the writer...-_-;)

ORIGINALLY, THESE TWO WERE GOING TO APPEAR IN VOLUME THREE, BUT DUE TO CIRCUMSTANCES WE'LL HAVE TO POSTPONE THEIR INTRODUCTION.

I WOULD LIKE TO INTRODUCE MY PUPILS.

FIRST UP IS SOMEONE WHO WORKED VIGOROUSLY ON VOLUME THREE, MISS IFREETA.

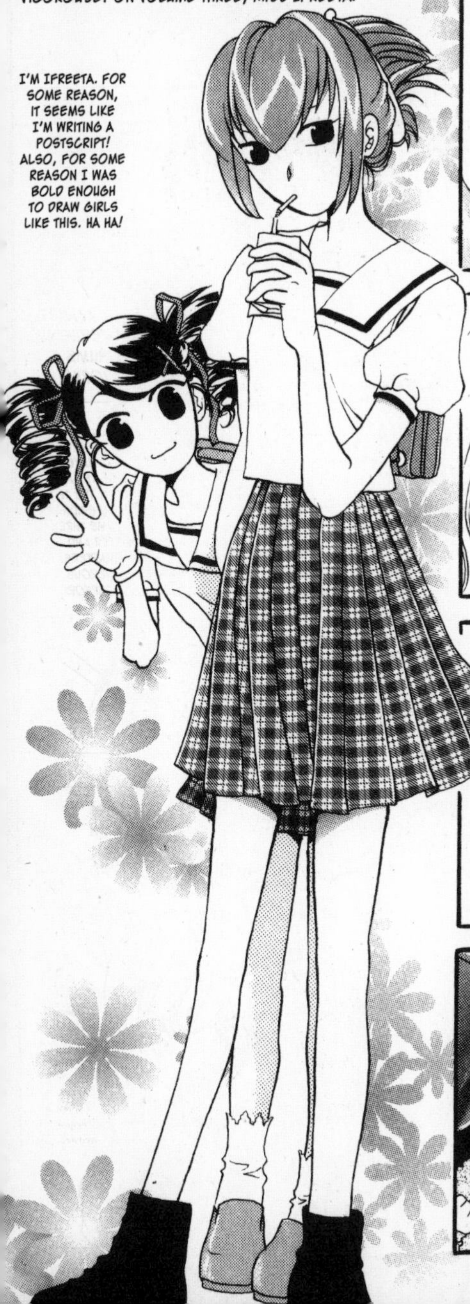
I'M IFREETA. FOR SOME REASON, IT SEEMS LIKE I'M WRITING A POSTSCRIPT! ALSO, FOR SOME REASON I WAS BOLD ENOUGH TO DRAW GIRLS LIKE THIS. HA HA!

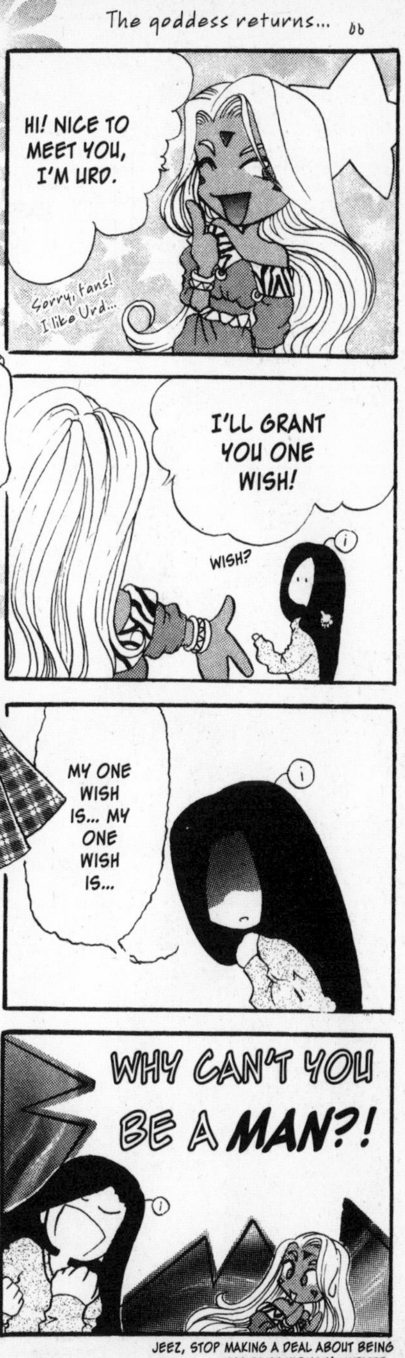
The goddess returns...
HI! NICE TO MEET YOU, I'M URD.
Sorry, fans! I like Urd...
I'LL GRANT YOU ONE WISH!
WISH?
MY ONE WISH IS... MY ONE WISH IS...
WHY CAN'T YOU BE A MAN?!

JEEZ, STOP MAKING A DEAL ABOUT BEING THE SAME WOMAN! -WRITER-

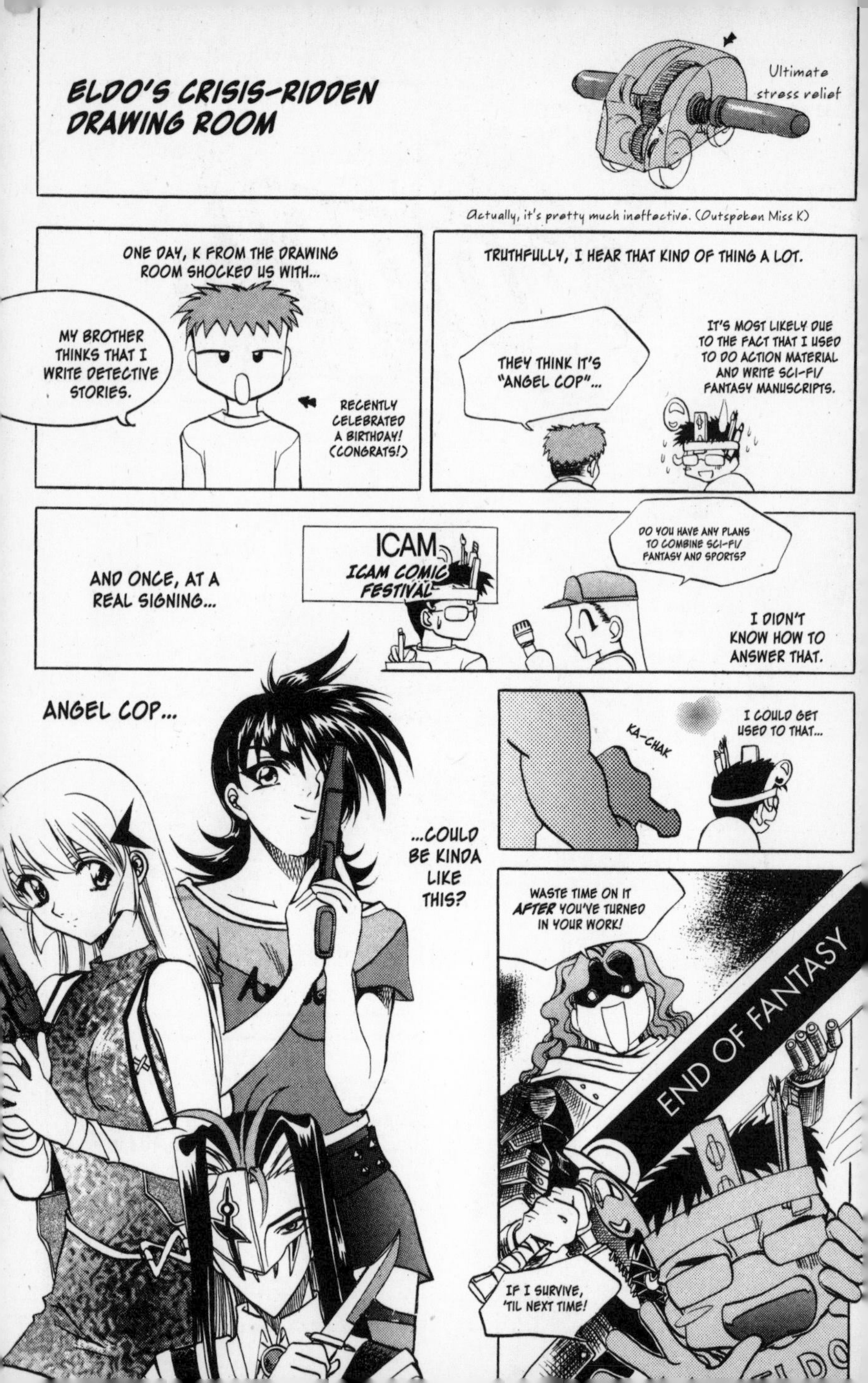
ELDO'S CRISIS-RIDDEN DRAWING ROOM
Ultimate stress relief
Actually, it's pretty much ineffective. (Outspoken Miss K)
ONE DAY, K FROM THE DRAWING ROOM SHOCKED US WITH...
MY BROTHER THINKS THAT I WRITE DETECTIVE STORIES.
RECENTLY CELEBRATED A BIRTHDAY! (CONGRATS!)
TRUTHFULLY, I HEAR THAT KIND OF THING A LOT.
THEY THINK IT'S "ANGEL COP"...
IT'S MOST LIKELY DUE TO THE FACT THAT I USED TO DO ACTION MATERIAL AND WRITE SCI-FI/ FANTASY MANUSCRIPTS.
AND ONCE, AT A REAL SIGNING...
ICAM
ICAM COMIC FESTIVAL
DO YOU HAVE ANY PLANS TO COMBINE SCI-FI/ FANTASY AND SPORTS?
I DIDN'T KNOW HOW TO ANSWER THAT.
ANGEL COP...
...COULD BE KINDA LIKE THIS?
KA-CHAK
I COULD GET USED TO THAT...
WASTE TIME ON IT AFTER YOU'VE TURNED IN YOUR WORK!
END OF FANTASY
IF I SURVIVE, 'TIL NEXT TIME!

In the next volume of:

Practice time's over for the girls as they get ready to face off in their first real soccer game! They've only caught a glimpse of their newest rivals, the behemoths of Gai Leung, but how will they match up on the field? And when everything's on the line, these animals will make the fur fly!

Anytime Anywhere

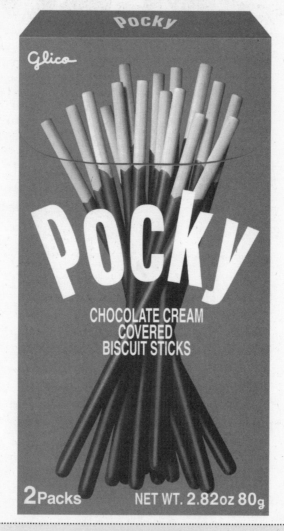

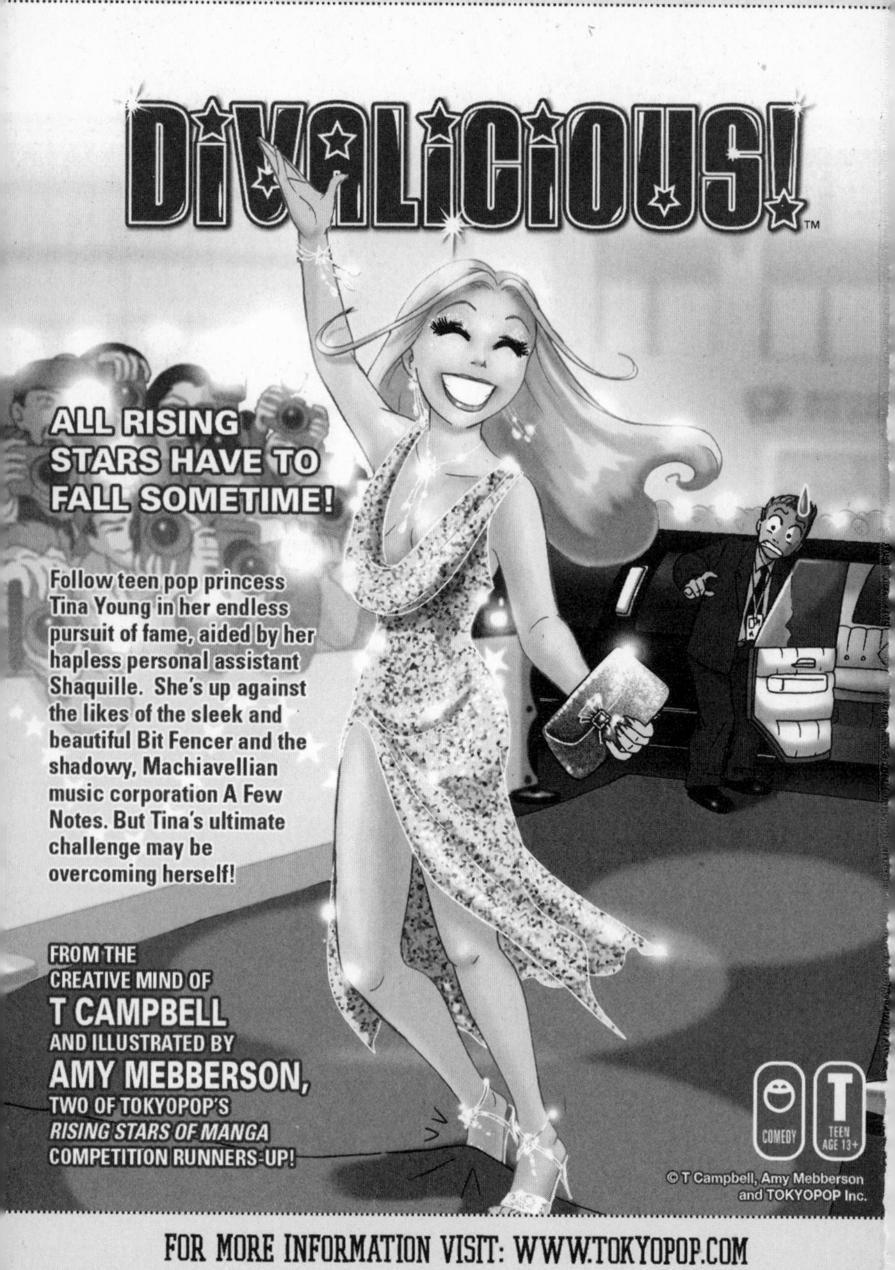
DIVALICIOUS!™
ALL RISING STARS HAVE TO FALL SOMETIME!
Follow teen pop princess Tina Young in her endless pursuit of fame, aided by her hapless personal assistant Shaquille. She's up against the likes of the sleek and beautiful Bit Fencer and the shadowy, Machiavellian music corporation A Few Notes. But Tina's ultimate challenge may be overcoming herself!
FROM THE CREATIVE MIND OF
T CAMPBELL
AND ILLUSTRATED BY
AMY MEBBERSON,
TWO OF TOKYOPOP'S *RISING STARS OF MANGA* COMPETITION RUNNERS-UP!
COMEDY
T
TEEN AGE 13+
© T Campbell, Amy Mebberson and TOKYOPOP Inc.